BOND

BOND

Terence Maher

William Heinemann Australia

First published 1990 by
William Heinemann Australia
22 Salmon Street, Port Melbourne, Victoria 3207

Edited by Sally Moss
Designed by Noniann Cabouret Lier
Typeset in 11/13 Cheltenham Book by Bookset
Printed in Australia by Australian Print Group

National Library of Australia
    Cataloguing-in-Publication data

Maher, Terence, 1948– .
    Bond

    Bibliography.
    ISBN 0 85561 336 X.

    1. Bond, Alan, 1938– . 2. Businessmen — Australia —
    Biography. 3. Millionaires — Australia — Biography.
    I. Title.

338.61092

Disclosure: Terence Maher owns 1000 shares in Bond
Corporation Holdings Ltd.

For Bosco who wanted this
and Belinda who will need it

Acknowledgements

The people who have helped me compile this information are legion. I have refrained from naming them for various legal reasons and because not all of them would necessarily agree with all the conclusions reached. I thank them anyway. I also want to thank the library staff of the *West Australian*, the *Australian Financial Review*, the *Age* and the *Herald* in Melbourne, the Fremantle City Library, Australian Archives and Australian Business Index, without whose help the task would have been almost impossible.

This story would not have been told had the publisher, William Heinemann Australia, not had the guts to back the project in the first place and the patience and strength to see it through to its conclusion. I am particularly grateful for the assistance of my editor Sally Moss of White Kite Productions, my agent John Timlin of the Almost Managing Company and Maryann Ballantyne of William Heinemann Australia. Finally I would like to thank the *Sunday Herald* for giving me time off to complete the project and Terry McCrann for the foreword.

Foreword

I met Alan Bond face to face for the first time as late as May 1989, although I had followed his corporate fortunes since the mid-1970s, and often spoke to him on the telephone (the first time, as I recall, being when he was in Newport on one of his early America's Cup challenges). My first and lasting impression of Bond *au naturel*, so to speak, was of a character straight out of *Alice in Wonderland* — in particular, the Mad Hatter's tea party — as this chubby, jovial, fresh-faced man with a seemingly all-encompassing grin bustled around his hotel suite, personally providing me with a cup of coffee. And I couldn't help feeling that this late meeting and consequent impression were so deliciously apt; for, if Alan Bond had not existed, we would probably have had to invent him, and we would have invented him exactly the way he was. In a way that is utterly unique, Alan Bond captures and projects the essence, the very spirit of 1980s Australia: our Alice in Wonderland age.

It is as impossible, even in today's heat of the moment, to understand this slice of our history without understanding the story of Alan Bond, and Bond Corporation, as it is to understand the Bond story in isolation from the broader economic, political and social streams.

Entrepreneurs, financiers, financial entrepreneurs, players all, have come and gone across the pages of the last decade: Judge, Connell, Skase, Yuill, and countless dozens of smaller, already forgotten names. But there is something special about Alan Bond. How was it possible for a man of his less-than-credible background to galvanise the decade by mounting Australia's first billion-dollar-plus takeover off the back of a company barely one-sixth of that size? How could a man build debts of more than $12 billion when the world's once-biggest and leading bank, Citibank, had black-banned him (and still does) after being burned in the 1974 property collapse?

The answers to questions of this sort provide telling insights into a less-than-glorious age — a decade in which Australia as a country spent $120 billion more overseas than it earned and, as a consequence, acquired a massive millstone of foreign debt and engaged in the biggest sale of the farm in its history.

On this measure alone, the Alan Bonds who borrowed the billions have to be considered a disaster of a magnitude not even imaginable in the Australia of Chifley and Menzies. The records show that such people have certainly not added wealth to Australia and did not lead us into a promised brave new world of productivity and international competitiveness. In large part, the 'profits' they generated were illusory and, worse, were then expended in an orgy of conspicuous consumption not seen in Australia since the land booms of the 1880s.

Yet there are shades of grey, perhaps even white. It is undeniable that the America's Cup victory injected a significant boost into our collective psyche. Along the way Mr Bond has also displayed a unique ability to see the emerging upside. His coup in seizing Santos in the dismay and disarray of the 1973 OPEC oil shock and his acquisition of the Greenvale nickel project stand out. Even his less-than-desirable foresight in tapping the great lending orgy of the 1980s showed a skill of sorts.

But none of these takeoffs has ever developed into a sustained healthy business. And that, writ small, is the story of Australia in the 1980s. At the outset of the 1990s nobody believes that the economic and corporate 'rationalisation' of the last decade has fitted us to compete even with likes of Thailand or Malaysia, far less Japan and Taiwan or the newly awakened economies of western and eastern Europe.

Mr Bond and his ilk are quintessentially creatures of Bob Hawke and Paul Keating and the policy structures and Faustian pacts which they entered to sustain the false boom of the decade. Also, of course, they are creatures of the tides of change that swept through the rest of the world's economic and financial systems. This is history on the run, and we need to learn and understand it before we can understand where we really are in the 1990s, if indeed we are to survive the new decade to prosper in the twenty-first century.

Terry McCrann, Associate Editor, the Melbourne *Herald*

CHAPTER ONE

1950: SS Himalaya, *London to Fremantle*

Alan Bond was born at Ealing, on the western edge of London, on 22 April 1938. That much is certain. The rest of his background has to be pieced together from often-contradictory sources. He was the second child born to Kathleen and Frank Bond following the birth of their daughter, Geraldine Kathleen, eighteen months earlier. Mrs Bond's maiden name was that most English of surnames — Smith, but her own Christian name and that of their first child indicates that there could have been an Irish connection in her immediate family tree. We are told her father was a physician and a conservative politician of some note, having at one time been lord mayor of Leeds.

Frank Bond was definitely Welsh and had a slight accent till the day he died in 1970. He and his three brothers (in one

interview there were seven) worked in the coalmines of Monmouthshire in old South Wales. Alan Bond says (through the
rhetorical flourishes of a journalistic medium)[1] that he remembers his uncles so saturated with coaldust that, even after they
washed in cold-water tubs in their backyards, the veins in their
arms stood out like thick black lines on a parchment chart. He
remembers the earth trembling as he stood in their spotless
cottages, the brassware burnished, the white lace curtains
stiffly starched and the floors all neatly scrubbed. He remembers them being simple men — honest, hard workers: 'They
were happy, because they knew nothing else. They were also
very, very poor.'

The place and time of Alan Bond's birth seem significant
to his later development. Ealing, a working-class dormitory
suburb on the western edge of the great metropolis between
Shepherds Bush and Heathrow Airport, is also home to Gunnersbury Park. This giant estate stretching down to the River
Thames was owned by the mega-wealthy Rothschild family
from 1835 to 1917. It is inconceivable that the young Bond
would have been unaware of this green island in the middle of
a sea of grey semidetached row houses and the wealth contained within its Georgian mansions. His mother later said that
Alan had been interested in boats and the water since he was a
little boy. 'He just loves the water,' she said.[2] The Thames at
Gunnersbury Park was probably the closest stretch of water to
his home in Ealing.

How and when the Bond parents met each other and came
to be living in London is not known. But the decision to have
two children at the height of the Great Depression seems a
particularly brave one; if, indeed, it was a decision. Kathleen
Bond would have been thirty when she gave birth to Alan. It
was the year the Nazis made infamous as *Krystallnacht*, the
night of the broken glass. Bond says his father started work in
the coalmines in Wales when he was twelve and was a physical
training instructor before and during the war.[3] Later reports
have him as a 'London builder'[4] but he was a painter and
decorator with English qualifications when he arrived in Australia in 1948 via a brief stint in South Africa. The Bonds cannot
have been too badly off despite the experience of raising a
young family during the Depression and a world war. Frank
Bond is said to have brought with him from England a new Ford

Zephyr sedan and sufficient cash to buy a house in Fremantle's High Street.[5]

There is little doubt which of the parents had the stronger influence over the young boy. Kathleen Bond is quoted as saying: 'His dad was placid and satisfied with just enough to get by on. But that has never been good enough for me. I think I've passed on my own canniness with money to Alan ... He was always an adventurous boy but one who loved his mum and liked to show it.'[6] Denis Sowden, a Fremantle butcher, says this about the father/son relationship: 'He was working for his father when Frank had to go into hospital for a week. His dad used to say, "I came out of hospital and was a partner in the business." Frank also told us, "If I'd known what he was going to put us through, we'd never have had him. But the Bonds would still be just plodding along in Fremantle."'[7]

It is not surprising that Alan Bond developed a Coriolanus complex, given his mother's strength of character and the limited exposure he would have had to his father during his formative years. It appears that his father enlisted as a PT instructor in the Royal Air Force very soon after Alan's birth and spent some time training commandos before fighting alongside Australian troops at Tobruk in the North African campaign. In 1944, he was badly wounded when the ship taking him and other military personnel to Algiers was hit and part of the blast was forced into his lungs. He lost one lung and was seriously ill for years. Service doctors finally warned Mrs Bond that he had no more than two years of life ahead of him if he stayed in London's damp climate. It is interesting to note that Alan Bond describes his dad as 'a great athlete and very oriented to sport',[8] when his first sighting of him after war service would have been as a TPI in a hospital bed. Still, his father is credited with providing Alan with his first great insight into the need to acquire wealth and power, even if the inspiration came from a negative example.

The maker of this particular myth was Bond's journalist friend of twenty years, Bruce Stannard, who, in the *Bulletin* on 26 November 1985, wrote about the time Frank took the boggle-eyed, seven-year-old Alan down a Welsh coalmine. That places the year as 1945 and shows that Frank Bond's injured lungs had recovered sufficiently for him to take the minor miner 'into the depths of a wet and foetid mine in Monmouthshire'. According to Stannard, 'The idea was to teach the child something about hard physical work and its rewards. But the experience did more than that. It kindled in the boy what was to become the man's single greatest obsession: the notion that if an individual used his energy and his initiative, if he were smart and tough enough, he need not be condemned to a life underground. It occurred to him that perhaps one day he might even own the mine. Alan Bond has always been nothing if not ambitious. In that black bedlam, far below the surface, he gaped in amazement at lumbering pink-eyed pit ponies that had never seen the light of day. He watched the sweltering miners with their feeble yellow head lights, relentlessly chip, chip, chipping at the coalface with picks and shovels, and he came away with impressions which, forty years on, remain seared in his memory.' Stannard concludes the parable with the seemingly apocryphal line: 'Poor was something Alan Bond decided then and there he'd rather not be.'

But in a *Playboy* interview five years earlier Bond spoke (in his own words) about the profound effect his mother had had on his approach to life: 'She is a very intelligent person and continues to be an example of the philosophy that you never stop learning. She is now seventy-one, but at sixty-eight she went to the University of Tokyo to learn to speak and write four Japanese dialects. Not many people would take on the awesome task of learning the many thousand Japanese characters at that age. I think too many people waste their time. She wastes none of her time. She travels constantly around the world. She spent two months in Russia learning about their culture and country and another two months in China last year. She is aware of the world around her — a lot more aware than most other Australians. My mother speaks of Australia as a paradise, but only because she has travelled the world and can make realistic comparisons with other countries. She is not only a mother in the maternal sense, but an interesting and intellectually stimulating person with whom to talk. She does set me an example. I think we are cast in a similar mould.'[9]

The origin of Alan Bond's drive and determination is clear in another story about his mother.[10] On 11 October 1982 Kathleen Bond had a stroke which was to leave her completely paralysed down her left side. Doctors told the seventy-four-year-old woman that her globetrotting days were definitely over. 'My left hand was like a lump of dead meat. I was in hospital for nine weeks. The doctor said, "Well, you won't be going to Newport this time." I didn't say anything. But that night I did my physiotherapy exercises instead of sleeping. I did them every night. I had such pain in my arm that I thought I couldn't carry on. But I told myself that that attitude was no good and I had better get on with it. I had never been ill before in my life and I didn't like it. So I persisted. Then I found I could move a finger. It's amazing, you know, how dead limbs can come back to life.' Mrs Bond was out of hospital in a wheelchair before Christmas and was walking, with the aid of a stick, along the Newport offshore jetty and clambering aboard her son's motor launch when I last saw her in September 1983. She was always her son's greatest admirer and sat in the front row of all Bond Corporation annual general meetings. When she collapsed with a heart attack at a Los Angeles hotel in late August 1987, Bond uncharacteristically left a business meeting in Europe, flew to her bedside and was with her when she died. She was seventy-nine and had lived a full life, thanks to her Coriolanus. Bondy had always looked after his mum and she took great pride in his achievements.

Like the man, Alan Bond's school days in England are shrouded in mystery. His entry in Debrett's has him attending Perivale School, for which the education section of the British Council has no listing. When he started school around 1943, the German Luftwaffe was systematically trying to level the city. A lot of children were evacuated from London during the blitz, including Steve Welstead, who now lives in Perth but claims to have known Bond in his Ealing days. 'My mum used to say that there was no way that the Germans would bother to fly all the way across London just to drop bombs on Ealing. One day she went up to the corner store and it wasn't there any more. We were sent to live with a family near Salisbury for the duration.' He vividly remembers the barrage balloons anchored overhead, the constant air-raid siren tests and the backyard air-raid shelters. All exciting stuff for a young boy, but hardly conducive to the learning process and the getting of wisdom.

Even as a boy, Bond bragged a lot about how good he was. He told Steve Welstead in clear and precise terms the first time they met in Ealing for a game of marbles: 'My name is Alan

Bond! B-O-N-D! I speak fluent German and one day I'm going to be the richest man in the world! I shall probably beat you at marbles, as well!' He did — at least Welstead thinks he did. And now Welstead would like his two marbles back from the rich man. (Bond played only for keeps.)

In May 1984 Alan Bond told Hugh Schmitt in the *West Australian* that from the age of eight (1946) he studied French, Latin and German at English schools and that, when he left to come to Australia as an eleven year old, 'his mathematics standard was equal to matriculation standard in WA'. He told Bruce Stannard in the *Bulletin* that he was 'a scholarship winner ... who excelled at mathematics, French, Latin and German'. In the 1980 *Playboy* interview he described his schooldays thus: 'I came from London, a thriving, exciting metropolis where I was keenly interested in my studies and doing well at school'. Keen he certainly was, but there is no proof that he was brilliant.

English education in those days was geared to the 11+. Alan Bond would not have had time to sit for it before coming to Australia as an eleven year old. It is also highly unlikely that he was learning German at school in 1946. With his father's life in the balance because of German actions in the Mediterranean and his own experience of having lived through the German blitz of London, why would he want to learn German anyway? He was an eight-year-old junior schoolboy, not a British intelligence officer. If Steve Welstead is right, Alan Bond attended Ealing's Lamos Junior or Lower Grammar School at some stage. He might have been sent to live with relatives in Wales or Leeds or got a scholarship to a private school or have done very well at Perivale School but there is no proof. He almost certainly never sat the 11+.

What is important here is that Bond thought he did well at school in the UK and that his problems with the education system began only when he left England in late 1949 to come to Australia as a ten-pound immigrant.

Twelve thousand miles away, in the year of Alan Bond's birth, the Hughes family of 31 Quarry Street, Fremantle, Western Australia, also had a new arrival. But Eileen Hughes of Freo (as the locals call it) was born into a world vastly different from that of Alan Bond of Ealing. As a fourth-generation Irish Australian born into a large, loving and honoured Fremantle family, Eileen Hughes was privileged and she knew it. Her father was a well-liked, respected, fit and healthy local sporting hero with a good job. He was a member of the Order of the Knights of the Southern Cross, a pillar of the community and of Saint Patrick's Catholic Church around the corner from his comfortable home. He was not an invalid with a death sentence over his head as a result of war wounds. He was a father figure to be looked up to.

Eileen Hughes was a slightly shy Freo girl with no need to be particularly concerned about or to exaggerate her school results from the Sacred Heart Convent in nearby Tuckfield Street. She suffered no deprivation and little could be done to improve the quality of her life or her standard of living. 'She was beautiful,' says Father John Hannah of Saint Pat's. 'She was thin and she had those beautiful eyes and she always had an exuberant nature. Eileen's always been a happy-go-lucky, welcoming person,' he says.[11]

She was born with the flaming red hair that is a racial characteristic of the Kerry men and women of western Ireland and indeed she thinks her great-grandfather sailed from Dublin in 1829. This would place her family among the pioneers of the State, the port town being named after Sir Charles Howe Fremantle who, as the twenty-eight-year-old captain of HMS *Challenger*, took possession of the west coast of Australia for Great Britain in May 1829.

Eileen says her mother, Mary, was also Irish and had a passion for green. Hence, the bedroom Eileen shared with her sister was painted a murky green during her seventeen-year tenure in the solid, three-bedroomed cottage, with verandah out the front and a grapevine and a fig tree in the backyard. She remembers a glass-bead curtain hanging halfway down the hall. On stinking hot days when the air refused to move between the open front and back doors, its tinkling would announce the arrival of the afternoon sea breeze which the locals know as 'the doctor'. Eileen, as a young whirlwind, loved nothing better than to charge through this glass wall at top speed, just to hear the bang and clatter of the beads crashing against the wall.

Eileen's father, William John Hughes (universally known as 'Doozer'), was born on 19 December 1903, to William and Alice Hughes. The young Bill Hughes was a busy man who seemed to strive tirelessly for the things he loved and prized.

He left school, at Fremantle's Irish Christian Brothers College, on his fourteenth birthday but was considered too young and too far away to serve as cannon fodder in the Great War. In 1918 he joined the wool-broking firm, E Antoine & Co., as a junior cadet to learn wool classing. In the early 1920s he moved to Wm Haughton & Co., where he stayed, in charge of the sheep skin department, until he joined Prevost & Co. just before the outbreak of World War II. He probably got the nickname 'Doozer' in the days when he played cricket and Australian Rules football for the South Fremantle club (he played forty-seven games with the red-and-white Bulldogs from 1925, which in football-mad Fremantle is considered dancing with the gods); but another theory says the epithet comes from his eagerness as a young wool buyer in the early 1930s to go to wool sales in the bush, with the expressed intention of having a good time and the rare use of a company car. 'I'll doozer,' he'd call, as quick as a flash.

During the war, when the government controlled the industry, he was with the Central Wool Committee in charge of the sample department. He rejoined Prevosts after the war as head of its Fremantle division. When Doozer Hughes retired after nearly sixty years in the trade in 1977, he was feted at a civic reception as 'the doyen of the Fremantle wool industry' and the progenitor of the Westwools empire.[12] His son Bill and Frank Blakiston had worked under him at Prevosts before going out and setting up their own companies — the Blakiston Group in 1955 and the Hughes Group in 1958. These entities merged in 1971 to form Westwools, and Bill Senior joined Bill Junior as a director in 1973. As a businessman, Doozer Hughes was a steady builder of skills and assets for other people, rather than an amasser of personal wealth on his own account. It was in the community sphere that he excelled as an administrator. Doozer was rarely seen without a hat because he was always between meetings. He served three successful two-year terms as president of the South Fremantle club in 1951–52, 1960–61 and 1970–71 and many times held aloft the West Australian National Football League premiership trophy. He was also a Fremantle City councillor for twenty-one years, including one term as deputy mayor, and was a commissioner of the Fremantle Port Authority for sixteen years. He was a director of the Fremantle Building Society for seven years,

including one as chairman. The Hughes family of seven celebrated the great Australian weekend together with two holy
days of obligation. On Saturdays, the whole family would dress
up and watch the game at the historic Freo Oval, sandwiched
between the prison and the markets. And sometimes, for a
treat, they would then promenade to the Roma Cafe in High
Street for lashings of minestrone, chicken and spaghetti, and
Coca-Cola. The ritual was repeated on Sundays but the home
ground was Saint Patrick's Catholic Church in Adelaide Street
and the prize was eternal salvation. With a large family, a sister
a nun and a son a priest, Bill Hughes was blessed in the eyes of
the Catholic Church.

If Doozer was the uncrowned King of Freo then Eileen was
his princess. He was very protective of his children, especially
his youngest, and she absolutely adored him. They formed an
exclusive mutual admiration society.

When Doozer Hughes died on 13 March 1988, most of the
town mourned the passing of a great Australian achiever of
the old school, an all-round good bloke. He had been sick for
a couple of weeks in St John of God Hospital and was quite
pleased with his weight loss. Eileen wasn't, but she didn't think
he'd die. 'He was eighty-four and he'd had a good life. He was a
fantastic person — calm, serene and terribly strong,' she
says.[13] Her dad's car number plate was 'WA 38'. She still has it
and she now travels with an Irish passport.

To gain any real understanding of Alan Bond, it is essential to come to grips with Freo's spirit of place. The small port
town's physical environment, its history, its traditions, and the
prevailing ethos of its 23,000 citizens provide the crucible in
which he was forged. This is Fremantle's story.

Being on the main European/Far East trade route around
the Cape of Good Hope, this treacherous New Holland coast-
line, battered by Indian Ocean winds that sweep in, unimpeded,
from Africa, was well known to Dutch and French mariners
before Captain Fremantle finally planted the Union Jack on
2 May 1829 and claimed the western half of the continent for
his king. (A mob of blackfellows had found it tens of thousands
of years earlier, after a walkabout from Asia, and figured that
where the river ran into the sea was a good place to catch fish.
It still is.)

It had strategic importance only because of the isolation

of its position. The Swan River Colony was set up in June when a second ship, the *Parmelia*, arrived; but the eager colonists and their sheep had a hard time of it for the first twenty-one years. A limestone bar at the entrance blocked the river to sea navigation, so everything to and from the new colony had to be landed at a long sea jetty near Arthur Head at Fremantle, then shipped upstream in shallow draught boats to Perth Water — a very labour-intensive operation. It didn't matter much, though, as the only exports were whale oil, wool, sandalwood and jarrah timber and the imports were goods and passengers.

The Swan River colonists built a prison called the Round House on the top of Arthur Head in 1830–31 and the Fremantle Whaling Company excavated a tunnel through the middle of it in 1837, to link the jetty and the merchants of High Street. Then, faced with a labour shortage, they did an extraordinary thing. They petitioned Her Britannic Majesty to send convict labour long after the other Australasian colonies had abandoned the practice. They claimed that, as free settlers, they had no one to build bridges and make roads for them (the blackfellows were still fishing or had gone bush) and so the English Queen obliged by sending some of her many petty criminals and Irish political prisoners.

The first white slaves landed in Freo in 1850; and when transportation stopped in 1868, 9668 people had arrived in chains. First they built the Warders' Quarters in Henderson Street, then, between 1851 and 1858, they constructed the sandstone prison which hovers, Bastille-like, above the town. In April 1876 crewmen from the *Catalpa*, a visiting Yankee whaling ship, grabbed six Irish Fenian convicts from this jail and attempted to slip out of Fremantle in the general confusion provided by Perth Regatta Day. The British gave chase in the steamer SS *Georgette* and soon overhauled the American boat. But by then the *Catalpa* was in international waters and flying the star-spangled banner. The skipper of the *Georgette* decided it would be 'impolitic' to fire on the American flag and so the Fenian convicts made good their escape to the United States before the lowered guns of the British Empire. The *Catalpa*'s bold escapade became a *cause célèbre* among Fremantle's convicts, and the folk song about it became so popular in the local pubs that it was banned by the British authorities of the day. There were no complaints from the prison warders, for it is said they were paid in American gold for their co-operation. In 1866 the convicts threw Fremantle's first bridge over the Swan River to give land access to Perth, twenty kilometres upstream, but the seaport's golden days were just beginning.

Self-government was granted to the colony in 1890 and in 1893 Paddy Hannan discovered the world's richest gold deposit at Kalgoorlie in the eastern hinterland. The rush was on. Fremantle's population almost doubled in the decade following 1881 and almost trebled again in the next decade. The labour shortage had been solved, but there was no water on the goldfields and the Arthur Head jetty had become a bottleneck.

It took another Irishman, Charles Yelverton O'Connor, to solve the problems created by Paddy Hannan. This brilliant chief engineer devised a scheme to pipe water from the coast to the goldfields and then had the vision to plan and construct an inner harbour at the mouth of the river by removing the bar. The first steamer to enter the new harbour and tie up at Victoria Quay was the SS *Sultan* in 1897. The port was complete.

Fremantle was declared a city in 1929, only one hundred years after Captain Fremantle's arrival, but it has always seen itself as a 'Struggletown', as well as Australia's Ellis Island. Wharf labourers dominated the port's population and they were as proud of their working-class traditions as they were of the *Catalpa* convicts. Outside the town hall is a memorial to Comrade Tom Edwards, who gave his life to the cause in a bloody confrontation with scabs and State troopers on Victoria Quay on Sunday, 4 May 1919. Another thirty-three were injured in the clash.

In 1938 when the Australian government allowed a shipment of pig iron to be exported to war-minded Japan, the Freo wharfies nicknamed the minister responsible 'Pig Iron Bob' and black-banned Japanese ships. Because of the campaign, the Lyons government was forced to bring in a total iron ore export ban that was to stay in place for twenty years and delay the economic development of the State.

London-on-Thames, Dublin-on-Liffey and Fremantle-on-Swan have something else in common besides Alan Bond and Eileen Hughes. There are all Arms of the Sea.

In 1851, as ships containing refugees from the Irish potato

famine and convicts continued to pour into Fremantle from Dublin and London, the gentlemen from Britain's Royal Yacht Squadron were busy conducting a regatta with a syndicate of gentlemen from the New York Yacht Club to see who had the fastest boat. At stake were national pride and an ornate silver ewer, twenty-seven inches tall and weighing 134 ounces, called the Hundred-Guinea Cup. The New York entrant, the schooner *America*, easily won the fifty-three-mile fleet race around the Isle of Wight and took home the ugly trophy, renamed the America's Cup. British yachtsmen have been trying to win it back ever since.

In July and August of 1937, the Golden Age of America's Cup yachting was coming to an end off Newport, Rhode Island. Despite the Great Depression, entrepreneurs such as the tea baron Sir Thomas Lipton, the builder of the World War I Sopwith Camel aeroplanes T O M Sopwith, and the very wealthy Harold (Mike) Vanderbilt were schoolboy role models of success as they played the one remaining rich man's game with magnificent J-class sloops. Only ten J-boats were built and only three matches were held — in 1930, 1934 and 1937. 'It was a happy conjunction of majestic boats, technological advances, sportsmanlike conduct, and some close and exciting races.'[14] The events of that summer would later provide new heroes in the firmament for a reader of the Boy's Own paper.

On 5 February 1950, when the SS *Himalaya* steamed into port, Fremantle was hot. Passenger No. 559, tourist class, was a precocious, pugnacious and plump English lad all trussed up in tweedy gear with little school cap and tie. He missed London and he didn't like this place one little bit.

The boy who would turn twelve in two months' time had just become the latest in a long line of 'whingeing Poms' — over a million and a half Britons, who came to Australia as assisted passage migrants after World War II and didn't like what they saw on the first day. You'd think the young man would have been grateful for the free trip and for the opportunities awaiting him in the New World; or at least that he would have been delighted to see his Da again after two years, to see how the hot, dry climate of Western Australia had suspended his death sentence for another twenty years.

Passenger 559, BOND, Alan, made his first mistake when

he gave his address at destination in Australia as 276 High Street, Perth. The timber bungalow his father had bought was in fact at 276 High Street, Fremantle. It was a mistake that later was to teach the young Bond much about doing business in Western Australia; for, culturally, the two cities on the Swan are worlds apart.

The migration experience was a particularly traumatic one for Bond, not so much because of what lay in front of him but because of what he was leaving behind. Maybe it's because he's a Londoner . . . or maybe it was because as an eleven-year-old Ealing hustler he was being plucked from his peer group and his pleasures and forced to live as a foreigner in another country on the other side of the planet. Maybe he left behind a girlfriend, other friends and relatives whose company he enjoyed. In a new neighbourhood, in a new country, he would have to fight all over again for a place in the junior pecking order. Having grown up independently in a matriarchy, perhaps he did not relish the prospect of living under his father's authority again for the first time in years.

Frank Bond's first long march in search of health and wealth had taken him from the valleys of Wales to the streets of London. His second shift, via South Africa, would not only give him a new life in the promised land but also provide a future for his wife and children. Although his health was the catalyst for the change, there was little to hold the working man in Britain.

Following the Great Depression, Britain had suffered six years of war, in which factories, homes and ports had been demolished or damaged by sustained bombing. The people had been subjected to severe rationing of fuel, food and clothing; services had been drastically reduced and there was little opportunity to replace essential goods that had been destroyed or had worn out. There was fear of another depression and another war in Europe in which the British Isles would be particularly vulnerable, and widespread doubt about Britain's capacity to recover from the economic difficulties caused by war, especially the decline in industrial capacity and loss of overseas assets.

The years 1947–50 were a period of lean austerity. Britons were forced to accept controls and shortages at least as severe as those they had suffered during the war, when sacrifice was the price for survival. Britons understandably looked beyond the shores of their homeland for a place to settle. In late 1947, over 400,000 Britons were registered at Australia House in The Strand, London, for free and assisted passage to Australia. Frank Bond was one of them. Kathleen, Geraldine and Alan Bond were not.

The rush was on, Frank had to go, but Kathleen and the kids stayed put and would not budge until the two-year term was up. Kathleen Bond would be on her own again. She would have to fend for the family and make the important decisions about its future. Frank had taken the brand-new Ford Zephyr car and enough money to buy the house in High Street, Fremantle, so there must have been a general consensus that the rest of the family would follow at some stage. Given her renowned 'canniness with money', it is inconceivable that Kathleen did not work, draw a pension and receive support from Frank as she struggled to raise the family single-handedly after the war. She had the house and Frank's compensation and every reason to stay. While thousands of her compatriots did want to go, she obviously didn't and no doubt her reasons were compelling at the time. Alan was definitely opposed and Geraldine was neutral.

As working-class Tories, Kathleen and Alan Bond's ears would still have been ringing from the speech Winston Churchill gave to the 1947 Conservative Party Conference. Churchill had acknowledged that some of the 500,000 Britons who had indicated interest in emigrating to Commonwealth countries needed to go for 'family and other reasons', but pleaded for others not to leave the sinking ship: 'Stay and fight it out. If we work together with brains and courage as we did not long ago we can make the country fit for all our people. Don't desert the old land: we cannot spare you. The socialist attempt to conscript labour is only a passing phase. Britain will rise again in all her strength and freedom.'

Frank would have written glowing reports from sunny Fremantle. Yes, there were miles and miles of empty golden beaches; he was learning to swim and get sun on his pit parchment skin; he was feeling much better; he had a job, a house and a car ... He had gone ahead to blaze the trail and set things up for them, proper like ... He had done them proud, finally. Kathleen accepted her fate.

The migration scholar, Eisenstadt, says that emigration is motivated by feelings of insecurity and inadequacy in a person's social setting. Kathleen, it appears, did not suffer such feelings. But she had been deserted by her husband, even if it was for health reasons and even if it wasn't his fault in the first place. Wives characteristically were much less enthusiastic about emigrating than their husbands. It was normal for the six-week period between notification of selection and departure to test their resolve and, in many ways, their marriages. It was a period of great stress. The unknowns in the venture were enormous. For the vague promise of better opportunities for their husbands and children, they were now dismantling all aspects of the only way of life they knew. As they were restricted to personal effects on the migrant boat, the home, the furniture and most household goods had to be sold within six weeks under buyers' market conditions.

The period was especially stressful for children such as Alan, who had to sever, perhaps forever, close friendships at school and in the neighbourhood. Leaving the only environment they had ever known, and giving away such precious possessions as a bike because it could not be taken, caused many youngsters to cry themselves to sleep in rooms where they had thought their most private thoughts and kept their most treasured possessions.

And so an eleven-year-old boy forms his last memories of Britain: his family's worldly possessions — two tea chests and four suitcases — stacked in the front room of their empty home awaiting the local carrier to take it to the railway station and then on to the Tilbury dock. The last English Christmas. The final goodbyes.

The ropes are tossed, the ship slides out . . .

They were very lucky to be on the SS *Himalaya* sailing from London's Tilbury Dock on that day in 1949. There was a tremendous worldwide shortage of shipping after the war and boats capable of bringing a thousand new settlers across the world in relative comfort were a rarity. She was P&O's finest and was on her maiden voyage.

Kathleen and the two children had a cabin to themselves. After the roughness of the Bay of Biscay, which fulfilled their worst fears about leaving home, came the calm but morbid

Mediterranean, where Flying Officer Frank Bond had been laid low by the Nazi Afrika Korp six years earlier. Their first port of call was Port Said in Egypt. It was hot and dusty and very foreign. Then through the as-yet-untroubled Suez Canal, past Aden, and on into the Indian Ocean to Bombay in India and Colombo in Ceylon. The sun didn't set on the British Empire until they had to skip Singapore because the insurgency against British rule in Malaya had created an emergency.

Fremantle was first landfall and the gateway to classless British Australia. Most of the ship's 938 passengers were due to disembark at either Melbourne or Sydney — the big cities that were more like London. But Frank had chosen for his paradise a fishing village called Fremantle, a small, close-knit community more like his mining village in the Welsh valleys. In the waters called Gage Roads, between Rottnest and Fremantle, he would have first felt the cooling effects of 'the doctor' and first laid eyes of the giant yellow-and-black Dingo Flour sign on the miller's silo at North Fremantle.

The Bonds were not among the 547 first-class passengers on the steamer. As the immediate family of a British ex-serviceman now resident in Australia, they travelled gratis, with the expense divided between the Australian and British governments. But the ambitious London working-class boy studying for the 11+ would have been acutely conscious that material things, life and times were better for the first-class passengers on the other side of the *Himalaya*'s plush rope barriers. Since he could not change the system, he must either cross the barrier or accept defeat.

The Freo beachhead. Day One. Ground zero. His first in the lucky country, but he doesn't appreciate it. The searing sun burns pale skin. The north-easterly wind blows in hot and dry from a real desert, a far cry from the piddling one at Port Said. After picking up the family and the luggage in the car at Victoria Quay, Frank decides to take the family for fish and chips in the High Street, a taste of the cornucopia available from the menu of the land of flowing milk and honey.

The boy's favourite meal is a bacon sandwich, no butter, heaps of HP sauce. He could always get it in Ealing. He could get it on the *Himalaya*, where the children were encouraged to have their meals separately from the parents. Why couldn't he get it in this Fremantle cafe? It was Frank's fault — it was all Frank's fault, he argued unreasonably. If it wasn't for Frank he wouldn't be here, without a bacon sandwich.

Frank was tolerant, he didn't push it. He knew the boy would eventually settle. He remembered what he had been through himself, when he first travelled up to London from Wales.

In an interview given in December 1988 to the *London Sunday Times*, Alan Bond said, 'When I get off the plane at Heathrow, I feel as if I've come home, and that's a very earthy feeling for me'. Indeed, the only time Alan Bond has 'earthy feelings' or becomes lost for words or emotional in public these days is when he is drawn, unexpectedly, into discussing and describing his migrant experience. In another interview he said the move from Britain was so 'horrific ... it's as if I don't have a memory past a certain point — can't feel it, can't touch it, can't revisit it ... Unless you actually have that experience, all of the trauma — and, of course, the exhilaration of succeed-ing — it's hard to understand ...' What he saw on his first day seemed as alien as the surface of the moon: 'Some low palms, a rattly old tram going past, and the sprawl ... There was this great wilderness that each house lived in. I thought they must be farming the backyards.'[15] He told Hugh Schmitt that 'Fre-mantle, with its sandy beach and palm trees, looked like a desert island. When we landed and I saw my first tram going up High Street I felt like I had arrived on the moon. There was a feeling of desolation and lack of development and people. It is a feeling you get when you return to Perth after a few months in a big city. At school I was ribbed over my English accent. I felt disoriented and even wanted to go back to London — it was a very unsettled period for me.'[16] If the inner Bond is the same as the outer Bond, and if trying to find out what fires his ambition is a bit like trying to unravel a molecule, then the *Himalaya* experience seems to represent Bond's soft underbelly. The journey itself should have been a delight for a boy who was supposedly in love with boats. Perhaps he didn't want it to end. Perhaps he wanted to go on chasing sunsets. Or perhaps he got fidgety and bored, homesick and seasick on the three-to-four-week voyage into the unknown.

CHAPTER TWO

1954: HMS Britannia, *royal yacht, royal visit.*
UK 1–OZ 1

        It's not there any more, the house that Frank bought for the family with his compensation money at 276 High Street, Fremantle. If the Academy of Distinguished Entrepreneurs from Boston University's Babson College had their way, the old timber, three-bedroom family house on a quarter-acre block would be enshrined as an international monument. For it was from here that the migrant schoolboy laid his plans for world domination. From here, he was going to 'show 'em'. Ironically, the house has been replaced by a freeway and is marked only by the point where the Leach Highway extension, at High Street, dissects the Stirling Highway extension after it crosses the Swan and cuts a swath through East Fremantle. It would have lounged under a big tree in a little depression that eventually slopes down to White Gum

Valley, just over the top of Fremantle's High Street high ground. The house was within a ship's whistle of the Fremantle Harbour, the Swan River, the Richmond Park Raceway, the old East Fremantle Oval ('Home of the Sharks'), the Fremantle Public Golf Course, East Fremantle State School, the Horrie Long Reserve, the war memorial park and lookout at the top of Monument Hill where East Street meets High, the tram downtown: High Street, like the shaft of an arrow, pointing at the wharf; the wharf pointing out to sea; the sea pointing back to England ...

Bond's initial assessment of the state of development in Western Australia was way off course. Later that year he would do a school project to show that the Port of Fremantle was thriving in 1950. If the only comparisons he had were Tilbury Dock in London and Port Said in Egypt, then it was more like Port Said. But it had a vigorous trade exporting gold from the eastern goldfields, wool from the backs of ten million sheep, and teaming tons of wheat from fields that stretched over the horizon. Everything the West needed (mostly settlers and sailors) was imported from the East of Australia. The city/village of Fremantle was a dormitory suburb for the thousands of waterside workers, mostly Irish Catholic, partly Communist, whose livelihood depended on the activity level on the docks. The goldmining and rural industries were booming. When there wasn't a strike on, the inner and outer harbours were crowded with migrant, cargo, fighting and tourist ships. There were plenty of strikes in 1950 as the Cold War hotted up. The new Menzies Liberal government had introduced the Communist Party Dissolution Bill. Many Catholics in the Labor Party wanted it to go through. The Communist-dominated Waterside Workers' Federation didn't. The wharfies challenged the Act in the High Court and won.

It was also an important fishing port with sizeable Italian, Yugoslav and Portuguese communities. Many Italian families migrated to Fremantle from Capo d'Orlando and Molfett after World War II. Everyone there was a migrant of one form or another. The locals were very friendly towards new chums, tolerating them but sending them up. The Italians were known colloquially as Dings, the English as Poms. But there was change in the air ... The Nationality and Citizenship Act of 1949, which followed ratification of the Statute of Westminster, meant that, for the first time, Australians were Australian citizens rather than British citizens. There was a new pride in the Freo locals, particularly the Irish Australians. No longer were they second-class British citizens; they were now first-class Australians. It was the Poms who were made to feel second class. The sins of the ancestors are nearly always visited on those who were last to leave the boat. The Dings had their own language, craft, culture and community. They were admired for their ability to fit in, they could handle both the humour and the iconoclastic style of the Aussies. But the Poms, as a group, had to fit in with the Aussies, or suffer isolation. Far from being united with their 'British brothers' by their language, they were singled out by their accents and regional dialects as foreigners, outsiders who needed to be taken down a peg or two. It was into this atmosphere that young Alan ventured as a schoolboy.

'Go Forward' was the motto of East Freo State School in Marmion Street, three blocks from the Bond home. It was built of solid sandstone and fashioned comfortably and practically in the colonial manner. It was a far cry from the bombed-out ruins of Ealing, London, but there were enough familiar symbols of the past for the outcast to feel comfortable in his surroundings. Pictures of the King adorned the walls. The school's colours were blue and white, the same as the local Aussie Rules footy club, East Fremantle, Old Easts, The Sharks, almost next-door in Marmion Street. Bond was not interested in Aussie Rules; he wanted to play Rugby. He was still unsettled. He was not interested in going to school straight away, especially a colonial primary school where the new school year had started in January. Had he still been in London, he could have been going on a scholarship to a proper English grammar school. He couldn't believe his family would do this to him.

Eventually, Bond had no choice but to go to East Freo State School and the school no choice but to take him in. Maybe Frank threatened him with the truant officer in an effort to focus his attentions. This suggestion had Alan mindful that, until then, the London air-raid warden, with his tin helmet and whistle, was the closest thing he knew to an authority figure, somebody to be frightened of. Teachers didn't frighten him at all. Kathleen eventually persuaded him. She encouraged him to do well and so earn his ticket of leave. Most of the locals went to the Catholic schools. The Protestants, the disbelievers and the children of devout Communists, used the secular State school system. He was no Communist but he was certainly no Catholic. As he had not sat the 11+ and had not yet reached the age of twelve, he was handed over to Mr E Hinchliffe, the hardened class master of grade 6A. The two were destined to clash.

The last thing Mr Hinchliffe wanted introduced into his large and undisciplined class in the middle of a school term was another reluctant student, another potential troublemaker fresh off the boat. It was a tough working-class port town and these were tough kids used to scrapping and giving cheek in the street to the world's best. The sixth-grade boys, many of them strapping young men, were the school bullies. Judging by contemporary reports, the mob in 6A (comprising twenty-one boys and eighteen girls) closely resembled an anarchists' convention. The school's head teacher, Mr T Minard, summed up the discipline and tone of 6A in 1950 thus: 'Mr Hinchliffe is striving well to lift tone and to gain co-operation which has been lacking with this class' (17.7.1950) and 'Mr Hinchliffe has effected considerable improvement in this, but the general attitude is not attractive' (8.12.1950). Most of the boys were bound for the trade schools, provided they could get through the final year of primary school without assaulting any teachers. The girls would go on to the Princess May Girls' School, then find a husband. A class like this was hard to emulate, but Bond managed to do it.

'When I'm older I'm gonna buy and sell people like you!' Bond is said to have screamed at Hinchliffe during a classic confrontation.[17] The witness, former tug master John Waters, is not listed among the twenty-one boys in grade 6A but nonetheless describes himself as having been a classmate of Alan: 'He was a very cocky, mature bloke ... While we were still playing cowboys and Indians he was more interested in girls. You could see he had a pretty good head on his shoulders. He knew what he wanted to do. His forthrightness brought him into conflict with the teacher. He stood up in front of the class to deliver the measured line directly at Hinchliffe.' Waters does not recall the outcome of this naked challenge to authority. 'The rest of the class was too busy ducking for cover ... We always knew Alan would either make a quid or have his head cut off. He thought he was better than us but we put that down to him being a Pom. Besides, he was diplomatic and could run fast.'

His achievements were certainly not evident in his school results from East Fremantle State in 1950. In the half-yearly examinations conducted between June 25 and July 4, he got a bare pass in five subjects (writing, mental arithmetic, English composition, grammar and oral reading), failed two (silent reading and written arithmetic) and didn't sit three (spelling, arithmetic accuracy and dictation). Bond was not in the class for the full five months before the June examinations but he was obviously not up to Western Australian matriculation standard as he had claimed. He was no boy genius.

However, there was a vast improvement from a low base in his results in the December half-yearly tests, failed two (spelling and grammar) and again did not sit for dictation. He was self-conscious of the fact that he was one of the worst spellers in the class. He could say the words all right but when he tried to write down the letters and the words, they came out in a jumble. It was a difficulty that would plague him in latter life.

What Bond lacked in manners and ability he made up for with boyish charm, confidence and adaptability. He gained kudos by standing up to Hinchliffe and, as he began to adapt his speech patterns to the less-animated local variety, he earned his first acknowledgment when kids started calling him by the more familiar 'Bondy'. He claims that the ordeals he endured as a migrant gave him an 'inner strength to survive and rebuild'. They made him believe in himself. 'Setbacks and adversities are part of life ... the difference between individuals is how they mentally get on top of the problems, how they lift themselves above that depression that can so easily come upon them.'[18] Others described him then as a brash know-all with a mediocre IQ but with a supreme confidence in his own ability.

His big mouth was bound to get him into trouble at Fremantle Boys' High School, the august institution to which he was soon promoted. But here, the rebel was to find his cause. Here he was to learn the fundamentals of making money, the art of buying and selling and the skills of dealing with people.

The sandstone building with its Dutch gables is now home to Western Australia's Film and Television Institute.

Bond turned thirteen in April 1951. He seemed to have been waiting all his life for this moment, his personal coming of age. For years his head had been bursting with wonderful ideas and dreams of fabulous wealth. Now he was a man he could set about men's business and put his ideas into action. And attending the Boys' High School provided his entry to the downtown Freo business scene and away from the close attentions of his family in East Fremantle.

The building, erected nearly 100 years earlier, was strategically located between the heart and soul of the Fremantle ethos. With its back to the Elders wool stores and Victoria Quay it confronted St Patrick's Catholic Church across Adelaide Street. Next door was the Princess May Girls' School (now the Fremantle Education Centre) but luckily for the girls, a high fence separated them from the boys' school. For both sexes, the fence only added to the allure of what lay beyond.

We do not have Bond's academic accomplishments from Fremantle Boys' but they are unlikely to have been spectacular. He left the school within two years, after continued confrontations with teachers and the other inmates. Bond's personality seemed incompatible with the institution's discipline code. It was another shackle he would have to break. Schoolmate Bob Maumill (now a Sydney broadcaster) recalls: 'Bondy always insisted he was better and smarter than the rest of us ... the reason he left school early was because he argued so much with the teachers.'[19]

He was obviously self-conscious and evasive about his lack of formal education and this came through in an early television interview in 1969: 'I did most of my schooling in London, and with the war everything got tossed around a bit of course, and I never did settle down to schooling again out here. I think it's fairly difficult in the first years when you come to a new country. You don't know anyone, it takes some time to adjust to different principles of life. And with this, I just didn't settle down to schooling here. I think this brought about the desire to go and work and earn a living, and I did this ... (I didn't have any) really formal education, as one can put it, although the standard of education I had in the UK was probably higher than what it was here at the time and I'd been

reasonably quick to grasp onto anything to do with accountancy and figures and so forth ... I finished [my schooling] at
Fremantle Boys', for one year.'[20]

At Freo Boys', he was in a bigger sea, which he liked, but
he was a small fish way down a pecking order that included
some substantial sharks. Being big and tall, like the heavies of
Freo Boys', helped your chances of survival around the tough
Fremantle wharves. He was small and squat. He would have to
learn either to run or to fight. As it turned out, the former came
more naturally.

It is unlikely that Bond was brutalised by coming off
second best in schoolyard punch-ups. These were part of a
painful learning process he would have to go through until he
won his freedom. They certainly didn't make him any less
fearless. At Fremantle Boys' School he was ribbed over his
English accent, which he consciously tried to shed. He was
nicknamed 'the Frog' — because of his jowls, because he made
a lot of noise and because he jumped all over the place. He
hated the name, which pleased its creators, because it denied
him his tribal dignity. He was English; he hated the French.

He was also working out how to make money in his spare
time. These were the beginnings of the heady days of rock-'n'-
roll consumerism, and a teenage boy in high school had a lot of
demands on his trouser pocket. As a matter of principle Frank
wouldn't give in to his son on the question of pocket money.
Frank tried to pass on to Alan the same ethical framework in
which he had been strictly tutored in the Welsh Chapel: no
work, no pay. (Not only that, it had to be a fair day's work for a
fair day's pay.) Never a borrower or a lender be, etc. There was
no communication, the ethical framework was never trans-
planted, and there was no pocket money from Da. The getting
of Alan Bond's wisdom at Freo Boys' would have to depend
very much on his success at extracurricular business activities.

Alan Bond's first entrepreneurial thrust was to cover the
after-hours waterfront with print. As the school was so close to
Victoria Quay, Bond, along with schoolmates John Waters and
Murray Shaw, became after-school newspaper sellers on the
docks. They received two shillings in the pound commission
for selling magazines to sailors from interstate traders.[21] Salesmanship has always been Bond's strongest attribute. He was
born a hustler and he honed these skills on the rough and

tough Freo wharves where a quarter had to be fought for. He was good at it. His first opportunity lay in the fact that the paper shop shut each day at 7 p.m. Bond still had peak demand from the suckers who poured in from the sea at that time of the evening; but he had no supply and neither did the other kids. In no time Bond had struck a deal with the shop owner, secured his own stock of papers and magazines and supplied the other kids, making them his employees.

It was as plain as the nose on his face. Bondy had filled his first market niche. He had become a capitalist. He owned a distribution system and controlled a market. He was employing people. He was making profits at the margin. He was on his way to becoming a millionaire. It was so ridiculously simple that it fuelled his growing ego and he began to scorn the dumb Aussies who didn't have his Pommie spunk, his insights, his get-up-and-go. The work was time consuming, but then so was spending the proceeds. Froggie had made it. He was his own man. The pursuit of pleasure had become a Bond obsession at high school although there is evidence of its having been already awakened at East Freo State. He had to make money to spend it. He had to spend it to make it. The lifestyle of a teenage merchant banker with a Bodgie haircut and long sidelevers was a full one. There was little time for home, there was even less for school.

The crunch came in 1952 when Bond was fourteen. 'I had done all the work in languages and mathematics they set me when I first went to school in Fremantle and I was bored. There was no challenge. I was restless and wanted to get out and do something for myself. Very wisely, my father said: "Well, let's look at what you can do well at this point." The only thing I could do well at that age was draw, so my father said, "Maybe you should be a signwriter." His philosophy was that I should always have something to fall back on. He'd started work in the coalmines in Wales when he was twelve so he thought it was perfectly natural for me to want to leave school at fourteen and start working. If there were jobs available, he saw no reason why I should not start to earn some money. After working for a couple of years and realising how little I knew, I went back to night school.'[22]

But this story has another side: 'You are too late,' said Fred Parnell, seventy-five, when I settled down to question him about a document he had signed thirty-seven years earlier. 'I gave his apprenticeship papers back to him when he was featured in "This Is Your Life" in 1980.' As Bond's first and only boss, Parnell has been pestered by the media for many years. He was interviewed by Ron Saw and got his picture in the *Bulletin*, they flew him to Sydney to film the episode of 'This Is Your Life'. He's bemused by all the fuss because he is still dumbfounded by Bond's success. 'I wouldn't have given him Buckley's chance. He showed signs of a good imagination, was very energetic ... but he was not an accomplished tradesman. While he was with me he showed only normal ability. When he went into business I thought he would last only a few months.'

As bold as brass, Bond had dropped in to Parnell's nearby workshop after school one day and asked for a job. 'He had a bright personality and could present himself well. I was looking for a new apprentice.' Parnell was impressed by Bond's vivacity and enthusiasm but his obvious lack of application to school work was a concern. He had brought in some promising examples of his drawing and lettering but he had no runs on the board with his other school results. Bond told Parnell he had had enough of school and wanted to get out and earn money. Parnell could relate to that desire but first he would need to talk to the boy's father, tradesman to tradesman. As a Freemason, Parnell puts great store on the ancient fraternity for mutual help and instinctive brotherly sympathy — in the skills of his signwriting craft and in a man's word.

Frank Bond, who had established his own business in Freo as a painter and decorator, was keen to oblige. He told Parnell that his son was a good worker and he guaranteed that the lad would knuckle down to his trade-class studies. Frank even claimed that Alan was a mathematical genius, a claim that was taken with a grain of salt. Parnell then agreed to take him on. Alan Bond's labour was indentured for a period of five years. In that time he was expected to become a proficient tradesman and to accept direction from his employer and his father. In exchange for the in-house training, he would work like a demon for below-award wages. The starting money was not generous but it should have been a fortune for a fourteen year old. Parnell recalls it as about two pounds a week. Bond has recalled it both as two pounds five shillings and two pounds fifteen shillings a week. He would not be able to give up his night job on the wharves, and this would become a sticking point later.

There is a suggestion that Frank railroaded his son into the signwriting trade; but given Alan's poor results, his lack of discipline and his inability to fit in, he had little choice. Frank didn't want his son to become a juvenile delinquent, a 'Bodgie', a Wild One of the 1950s. His Depression-bred desire was to see his son go out into the New World with proper qualifications, with something to fall back on. If he couldn't get it at school, then he would have to gain trade qualifications.

Not only was Alan in total agreement with his father on this issue, it appears he initiated the move and presented it to him as a *fait accompli*. The impetuous youngster was impatient for social success. He had had a taste of money on the wharves and he was addicted. Through the self-respect that comes from work he thought he would find the freedom from his strange persecution complex. He hated life at school. He was too clever for school, and it interfered with business. He had a fierce desperation to get out and make a name for himself.

Only later would he realise that he wasn't as clever as he had thought, that he had entered a new entrapment, that he had locked himself into long-term low wages and diminished his earning potential. For the moment, he relished his new freedom. He had time to work, time to do business and time to play. The boy was a new man at work, a happy man. He found dignity in labour. The work was mostly mundane general signwriting for the port town. Oil company signs were a staple diet for Parnell Signs (which still does business today in Queen Victoria Street). A gofer like Bond would have spent much of his time doing menial work at the behest of the tradesmen: running messages, holding, carrying and erecting signs. There were trade classes to attend for half a day once a fortnight, a valuable source of contacts in the building industry. Here he met and cultivated like-minded individuals with an eye for the main chance who were in the know about the various jobs their employers were tendering for.

Fred Parnell retired from Parnell Signs in 1977. When he went to the family firm as a fifteen year old in 1928/29 the work was repetitive and irregular and the pay was ten shillings a week. By the time he left, the signwriters' artwork was being generated by a computer. Parnell does not claim credit for either discovering or creating Alan Bond: 'Alan had a will of his own.' He does not resent the success of his former pupil but sees the distinction of being Bond's only boss as a dubious one. Bond had not finished the five-year apprenticeship, he had not become an accomplished tradesman, and there were rumours that he was organising the other Parnell apprentices to do outside jobs.

Parnell says Bond could pick up the gist of a thing fairly quickly, and was a good worker who gave him little trouble, but when he took telephone messages his spelling was atrocious. This was not one of the attributes he liked to see in his young signwriters.

There were happier moments, though, and the one Parnell related to the cameras from behind the sight screen in the 'This Is Your Life' studio seems somehow symbolic: One day Alan was assisting tradesman Keith Pittaway do a sign on a verandah on the corner of Pakenham and High Streets. His task was to help shift the trestlework from which Keith was working as the job advanced around the corner. Alan was either daydreaming or, more likely, standing on the corner, watching all the girls go by. Keith moved his end of the trestle, Alan failed to respond, and the poised paint tin toppled on his head and laid him out cold in the gutter. He was carted off to hospital and everybody laughed.

Meanwhile, back at her Quarry Street ranch, Eileen Hughes was blissfully unaware of the existence of Alan Bond. She was enjoying school at Our Lady of the Sacred Heart, becoming involved with the Society of Mary and enjoying reading. She was dreaming of a distant Notre Dame with Boston lace, dreaming of dancing, dreaming of tall, dark, handsome strangers on white chargers ... If anything, her life was too cloistered, she was bored and looking for some excitement. Eileen didn't have to do anything; she didn't have to prove anything.

Because of the war, there had been no America's Cup sailing since 1937. No one saw fit to revive the competition. The winds of change had since blown away the sheltered world of elegance and privilege that had nurtured the J boats and their swashbuckling tycoon owners. In 1949 the Cup was removed from the vaults at Tiffany's to the NYYC's landlocked clubhouse at 37 West 44th Street. A special wrench was used to secure it to an oaken table in the crypt-like trophy room. The wrench was placed in the club's safe, along with the Deed of Gift.

One yacht did come to Fremantle in 1954. It was the royal yacht *Britannia*, and its arrival in the harbour caused great excitement in the Bond household. The Queen of England and Australia was in the Port of Fremantle! It was the first visit by a reigning monarch to this colonial outpost.

CHAPTER THREE

1958: Colombia vs. Sceptre, Colombia, *4–0*

It is 1955. The world (and, in its microcosm, the Australian Labor Party and the port town of Fremantle) is dividing bitterly on fundamental ideological grounds. Little Aussie Alan, seventeen, has grown into a man-on-the-move around Irish Catholic, working-class Fremantle. He is still extremely small beer, but beer nonetheless. The weekly wage he draws at Parnell Signs wouldn't cover his bills from one night out on the town. Consequently, he is always looking for a quid. He doesn't have a starving family to feed and he isn't saving to go back to England any more. He just thinks that money should be acquired rapidly and disposed of rapidly. He's started to say, 'You've got to move a quid, move a quid. Keep the money rolling.'[23]

Locals say he was always enthusiastic, always looking for

work, and this irritated some of the more leisurely Fremantle folk. This was a pretty easy-going place, a union town devoted to its inalienable right to the pursuit of pleasure and the eight-hour day. This was the Lucky Country. Work was something you did to fill in the gap between the great Australian week-ends. Unless you had a special need, like an expensive illness in the family, it was considered unnatural in Freo to go around touting for work when you already had a job. But Bond was something completely different. 'It soon dawned on me that there were few people who really wanted to go out and tackle the difficult work. I found there was money to be made in solving other people's problems.'[24]

Bond had no seed money, no capital, no collateral. It wasn't needed in freewheeling Freo where everyone operated on credit. (In Dingville, the Italian quarter between Essex and Norfolk Streets, it was not uncommon for weekly rent to be paid in kind, in snapper and crayfish.) Whether by default or intent, Bond's early wheeling and dealing revolved around his ability to buy and sell labour. Remarkable as it may seem in a town with a strong trade union culture, Bond became an organiser and facilitator of non-union, unskilled labour: a one-man labour exchange, a labour contractor for technical college apprentices.

In a television interview in March 1969, Bond told of his early business acumen in this way:

> BOND: Together with a few other fellows which were at the technical school I was attending as part of my job, we got together a small group and we used to do what we called 'foreign orders'. These were jobs we did in the weekend and evenings and night-times ... DONAVAN: Did you prosper? BOND: Yes, yes, we went ahead and as a matter of fact, I think that from that beginning I got the idea that I should have my own signwriting, painting and building business. And it was only about three years later when this came about ... We formed a company called Nu-Signs, which had all sorts of ramifications of working, renovating buildings, most of the awkward jobs which other people didn't want to do. At that time there was a great shortage of skilled people and we gathered these together to do jobs ...

To organise these 'foreign orders' Bondy needed some basic ingredients: intelligence on work available, a pool of semi-skilled labour, someone with established business, trade and union qualifications to front his illegal organisation and someone with a car. Freo Tech. provided the first few, and Frank Bond's current union ticket and English Ford Zephyr, with a wheel wobble, completed the picture. Now, you could argue that Bond was also cheating on Parnell Signs and his employer, Fred Parnell, in that he was organising his apprentices, behind his back, to do outside jobs. No doubt his accomplices, under Bondy's urging, did the same thing to their employers. You could also argue that they were merely enterprising, indeed civic-minded, youngsters who were doing their bit to clean up the run-down port town in their spare time.

In Bondy's own words, 'After a couple of years at Parnell's, I decided I needed to go back to school, so I enrolled at Fremantle Technical School and attended four nights a week for five years ... I learnt all sorts of things, English, tinsmithing, carpentry ... and when I wasn't at night school I went to Wrightson's dance studio to learn ballroom dancing.'[25] He has also said, 'I went to night school for five nights a week for three years, in which I did various things, including bookkeeping and accountancy.' Apart from the contradictions in the two statements, one wonders where he found the time to fit in all this study with his extramural activities.

The truth is that Bondy used Freo Tech. the same way he used Freo Boys' and Parnell Signs: as a base from which to launch various business ventures.

Perhaps it was his desire to be seen and noticed that caused him to hustle so in those early days as an apprentice. After five years in the country, he was definitely assimilating and even picking up a few of the nasty local habits to combine with his London street skills. Was he proving things to himself or to his peer group? Bondy uses the royal 'we' often when he means 'I', and the small groups that he gathered for these 'foreign orders' seem more like convenient arrangements than a concerted attempt at group profit sharing. Using his charm and guile, Bondy press-ganged specialist units for specific projects. He made the connection, did the hustling, and arranged the actualisation. *He* did it, he figured, therefore the difference between costs and contract price was *his*.

Bond won work from regular contractors, the apprentices' masters, by undercutting on price. He did not have to pay his contracted labour full award wages or penalty rates. The work would be done outside normal business hours, to minimise inconvenience, and he would guarantee that it could be finished on time. During this period he painted the Burns Philp Building, the Federal Hotel in William Street and the Bushells Tea headquarters in Queen Victoria Street. He also painted a large number of houses in and around Fremantle.

It was the sort of practical, hands-on experience some fathers send their sons to expensive international business schools to learn. Bond pitched in with the other kids but he was also the driving force behind each endeavour. He saw himself as providing the brains and determination that got the show on the road. He was the only one tough enough to crack the whip and lull the lags out of their apathy. Profit margins would have been narrow but he did manage to create wealth for himself and his small group of co-conspirators at a time when, and in a place where, affluence was conspicuous when it was consumed in vast quantities.

'All he seemed to do was work and drink buckets of beer — until he found that the beer interfered with business. Then all he did was work,' says Denis Sowden, whose family of wholesale butchers had the first refrigerated shop window in Fremantle, which young Bond was to paint. 'We said he should turn up at 12 on Saturday, when we were closing. He was there at 11.30. It was typical.'

Before it eventually evolved into Nu-Signs Pty Ltd in 1957, Alan Bond Enterprises was a hydra-headed monster in its illicit early days of moonlighting, mumbles and 'foreign orders'. Sometimes it acted like the unofficial night shift or overtime division of Parnell Signs, at other times it was Bond and one or two like-minded mates from the tech. school. More often than not, especially on the little jobs, it was Bond alone or Bond acting in some form of concert with a seemingly reluctant Frank Bond.

Like a scene from the 1950s motion picture, *High School Confidential*, Frank (easy-going but 'concerned father of two') would have had many arguments over the keys to the Ford Zephyr with his rebellious 'Wild One' Alan, whose business, social and educational opportunities depended on having access to the family 'wheels'. The generation gap between Frank, from the Welsh Valleys, and Alan, from freewheeling

Freo in the fifties, was considerable. It was exacerbated by more than just the keys to the car. If Alan Bond gave the best years of his life to the pursuit of young love and its lubricant, rock-'n'-roll music, if he stayed out late every night on some excuse or another, if he didn't contribute housekeeping money, then all of this meant nothing to Frank Bond compared with the lad's lack of discipline and moral fibre. He would not do anything by the book, Frank's book; he always wanted to write his own book. He felt in charge of his destiny, and he thought his destiny was to have a good time, pull a few chicks, and become a millionaire by the time he turned twenty-one. The ultimate teenage boy's fantasy.

He had certainly picked the right industry growth corridor and understood the basics of supply and demand (with labour) and debt-funded project financing (with credit). Because of the postwar housing shortage and industrial regeneration, painting and decorating Freo's substantial and decrepit housing stock and industrial symbols was work crying out to done. Bond's ability was to see the obvious and have the resolve to carry it through.

As Alan Bond approached Doozer Hughes's Quarry Street castle that July evening in 1955, thoughts of the Spanish inquisition surged painfully through his brain. This was more scary than the Nazi V2 ballistic missiles he had fronted ten years before in the London blitz, or stepping off the *Himalaya* and onto a strange land five years previously ... For the first time in his life he was in really big trouble and there was no way he could talk his way out of it.

Doozer's daughter, Eileen, was pregnant and young Alan was marching off manfully to accept responsibility for his part. His anxiety was accentuated because this was a time of high sectarian tension between Catholics and Protestants. He was studying to be a Freemason. Doozer was probably Freo's leading Catholic layman. There were bound to be sparks and bitter recriminations. Frank had been flabbergasted; Kathleen had urged him to do the right thing. He was brave enough to face up to it. What he didn't like was the thought that the birth of his brilliant career could be curtailed because of his stupidity in causing an unwanted pregnancy.

The Orange and the Green had met on neutral ground at Wrightson's Dance Studio at Victoria Hall in High Street on a balmy night a few months previously. 'He was kind of forward,' Eileen says of the encounter that was to leave her expecting a baby at age seventeen. (John Bryan Bond was born on 26 February 1956, six months after his parents' wedding on 13 August 1955.) 'That's where I met my wife, Eileen. She was a teacher there, and I also became a teacher,' says Alan, sounding pretty pleased with himself.

Two of the many Bondy myths are destroyed by these revelations of pre-marital hanky panky. The minor one is that Eileen initially rejected Alan's marriage proposal because he was not a Catholic. But the major myth surrounding Alan Bond's early career and subsequent success has him marrying Eileen for her money. This is a massive misunderstanding of his motives on approaching Doozer Hughes's door that fateful night. To be sure, there was rage at first, and a right dressing down. Eileen's mother, Mary, was distressed and Doozer uttered a curse not normally uttered away from the South Fremantle Football Club. But in the end what Alan Bond got from Doozer was kindly understanding and a resolve to sort out the mess.

Doozer Hughes simply adored children. According to Eileen, he was happiest when perched on the best lounge suite in the front sitting room at Quarry Street and inviting his children to seat themselves on his lap. At fifty-two he was also wise in the ways of the world, especially the ways of Fremantle. It is hard to find a community activity he was not involved in. As head of the Fremantle division of the wool brokers, Prevost & Co., he was used to solving labour disputes. As president of the South Fremantle Football Club, as a Fremantle City councillor and as a commissioner of the Fremantle Port Authority, he was adept at solving problems with honour. His honour was at stake along with his young daughter's reputation. Mr Hughes was an honourable man. Bond had found his father figure in Fremantle.

Of course, Bond would have to marry the girl as soon as possible; there was no question of anything else. He would also have to renounce his Protestant past and embrace Catholicism. This was a sticking point but Doozer was adamant that a mixed marriage was definitely not on. He would also have to agree to the child in question (and any other offspring from the union) being likewise brought up Catholic. Bond was still in a state of shock and at Doozer's mercy. He had no choice but to agree.

It is a definite understatement to say that there is no love lost between Catholics and Freemasons. Each group considers the other to be the personification of the Antichrist. Bond had flirted with freemasonry because he thought it would be good for business. His father was one and so was his boss, Fred Parnell. The Catholics even had their own version of it, called the Order of the Knights of the Southern Cross, of which Doozer was a member. Bond drank at the Freemasons' Hotel over the road from the Tech. and is said to have studied the elaborate rituals and secret signs of freemasonry during his crowded evenings. Fred Parnell says that Frank Bond had once asked him to nominate Alan for the local lodge but he had declined because he didn't know him well enough. Changing ships in such a dramatic fashion, midstream, was not a common occurrence but Bondy managed this historic compromise with what appears to be the minimum of fuss.

When I talked to Father James Sullivan, the priest who baptised Alan Bond (and John Bond, a few months later) into the Catholic faith and married the loving couple at St Patrick's Church, he denied all knowledge of Bond having been a Freemason, which is an impossible proposition but is one way of making the problem go away. Fred Parnell, who was not invited to the wedding, was not even upset by his having changed camps. His view was that a Freemason who married a Catholic would have the best of both worlds. Bondy probably saw it that way as well. Mr Hughes had done the right thing by Bondy and Bondy was keen to do the right thing by Mr Hughes. He had been fulsome in his response to Mr Hughes's enquiry about his prospects, even though the question smacked of shutting the gate after the bull had bolted, and Mr Hughes was merely going through the motions of formality and politeness in asking it. This was Bondy's big moment, his first chance to take centre stage and impress his future father-in-law. Naturally, he bragged about his trade and his desire to be a millionaire by the time he was twenty-one, but these empty words fell on deaf ears. Sensing the mood of the audience he was playing to, he then produced something more concrete to offer an aggrieved father who was desperately seeking some positive outcome to the sordid little affair. Bondy solemnly promised to love and care for Eileen and to buy a block of land the day after the wedding and commence building a home for his new Catholic family. The deal was settled with a handshake. The road to Damascus was but a short trip down Quarry Street. The Orange and the Green had come together beneath a sprig of wattle in faraway Fremantle.

True to his word, the day after the wedding on 13 August 1955, Bondy purchased his first piece of Australia and launched himself into the property business. It was a quarter-acre block on the corner of Maclean and Isaac Streets, Melville, a short distance inland from Freo. The list price was 350 pounds and he slapped a brand-new five-pound note in the hand of the estate agent from T M Burke as a money-down deposit. The land shark had taken his first bite and he liked the taste. It gave him a warm feeling. It was the start of a lifetime's habit.

The one humanising aspect in Alan Bond's perceived personality at this time is the sheer joy he seems to have derived from living out the great Australian dream. He was prepared to be resourceful and have a go in the cause of emancipation. The 'Aussie battler' experience he gained then as a struggling, newly-wed, homeowner-builder was genuine. If he had 'married into a lot of money', as many believe, it was certainly not evident at this stage of his career.

'I built a double garage to live in while I built the house. I became a stonemason, bricklayer and carpenter and joiner, and some of the walls were not too straight, I must admit. It is not easy.'[26]

The fact that the house at 36 Maclean Street is still standing bears testimony as much to the substantial subsequent renovations and additions that have since taken place as to Bond's skills as a home builder. The outline of the old house can be discerned only by observing the different colour of the roof tiles. Melville Heights, as it is now known, has become a leafy, green suburb. Then, it would have been a dusty, brown sand-belt estate on the edge of civilisation. It has no view of the Swan River. It has no view of the sea.

Besides building the house, Bondy did other things to ingratiate himself with the Hughes family. Cousin John Hughes says he first heard of Bond when his grandmother told him Eileen was going out with a 'brash young Englishman'. Bond later quoted her thirty shillings to paint her kitchen, which would not have gone down too well in a family more used to giving than to taking. There was suspicion and resentment in the family at the arrival of a foreign devil in their midst. Bondy decided he should make another grand gesture to win the moral high ground. He painted, gratis, an original landscape on the back stage wall of the new St Pat's parish hall. The work is a simple scenic backdrop of blackboys and scrub, much like the desert island environment he saw as he gazed down Cockburn Sound on his first day in Australia. The work is not nearly as good as the Vienna architectural drawings and watercolours done by that other house-painter-turned-artist, Adolf Hitler, but it appeased the Hughes family. There could be peace, this time, for Eileen's sake. Besides, they were practical people and they figured that any Pommie Freemason who chose to praise the Lord by using his God-given talents to decorate an Irish Catholic church can't be all that bad.

He was no artist but he was still surprisingly intent on giving up his day job and making a living out of his talents. By moving out and shacking up with Eileen, Bondy finally broke the chains of unhappiness that bound him to England and his English family. His next task was to seek emancipation from indentured labour and really become his own man. He could not do the latter until he had completed the former. Frank would never have approved; but then Frank never approved of anything . . .

In 1956 the Suez Canal came to a standstill and the world came to Melbourne for the Olympic Games; the Russians crushed Hungary when they reached Budapest; and Alan Bond turned eighteen and came to the conclusion that he must abandon his apprenticeship and pursue a career in business. According to Fred Parnell, the apprenticeship was terminated after three and a half years by mutual agreement but against advice. Alan wanted out and Parnell was not going to stand in his way. He didn't think all that highly of the standard of his work or give him much chance of success but young Alan seemed to want to prove something to himself and to everybody else. (Parnell says that if Bondy goes broke, he can always come back and finish his apprenticeship.)

Parnell was not to find out until later that Bond had been 'involved in a few activities for his own benefit' while still in his employ. In fact, Bond's outside work had become the norm and his apprenticeship at Parnell Signs had become a time-

consuming and low-paying 'foreign order'. Bond sees it differ-
ently. Big and bold as he is, he is quite squeamish about facing
up to his lack of educational and trade qualifications (and the
illicit nature of his early business ventures). It is as if he cannot
abide his own ordinariness in this regard. Whenever challenged about why he never bothered to take exams, Bond has
waxed defensive:

'That's not quite right. I took a five-year examination after
three and a half years' study and passed. But I believe the term
"academic qualification" is an ever-changing thing. Quite
frankly, a lot of people who've had ten years' experience in
academia know very little other than what they have read
in books. They are not really taught to think about their place
in the environment, about which they know very little. As far as
my own family is concerned, I have made my four children
aware of the need to have a background of achievement behind
them, as I have a trade.'[27]

Technically, he did have a trade, he was in the same
painting and decorating business as his father and he had a
union ticket to prove it. (Not much can happen in Freo without
a union ticket.) He had trained with a recognised tradesman
and he was working with a recognised tradesman. He had not
come by these qualifications through the normal procedures
but this was unlikely to be detrimental to his career prospects.

It was about this time that Frank had to go to hospital for a
week for a check up on his remaining lung. He returned to find
himself a partner in his own business. The Alan Bond band-
wagon was beginning to lurch forward.

And so it came to pass that Alan Bond Enterprises forsook
the bourgeois comforts of Adelaide Street, where Freo Boys',
Parnell's and St Pat's sat snuggled (perhaps smugly) side by
side, and ventured bravely into the land of mammon. To be
precise, he shifted into the proletarian delights of a tin shed
behind the Fremantle headquarters of the Communist-ruled
Waterside Workers' Federation, on the corner of Mouat and
High Streets, in the seedy Freo West End. It was not the most
auspicious beginning for a man eventually to be regarded as
one of the world's supreme capitalists; but then, beggars can't
be choosers ... It was cheap, it was downtown, it was convenient and it was available. The P&O Hotel, a lair of lags, was a
thirsty spit away over the road. The Roma Cafe, renowned by

the locals for its unusual chicken and spaghetti dish as much as for its wholesome minestrone, backed on to the workshop. For a man who liked to work, drink, eat, and talk, it was perfect.

But there must have been a political price to pay for this accommodation and Bondy freely admits it: 'I have always had an interest in power, the bases of political power and its various factions. In the early days I got to know a lot of the waterside workers as individual people and have always understood their point of view. Mind you, I was well grounded in the labour movement. My father was a labour man who had worked in the mines and was conscious throughout his life of the need to work hard for his wages and of the balance of community involvement between those who have and those who don't ... I am still a member of the painters' union and I still pay my dues. I like to get the union magazines and read and feel part of the union. It is important to me.'[28]

This may seem a reasonable position to take if you are renting a workshop from a trade union but these were not reasonable times. The Cold War between East and West was blowing hot and Australia had sent troops to fight Communists in Korea and Malaya. The Russians had just ruthlessly crushed a revolt in Hungary and the world was in ferment. This passion was reflected and felt with no less intensity in Fremantle, where the loyalties of the wharf labourers and their families were torn between the Church and the union. As the most powerful union in Freo, the Communist-led Waterside Workers' Federation was constantly up against the Catholic-led Anti-Communist Australian Labor Party, which changed its name to the Democratic Labor Party in 1957. It was the wharfies' union that had successfully challenged the Menzies government's Communist Party Dissolution Act in the High Court. Antipathy toward all things Communist had intensified since 1954 when KGB agent Vladimir Petrov defected and claimed he had evidence of Soviet espionage in Australia. A Royal Commission was set up and diplomatic relations with the USSR were severed. This was not the time or the place to be showing a red rag to the bulls.

How Bondy managed to walk this political tightrope without falling to the prods from the polemical protagonists below remains a mystery. His ability to adapt and accommodate was certainly apparent during this Cold War in a hot place, as he continued to do business with both Catholics and Communists.

The Hughes family must have been aghast. There was no question about where they stood on the issue of fraternising with Communists and their fellow travellers. Poor Doozer copped it every time he went to St Pat's and the footy club. What had he done to deserve a son-in-law like Alan — a Pom, a Freemason, a big mouth and now a Pinko? Surely Doozer would go straight to heaven when his time came.

The wharfies are still there in High Street but the tin shed has made way for a bitumen car park. You can see the outline of the shed roof etched into the masonry high up the back wall and, at the entrance to the yard in Mouat Street, you can just make out the old Nu-Signs sign. It has been painted over. Around the corner at the Roma they have an original relic of the master signwriter's early craftsmanship framed on the wall of the restaurant. It advertises takeaway chickens for one pound. As examples of his ability at the time, neither sign is particularly good in its execution. This confirms Fred Parnell's view that Bondy was not yet accomplished, but very ordinary, when he went out on his own.

Bondy's thick skin made him impervious to the jolts from his detractors. He would salute them with one upthrust finger and shout 'Up yours!' Then, with a flourish of the hands, he would whistle loudly to draw attention to his new set of wheels, his first car: a brown-and-cream FC Holden station wagon, with a rack on top for his gear and a rabbit's tail hanging limply from the aerial. He knew that success had its ultimate test on the scoreboard of life's major acquisitions. He had evidence to show he was doing well. He had to *have*.

There were some very good times. He liked to enjoy life to its fullest, when he could, as a reward for his hard work and continued success. He would swim at the beach, he would throw arrows at a dart board in the pub and he would moon to the debonair delights of ballroom dancing where he, more often than not, came to grips with the opposite sex. 'Dancing was one of the few things you could do in those days,' says Eileen.

By coincidence, Alan Bond's business career was getting off the ground just as the America's Cup competition was getting off the rocks. Having undergone the longest hiatus in its history, the America's Cup Deed of Gift was amended in 1956, with the approval of the New York State Supreme Court, and in 1958 the competition was reborn in the smaller and more moderately priced twelve-metre yachts. It was still between the Royal Yacht Squadron and the New York Yacht Club, though, and a yachting writer of the time described the British syndicate, headed by Hugh Goodson, as 'a group of kindly, elegant, elderly British gentry, whose sense of loyalty and gallantry was infinitely superior to their sense of competition and their critical understanding of boat speed.'[29]

Not surprisingly, the Poms were hopeless and *Colombia* thrashed *Sceptre* in four straight races by margins of seven to almost twelve minutes. On 20 September, President Eisenhower watched the first race from a destroyer but left to play golf before the final gun. The New York *Herald Tribune* described the last race as 'a spectacle calculated to make the tea break at a cricket test seem wildly exciting.' In Australia no one had been interested in the event until they heard those magic words, *cricket test*. Then Sydney media mogul Frank Packer sniffed the wind and decided to have a go on the grounds that Aussies were, by nature, racially superior to Poms. His challenge for the next Cup was announced in October 1959. When asked what hàd inspired the challenge, he replied extemporaneously, 'Alcohol and delusions of grandeur.'

CHAPTER FOUR

1962: Weatherly vs. Gretel, Weatherly, *4–1*

Nineteen fifty-nine was a big year for Bondy. He turned twenty-one, turned his first million, worked in every corner of the State, spent three months overseas, did his first big real estate deal and fathered his first daughter. It was another turning point for a man who was establishing a modus operandi for not going in a straight line.

Setting the target of becoming a millionaire by his majority seems admirable for a young businessman. That he planned ahead and budgeted at this age is good. (He now says Bond-Corp is working to a fifty-year business plan.) That he planned to make (in profits) and amass (in assets) a million pounds in the four years to 1959 seems an idle boast but one he proudly claims to have met.

While it is entirely possible, given Bond's level of activity at the time, that the value of all the work done by Nu-Signs over the four-year period may have totalled about $2 million, it is highly unlikely that he had accumulated assets or cash that would even approach this figure. Often with Bondy, finding the real profit figure can become a pea-and-thimble trick, especially when it is said that he didn't pay a penny in tax in his first seven years in business. He would argue that cash flow is king and that we are comparing apples with pears and denigrating his substantial achievement; and he would be partially correct. He did turn over a lot of business in these first few years under his own steam and he did achieve the critical mass required for business take-off. For this he should be given due credit. He was certainly a success in his own eyes, which is the important thing here. But was Nu-Signs really the raging success he claimed it was, or just a tin-pot show?

He tried to make a go of it and, at one stage, had five or six employees on his payroll. His earliest business plan was to take advantage of the cost savings in mass production by using an automated silk-screen printing process which he says he developed. But producing the signs was only half of the economic equation. His general problem was in selling them, and his particular solution was to rent them and recycle the used ones.

The market was real estate agents and builders, and for them Bond provided a unique service: 'We'd deliver and put up the signs and take them down again when the property was sold.'[30] This was a boon for the local agents who hated nothing more than having to put up and pull down property signs. He sold it to them on the basis that they were also getting a good financial deal. Instead of buying a sign from him for say two pounds, Bondy would rent them one for ten shillings and also charge them ten shillings for erection and ten shillings for removal. It was a clever piece of marketing and quite pioneering in its use of rental leverage. But, good as it was, it was never going to make him a million pounds.

The reality of the Fremantle signwriting business in the late 1950s was that it was too small, even during a property boom, to sustain all the participants and that the growth of one was at the expense of the others. Fred Parnell says, after prompting, that Nu-Signs undercut Parnell's on some signage tenders 'but [the clients] had to pay the extra in the end to come back to me for quality work.' So Bond's bread and butter came from the small stuff he attracted from around his WWF tin shed workshop off High Street.

The work was mostly mundane: houses, shop windows, takeaway food billboards, and flag-fall and tariff signs for cabbies like Mick Vodanovich. 'I used to go around to his shed on a Sunday, he'd slap on the new prices and we'd knock off two bottles of beer.' Doing these fiddly little bits was a living, but not much more. Given that the man's prime objective upon setting up Nu-Signs was to make as much money as quickly as possible, it must have gradually dawned on him that the small-brush approach was proving deficient in attracting large-scale mammon.

He sold the signage business to a builder in about 1962, having failed to set the world alight. Though he had been full of ideas and energy and prepared to work extremely long hours, his artistic skills were crude and there just wasn't the work to go around. Had Bond stuck exclusively to his signwriting trade, the world may never have heard of him.

Bondy decided to raise his sights and broaden his corporate horizons by becoming a bulk painting and decorating contractor, a jack-of-all-trades, a go-anywhere, do-anything sort of fellow. His mark now shifted to the bigger corporate and government contracts. It was a return to the methods of his likely lads when they were moonlighting on 'foreign orders'. He was buying and selling labour, just as he had done when his after-hours gangs had painted the Burns Philp building, the Federal Hotel (that contract was supposed to be worth 3200 pounds) and the Bushells Tea Company office in Queen Victoria Street.

Bond would have us believe that the name Nu-Signs had all sorts of connotations beyond its more obvious reference to modern advertising. To him there had always been two aspects to the Nu-Signs business — signage and contracting — and they ran as separate operations, side by side. He would reject the proposition that the former was but a front, or cover, for the latter. The diversity of the work undertaken by Nu-Signs at this time is indicative of Bond's innate ability to consider any business proposition, no matter how bizarre, so long as he can see a quid in it. An early project that made Freo folk sit up and take notice of the upstart Bondy was when he and his boys painted the biggest crane on Fremantle Harbour one long weekend while the town's good unionists were at rest and play. 'They had a boom which went out some 200 feet and there weren't many people interested in climbing this boom to sandblast it and paint it. We took on this job and we started by doing one and we did about thirty of them.'[31]

How he pulled this contract from the Fremantle Port Authority (FPA) is not known but, by coincidence, his father-in-law, Doozer Hughes, was a commissioner at the time. We do know that when officials from the Ship Painters' and Dockers' Union and the Waterside Workers' Federation arrived at Victoria Quay on the Tuesday morning they were furious. They demanded to know whether the work had been carried out by union labour on full penalty rates and whether safety regulations had been enforced. No answers were forthcoming.

Bondy didn't give a stuff what his detractors said, so long as he got the job done and kept his client happy. He seemed delighted with his notoriety and dauntless in his desire to upset the applecarts of established business and union morality. He was discovering new ways of doing things all right, but he was doing it in a town which was very set in its traditional ways and resistant to change. It helped that he had no fear of heights.

The story is told that when he won a contract to paint the forty-metre hot stack at the Jandakot Wool Scourer's plant (possibly another Doozer connection) his quote included the cost of scaffolding he never used. 'Instead, he scaled the stack on a ladder, rigged a bosun's chair at the top and, despite the danger, swung out and around with his paints and brushes.'[32] He did chimneys, tidal flumes and some P&O ships, and even cracked an excavation contract with BP Refineries at the nearby Kwinana industrial estate. 'I built the concrete bunkers round the BP Refinery, developing a new method for concrete construction — I'd put chicken wire over the job and spray the concrete on.'[33]

His biggest contract was also his first contact with a government agency. It was to renovate and paint every railway station down the State between Broome and Perth. No one seems to know how a corporate pipsqueak like Bond managed to swing this massive deal but we presume it was because he tendered the lowest quote. (We do know that the staunchly pro-development Liberal premier to be, (Sir) Charles Court, numbered Doozer Hughes among his mates, but that may not have been relevant.) Having swung the deal, Bond then required the West Australian Government Railways to provide him with a boxcar and free cartage to allow the job to be completed on schedule. It was, and Bond said it paid well.

Interestingly, this was not Nu-Signs' most controversial project. That distinction belongs to 'the painting of the dingo', a *cause célèbre* in parochial Fremantle. The Dingo Flour sign on the Goodman Fielder silo on the North Fremantle headland is much more than an advertisement for a commercial product. It is an Indian Ocean landmark. Like the Colossus of Rhodes, this giant red native dog standing, with its head held high, thirty metres off the ground symbolises the port town's suspicious stance to the outside world. Without ascribing mystical properties to the emblem, it is a more metaphorical representation of the characteristics of the local inhabitants than the seahorses and black swans on the city's coat of arms or the bulldogs and sharks of the local football clubs.

To have created and executed such a powerful symbol, etched so deeply into the local psyche, would be a magnificent achievement for any signwriter, but the credit does not belong to Bondy. It was there, sniffing the wind and staring alertly out to sea, long before he was born. The design is the work of another local artist named Les Nash. He did a scale drawing of the dingo logo for the flour mill in the early 1930s and the sign was then erected by Davies Sign Services as a black animal on a yellow background. The Australian Army painted it out with camouflage during the war but the crafty dingo was merely hiding in the scrub. After the war, he gradually reappeared as the camouflage wore off. Then Fred Parnell repainted it, red on white, over the visible outline, adding an eye and the words *Dingo Flour*. He did this on instructions from the miller who was worried that people thought it to be a nice dog and were missing his message about buying the flour. Nu-Signs were the next to have retouched this work and so purloined the authenticity of its creation. Recognising the power of the symbol, Bondy later exaggerated his feat to heroic proportions when entertaining out-of-towners and so, through omission, perpetuated the myth which cannot be put down because it is both true and false at the same time. It is part of the Bondy mystique that he 'painted the dingo' and it seems churlish to deny him this moment of glory.

Bondy's dogged determination and broad-brush approach were by now paying reasonable dividends and he was acquiring valuable management skills along the way. He was collecting intelligence on tenders and forthcoming contracts by hanging around the traps, he was profitably exploiting his Doozer Hughes connection, he was learning to budget and quote for big jobs, he was clinching deals with well-thought-out presentations and he was applying a form of lateral thinking when confronted with difficulties. But his best skill was still his ability to organise labour. Bond claims he eventually employed about 400 men but even getting a gang of fifty on a project site would require many hours of consummate negotiations.

At the time there was a shortage of skilled labour but Bond still had on tap his pool from night school. Here he had kept a contact book and taken down the names and addresses of all the budding tradesmen with whom he came into contact. 'When the time came, he employed them together with the migrant Italians and Slavs who had experience and skills but no formal qualifications.'[34] But the contracting business also had its drawbacks. He was expected to roll up his sleeves and pitch in, and the hours he worked were ludicrously long. Hugh Schmitt relates that Bond 'and a mate were painting the Caves House Hotel at Yallingup once and it started to get dark. The mate said, "We won't finish this." Alan said, "I'll fix that." He went away and came back with two hurricane lamps.' While digging a trench with a pick in Derby in the arid north-west of the State, Bond had an unfortunate accident: The scorching sun had baked the ground so hard that his initial swing with the pick rebounded on him. Bond says he became a lot less hands-on with the manual work after that.

Finally, the ever-narrowing profit margins on this sort of work forced him to look for greener pastures. 'I soon realised that this wasn't my vocation. There was little future in buying and selling labour. As a commodity it was highly priced and in short supply.'[35] Perceptive as this comment may seem, the reason for his change of focus was that his sights were now firmly set on another commodity which was relatively cheap and in abundant supply in his country of adoption — land. More importantly for Bond, who was running out of time to fulfil his make-a-million vow, it was returning spectacular short-term capital gains.

Bond had been in love with the potential of Australia's wide-open spaces since the day he landed in the country. 'There was this great wilderness that each house lived in. I thought they must be farming the backyards.'[36] He bought his first house with a five-pound deposit after being in the country for a little over five years. 'Buy land son,' he used to quote, 'they have stopped making it.' And it didn't take him long to put two and two together when he was running the rent-a-sign business for the estate agents. 'I began to learn which types of properties sold best.'[37]

Housing starts jumped from 66,000 in 1956 to 81,000 in 1960 as returned servicemen and immigrants battled for space to grow. Bond turned to capitalise on the perennial metropolitan housing shortage and it became his avenue to wealth. He began talking up the property market with the zeal of a missionary: 'I just love to have my own piece of land. As a person who has come to Australia from another country, my piece of land makes me feel more Australian. I think it is wonderful that Australians should strive for ownership of their own home and land. They see it as their heritage.'[38]

His first property development is believed to have been a shopping complex on the corner of High and Josephson Streets in beautiful downtown Fremantle, and again the financial muscle is said to have come from Doozer Hughes (not that this help was extended liberally by Doozer; in many incidences Bondy used Doozer's name first then asked for permission in hindsight).

According to a local, Bond had first tried to gazump the Stricklands into parting with the derelict old Potato Board building next-door to the Victoria Hall in High Street, where he had danced his way into Eileen's life. While the Stricklands were dithering in the negotiations over his take-it-or-leave-it offer for the property, Bondy decided to enliven the proceedings by uttering a vile dockside curse and storming out of the talks, saying he would buy the local Hoyts picture theatre in the West End instead. It was pure bluff and a negotiating technique he was to perfect in later life. The local recalls: 'I couldn't believe it, here was this plump little fella who had just learned how to shave and was not yet old enough to vote, telling the local elders to get stuffed and threatening to buy the most culturally significant building in the town. I thought he must be from cloud cuckoo land.' Bond ended up with the service station over the road and developed it into shops and offices in conjunction with the property on the other corner of High and Josephson Streets.

Bondy's next endeavour on his personal road to Damascus was to take in the world. 'When I was twenty-one I spent three months travelling through other countries. I saw the sorts of things that were being done overseas and visualised doing them in Australia.'[39] He had now travelled further in outback Western Australia, courtesy of the government railways, than he had on his entire trip from England. It was time to broaden his horizons and finally free himself from the psychological hang-ups he suffered as a result of his forced emigration. Television had come to Perth in 1959 and a cashed-up Bondy was ready for some bright lights and big cities. This was his first overseas trip from Australia and was followed by another in 1960 when the Australian Jaycees sent him as a delegate to a world conference in Paris. These days he is rarely off a plane; but that first flight, like the first million, is always the hardest and probably the most significant, for without it there may not have been others.

We are told that, as a stranger in the American paradise, Bondy was particularly impressed with the cliff-top housing developments that clung to the walls of the Greater Los Angeles valleys. It was to inspire him, we are led to believe, to construct a Hollywood Hills-style residential development in the Darling Ranges to the east of Perth, called Lesmurdie Heights. This was the project that was finally to make him his fortune.

As cities, Los Angeles and Perth have about as much in common as chalk and cheese. Both have western-ocean sunsets which means you can drive home to the east in the evening without getting the sun in your eyes, but that's about all. But Bond says he has this ability to look at a greenfields site and visualise it as a finished suburb, complete with houses, roads, lawns, trees and washing on the lines. He reckoned he could sell a west-coast (USA) lifestyle to the people on the west coast of Australia.

He had the bit firmly between his teeth and was off and

running as soon as his plane touched down again in Perth. While circling Perth Airport, the panorama of metropolitan development unfolded below him. Even for a small city, Perth was bursting at the seems. Restrained in the west by the Indian Ocean and thirty kilometres away in the east by the wooded Darling Ranges, the suburban sprawl could only spread tentacles out in ribbons along the Great Northern, the Great Eastern and the Albany Highways. He knew the western boundary like the back of his hand; it was time to head for the hills in the east.

He found the land he wanted — 150 acres in the Darling Range foothills below Mount Gungin, which stands only limply at 409 metres. Here, beneath a backdrop of new television transmission towers, the Woodlupine, the Yule and the Bickley Brooks trickle down from their headwaters in the scrub-covered foothills and deposit their puny contribution in the Canning River, which gives way to the Swan as it swells Melville Water. The Yule Brook cascades over the falls at Lesmurdie and here only a small part of the bush wonderland has been set aside as a National Park.

It could be argued now that the whole area should have remained an urban greenbelt, but such arguments then would have been seen as flying in the face of progress. In the late 1950s, the only things more certain than the wheels of progress were death and taxes (and Bondy didn't like either of them). It was inevitable that somebody would eventually subdivide the nearest habitable land to the edge of the metropolitan sprawl. It was fortuitous, indeed, that that somebody just happened to be the young Alan Bond, Esquire.

We know it was former Crown land; a big tract of land like that, so close to the city, had to be. And we know he paid the then-staggering sum of 100,000 pounds ($200,000) for it. The question is: How did he get it re-zoned from rural to residential? Perhaps the local authorities thought he would never make it. 'Laying bitumen roads in the hills area of the Darling Ranges east of Perth was the first scheme from which I made money. I opened up land they said couldn't be opened for development. They told me it was an engineering impossibility to build a road around a mountain. But I knew it was possible . . .'

The money for the deal came from the Finance Corporation of Australia (FCA), a non-bank financial intermediary associated with the Bank of Adelaide (alas, both companies are now gone). The three-year loan, secured with first and second mortgages over the 150 acres and probably subject to planning approval as well, was guaranteed by Doozer Hughes. Bond's chances of getting it without Doozer's backing were about zero. His palms were already getting sweaty over the risks involved in this deal, as he was later to admit: 'I think, possibly, if ever I gambled, that was the time.'[40] In those days banks would lend you money only if you could prove that you didn't need it. The newly emerging, less-regulated finance companies, on the other hand, were facilitating the easiest credit terms in living memory. It was known in English as hire purchase, or in the native tongue as 'the never-never'.

Persuading FCA that the Lesmurdie Heights development was a bankable proposition (its business was extending credit for consumer durables; it had never backed a land development before) had been a harrowing experience for the asset-less Bond, but it was a process that he was to become extremely familiar with over the next thirty years. He finally convinced these gnomes of Adelaide when he offered them a double bite at the cherry. If they backed him with the 100,000 pounds to secure the site, he would also direct the block buyers to FCA for housing finance and they could collect interest from him and interest from them and have security over both the land and the homes. It was a convincing argument and FCA bought it. (The ruling hire purchase interest rate was 1 per cent a month, or 12 per cent a year.)

Doozer had been no less enigmatic than the officials from the FCA. He made it clear that his neck was on the line, along with the guarantee and his reputation. If it didn't work, his only option would be to pack his bags and head back to England, for there would be no more doors opening to him in Fremantle. This fear probably galvanised Bondy's frantic efforts at bituminising the gravel tracks of Lesmurdie to a greater extent than the profit motive.

Now, there was no way he was going to let a mere shire council or a mountain stand in his way. Even as the project rapidly came to fruition, his body ached and his mind was racked with doubts and anxiety. What if he put the 500 or so lots on the market and nobody was interested in buying because they were too far away and the idea was ahead of its time? The road to Lesmurdie was no Sunset Boulevard. What if they didn't want to wake up with views overlooking Perth and drive home without the sun in their eyes? What if they realised the outskirts had no facilities, like schools and shops, and no community to fall back on in times of trouble?

He needn't have worried. 'It was a bonanza,' says Jim Brewer, a Perth car salesman who helped Bond (who he said was 'actually dribbling with enthusiasm') with the selling when Lesmurdie Heights Estate opened in 1960. 'It was open slather. We had a few tents on site, and all these car salesmen selling land. People would walk onto a block and you'd just rush them into a tent to the finance guys, then go and grab another one!'[41] Eileen Bond remembers sitting in a marquee on the site while people queued up to buy the blocks: 'I'll never forget that day. I had a bag and it was stuffed full of money. It was like selling fish and chips. Most of the blocks sold before lunchtime.'[42] Another Bond acquaintance of the day says the subdivision 'represented the application of today's voracious business principles ahead of their time ... It was classic white-shoe stuff: buy the cheap rural land [seek and obtain] a zoning change and sell it off in blocks.'[43]

By making the roads and putting up the signs, Bondy became a made man; Lesmurdie had made him. He repaid the 100,000 pounds FCA loan in full within six weeks of taking it out and was naïvely bemused that the finance company did not thank him for his thrift in not sticking to the three-year term. We don't know what the capital gain was on the deal (and we doubt that the tax man does either) but if he sold, say, 500 quarter-acre lots at an average of 2000 pounds a block, then, all up, Eileen's bag would have been bulging with a million pounds in it (the magic million). Take off the 100,000 pounds owed to FCA and a generous 50,000 for roads, kerbing and guttering development and other marketing costs borne by Bond, and you've got some idea of why Alan Bond laughed, and laughed, and laughed all the way to the finance company that afternoon.

Not only had Bondy made a big quid, his timing had been impeccable. He had managed, without capital, to get in and out of a huge, boom-time residential development just before the Federal-government-induced credit squeeze of 1960–61 slammed shut the window of opportunity and crunched the fingers of other speculative land developers. To be fair, credit for the timing of the squeeze belongs just as much to Treasurer Harold Holt as it does to developer Alan Bond, who didn't know a damn thing about economics at that stage. Like a latter-day Paul Keating, Holt had warned in his 1960 August Budget that the economy was overheating and that if it didn't stop, the government would be obliged to curb over-optimistic expectations. Among other indicators, the government had been alarmed by the sharp escalation in the price of property on the outskirts of Australian cities in the late 1950s, a campaign/ event that Alan Bond was proud to have played his part in. Pent-up demand from returned servicemen and 'New Australians', still frolicking in the delights of postwar, baby-boom family-making, was causing the country to over-reach its resources, and consumer debt had ballooned to an historic, all-time high.

On 15 November the government struck. Holt announced a package of economic measures designed to tighten credit ... Overdraft rates rose from 6 to 7 per cent, higher sales tax was imposed on cars and the pip squeaked as the credit was squeezed. There was a sharp rise in unemployment and share prices fell 20 per cent in the December quarter — the first major fall in nine years. Bond had been lucky: 'The season in 1961 was a very difficult period for us. We had to close down our ideas of great expansion that we had at the time and we certainly had to control our activities. As a matter of fact we were rather fortunate then, more so than other people, and where large companies did falter, we were able to pick up some of the properties and pieces they couldn't handle.'[44]

Although not unscathed by the sharp contraction caused by the credit squeeze, Bondy felt he had been blessed by Saint Jude Thaddeus, patron saint of hopeless causes ... the one Catholic icon he could readily identify with. He had survived and was now convinced that he was destined to lead a charmed life. And he praised all the Lords that he had been born impetuous, and not the cautious sort who would have delayed the Lesmurdie plunge. He now had a bankroll, his own seed money, and a self-made reputation that he could trade off in the coming years. For Bond, the most important lesson to come from Lesmurdie was that you didn't need money to make money. All you needed was access to other people's money and a fierce determination to make your dreams come true.

From this first taste, he had become addicted to credit. It was a habit he was to carry with him throughout his corporate life. He must have missed the lesson on prudential standards when he was studying accountancy at night school.

It is doubtful that all Eileen's dreams had come true upon marrying Alan Bond. She might have got to play the Lesmurdie bag woman but she didn't get to go on the three-month overseas trip. Someone had to stay home and look after the kids, and with the birth of Susanne in 1959 there were now three of them. Although Alan never spent much time in his home he bought Eileen a new one (this time, constructed by a decent builder) at 10 Knox Crescent in Melville Heights. It's a lovely solid brick number overlooking a pleasant park, which would have been great for the kids. It's a pleasant street in a nice neighbourhood — everything you needed, really, to live out the middle-class Australian dream. But soon it was not enough for Bond. This move was to be the first of many changes in domicile as the Bonds climbed their way up the social and corporate ladder. (Bondy had sold 36 McLean Street to Eileen's sister Maureen and her husband (for a profit, naturally) and moved his mum and dad into Lesmurdie Heights.) Bob Hicks, next-door at number 12 Knox Street, saw them come and go and remembers Bondy for wanting to build a dirty great big brick wall between the two properties. He reckoned Eileen was all right though. Everyone does. Her large, loving family, especially. Alan was not in the Doozer mould as a husband and father but he was working terribly hard to make a better life for them. Things would get better, Eileen assured herself. In the meantime, there were nappies to wash, meals to cook, arguments to settle ... A housewife's work, like an entrepreneur's, is never done.

In 1962 Australia came out of its shell and went for the America's Cup with swashbuckling media mogul Sir Frank Packer at the helm of *Gretel*, a twelve-metre yacht named after Lady Packer. As a businessman, Packer was idiosyncratic and authoritarian, a self-made man, a hands-on leader fashioned after Bond's own heart. His empire was built on newspapers, magazines, television and radio stations, and he ran it and the Cup challenges with an iron fist in a steel glove. One day Bond would get to own those television and radio stations and inherit Packer's mantle as Australia's Sir Thomas Lipton, the tea tycoon who launched never-ending challenges for the Cup. Packer would also set Bond an example in the blustering, never-say-die, hands-on management style that would eventually take the Cup.

Packer put up his hand in October 1959, when his Royal Sydney Yacht Squadron syndicate announced they would be coming to challenge in 1962. The Poms took no notice of this colonial upstart. Since 1851 they had come to view the sporadic contests for the Cup as their personal grudge match with the New York Yacht Club. It was their honour that was besmirched when the schooner *America* took the 100-Guinea Cup from them in the first place. Despite the fact that the Cup's Deed of Gift specified that it was an international challenge trophy (and, indeed, the third and fourth challenges had come from the obscure Bay of Quinte Yacht Club of Belleville, Ontario, in Canada), they saw the challenge of 1962 as their prerogative; but they had not counted on the wily ways of Frank Packer.

Although an empire loyalist at heart, Packer was first and foremost a competitive Australian who understood the communications business. When he got the word from his London contacts that a member of the Royal Thames Yacht Club was on his way to New York to deliver a written challenge, he cabled ahead of him and got the nod from the New York Yacht Club. It was a moment of great national pride for Australians when the challenge was accepted. The Poms were furious and tried everything to get the Aussies to stand aside or accept a Commonwealth elimination test to choose the ultimate challenger. Packer rightly refused but attempted to placate the Poms by telling them: 'Maybe we won't do any better, but every now and again you have to give the young fellow in the family his head.'[45]

As well as having no America's Cup tradition, Australia had no twelve-metre yachts to take to Newport. Packer soon chartered 1958 America's Cup contender *Vim* as a trial horse and got Australia's only full-time naval architect, Alan Payne, to design *Gretel*. She had a fast hull and a strong crew but was handicapped by Packer's heavy-handed interference. As was his wont, he delayed naming his final crew and skipper until the eleventh hour. Instead of honing their match-racing sailing skills under eventual skipper Jock Sturrock, Packer had them test a bewildering inventory of eighty-five sails. His best trick was to replace the navigator (with one who had little knowledge of the Newport waters) on the very morning of the first race.

A huge mob, estimated at 2500 spectator craft and including United States President John F Kennedy on a destroyer, turned up that day to see the cheeky Australians take on the might of America for the first time. The indomitable Bus Mosbacher had the wheel of the New York defender *Weatherly* and she crossed the finish line three minutes and forty-three seconds ahead of *Gretel*, which had suffered from a navigation error. Packer treated the navigator the same way he would an editor of the Sydney *Daily Telegraph* during a circulation drop — he sacked him. But things were to improve in the second race. *Gretel* started from behind but on a downward leg under spinnakers and with the wind blowing in at twenty-five knots, *Gretel* caught a series of huge rollers and surfed past *Weatherly* to take the race by forty-seven seconds and go into history as the first challenger to win a race against New York since 1934.

Gretel was to lose the third, fourth (by only twenty-six seconds) and fifth races to Mosbacher's *Weatherly* but it didn't matter. The Australians had made their point and they celebrated long into the night at the Cameo Bar in Newport. Back in Australia, Packer's newspapers, magazines and television stations went crazy with delight for their boss's good fortune. Bond knew about it but he wasn't all that interested; he had other things on his mind.

CHAPTER FIVE

1964: Constellation vs. Sovereign, Constellation, *4–0*

It is tempting to assume that Bondy took a siesta in the early 1960s as he digested his Lesmurdie windfall and weathered the tighter economic times engendered by the Holt credit squeeze. But perpetual-motion machines, like the one that Bond had turned himself into, rarely stand still — even when their gears are set to neutral. At any one time he had dozens of property developments and other schemes either in the pipeline or coming to the boil. He was indefatigable, especially in the face of adversity, and just as hungry for his second million as he had been for the first.

During this 'quiet period', when little is widely known of his activities, he was constantly expanding his repertoire and becoming louder in his personal tastes and desires. 'Bondy', 'The Frog', became 'Nonpareil' to his friends, enemies and business acquaintances in the know around Fremantle and even beyond. This was on account of his constant reference to hundreds and thousands in everyday speech as well as his ability to juggle myriad money-making schemes in his not-too-pointy head. Armed only with his seed money from Lesmurdie and the rudimentary financial skills he had acquired from his night-school bookkeeping and accountancy classes, Bond left the signwriting trade behind him and charged headlong into the world of business.

His corporate strategy ('you've gotta move a quid, move a quid, keep the money rolling') was still in place and his focus set firmly on property development. He knew he could sell land, now he wanted a slice of the value-added value that went with selling land with new buildings on it. First, he would have to learn a bit more about the construction business. To this end, he undertook contracts to rebuild the airstrips at Derby and Broome in the north-west. Presumably these were with the Federal Department of Civil Aviation and presumably they were awarded on tender price alone. The job was a bit like the old days of labour contracting; but this time it had a purpose, and that was to gain valuable experience in cheap construction techniques.

The overt signs of Bondy's change in status from trades-man to entrepreneur came in his choice of cars, the Australian male both expressing himself and being defined by the quality of the wheels underneath him. Gone was the old man's Ford Zephyr and his first brown-and-cream FC Holden station wagon. On the way up to the first Roller he drove into the ground at least one Belair Chevy, a white Cadillac convertible, a blue Mercedes and no doubt many other vehicles. Such was the tyranny of distance in Australia that the best way to overcome it was to go over it rapidly in the best means possible. Cousin John Hughes worked for a car dealership where Bond indulged his liking for fast cars. He was generous with his expensive toys but Hughes was dismayed by the way he treated them. 'He bought a new Mercedes, a very costly long-wheelbase model. A week later he took it across a paddock — probably showing someone a development — stacked it on a rock, drained all the oil out of the sump and did some $4000 damage. I thought that was a pretty cavalier attitude to worldly possessions.'[46]

Some time after disposing of his Nu-Signs persona Bond

began styling his business interests by the pretentious-yet-pertinent title of the Progress Development Organisation (PDO). Although this sounds very much like a body given to the espousal of pro-development political philosophy at a local council level it was, in fact, meant to be a statement of his business intent. All right-thinking people of the time believed in progress. Progress was to be the altar on which he would offer up his developments and the PDO was to be the organisational instrument for achieving the tribute. The PDO eventually evolved into the Bond Corporation but it is hard to reconcile the quantum leap between the latter's towering corporate edifices and the former's primitive early offices.

After moving out of the tin shed behind the Waterside Workers' Federation branch office at Mouat Street in the West End, Bond initially returned to his old stamping ground closer to Victoria Quay. The City of Fremantle's electoral roll for the year to October 1960 has him occupying a shop and workshop at 3–5 Queen Victoria Street, a stone's throw from the Boys' School, Parnell's, St Pat's and Doozer's place. It is believed that he shared this space with his mother, Kathleen Bond, who had been running a retail furniture business from the same address during Alan's painting years. Old man Parnell recalls it as a fair-sized show selling both new furniture and antiques to home-makers. This information provides further proof of the font of his commercial instincts.

We don't know the quality of this business relationship with his mother but after a short period at Queen Victoria Street, Bond set up shop not far away at 30–32 Queen Street. Here he was closer to the markets in Henderson Street, the technical school in South Terrace, and the 'traps' which were the source of his commercial intelligence and the places where he conducted a lot of his business. These were the Freemasons' Hotel over the road from the tech., the Park Hotel in Parry Street, the Federal Hotel in William Street, the Commercial Club in Cantonment Street and the Willagee nearer his home in Melville.

When the second stage of the High and Josephson Streets development on the Mobil garage site was completed, he moved into an office above the shops on the north-east corner. Now, he was not only above the rabble but also in his own building for the first time and he wanted to be known as a big-

time operator. Perth journalist John McIlwraith recalls visiting
him: 'I did a profile on him ... In his small but lushly furnished
private office, he had a wide desk and he had the most
elaborate coffee table and, on it, an even more elaborate cigar
box. The moment I walked in he said, "Have a cigar." I declined
and he looked a bit despondent. A bit later he offered the cigars
again. Seeing my quizzical look, he said, "Well, they all expect
you to have these things in your office." That was his idea of
style.'[47] He presumedly got it from the latest glossy American
magazines which lined his waiting room along with 'his attractive, well-groomed secretary'. (This was Maxine Fishwick, his
first receptionist and girl Friday.) According to McIlwraith, the
recent magazines in the waiting room were 'symbolic of his
distaste for delay, conservatism and timidity'.[48]

Others who manned the office in the early days were
accountant Ron White and salesman Cam McNab but neither
will confirm what their duties involved or discuss the formative
years of the PDO. White was Bond's right-hand man and had
been the secretary and one of the three directors of Lesmurdie
Heights Pty Ltd (the others were Bond and Doozer Hughes). He
went on to become deputy managing director of BondCorp and
set up Bond's family holding company, Dallhold Investments
Pty Ltd. (There is a theory, probably apocryphal, that Dallhold
is short for Doozer and Alan's Land Holdings.) McNab was a
sort of second right-hand man who stayed on with White for
the ride until the late 1960s.

White is believed to have kept extensive files on the early
land and unit projects of the PDO but will not divulge their
contents. This is unfortunate as there is little in the way of a
paper trail to unravel the spasmodic chronology of events that
followed the Lesmurdie hoist. We know that Bond developed
another eastern suburban broadacres project at Gooseberry
Hill, just north of Lesmurdie, in March 1962 and in February
1963. We believe he obtained the land after an executor's
auction but that's all we know about it. Also in the early 1960s,
he bought up five or six ten-acre poultry and pig farms each
side of North Lake Road at Kardinya, south of Melville, which
was closer to Fremantle but still on the outskirts. He later
added to this subdivision when he acquired the adjoining
ninety-acre Welby's vineyard as a further development stage.
There was also another land deal in the southern suburbs at

Hamilton Hill, where, we are told, the sales were aborted and the deposits returned without a reason being given.

But it was away from the wide-open spaces of the hill and sand-belt broadacres, among the cramped blocks of flats and modest home-unit complexes of the older, inner suburbs (which Bondy was also building throughout this period) that his fledgling PDO was to make its most indelible mark. The first of these was a block of twelve units at 439 Canning Highway, Melville, called Melview because of some perceived vista over the Melville Water which is not obvious. This modern, 'saw-tooth'-design, two-storey town house complex was whipped up by Bondy in about 1961–62 and is remarkable for the density of the space allotted to each unit in the long, squat row occupying the land where one house once stood in the middle of big front and back yards. At the front it is cheap brick shoe-box architecture that could have been borrowed from the working-class terrace rows of South Wales or Ealing. At the back it is all-Australian light, glass and angles, with verandahs overlooking a strip of greenery and colour. No doubt the City of Melville had building regulations at the time which specified the minimum height requirements needed for swinging a cat and these seem to have been observed to the letter. Construction was achieved quickly and cheaply after planning approval and Doozer was said to have assisted with the financing by advancing to his son-in-law funds secured by a second mortgage over the property.

The second of these PDO unit developments took place at 43 Preston Point Road in the town of East Fremantle. It was erected in three stages some time between 1962 and 1963 and called Preston Towers by somebody with a sense of humour if not the ridiculous. There are eighteen units in the low-slung, two- and three-storey cream-brick buildings that comprise this oddly shaped lot and again they seem to have been built with the physical dimensions of the Pigmy in mind. One unit buyer is said to have refused to settle until a broom cupboard was included in her fittings. The story is told that Bond picked up the block for about three thousand pounds at an auction attended by only half a dozen people during a downpour of rain. Bond is also said to have reached an accommodation, pre-auction, with a nearby wealthy resident (George Evans) in an effort to keep him out of the bidding for the property.

North of the Swan, another small block of slightly more prestigious units was constructed at Overton Gardens, in seaside Cottesloe, as Bondy appeared to be testing the top end of the market. Again, there is the economy of space that seems to be the hallmark of all his housing projects of this time. At Overton Gardens he maximised the development potential of the site by taking the building to the three-storey height limit specified by the Cottesloe Council but roundly condemned by other residents. Although he was later to do some home units in the trendy, nearby town of Mosman Park, when some former industrial land was re-zoned residential, it is believed the PDO found the North Shore a bit rich for its tastes. Obtaining planning approval was more difficult and the returns were marginal because only small-scale developments were possible.

From 1963 some of the Lesmurdie loot was also being diverted into the acquisition of rural properties. It is believed that Bond picked up some of these cheaply in the recession that followed the credit squeeze and that he swapped city-based assets for country ones. He tells us that these were difficult times for him but within three years he had amassed a sizeable portfolio of six rural properties and had appointed Alan Utterson his full-time farm adviser. His motives for this move are unclear but are probably connected with the tax breaks available to primary producers. As a street kid he knew nothing about farming sheep and cattle, growing wheat and lucerne and the fickleness of Mother Nature, yet he had grandiose plans to turn them all into money spinners through the liberal application of superphosphate using aerial top-dressing.

One of the farms, 1300 acres at Beechboro, just twelve kilometres north-east of the city centre, was obviously purchased for its development potential as it was in the direct path of metropolitan expansion. But the rationale behind the purchase of the other properties is more difficult to fathom. There were 7000 acres at Brookton, 7489 acres at Marchagee, 8300 at Ballidu, 8000 acres at Badgingarra and several thousand acres at Safety Bay, each staffed by a manager and an assistant manager. Although Alan didn't have a clue about the marketing possibilities of running 50,000 to 60,000 sheep, Doozer and the Hughes family did. We are told that the Safety Bay land and another block at Buckland Hill were taken over by Bill Hughes and sold through his development company.

It is doubtful that jackeroo Bond was seeking a place by the fireside of the landed Perth Establishment by becoming a respectable farm owner at age twenty-five. More likely, he was acting on advice which said that the depressed rural property market was a good counter-cyclical investment and a safe storehouse for his new-found wealth. Much as he loved Western Australia's wide-open spaces, he had no intention of living in them.

It was in the early 1960s that Bondy developed his obsession with personal image and style and it is interesting to speculate on why he felt the need to become so conspicuous in his consumption and lifestyle at this early stage in his career. Obviously he felt the need to set behind him the deprivations of the 1950s and his migrant working-class origins. He wanted to be seen as a changed man, a man of substance, someone who had credibility as a businessman who had 'made it' through the Protestant work ethic. He saw worldly possessions and the pursuit of personal pleasures as the rewards for, and the yardsticks of, success. His personal philosophy was as succinct as it was simple: 'The good things in life come to those who dare to strive. Anyone who is prepared to work harder and longer hours than the next person must succeed.'[49] He worked like a Trojan; therefore, it followed, he should live like a Roman.

He was also strongly influenced by the cultural icons of the time. The Beatles, four English working-class musicians from Liverpool, near his mother's home town of Leeds, had 'hit the big time' and he had their records to prove it. That they had 'made it' was reflected in their fame and fortune for all the world to see. His namesake, James Bond, the British secret agent 007 created by author Ian Fleming, was also all the rage at the time and was one of Bond's cinematic heroes. Identifying with James was easy for Alan. Not only was the star-spy always conceiving ingenious plots to stay one step ahead of his deadliest foes but he lived a flamboyant life surrounded by technological toys and glamorous flirtation. There were American heroes, too, for that is where his business philosophy came from, but the Beatles and 007 held a special place in his English heart.

Bond's life was beginning to imitate the art of a James Bond movie. As well as the fast cars, there was the phone in the loo and a succession of fast boats. Rottnest Island and the Swan foreshores were the playgrounds of the Perth *nouveau riche* and Bond was a player. It has been suggested that Frank Bond advised his son to temper his passion for business with a little sport but it is doubtful that this was the sole motive for his interest in speedboats. Like Frank, Alan loved to swim. He had been a member of the Leighton Beach Surf Club at North Fremantle and an inaugural member of the Port Surf Club when that formed. But whereas Frank used the water for its therapeutic benefits, Alan used it for show.

He had taken lessons to become proficient at water-skiing. Stories are told of his fearlessness in skimming over the waves — and through the middle of a mob of dorsal fins — off the beach at Rottnest and how, one Christmas, he lost a little toe while water-skiing on the Swan dressed as Santa Claus to amuse his young children. He treated his boats the same as he treated his cars. He ran one new speedboat aground one day as he paced himself against the cars coming out of the city along the Stirling Highway. Although it was his fault that the boat had its bottom ripped out, he rang the dealer who had sold it to him, told him where he could find it and then demanded to know what he was going to do about it.

A fast speedboat was a status symbol for the Rottnest Island social set, the car you drove when you were on the water and the bed you slept in after a wild time at the regular Saturday night dances held on the island. We are told that Bond loved the dances and loved nothing better than to caress the dance floor with a beautiful woman in his arms. We are also told that he used to brag that he had never left a Rottnest dance on his own and had never managed to be there when the band stopped playing.

Eileen Bond cannot have been oblivious to his demands for instant gratification but she was grateful that he wasn't playing in, or managing, a rock-'n'-roll band. Apart from his mother, Eileen was regarded as the only individual who got really close to the fast-moving Bondy, but even she had no idea what he was up to half the time. She had three young children to worry about and a hyperactive husband who, more often than not, was away working on a new deal. It wasn't the perfect relationship but it was a working relationship and the only one she had. When he was home they seemed to enjoy their time together and he doted on the children, which was her criterion for dedication.

She was stuck away in the sticks at Melville Heights but Alan had given her a car along with all the modern conveniences supposedly required for domestic bliss. She liked living in her modern house in a new neighbourhood and didn't seem to miss some of the old-world charms that Freo offered: 'When I lived in Freo there was a lot of wealth and all these delightful things but no one was doing anything and we went through a most depressing stage.'[50] She would still go down there to see her family, to go to Mass on Sunday and to shop at the Fremantle markets. She would take the children to the amusement park at South Beach, where she had gone as a child with her father, and the boys to the occasional game of footy when South Fremantle were playing at home.

Eileen tells us that she loved nothing better than to spend the day in bed with a good book and a box of chocolates. She had been deeply affected by the assassination of US President John F Kennedy in 1963 and the horror stories coming out about thalidomide, the drug (widely used to combat depression in expectant mothers) that was causing deformities in new-born children. When conscription was reintroduced in 1964 she worried that her sons would one day be forced to go off and fight and die. Australia had had troops in Vietnam since 1962.

Having been beaten to the punch by Packer's astuteness in 1962, the Royal Thames Yacht Club was determined not to miss out on the America's Cup party again. This time London cabled a formal challenge to the New York Yacht Club as soon as *Weatherly* had finally disposed of *Gretel* in the best-of-seven series off Newport and this time it was the Australians who were too slow off the mark. The English had wanted the match to take place the following year but New York rejected the challenge on the grounds that it would be held too soon after the last contest. Interestingly, Anthony Boyden, the 35-year-old business tycoon heading the British challenge, threatened to take the NYYC to the New York State Supreme Court on the grounds that the club had no right to reject a challenge under the Deed of Gift governing Cup competition. The issue was resolved only when Boyden issued a new challenge for 1964 which New York accepted.

Although the Australians had missed the boat this time around, they gained some satisfaction from the fact that the British put in their worst performance since 1886. They were thrashed decisively in four straight races and lost the second race by the mammoth margin of twenty minutes and twenty-four seconds. Earlier that year, the Australian Navy had shown the world we meant business on the high seas. During exercises off Jervis Bay, New South Wales, on 10 February, the Navy's flagship, the aircraft carrier HMAS *Melbourne*, collided with the destroyer HMAS *Voyager*, slicing her in two and sending her to the bottom. *Melbourne* managed to limp across the line in Sydney Harbour with a huge gash in her bow.

CHAPTER SIX

1967: Intrepid vs. Dame Pattie, Intrepid, *4–0*

In the mid-1960s in Western Australia the pace of progress seemed rapidly to accelerate as the sleeping rural giant awoke to a new age of mineral discoveries and fabulous wealth. Alan Bond had just made it into the back seat but he was along for the ride. Optimism, never a commodity in short supply in the State of Excitement, bounded ahead. Speculation was rife and new money vied with old for control of the State capital.

The excitement generated by the unlocking of the State's huge mineral and energy potential was reflected more on the pristine streets of Perth than in the dusty, outback regions and obscure shanty towns where the resources were found. Along St Georges Terrace particularly, the Perth Stock Exchange and the mining houses began erecting obelisks to Lady Luck. As percussion drills rapidly turned the outback into a Swiss cheese, giant metallic corporate-claim pegs were being hammered into the St Georges Terrace streetscape on the banks of Perth Water. It was a process in which Bondy was to play no small part.

Fortunately, the West had experienced such mining booms before and so the trauma associated with these tumultuous events was easily absorbed into the laconic local psyche. In the 1890s, when the eastern goldfields around the Kalgoorlie Golden Mile opened up, Australia became the free world's largest gold producer — with all that that entailed. Although Kalgoorlie's golden title was supplanted when South Africa later brought the rich Johannesburg Rand mines into production, the area continued to regurgitate the precious metal and, in the grim years of the Great Depression, mining was the only industry to expand. However, rich rewards from the industry were still restricted in the mid-1960s by the pegging of the international price of gold at US$32 an ounce.

Now there were new gods being worshipped in Gomorrah-on-Swan and their names were Iron Ore, Oil, Bauxite and Nickel. The people who went in search of these gods were called explorers and their 'discoveries' ignited the public imagination in 'rushes' that caused 'booms' on the stockmarket. The process swelled company balance sheets and individual bank accounts like never before.

One day in November 1952 a Pilbara pastoralist named Lang Hancock discovered a mountain of iron ore in the Hamersley Ranges by accident while flying home from doing the shopping with his wife in his single-engine Auster. Hancock was forced to sit on his hands until the Federal government lifted the iron ore export embargo in 1960. It had been imposed in 1938 to circumvent opposition to the export of pig iron to prewar Japan and to conserve what were thought to be Australia's dwindling reserves. When Canberra's stranglehold was released, the 600 million tonnes of high-grade ore in Hamersley's Mount Tom Price mine were developed for export to postwar Japan. Other deposits were opened up at Shay Gap, Mount Newman and eventually Robe River as the West became a major force in the world iron ore market from a standing start.[51]

On 4 December 1953 Ampol Exploration Ltd discovered

oil while drilling at Rough Range near Carnarvon in the West. Finding indigenous oil in a country that was not producing it but was consuming it in ever-increasing quantities was indeed a wondrous event; and, to celebrate, company chairman Bill (later Sir William) Walkley 'stopped traffic in Pitt Street as he walked along it in a blazing red ten-gallon hat.'[52] The effect on the stockmarket was to send Ampol Ex shares soaring up from eighteen shillings to six pounds five shillings (A$1.80 to $12.50) in a single day. Rough Range proved too small to be commercial but in 1963 oil flowed offshore at Barrow Island for West Australian Petroleum Ltd, well before the 1966 Esso-BHP discoveries in Bass Strait.

In 1957 Western Mining Corporation uncovered bauxite's hiding place in another part of the same Darling Ranges where Bondy was to make his Lesmurdie fortune. This mineral was the raw material of aluminium, then the world's strongest and lightest metal. Until Alcoa of Australia started the first major bauxite mine here in 1961, we were importing the stuff from Malaysia.

Then, on 28 January 1966, Western Mining struck nickel at Kambalda, thirty-five miles south of Kalgoorlie, and caused the greatest excitement in the West since the 1890s gold rush. Nickel, known as the devil's metal, was hard, lustrous and in short supply owing to a labour dispute at the Canadian mine of the world's largest producer, Inco of Canada. It was used mainly as an alloy in the production of stainless steel, for which demand was expanding rapidly in the booming Western economies. But it also had many applications in the munitions industry (the Vietnam war was all the rage in 1966 and the first regular Australian troops hit the beaches in May 1965) and in the fledgling aerospace industry. Western Mining's share price took off like a rocket and set the scene for the frantic Poseidon share boom to come in 1969 and 1970.

The cumulative effect of these discoveries was to turn Gomorrah-on-Swan into a hotbed of entrepreneurs and money miners of every conceivable shape, size and description. It was argued at the time that if you couldn't make a quid during a boom like this in a wide-open frontier town like this one, you were probably doomed to never make one and should give the game away. Even the money changed colour on 14 February 1966, when the pastoral green pound of the Menzies era gave way to the dusty brown dollar of the Age of the Main Chance.

It acted like a magnet to Bond, who had outgrown the Freo hicksville of his formative years and yearned to have a crack at the big league on St Georges Terrace. He made the move in about 1964, leasing a floor of a building in Sherwood Court, a lane running between St Georges Terrace and The Esplanade, conveniently in the heart of the city's then-burgeoning legal and financial district. But by 1965 he had shifted his small PDO outfit to offices on the east side of Mill Street, behind what was to become the Parmelia Hilton Hotel.

In 1965 he lashed out and bought his first property on the Terrace, the old ANZ Bank building on a prime site at number 68, which he was to rip down and redevelop as Stock Exchange House, the high temple of Gomorrah-on-Swan. He picked it up at auction for $350,000, at that time the record price for a CBD property. This acquisition forced the aloof Perth Establishment finally to sit up and take notice of the swaggering, stocky twenty-seven year old from Fremantle and the first clippings about him went into the newspaper library files of the *West Australian*. He recounts the incident with the unrestrained glee of a schoolboy entering a lolly shop for the first time: 'The bidding was going up slowly in $10,000 lots. It was 320,000, 330,000 when I stood up and my first bid was $350,000. Bang. There was this terrible gasp of disbelief. Everybody looked around. They didn't know what to do. In the meantime the auctioneer knocked it down. There were no other bids. The old president of the Real Estate Institute shook his head and said, "This boy's gone too far. Comes from Fremantle y'know. Doesn't know the values." '[53] This charge would be levelled at Bond again and again during his career.

Bond knew the potential values all right, and his foresight and daring were tempered by solid preliminary groundwork on the up-sides and down-sides of the proposal. While diligently poring over the contract of sale he found a catch that was to help underwrite any initial risk involved in the venture. The contract of sale specified vacant possession within ninety days but both Bondy and Blind Freddy knew that the ANZ Bank's new building was hopelessly behind schedule and they could not fulfil the contract. Bond claims to have leased the old building back to the bank at a figure so high that it paid all his holding costs on the site for two years.

Right place, right time ... Maybe. In 1966 he paid $400,000 for the Steamship Buildings on the north side of St Georges Terrace, one building from the corner of King Street. On 22 February 1967 the PDO announced a $2-million-plus building program for its terrace territory. More than $1 million would go on building 'a new thirteen-storey, fully air-conditioned and carpeted office block' on the ANZ Bank site and extensions worth $450,000 would take place on the Steamship Buildings. Flash in the pan? Obviously not. Bond was to move his corporate headquarters first to the Steamship Building and later to Exchange House when it was completed in December 1968. But let us go back to the farms and the suburbs for a moment in an attempt to find the source of the relatively massive funds he would have required for this push on the town.

Bond added two other rural properties to his portfolio in the late 1960s and neither of them was cheap. One was Daisy Downs, a 57,000-acre wheat-and-sheep farm fourteen miles east of Mullewa, which would never be heard of again; and the other was a 20,000-acre pastoral property at Yanchep, thirty-five miles north of Perth, which the whole world would get to hear about. With so much of his assets tied up in idle rural retreats at a time of great capital need, his PDO was no doubt feeling financially strained. When he was forced to make a choice between the city and the bush, the city won hands-down. It appears he kept the cream of the near-metropolitan development sites and handballed the scrub and spinifex acreages to an anonymous group of English investors. 'We've been able to interest substantial funds from UK investors to buy a farming kit and from this we've been able to form a department that does this.'[54]

Access to large licks of development capital has always been the main restraining factor in the growth of Alan Bond's ambitions. It has been his life's blood and as the Australian banks would not let him so much as sniff at their supplies, he became very adept at locating and lining up alternative sources. In July 1967 he went overseas on a study tour to Thailand, Japan, the US, Canada and Britain. He was supposed to be looking at the latest developments in home units and office buildings but he was also flogging his wares and soliciting funds.

By 1969 he had seven round-the-world trips behind him.

'On trips to London I was lucky enough to meet men whose whole lives had been devoted to investing large sums of money. Listening to them, you can acquire knowledge that would take you ten or twenty years to gather.'[55] But he acquired more than just knowledge from these shrewd British financiers in the city of London. He claimed to have raised $1 million in bridging finance at 6 per cent interest for two years with further credit lines available to him at 8 per cent. The money is believed to have come from a group called Chaddesley Investments. London money, he said, had been investing 'big sums' in his enterprises for some years and this obviously gladdened his London heart.

Bond's other way around the perennial funding crises facing the PDO was to develop a creative accounting technique that relied very much on the pull of inflationary values to justify and pay for the initial plunge. Again and again he would buy something, borrow money to develop it, capitalise the development costs into the asset's value, revalue the asset and borrow further money against the higher value. As long as the values kept rising, the PDO could easily service the debt and consolidate its equity in the asset. Most of the Progress Development Organisation's estimated turnover, or operating cash flow, of about $500,000 in 1967 was still in the form of sales from its outer-suburban land subdivisions and inner-suburban home unit developments. By judicious use of the frequent revaluation technique he was able to keep these projects largely self-financing and so concentrate his limited capital for the big hits on the Terrace.

After the initial flurry in the eastern outskirts at Lesmurdie and Gooseberry Hill, Bond seems to have abandoned the Hollywood Hills syndrome and followed popular sentiment towards the fill-in western suburbs between the city and the Indian Ocean beachfront. The 1500-acre Beechboro farm, near the north-eastern suburb of Morley, was put on hold for future growth and left as grazing land for 500 head of contented beef cattle.

In the south-western suburbs, between Fremantle and the new industrial port of Kwinana at the bottom of Cockburn Sound, Bond's PDO is said to have amassed a stock of 800 building blocks. Most of this was in the Kardinya area, south of Melville, and the ill-fated Hamilton Hill development. But he also started acquiring acreage further south, near Lake Bibra, and picked up 150 acres of industrial land near Kwinana itself. The Safety Bay farm land, even further south, no longer appeared to be in the portfolio.

North of the Swan, he seems to have concentrated on high-density residential developments. He built his first high-rise apartment block in this period — eighty-odd classy near-city units with park views and underground parking, called Kingsway Gardens, at 38 Kings Park Road, West Perth. He began acquiring land near Herdsmans Lake at Glendalough, about six kilometres north-west of Perth, where he planned a massive 700-unit development. He also had home units on sale at Mosman Park. Television advertising, with a PDO jingle, was being used to drum up interest in the blocks and units.

Back on the Terrace, Bond was beginning to flex his muscles on the stockmarket. On 11 July 1967 Lesmurdie Heights Pty Ltd announced a speculative $500,000 cash bid for a city property-owning company called West Australian Finance Ltd. Bond has often stated that he made his first company takeover when he was just twenty, but this appears to be his first offer for a publicly listed company. Although he pursued WA Finance for several years, the bid ran into stiff opposition and ultimately failed. He could not acknowledge this outcome, as the word *failure* had been removed from his vocabulary: 'We have never had a proposition that hasn't been successful.'[56] He could, however, admit to a few mistakes: 'When you're head of a small company struggling to get established, you are likely to hurt other people. Later, you learn a little finesse, discover ways to reach your goals without doing this.'[57]

By now, Bond in his dark-blue Mercedes 600 saloon was a familiar sight around the streets of Perth — 'a short, stocky figure hurrying from one boardroom to the next', according to a contemporary report. He wanted desperately to be seen as a success and was as conspicuous in his new-found wealth as he could possibly be. When he parked the Mercedes in town at night he was said to leave the interior lights burning so passers-by could admire its lavishness.

Eileen Bond was also kept busy by Alan's rapid rise. Each step he made up the social ladder was accompanied by a new house and a new neighbourhood for her. From the solid suburban redbrick in Knox Crescent, Melville Heights, the Bonds moved first to 25 Melville Beach Road, Attadale. Here they had a pool and a view of the Swan River, which was good but not good enough. In the mid-1960s they acquired a southern-Colonial-style mansion on the foreshore at Applecross from the spec builder, Tom Plunkett. This mini-Tara was more like it: pillars, verandahs and a sweeping driveway to the front door. But grand as it was, it was on the wrong (south) side of the river. Perth society — the people with taste as well as money — perched only at Dalkeith, across the river from the Bonds' new house.

By the time the 1967 America's Cup defence came around, other Australians besides Sir Frank Packer were suffering from the 'alcohol and delusions of grandeur' that inspired Australia's first tilt at the Auld Mug in 1962. The comparatively low cost of the twelve-metre-class sloops used in the regatta since 1958 had helped democratise the event to a certain extent. Now, you didn't have to be super rich, just someone with time and money on your side. Any bored businessman with a lazy hundred thousand or so dollars who could prop up the bar at the local yacht club was in with a chance.

Gretel's valiant defeat had raised the consciousness of the nation's sailing enthusiasts and sports fans beyond their devotion to the annual Sydney-to-Hobart bluewater classic and the eighteen-foot skiffs on Sydney Harbour. Sir Frank and the Gretel gladiators had also shown that there was personal and commercial kudos to be gained from being associated with a Cup challenge. Furthermore, the total ineptitude shown by the Poms in their 1964 challenge acted as a spur to the Australians.

But Packer's heavy-handed approach had not won him many friends among the local sailing fraternity. Some of those with him in Newport in 1962 actually thought Gretel could have won the Cup if he hadn't stuffed it up with his dictatorial pig-headedness. They were prepared to have another go and they coalesced under the leadership of Emil Christensen as the Dame Pattie America's Cup Yacht Challenge. Christensen was chairman of Petersville Australia Ltd, the makers of Peter's ice-cream, and a Melbourne-based businessman with a reputation for more level-headed decision making. Dame Pattie was the wife of Sir Robert Menzies, Australia's longest serving Prime Minister, who had just retired in 1966. The boat was to be designed by Warwick Hood, Alan Payne's former assistant, and skippered by Jock Sturrock.

Packer, meanwhile, got Alan Payne to completely re-design *Gretel* below the waterline. He had handed in a challenge following the 1964 races and was attempting to take advantage of a grandfather clause which allowed him to keep *Gretel*'s American Dacron sails from the 1962 campaign. Following the great *Gretel* scare, the New York Yacht Club tightened up the rules to keep its technological advantage over foreign challengers. It decreed that henceforth all equipment, sails and design research had to originate in the country of challenge and it was a decided disadvantage to those challengers. Packer's devious search for a loophole was typical of the resolve that would be required to wrest control of the Auld Mug from its holders. The contest no longer had much to do with sailing. It was now a test of management ability and technological excellence between the US and the rest.

Unfortunately, the re-jigged *Gretel* was not up to it. Christensen's *Dame Pattie* whipped her eleven times in thirteen starts and *Dame Pattie* was shipped to Newport to trial on her own. Even if they had been smart and taken both boats, it would still have been to no avail. For the 1967 defence, Olin Stephens had designed a breakthrough superboat called *Intrepid* which was faster and more manoeuvrable than any twelve-metre before it. Skippered by Bus Mosbacher, *Intrepid* took four straight races off *Dame Pattie* by margins of 3:36 to nearly 6 minutes. The Australians had picked a bad year to take on the might of American technology.

Alan Bond didn't go to Newport in 1967 but a mob of assorted Australians did, and they declared the *Dame Pattie* a 'Damn Pity'. They appear to have been received with warmth and bemusement by their American hosts: 'It was as if a bunch of boisterous fraternity brothers, from a school no one had ever heard of, had crashed a very exclusive, very traditional and rather dull tea party. The perennial guest of honour was miffed, the host was apprehensive, but everyone else was grateful for the diversion. Within hours, so it seemed, these brash newcomers had completely captivated the town, from the society matrons on Bellevue Avenue to the pub-keepers on

Lower Thames Street. They were so very down-to-earth, so charmingly oblivious to the stuffy nonsense that surrounded the Cup, so ... American. All they wanted to do was make friends, lift a few beers, get on with the regatta, win the thing, and take it home.'[58]

CHAPTER SEVEN

1970: Intrepid vs. Gretel II, Intrepid, *4–1*

In 1968, when Alan Bond turned thirty, he ascended into a kind of entrepreneur's heaven, the material fountainhead of the limousine, the cruising yacht, the mansion and the visibility. The proprietor/founder had transcended the mortal world of the working stiffs, the battlers and the losers — those who didn't count. He now counted, was counted upon, and should have been held accountable. But from now on his benefits to society, both real and imagined, would be trumpeted from the rooftops in public relations gestures while his shortcomings would be hidden in a cellar guarded by the best lawyers money could buy. Spiritually Alan Bond would always remain a man-of-the-people by dint of his humble working-class origins, but his worldly actions would now be amplified and distorted by his ego, his drive and his material possessions into an image of himself as a cut above the rest.

We are told that at an early age he had discovered in himself a certain eloquence that allowed him to be very persuasive in negotiations and forceful as a salesman. He saw this, his vision and his leadership qualities as innate. He had a cast-iron belief in his own infallibility. He was always successful; therefore it followed that he could never be wrong. As well as being a strength, this characteristic was also a weakness and a flaw. He was mistaken to believe that he could never be wrong because it frequently left him without a fall-back position. Because he believed in his own sales pitch, failure was incomprehensible to him; he thought he was too good for it.

And so it came to pass in 1967 that he became chairman and managing director of the Bond Corporation Pty Ltd (Bond-Corp), a name better suited to his intentions and better reflecting his new status than the cold and cumbersome Progress Development Organisation (although for a while he continued to use both names). By renaming the company after himself he was making the obvious statement that he *was* the corporation, and his ability and skills as an entrepreneur would determine its future success. Perhaps he was advised to take this course of action by his London backers in the belief that it would make his future loan and equity capital raising more identifiable with his activities. He was certainly mindful of having his name up in lights on St Georges Terrace once his companies became listed on the stock exchange. (It is hard to recall another entrepreneur in corporate history who has ever named so many companies after himself.) But the embryonic PDO/BondCorp was more than just Bond. In the Steamship Buildings he was assembling the beginnings of the executive team he would need to put his grandiose proposals into practice. As the owner and skipper he saw his role as that of ship's navigator, helmsman and chief provider. Crewmen were necessary to hoist the anchor, set the sails and pull the ropes. His endeavours required an enormous amount of back-up research, legal documentation and organisational follow-through. Bond liked to initiate deals, bring them to a head, then leave the details for others to sort out while he moved on to the next.

The early BondCorp head office staff consisted of only five or six people, and the chief executive was believed to be paying himself about six hundred dollars a week. On 4 July 1968 Bond announced BondCorp's new administrative structure 'to handle current group expansion'. Ron White became deputy managing director, Kevin George Benson-Brown (formerly of C P Bird and Associates) became finance director and company secretary, Clive Hartz was development director and Max Cunningham (formerly district manager of the Shell Company of Australia) was made development manager of the Yanchep satellite town project. Peter Mitchell (the only executive still with Bond) was appointed personal assistant to the chairman and managing director. As the 'current group expansion' was a hydra-headed monster that gobbled up land, buildings and companies on many fronts simultaneously, and as these executives ended up running three public companies as well as the private BondCorp, it is more illuminating initially to concentrate on the growth of the various corporate entities that came under Bondy's control during the Poseidon stockmarket boom years between 1968 and 1970.

It is impossible to understate the magnetic attraction the new world of stock exchange investment held for Bond in this period. As a land boomer he had profited handsomely from the 450 per cent increase in Perth land prices in the ten years since his Lesmurdie development. (He had claimed a steady rise in operating cash flow from his various enterprises from $500,000 to $5 million in the last few years, and assets totalling $7 million.)[59] But these figures paled by comparison with the capital returns then coming from the stockmarket mining boom. He could hardly have missed it. When the BondCorp Exchange House project opened at 68 St Georges Terrace on 16 December 1968, its first tenants (along with BondCorp) were the Stock Exchange of Perth and most of the city's stockbroking fraternity. The stock exchange's shingle was hanging at street level but Bond's name was on top of the building in red neon. The signwriter, having made his mark on the outside of the building, proceeded to do the same on the trading floor.

Western Mining's 1966 nickel strike at Kambalda had set the scene for the share boom. The company's share price, which had languished as low as 10/3d ($1.02) in 1960, climbed to $6.96 by the end of 1966, then raced to $43.50 in January 1968. But if 1968 had been a good year for stockbrokers, it was merely the calm before the storm. On Wednesday 1 October

1969, a penny dreadful nickel explorer called Poseidon NL set the world on fire when it reported the atomic absorption spectrophotometry assay results from its second percussion drill hole at a prospect called Windarra, far from anywhere in Western Australia's Great Victoria Desert. The company told the stock exchange that the drill had encountered 'massive' nickel sulphides and it sparked 'the wildest phenomenon' ever recorded on Australian stock exchanges.[60] The small number of Poseidon's shares on issue went from a nominal two or three cents in 1966 to nearly $300 during the four-month speculative spree that followed. Most gambling-prone Australians were affected in some way or other by that stockmarket boom — none more so than those close to the centre of the action in Exchange House. Bond's first foray onto the stock exchange had been in search of undervalued property assets rather than for capital gains, investment income or even as a source of equity capital raising.

When Lesmurdie Heights Pty Ltd made a $500,000 cash takeover offer for West Australian Finance Ltd in July 1967, the object of its desire was WA Finance's ownership of the freehold title to the land in Adelaide Terrace on which stood the Attunga flats. This central city property was valued in the company accounts at cost price of only $50,346. It was an opportunistic grab but it failed because Bond was outnumbered by Bernie Prindiville, whose Prindiville Holdings controlled the shareholders' register of WA Finance. Prindiville was not a seller and so Bond could not obtain his minimum 40 per cent of the issued capital which was a condition of the offer.

Bond was again gazumped by Prindiville when in January 1969 he made a bid for Metro Industries Ltd, another company with extensive interests in undervalued city properties and the target of several unsuccessful takeover bids in the previous year because of its wide-open share register. A BondCorp subsidiary called Landbrokers (Perth) Pty Ltd quickly obtained a controlling 32-per-cent interest in Metro through an on-market raid, a first-come-first-served bid at $1.40 a share. This time Prindiville out-manoeuvred Bond by organising a reverse takeover of Metro by WA Finance. In effect he swapped his controlling interest in WA Finance to Metro for a controlling interest in Metro. Prindiville Holdings ended up with nearly 50 per cent of

July 1966. Young Bond swings on the gate of his Beechboro farm in Western Australia. The city slicker moved into farming with his profits from Lesmurdie Heights. (Photo courtesy of the *West Australian*.)

36 McLean Street, Melville Heights — the first house that Bond built. He and Eileen lived in the garage at the back while the rest of the house was completed. It has been extensively modified since.

An early example of Bond's skill as a signwriter, this sign hangs in the Roma Cafe in High Street, Fremantle, where the young artist was a frequent patron.

Fremantle Technical College in South Terrace where Bond studied accountancy at night school. It was here that Bond obtained labour for his 'moonlighting' contracts.

Nu-Signs, Bond's first office and workshop, was located in a tin shed behind the Waterside Workers' Federation in High Street, Fremantle. The Nu-Signs sign is still visible on the back wall to the left.

10 Knox Crescent, Melville — the house the Bonds moved to after the success of Alan's Lesmurdie Heights development.

'Melview' at 439 Canning Highway, Melville, was Bond's first housing development. The small units brought big profits.

These shops and offices on the corner of High and Josephson Streets in Fremantle were Bond's first retail development. The office upstairs was the company's last in Fremantle before the shift to Perth in the late 1960s.

Bond, singer Jackie Love and Laurie Connell kick up their heels at the opening of Observation City Hotel on 3 October 1987. Three weeks later Laurie Connell's Rothwells merchant bank would be ruined by the sharemarket crash. (Photo courtesy of *News Limited*.)

Bond's sister, Geraldine, and his mother, Kathleen, celebrate the America's Cup win in 1983. (Photo courtesy of the *West Australian*.)

Alan and Eileen and the Auld Mug. For the preceding 132 years it was in the possession of the New York Yacht Club. (Photo courtesy of the *West Australian*.)

Bond and President Reagan at the White House after the 1983 victory at Newport. (Photo courtesy of *Associated Press*.)

Metro (and WA Finance) and BondCorp's holding was watered down from 32 per cent to around 18 per cent, the shares being worth a lot less because there were now more of them. Prindiville struck on 17 January, the day Bond flew to London to arrange British finance for his Yanchep development. When he flew out, Bond was confident that he had Metro Industries in his pocket. Thanks to Prindiville he returned red-faced and nearly $1 million out of pocket on the Metro play. Furious at being outsmarted a second time, Bond issued a writ out of the West Australian Supreme Court seeking to stop the issue of new Metro shares and made a direct personal offer for all the old capital at $1.50 a share. This bid valued the company at around $2 million, more than double his original exposure. Both moves failed but Bond's two encounters with Bernie Prindiville had taught him some valuable lessons about the stockmarket and takeovers.

He had been more successful in 1968 when he engineered his own complicated reverse takeover of a small listed hardware merchant called W Drabble Ltd. In effect, BondCorp sold two of its subsidiaries to Drabble in exchange for a majority shareholding in the company. The first step came in September 1968 when Drabble shareholders agreed to acquire from Bond-Corp a seventy-per-cent interest in a Middle Swan brick maker called L Whiteman Pty Ltd. At the annual general meeting on 3 October, Alan Bond was elected to the Drabble board, his first directorship of a listed public company.

After only a few months in such esteemed company Bond began to get the hang of stock exchange life and figured you had to be listed on it to win at it. Having entered initially by the back door, he now mused about the front door. By December 1968 he was talking about plans to list two new public companies — but not the core BondCorp business, which he wanted to keep private. He had in mind the wholly owned subsidiary, Residential Developments Pty Ltd, and the other 30 per cent of Whiteman Bricks which he had not sold to Drabble. Neither float came off. Residential Developments ended up holding BondCorp's fifty-per-cent interest in the Ocean Beach Hotel at North Cottesloe. This property had been purchased for a reputed $500,000 in 1967 by a syndicate with grand plans for a new ten-storey palace for weddings and retreat for honeymooners on the site. Unfortunately, the local council did not share the syndicate's *joie de vivre* and was apparently not prepared to compromise on its foreshore building height restrictions. Without building approval, the project became a dodo. Residential Developments, along with the rest of Whiteman Bricks, was eventually transferred into the Drabble group in exchange for more shares.

When the first Bond float did happen in 1969, it was by way of helping to pay the deposit on a particularly expensive and speculative, long-term broadacre investment rather than a profit-making core business that could immediately generate dividends to satisfy shareholders. West Australian Land Holdings Ltd (the company that was to become Bond Corporation Holdings Ltd) was incorporated on 15 June 1969, with a paid-up capital of $3. In July it lashed out $4.1 million for the 5061-acre Santa Maria estate near Hamersley on the city's north-western outskirts.

According to Robert Gottliebsen, 'Bond bought the Santa Maria property for $3.55 million from three beneficiaries of a trust. Bond agreed to pay around $615,000 down and the rest over extended terms. Before he signed the contract, Bond got a valuation of the property. This showed it to be worth $4.6 million. On the strength of this he bounced over to CAGA [Commercial and General Acceptance] (a subsidiary of the then Commercial Banking Company of Sydney), who lent him $750,000 on the size of his equity. This was enough to meet the $615,000 down payment and provide Bond with a $100,000 commission. Deals of this sort were going on all around the country with a host of developers at the time.'[61]

When Bond first looked at the Santa Maria estate he could see only the big expanse of blue sky above the land-for-sale signs. If 5000 acres about fifteen kilometres from Perth could be subdivided into 20,000 quarter-acre building blocks and these could be sold for $3000 each, gross revenue from the development would be in the order of $60 million. But almost from day one, an even bigger black cloud in the form of the Metropolitan Regional Planning Authority (MRPA) eclipsed this vision and the prospects for WA Land (WAL). Mr M E Hamer, the MRPA chairman, said he could not see the authority agreeing to re-zone the land from rural to urban either now or in the immediate future. 'Predicting re-zoning was a matter of crystal ball gazing. One could talk of the inability of the government to supply the services to the area, of the way the area was unrelated to existing urban development and other factors against re-zoning.'[62]

But both Bond and the Perth Stock Exchange seemed unperturbed by any clouds in their crystal balls. BondCorp enticed fellow developer Landall Holdings Ltd (since liquidated) to joint-venture the Santa Maria development with it and WAL offered its shares to the public in a prospectus dated 19 November 1969. By coincidence, this was the very day that Poseidon chose to give the stock exchange its first substantive report on drilling at Windarra since the nickel strike was formally announced on 1 October. Poseidon shares closed in Perth at $55, opened in London overnight at $57.50 then traded up to $62 the next day.[63] With the share boom upswing about to reach full crescendo, it is not surprising that the Perth exchange listing committee appears to have given the WAL prospectus only scant attention. Had they examined the prospectus more closely, they may have concluded that without planning approval for the Santa Maria land, the 5.2 million WAL shares issued to the public and the 3.2 million issued to the promoters had no visible means of support. True, there was a slight income from leasing the property for pastoral purposes but it went nowhere near offsetting the holding charges on the debt-funded purchase which were being capitalised. WAL lost $26,896 in its first year to 30 June 1970, so the directors decided to diversify into other property investments while awaiting the fate of the nationalised Santa Maria development. Chairman Alan Bond was only too willing to lend them a hand. In September 1970 BondCorp sold WAL three city buildings — including the jewel in Bond's crown, Exchange House — for an undisclosed cash sum and the issue of 860,000 fully paid WAL fifty-cent shares. Combined with the 1.7 million shares it picked up in the float, BondCorp now controlled WAL's capital and got to walk away with a bag containing about $3 million in cash. That cash came, in part, from the WAL public shareholders who had to cough up another $1.3 million on the twenty-five-cent balance due on their fifty-cent shares on 19 November 1970. In exchange WAL shareholders got the immediate rental income from the fully leased Exchange House and from Tyre House (on the corner of Milligan and Wellington Streets. Bond-Corp had bought it from Dunlop Australia Ltd for $180,000).

They also got lumbered with the New Zealand Insurance building site in St Georges Terrace which BondCorp had picked up in March that year for $700,000. They already had plenty of development potential at Santa Maria; it was income that WAL desperately needed.

At the other end of the trading-room floor, Bond's other listed company, W Drabble Ltd, was also undergoing significant changes. In 1970 the little hardware group changed its name to the much grander sounding Amalgamated Industries Ltd (AMIN) and BondCorp busily backed other assets into it in exchange for more shares and cash. Bond had in mind that AMIN would provide the diversified industrial muscle needed to drive his twin obsessions of real estate and mining development. He was seeking some vertical integration by having AMIN become a supplier to these trades. Whiteman Bricks, Drabbles Hardware and the newly injected Skipper Mayday plant hire group could provide his construction projects with materials and equipment. AMIN was listed on the industrial boards but at times it walked and talked like a mining company. Two of its subsidiaries were Pilbara Ice and Delta Earthmovers.

But like WAL, AMIN was also used as a dumping ground for BondCorp development projects that had not got off the ground. To AMIN's holding in the Ocean Beach Hotel (Residential Developments Pty Ltd) Bond added a controlling interest in a company that owned a ten-pin bowling alley centre sitting on nearly an acre of land in Adelaide Terrace (Fairlanes (WA) Pty Ltd). BondCorp was prepared to park these slow-moving assets in the two listed companies so that Bond could access the cash and use it to greater effect during the mining boom. During the share boom the combination of instant wealth and mass hysteria induced some mineral exploration company promoters to behave in a manner which suggested they were completely without ethics, honour or decorum as they desperately grasped, first for a share of the new Eldorado, then to avoid falling into the black hole that inevitably followed its passing. It was an age of rank opportunism, characterised by shady deals, core salting, insider trading, blatant share ramping, dubious share placements, fraudulent disinformation and criminal neglect for the rights of small investors. It exposed serious weaknesses in the self-regulation of the Australian securities industry and led, through the Rae Senate Select Committee on Securities and Exchange, to the setting up of the National

Companies and Securities Commission and hence, the Australian Securities Commission. With the benefit of hindsight and a
changed legal and moral framework, it is easy to look back and
say that some of Bond's words and deeds of that time would
not pass muster today.

Bond played the mining stockmarket with the same fero-
ciousness that he applied to his other business ventures. To
him the basic difference between buildings on top of the
ground and minerals below the ground was that there was
more money to be made in the latter. You didn't have to be a
geologist or a mining engineer or even have an ore body to
make a killing on the stock exchange. The profits here were all
in paper shuffling. The game was to do a deal and then sell it to
the market, two things that he was very good at.

Considering the important role that mine-owning was to
play in the later career of this coalminer's son, very little is
heard about Bond's early ventures into mineral exploration.
This is simply because he was not good at it. BondCorp
(probably through the Bond Mining Pty Ltd subsidiary) is said
to have been dabbling in mineral exploration since its inception in 1967. A company called Murchison Minerals Pty Ltd was
formed and launched an iron ore exploration program in the
Jack Hills area of the Murchison River, about 700 kilometres
north-east of Perth. Nothing commercial was found but Bond
was convinced he had discovered an ore body containing
'more than 200 million tons of ore with an iron content of
between fifty-seven and sixty-five per cent.'[64] A 51-per-cent
interest in Murchison Minerals Pty Ltd was sold to Pacific
Island Mines Ltd (PIM) in exchange for a share placement and
Bond subsequently became chairman of PIM. His attention
then shifted to the Durack Ranges, the headwaters of the Ord
River, south of Wyndham on the West Australian/Northern
Territory border. The prospective area was about as far away
from St Georges Terrace as you could get, but Bond made sure
the brokers heard about it.

On 11 September 1970 Bond announced that 'a major
international company' had reached agreement in principle to
join PIM's exploration program in the area. He said PIM had
found indications of a major low-grade copper occurrence,
lead, zinc and silver mineralisation and ilmenite in the Durack
Ranges 'as well as uranium mineralisation and heavy mineral
bands containing uranium-bearing monazite, zircon and rutile.'

Bond's discovery of exotic and precious hot rocks was accompanied with the information that PIM would float off a new company, Durack Mines Ltd, to take over the area and that the move would be 'beneficial to PIM shareholders'. Durack Mines subsequently raised $8.5 million by issuing nineteen million fifty-cent shares but Bond appears to have had a change of mind about the efficacy of his own advice. He was able to negotiate his way out of two million Durack shares a matter of days before the fifty-cent shares made their market debut at less than half the issue price.[65]

Bond had been too slow off the mark to exploit the Poseidon boom to full effect. Poseidon shares peaked at $280 on 5 February 1970, and the market was in free fall by the time he was cranking up PIM and Durack. Both companies were eventually merged into the Planet Resources group. But while BondCorp had poured a lot of money into mining ventures without success, Bond himself had a 'Poseidon windfall' which supposedly helped build and maintain the yacht *Apollo*, named after another Greek god.[66]

While his public AMIN, WAL and PIM were busy dancing the Poseidon jig on the stock exchange and earning him the ironic nickname 'the shareholders' friend', his private Bond-Corp ploughed on with its property developments, each one grander than the last. He began the five-million-dollar housing and flat development of 700 living units on a sixteen-acre site at Glendalough and had two close encounters with religious organisations over land. The first of these was a vain attempt to buy a boys' home at Clontarf from the Catholics and the second was a vain attempt to sell the Greenwood Forest estate at Hamersley to a Protestant group. Both offer fascinating insights into BondCorp at work.

The Christian Brothers' boys' town at Clontarf is on a prime riverside site hidden by a pine plantation on the middle reaches of the Canning River, only six kilometres from Perth. Bond offered to build his Catholic brethren a new boys' town in the barren sandhills of Yanchep in exchange for the title to this redevelopment dream. He is also believed to have offered the Christian Brothers a trip to Europe to look over similar institutions. They sensibly declined the kind offer and stayed at Clontarf.

The Protestants of the Christian Service Foundation in WA

Inc. appear to have been gazumped in their attempt to buy the Greenwood Forest land at Hamersley. BondCorp subsidiary, Dalston Development Pty Ltd, bought the 283-acre estate in the north-western suburbs for $2,183,000 in 1969. (The seller was Victorian orchardist Kenneth Anthony Hall, who had purchased it in 1961 for only $16,000.) Dalston quickly on-sold the property to an offshoot of the Christian Service Foundation called Group Ownership Land Development Ltd (GOLD) for the tidy sum of $4,268,000. GOLD proceeded to raise $800,000 by provisionally selling 389 lots to young Christian families on about $2000 deposit — in most cases their life's savings. The sales were provisional in that the subdivision had yet to receive planning approval and Hall had died. His estate had to be lodged for probate in both Victoria and WA and neither Dalston nor GOLD held the title. However, GOLD's contract with Dalston for the Greenwood Forest land required that a substantial amount (believed to be $1.3 million for the first seventy-one acres at $14,000 an acre plus development costs of $652,000) be paid to Dalston by 30 September. GOLD claimed that it turned up late on the day and Bond refused to accept. Dalston claimed it was forced to rescind the contract when GOLD failed to met its contractual commitments on 30 September and had, subsequent to that, sought to vary the contract. The $1.9 million figure for the total down-payment due on 30 September is significant. Dalston had borrowed $1,929,340 from financier IAC (now Citicorp Australia) to pay Hall. If it could retire the debt quickly, it would have a free ride to a $2-million profit. If GOLD defaulted it could make even more — and be able to borrow even more based on the higher value it had put on the asset by selling it to GOLD for $4.3 million in the first place. By late October 1969 Dalston had ousted GOLD as the landlord, gained the $800,000 deposit money, and had 900 building blocks on the market at an average price of $5250. At that price the entire estate had a paper value of $4,725,000. If it then followed the normal BondCorp modus operandi and capitalised the $652,000 cost of the roadworks, drainage and sewerage into the asset's value, it could say the estate was worth $5.4 million. In theory then, Dalston's profit from sub-dividing and selling Greenwood Forest itself was closer to $3 million.

But the big daddy development of all was Yanchep — a

19,600-acre patch of windswept Indian Ocean foreshore about fifty-five kilometres north of Perth which would take Bond's name around the world. This was to be BondCorp's corner-stone project and the ultimate test of Bondy's skills as develop-er and salesman. If he could persuade people to buy these God-forsaken shifting sandhills and actually use them for human habitation, then surely he could sell anything to any-one. At the time, the proposal was so outrageous and the prospect so preposterous that it stands today as living proof of the power of the mind and the dollar over matter and nature.

Bond is believed to have picked up the Wydgee Pastoral Company Pty Ltd, which owned the Yanchep land, for a relative pittance in the late 1960s while he was still going through his tax-effective farm acquisitions phase. By Western Australian standards it was a small cattle station, running only a few hundred head on a poor-quality scrub of stunted banksias and blackboy bushes. The only thing the treeless property had going for it was its western boundary — sixteen kilometres of beachfront where crystal-clear water washed over fine white sand. Based on the issued capital of the three companies that ended up owning the land, it would have cost him not much more than about $300,000.

Only a particularly vivid imagination could see Wydgee as anything other than an arid wilderness area dedicated to the breeding of dugite snakes and blowflies with the capacity to bite chunks out of them. But Bond had a vision of a new satellite city where 200,000 happy souls drawn from around the world would live and frolic by the seaside in harmony with nature and the economy. More specifically he saw it as a $250-million subdivision of 60,000 building blocks called Sun City. Alchemist Bond would wave his wand of energy and optimism and transmute the sand into gold. He had surely gone too far this time. What migrant in his or her right mind would see this desert backblock as paradise found? Indeed, Yanchep had everything Alan Bond had hated about Australia when he first stepped off the *Himalaya* in 1950. It was hot, dry and off the beaten track. If Fremantle then was like Port Said, this had to be a whole lot worse. It is doubtful that the contradiction even crossed his mind. When it came down to doing business, Bond was as adaptable as a chameleon. He had already changed his religion, politics and football club allegiance overnight.

Changing his mind required only a slight shift in consciousness, a different way of seeing things. He didn't see Yanchep as
a pipedream. He saw the opportunity there to plan and control
the development of his own city free from government interference and the meddling of the Metropolitan Regional Planning
Authority. To him it was a straightforward business proposition. Admittedly it was more ambitious and longer term than
any other project he had conceived before but that only meant
that the rewards for success would be greater. The only
problem he saw was in financing the massive development
costs required to set up the land bank. His own puny resources
would need to be augmented by a major international operator
with access to large licks of long-term development finance if
he were to get this one off the ground.

His first partner was the English developer Taylor Woodrow International. Bond had been cultivating this contact on
his many trips to London and was associated with them in the
redevelopment of the Celtic Club site. In January 1969, Bond
and BondCorp finance director Benson-Brown flew to London
for talks with the Taylor Woodrow parent board on the Yanchep project. He returned confident of 'a continuing flow of
British funds' for his organisation but sounded a note of
warning. 'English investors were eager to invest in Western
Australia but were selective in the nature of their investment.
Rather than looking to risk ventures, they saw their future with
established companies operated by sound management.'[67]

Bond must have convinced the Taylor Woodrow board
that he was running a soundly managed, established company
and that there was no risk in the Yanchep development,
because they formed a joint-venture company called Taylor
Woodrow Bond Pty Ltd to acquire the Wydgee Pastoral Co. Pty
Ltd and another called TWB Pty Ltd. Taylor Woodrow Bond
was given title to areas earmarked for development and Wydgee was left to run cattle on the other half of the property. The
cornerstone of Yanchep Sun City was now in place. Building on
it would take some time.

Throughout this period of great activity, Alan Bond was
engaged in a personal struggle to attain respectability and
acceptance in Perth society. His London backers could forgive
his youthful enthusiasm but his lack of connections in polite

society was proving a distinct drawback to his business aspirations. The Perth Establishment had laughed at him in 1965 when he bought the Exchange House site. He didn't give two hoots then. He had an abiding resentment of those in established positions, especially if they got in his way, and he loved nothing better than to bore it up the old school ties and silver spoons at the wild Friday-night parties held in the boardroom atop Exchange House. He saw their resentment of him as pure jealousy and he used it to spur himself on to greater heights. The only time they managed to wound him were with references to his lack of formal education. 'There was a small-mindedness in Perth in the early days. There were people who looked down their noses at you if you hadn't gone to school.'[68]

Bond appears to have responded to these barbs by exaggerating his academic endeavours and achievements in England and at Fremantle Technical School. This is a surprising reaction as most business contemporaries at least give him credit for having been intellectually astute and as sharp as a tack when it came to money matters. His knowledge of company law, contracts, planning codes and building regulations was second to none. Combined with his considerable financial skills and impeccable commercial judgment, he had no need to feel the intellectual inferior of any he had crossed swords with so far. But Bond was missing the point. There might have been a handful of old established families on the Swan who adopted the airs and graces of a bunyip aristocracy, but Perth was evolving into a meritocracy as a result of the mining boom. New money freely vied with old money within the Perth business community and on the social scene. If the Establishment within the business community had an objection to Bond, it was based on their disapproval 'of both the substance and style of the brash young signwriter from Fremantle.' In the early days the old guard dubbed him a 'flash in the pan' and muttered darkly about his business dealings ... 'People were saying "Alan Bond is going to come unstuck" from the day I started in business. I've learned to live with that.'[69] They had taken to the high moral ground to judge the upstart on the propriety of his rapid rise. 'He trod on too many people on the way up. But more than this, his personal style upset them ... He used to be quite coarse at times and pretty brash,' says one of his closest friends. 'He's made a lot of enemies in business and a lot of people say they'd never do business with him again.'[70] Bond cheerfully admitted he had detractors, 'people who detect in his hustling something a little ungentlemanly.' But, he reasoned, 'When you climb a 100-rung ladder, you'll inadvertently step on some hands. So you have these people striving to push you back down the ladder. A lot of people saw us make a lot of money and there were jealousies.'[71]

Many of the people supposedly hurt by Bond on his way up the ladder were ordinary people who had come to him with specific business ideas and propositions which, they later claimed, he had expropriated for his own benefit. They had approached him with the information because they trusted his financial acumen and because he was renowned for his ability to get things done. Their gripes seem to centre on his lack of acknowledgment or compensation for their contribution to various windfalls.

That Bond was an outsider, from humble origins in Fremantle, would not have helped his assimilation into what passed for high society in parochial Perth. 'There is still enough of the English working-class in his voice for him to lapse occasionally into "somethink" or "uvva" and he has had to overcome friendly Perth's own brand of freezes that it reserves for upstarts who do well.'[72] But Bond's problems with fitting in were mainly of his own making. He was capable of being rude, crude and unattractive. He was frequently obnoxious at restaurants and had the irritating habit of parking his limousines on city footpaths. He eventually acknowledged that he needed to acquire a little finesse in the interests of promoting a better business image. He resolved to tame down his crudeness and rudeness in public and allow joviality to replace his usual surliness and aggression. To enter Perth society he would have to flatter the doorkeepers rather than break down the door.

From 1968 on, he liked to see his name in print and this happened with regularity as he indulged in some pretty conspicuous consumption. He first hit the front page of the local press when he paid a then-record amount of $100,000 in May 1968 for the Victoria Avenue, Dalkeith, home of the former 'Mr Big' of the betting world, SP bookmaker Pat Healy. The attraction of the property was not the two-storey mansion but the location of the three-quarter-acre river frontage block in this

exclusive enclave of established Claremont. This was his statement that he had crossed the railway tracks (in this case, the
Swan River) and he was here to live among them for better or
worse. He became a member of the Claremont Football Club
(he was to switch to South Fremantle in 1970) and the Claremont Yacht Club (the Royal Perth Yacht Club blackballed his
first application). He had taken up sailing in 1968 to help
advance his business interests but also because it was the
done thing in Claremont. His first yacht, the forty-seven-foot
Bermuda sloop *Panamuna*, literally fell off the back of a cattle
truck: 'Bond owned a couple of farms which a man wanted to
buy, but who hadn't got enough money for a cash down-
payment. He offered instead a boat as the deposit. Bond
accepted and found himself the owner of *Panamuna*, which
happened to be the largest and fastest craft on the river.'[73]
(There was talk of him having another yacht, *Thera*, but
Panamuna is generally regarded as his first.)

He made news again in August 1969 when he announced
he was spending $100,000 to have a new ocean racer built. It
would be named *Apollo* after the Greek sun god of great beauty
and it would be paid for out of his Poseidon windfall. As this
followed so closely on his $100,000 for the Healy mansion, the
good burghers of Perth had to be impressed. But Bond's
intention was to impress his business clients: 'Sailing helps me
communicate with clients on common ground. This is particularly so with overseas business acquaintances. Quite often
these people find it hard to relax in an office. But sailing is
universal and most people like it, particularly when you take
them yourself.'[74]

Eileen's cousin and Alan's friend, John Hughes, is more
candid about Bond's motives then: 'I think Alan got involved
with the blue water scene for image. I don't think he was the
slightest bit interested in becoming a sailor, but it seemed
the "nice" thing to do. Then, consistent with the desires
and ambitions of the man, he wanted to be the biggest and
the best.'[75]

But Bond would not find it easy to get people to like him.
In May 1970 he stood for election to the Perth City Council but
failed to take the central ward seat. Two events that took place
on Friday 22 May conspired to defeat his campaign. The city
awoke that morning to find its hoardings and bus shelters
covered with anti-Bond posters. These depicted Bond with

horns, glasses and a beard and carried the slogan 'Feed Perth's Top Land Shark — Vote Bond 1'. The posters were ripped down and Perth CIB detectives called in, but the damage had been done. Peter Mitchell, Bond's campaign manager, decried the malicious smear campaign. 'Why anyone would do such a despicable thing is hard to understand ... We are confident that the public generally and central ward electors have sense enough not to be influenced by the content of the pamphlet.'[76] Later that black Friday, Eileen Bond was pulled over by a traffic patrolman and a yellow sticker reading 'vehicle unfit for use' was slapped on the car's windscreen because the front tyres were bald. She was driving the Bonds' new $24,000 maroon Rolls-Royce, EUL 555, which had only 9000 miles on the clock. The incident quickly became Perth's major talking point. No one had ever heard of a Roller being booked for having bald tyres before. The connotations were horrific for Bond. This was the exact opposite of the image he was trying to project.

His father died that year, too. The two were never particularly close but Alan must have grieved Frank's passing. It was Frank who was responsible for bringing him to Australia and it had taken him some time to come to terms with that fate. The story is told of a zealous BondCorp accountant who one day threatened to terminate Mr F Bond from his sixty-dollar-a-week retainer after he had failed to show for a few weeks. He was evidently mindful of his relationship to the chief executive but equally observant of his boss's directive that all 'bludgers' be pruned from the payroll. His mother was also a frequent visitor to the BondCorp bunker but appears to have received a warmer welcome. 'How's my boy?' she would call to the huddle of beavering executives guarding his doorstep as she barged cheerily into his office.

Once he turned thirty he became conscious of his own mortality, and he attempted to get fit and lose weight. Despite his energy, he had problems keeping his weight down because he ate to excess. 'I'm typically Australian: I like steak, fish. If I'm talking to you I can just sit here and eat without even knowing I've eaten. And I'm a moderate drinker.'[77] His friends were of the opinion that he wasn't a big drinker most of the time but when he hit the grog, he hit it hard. For a hobby, he began collecting coins, antiques and paintings but he claimed he only bought paintings that he liked.

Eileen Bond could be just as flamboyant as Alan. She used

to have a white Mini Minor with a chandelier welded on the roof which she drove around as an expression of her individuality. Their fourth child, Jody, was born in 1967 and though Eileen's role was the traditional one of mother and homemaker, Bond began publicly to acknowledge the importance of her skills as an adjunct to his business. 'We bought the Healy house because we have to entertain and look after investors coming to Australia in our home, as this is the way business is done in other countries. People of a mature age don't want to go to a little divy nightclub. My wife is a very good cook, she entertains very well at home, and we get her to do the entertaining at home rather than take people out to a hotel bar or a restaurant.'[78] Eileen got to decorate the Dalkeith mansion and exhibit her flair for ostentatious decor. Alan said he and Eileen liked the same sort of things. She also helped her friends with decorating ideas and renovated a terrace house in North Fremantle. Husband Alan was still apologising for not spending as much time as he would like with his wife and children because of his extensive travels. Despite all the talk about her cooking and wonders of home life, he was a frequent visitor to a North Fremantle dive called Hamburger Heaven.

Poolside seemed to be how the family relaxed and entertained friends — a small group that included fellow businessman Peter Young, who married 1961 Miss Universe Tanya Verstak; Eileen's cousin John Hughes, who had a large car dealership; and Yosse Goldberg who, like Bond, was into everything. 'I've had numerous people come and just enjoy the pleasure of seeing my pool,' Bond said in 1969. It was also the place for playful high jinks. In one incident that entertained the troops, Bond pushed Goldberg into the pool only to discover that the joke was on him as Goldberg was wearing Bond's suit.

As the Bonds were severing their connections with hand-to-mouth Fremantle and embracing the creature comforts of Claremont, the one constant for Eileen remained the South Fremantle Football Club. Her dad, Doozer Hughes, was beginning his last term as president in 1970 and Eileen appeared determined to make it as successful as possible for him. By hook or by crook, she dragged her husband away from his allegiance to the Claremont Tigers and chained him to the South Freo Bulldogs enclosure before the start of the season.

We have no evidence that Eileen used Doozer's significant contribution to the rise and rise of BondCorp as a bargaining chip in the ensuing pillow talk but Bond's conversion was as complete as it was sudden. Within weeks he had the South Fremantle players on a bonus for each win, was employing their star recruits at BondCorp and was running film nights devoted to his yachting prowess.

The sea discovered Alan Bond a lot faster than Alan Bond discovered the sea. He suffered endless bouts of stomach-retching seasickness when he first ventured out onto the rough Gage Roads waters on *Panamuna* and he seemed to have the curse of Neptune on him. He broke two masts in the first two months through carrying too much sail and the boat sank twice in the Swan. Within weeks of taking over the forty-seven-footer in 1968, the pugnacious landlubber was prepared to take on the world. 'Let's have a go at the Sydney-to-Hobart race,' he said to *Panamuna*'s sailing master Peter Nicol. 'Line honours or handicap?' enquired Nicol. 'Line honours,' responded Bond. 'We don't want to wait three days for a result.'[79]

Nicol contacted Sydney designer Bob Miller (later to change his name to Ben Lexcen) with Bond's request for a new yacht — he wanted the biggest and fastest boat in Australian waters. Miller came up with the state-of-the-art, fifty-six-foot *Apollo* within eighteen months, just in time for the 1969–1970 Sydney-to-Hobart. Bond was pipped for line honours in that first big yacht race by English publishing tycoon Sir Max Aitkin, whose sixty-two-foot *Crusade* beat *Apollo* into Hobart town by thirteen minutes.

Rather than allowing his spirit to be crushed by the narrow loss, Bond was smitten by the whole bluewater scene. It flattered his ego to be lionised and duchessed by the eastern seaboard Establishment and he was beginning to savour the business fringe benefits of being in the sport. He knew he was on a good wicket when he (and *Apollo*) scored invitations to regattas at Newport, Rhode Island, in June and Cowes, Isle of Wight, in August as a result of his modest charm and the boat's impressive performance. Bond returned to Perth on 9 January 1970 with a decided swagger in his step: 'We had several other invitations after the Sydney-to-Hobart race but will not be able to compete in all these races. Sir Max will be sailing on *Apollo*

when we race at Cowes after competing at Newport and
Bermuda. If shipping arrangements can be completed after
Cowes, we will take *Apollo* to Sydney to race in the selection
heats for the Admiral's Cup.'[80] Bond knew absolutely nothing
about yachting at this stage but he was now willing to learn
from those who did so that he could access the business
contacts. 'I pride myself on being able to absorb the experi-
ences of others quicker than the average person. Now I intend
to use that in learning all I can about yachting.' But he sailed
yachts in much the same manner as he ran businesses. 'In one
Cap Naturaliste blue water race, while competitors were jog-
ging sedately on the line, Bond put *Apollo* right along the line,
sending the fleet sprawling and winning the start. As one
affronted yachting buff put it, 'It was as much as to say "I'm
Alan Bond. I've got the biggest yacht. Get out of my way."'[81]

Bond arrived in New York, en route to Newport, Rhode
Island, early in June 1970 completely oblivious — we are
expected to believe — of the very existence of America's Cup
twelve-metre yachting. *Apollo* had been shipped to New York
and was being reassembled at the Robert Derecktor shipyard
when, legend has it, Bond spotted a twelve-metre on a nearby
slipway. It was the new Olin Stephens-designed *Valiant*, a hot
favourite to defend the Cup a few months hence. Bond was
having a good stickybeak at the twelve's open cockpit when he
was told to rack off by *Valiant*'s foredeck captain, Victor
Romagna. 'He snapped Bondy's head off,' according to Miller/
Lexcen, who was with him at the time. 'He said, "How would
you like me to come shove my face in your living room
window?" Well that really got Bondy mad. He said something
like, "What is that bloody thing anyway?" I explained to him
that it was a twelve-metre boat, an America's Cup boat, and he
asked me, "What is the America's Cup?" I told him and he said,
"Right, you design me one of those twelve-metres and we'll
come back here and win their bloody America's Cup." I didn't
think he was serious, but he was. When we got back to
Australia he got his sailing master to ring me up to confirm it.'[82]

It is a lovely story but it can't possibly be true. In 1968
Bond had unsuccessfully negotiated to buy *Dame Pattie*, the
1967 Australian challenger, before deciding to have *Apollo*
built. There were constant comparisons between *Apollo* and a
twelve-metre yacht in the Perth press in 1969 and even talk of a
possible match race between *Apollo* and *Gretel* on Sydney

Harbour. Ted Turner's twelve, *American Eagle*, was being chartered by Sir Frank Packer at the time and took part in the Sydney-to-Hobart race with *Apollo*. It is simply inconceivable that Bond, the quick learner, had not seen a twelve-metre yacht or heard of the America's Cup until that day in New York in 1970. Packer had certainly heard of Bond and *Apollo* as he prepared for this third and last America's Cup challenge in 1970. (He died before the 1974 series.)

Four countries — Australia, Britain, France and Greece — had challenged the New York Yacht Club for the Cup after the 1967 races. Britain and Greece pulled out, leaving Australia and France to fight out the first formal challenger series races off Newport. Enter Baron Marcel Bich, the French Bic ballpoint pen tycoon, with more money than sense. 'Having gained fame and fortune, he yearned for class. So he bought his title and took up yachting.'[83] It is estimated that he spent US$4 million on his twelve-metre yacht, *France*, and his 1970 campaign but it was a disaster.

Packer had got smart. He had Alan Payne design him a fast new twelve called *Gretel II* and he appointed Adelaide wine-maker James 'Gentleman Jim' Hardy as skipper and left him to get on with it. He had Ted Turner's *American Eagle* to trial against as well as *Gretel I* and *Vim* but he kept her true speed a secret. *Gretel II* ate *France* in four straight races, the last one being the most hilarious yet witnessed at Newport: 'Dressed in formal white yachting attire, complete with white gloves, the Baron steered into thickening fog. When he emerged forty-two minutes after the Aussies crossed the finish line, it was at the end of a tow, heading back to port. He insisted he had NOT gotten lost; it was just that with the fog and the crowding spectator boats, the conditions were little short of impossible. When he reached the dock, he was damp and hopping mad because the race committee hadn't cancelled the race. (It probably should have.) On the walk back he punched a French TV cameraman. He was even madder later, when the papers said he had gotten lost and that he had "abandoned" the race — a word which, translated into French, has unsportsmanlike connotations. He said he had been "dishonoured" by the challengers' race committee and vowed he would never set foot or sail in Newport again. But he did — in 1974, '77 and '80. He lost again each time, extravagantly.'[84]

Intrepid, the NYYC's 1967 defender, got the nod again in

September 1970, having dismissed *Valiant* (the one Bond saw in New York), *Heritage* and *Weatherly*. She was skippered by Californian Bill Fricker. (Bus Mosbacher was attending to his duties as President Nixon's chief of protocol that year.) In the first race *Gretel II* snarled her spinnaker, broke her spinnaker pole, lost a man overboard, lost a protest and came in nearly six minutes behind *Intrepid*. In the second race there was a collision at the gun and though *Gretel II* won by 1:07 minutes, it lost the protest and the race. *Intrepid* won the third race, *Gretel II* the fourth and *Intrepid* the fifth to take the Cup 4–1. It was a creditable performance by Packer and Hardy, the winning margins in the last four races all being under two minutes; but it was not good enough.

Bondy struck on 7 October 1970, announcing a surprise $1-million bid for the next Cup by his Spirit of the West syndicate at a press conference in Perth. In typical Bond fashion, he had already cabled his challenge to New York before he had informed the Royal Perth Yacht Club that he was doing it under their name. He refused to name the member corporations of his syndicate until the challenge was accepted but he said they were out to win the Cup at any cost. 'I have analysed what the Americans needed to do to win the latest series, and I'm prepared to accept the game on their terms. Australians generally lack the killer instinct found in the American defenders.'[85]

Bond said his syndicate would build two new boats designed by Miller/Lexcen and buy *Gretel II*, *Gretel* and *Vim* from Packer. There was no mention of Yanchep Sun City at this stage but Bond was proposing to trial his five twelve-metre yachts off the Western Australian coast.

CHAPTER EIGHT

1974: Courageous vs. Southern Cross, Courageous,
4–0

Making money in the property boom of
the early 1970s was easier than squashing snails after the rain
and considered just as distasteful. Artificially created land and
building values went through the roof as the property boom
followed the share boom in the first few years of the new
decade. It was built on a ready supply of cheap credit from
bank-associated finance companies and was going swingingly
until the Whitlam Labor government put up the cost of money
and brought the roof down with a sickening crash in late 1973.
One by one from 1974, the biggest land speculators and their
financiers began to fall over. But nobody cried for them.
Property developers had a thoroughly disreputable public
image, being seen as the catalysts for the roaring inflation
that then gripped the nation and for their crude exploitation

of the great Australian dream of home ownership.

Alan Bond was foremost among the Perth property developers at that time and his survival is still looked upon with a mixture of disbelief, awe and bewilderment. He won and lost millions as he shuffled paper like a possessed poker player; but it was his ability to get into, and out of, debt that turned heads in the eastern States and gave him his reputation as a great survivor. Bond claims that he saw the crash coming and diversified in the knick of time to save the day. The truth is even more fantastic.

When Lesmurdie Heights Pty Ltd changed its name to Bond Corporation Pty Ltd in 1967 its shareholders were Alan Bond, his family company Dallhold Investments Pty Ltd, Ron White (through White Investments Pty Ltd) and Kevin George Benson-Brown. In 1970 White and Benson-Brown's five-percent holdings were acquired by Dallhold's making BondCorp a one-man band. Bond held one $2 share, and the other 1,249,000 were owned by his family company. Dallhold's share capital was split into A, B, C, D, E and F ordinary shares. Alan Bond held the A-class shares, Eileen the Bs, and the four children (John, Craig, Susanne and Jody) the Cs, Ds, Es and Fs. We don't know whether he expected a rebellion in the ranks but he made his A share the governing share, entitling him to three times as many votes as the rest of the shares put together, plus one vote. A similarly structured second family company, Shield Enterprises Pty Ltd, held 10,000 ordinary shares in Dallhold and the whole operation was firmly under Bond's command.

Apart from him, BondCorp's major assets were the half interest in the Yanchep land and its controlling interest in the two listed companies, WAL and AMIN. At 30 June 1971 its total assets stood at $16.5 million and net tangible assets at $6.2 million after deducting just over $10 million in liabilities. Issued capital was $500,000. It was still small beer in terms of debt but it was to make a quantum leap into the never-never.

In October 1971 BondCorp regained total control of Yanchep when it took out English developer Taylor Woodrow's half share for about $1.5 million. Taylor Woodrow appears to have been a willing seller at this price. The task of financing and building the Yanchep resort was daunting and it obviously didn't share either Bond's enthusiasm for the project or an enthusiasm for working with Bond. It had been a short and sweet relationship but the dissolution of the arrangement was as enjoyable for Bond as had been the courtship and the intervening experience. Taylor Woodrow Bond Pty Ltd changed its name to Yanchep Estates Pty Ltd and along with TWB Pty Ltd became a wholly owned subsidiary of BondCorp.

The benefits of this takeover were several. BondCorp could now mortgage the estate to the hilt and gain full access to the sales income from the project. (The first 350 blocks were due to be released onto the market on Boxing Day, 1971.) There was a bonus in that TWB Pty Ltd had an issued capital of $200,000, twice that of Yanchep Estates, because it owned International House, an eighteen-storey office block and hotel complex on St Georges Terrace that was more in Taylor Woodrow's usual line of business and was being jointly developed with them on the old Celtic Club site. (It was to become BondCorp's new corporate HQ and the Ansett Gateway hotel.) If the two subsidiaries were worth $3 million all up and we impute a nominal $2-million value on International House, then in October 1971 Yanchep was worth no more than $1 million. But by 30 June 1972, the same land would appear in the notes to the BondCorp accounts with an independent professional valuation (by Jones Lang Wootton) of $6 million 'subject to the completion of a boating marina of the standard advertised.'

In early 1972 Alan Bond was ready to play his hand. He outlined to the world his multi-million-dollar gamble to align his business career with America's Cup yachting when he told a London press conference that Yanchep would make an ideal venue for the 1977 America's Cup series if he was successful in 1974. Not only would his Cup campaign now cost $4 million but BondCorp was spending $6.6 million on a marina for twelve-metre yachts at Yanchep. (It had no natural harbour or inlets.) He went on to say: 'One of the problems is that the United States is making it almost prohibitive for a country or an individual to challenge for the America's Cup. But we went into all this before we started. Under Australian law some of the cost of yachting could be a tax deduction when linked to a commercial development such as Yanchep Sun City.'[86]

It seemed that every time the subdivision was mentioned it underwent an exponential growth in value. In January 1972, with seventy brick-and-tile houses under construction, the project was spoken of as costing $25 million over five years and including a major hotel complex, a tavern, a marina and docking facility for 600 boats and an international golf course. In later publicity handouts, BondCorp put a total figure of $250 million on its cornerstone development.

In the first half of 1972 the shuffling began in earnest. BondCorp sold WAL (controlled by BondCorp) a half interest in the development and sale of 1450 lots at Yanchep for $1.05 million. The money was handy but BondCorp needed to get its hands on a lot more than that just to pay holding costs, let alone development costs, at Yanchep. It raised most of the money it required by plunging spectacularly into deep pools of debt. At 30 June 1972, BondCorp had an issued capital of only $500,000 but total liabilities of $27,325,595 — a somewhat risky gearing of 550 per cent (a debt-equity ratio of 55:1).

This money was costing a fortune to hold at a time when interest rates were fairly steady at 7 to 8 per cent. In 1971–72 BondCorp shelled out a total of $1,581,844 in interest payments. It capitalised (added to the cost and asset value of a project) $572,515 of this and charged $719,546 against its profit and loss account. Not surprisingly, then, profit that year was a paltry $64,886 and its accumulated losses stood at $1,565,075.

Why were financiers prepared to lend to BondCorp? Of this total indebtedness, $23,422,319 was in the form of secured loans, a staggering 221-per-cent increase on the previous year's $7,286,604. These borrowings were secured with mortgages over land and buildings, the value of which was rising in the BondCorp books at an even faster rate. At 30 June 1971, the value of land and buildings was in the books at $6,726,006. By 30 June 1972, it had risen to $24,824,150. In theory, the added value of the property balanced the new lending and secured the financier's position. BondCorp's ability to borrow then was limited only by the future value it put on its property holdings.

And how were these values set? In the 1972 accounts the great bulk of the $24.8 million ($16.6 million) was at directors' valuations. Only $8.2 million was set by independent professional valuation and this figure included the $6-million revaluation of Yanchep. Other projects making up the value would have included the new Tranby-On-Swan thirty-three-acre housing estate on the river in inner suburban Maylands; Glendalough; Bibra Lake; the Windsor Towers apartments in South Perth; and International House in the city.

Alan Bond should have picked up enough accounting

knowledge at night school to know that he would have been over-extended if any of these assets were overvalued. Their values were meaningless if the land could not be developed or no market existed for the developed properties. In 1972 WAL had the Santa Maria land in its books at $4 million but the value of the asset could not be realised because the State government would not re-zone the land for subdivision. Even though WAL was capitalising the holding charges on Santa Maria and not charging them against the profit and loss account, it made a loss of $250,643 in 1971–72.

It was from this highly geared and lowly earning base in late 1972 that Bond gambled $6 million on a major interstate expansion of his land bank in the hope that it would unlock even further lines of credit to help him exploit the now raging property boom. In December WAL launched a raid on the Melbourne-based, listed property developer, the Savoy Corporation Ltd. Savoy had other strategic assets, but its basic attraction was its control of 1780 acres at Taylors Lakes, in the outer Melbourne suburb of Keilor. The real prize here was a 1970 valuer's assessment that, as developed land, it had a possible market value of more than $48 million yet no part of the value of the asset (or the subsidiary that owned the land) appeared in the 1972 accounts.

The risks of getting done over in this deal were still quite high. Bond was from out of town, he wasn't in on the development from the ground floor and the deal had already been picked over by some of the smartest land sharks in the business ... Had he come into the Savoy market like the proverbial lift boy who is always the last to hear of a market run and consequently the first hurt when the market turns?

In mid-November, entrepreneur extraordinaire John Rogerson Hall had sold Slater Walker subsidiary, St James Properties, a 37-per-cent stake in Savoy for just under $1 million. Within six weeks it would on-sell this parcel to WAL for just under $2 million. This sparked a short, sharp market war between WAL and Cambridge Credit Corporation for control of Savoy. Cambridge, a developer/financier of some stature before its celebrated collapse in September 1974, was protecting both its 47-per-cent stake in Savoy and its direct eighteen-per-cent holding in Development Estates (Keilor) Pty Ltd (DEK), which owned the land. However, Bond found that Cambridge, like everyone else, had a price. On 22 January 1973 WAL emerged with 90 per cent of Savoy Corporation and 80 per cent of DEK for a further outlay of about $3.4 million to Cambridge. By the time minorities were taken out the bill was over $6 million.

If it were an expensive Pyrrhic victory that WAL could ill-afford to win, nobody was letting on. BondCorp director Peter Lucas described it at the time as possibly the biggest financial coup of the last decade. At the Savoy annual general meeting in Melbourne the next day, Bond disclosed that Savoy had been made an offer of $9,614,000 for the Keilor land. The salesman was at work on his new property and soon he would weave his magic over the balance sheet to find added value in the deal.

How could WAL afford to pay for the Savoy acquisition, though? Simple. It sold its Perth city property portfolio back to BondCorp and associates for their book value of $8.7 million. (WAL immediately lent $1.3 million back to BondCorp as an unsecured note repayable at call.) Savoy also paid for its own acquisition by selling its entire holding of $2.3 million worth of debentures and unsecured notes in unrelated companies during 1973.[87]

But the best was yet to come. On 27 June (three days before the 1973 balance date) the WAL-controlled Savoy received an independent valuation from Mr William J O'Conner that the Keilor land was worth $10,042,000. It was included in the 30 June accounts for the first time based on that 27 June determination.

Notes to the accounts show Savoy's breakdown of this valuation as land acquisition costs at $2,175,827, development expenses capitalised at $385,743, and rates, taxes, interest and other amounts capitalised at $1,598,341 for a total of $4,159,641. The remaining $5,882,359 was credited to the asset revaluation reserve and other provisions.

But the value was drawn against at the same time as it was added to the Savoy balance sheet. The same accounts show that on the strength of the Keilor revaluation, Industrial Acceptance Corporation (IAC) was prepared to advance Savoy a $12,667,000 credit facility secured by a mortgage over the Keilor land. At 30 June 1973, $8,287,800 of this facility had already been drawn down. In a sense, Bond got his money back from Savoy as soon as he got in there and started to crank up the Taylors Lakes action.

According to a 1974 BondCorp promotional document,

development of Taylors Lakes began on 1 June 1973 when town planning and engineering design consultants started work on the project. It was to be subdivided into about 8300 home sites and a value of $50 million was put on the development. (Sixteen years later, it still features in the 1989 BondCorp accounts – but as an estate of 4400 home sites with about 2000 sites still awaiting development.)

Bond had previously done business with the financier IAC in 1969 when he borrowed $1.9 million for the Greenwood Forest land at Hamersley, and it almost certainly had some exposure to Yanchep borrowings. In those days IAC was associated with the ANZ Bank but in May 1971 ANZ sold its holding to First National City Bank of New York which is now known as Citibank.

As Australia's second largest non-bank financier, IAC had plunged heavily into property, and property developers, in the early 1970s. Nearly half of its new lending of $531 million in 1972–73 was in the form of mortgage loans. The financial deal Bond struck with IAC over the Keilor land was good for Bond but was to prove not so good for IAC and Citibank over the short, medium or long terms.

'Under the terms of the deal, IAC will provide all finance for the development for 10 years. No principal or interest will be repayable for 3 years. IAC will get 11.5 per cent on its money and 15 per cent of the profit. This means Savoy Corporation is virtually getting a free ride on the subdivision — provided, of course, the company can sell the land at a large enough mark-up to cover the interest charges. Mr Bond told the *Australian Financial Review* that the deal was based on cash flow financing and that the agreement with IAC provided for two-thirds of the money to be raised as bill finance. The bills would presumably be long-term, drawn on Savoy or other companies in the Bond group and endorsed by IAC, which would either hold the paper or sell it in the rediscount market.'[88]

To complete the expanded land bank picture, Savoy also brought to WAL/BondCorp a Queensland connection through its Plantation Management Pty Ltd subsidiary. This owned management agreements for 'the design, development and sales' of three co-operatively owned forestry plantations on the Queensland Gold Coast. These were 'The Pines' subdivision of 1748 lots behind Palm Beach, 2885 acres at Oxenford and 1022 acres at Burleigh. The Burleigh estate would become Bond University. BondCorp had gone national with real estate on offer in three separate States. It was up there playing with the big boys at last.

Following his successful seizure of Savoy, Bond now had more development land than he could poke a stick at. He also had more debt (about $30 million at this stage) than he could comfortably jump over. Had he become a victim of his own success, as well as the success of others, in the raging property boom market of early 1973? How long could it and would it last?

A slightly nervous Bond sniffed the wind and allowed his business instincts to get the better of his enthusiasm for a change. His thirty-fifth birthday was approaching and he remembered how miserable his twenty-fourth had been in April 1962 as a result of Harold Holt's credit squeeze of November 1961. Increasing political stress had been placed on his chosen profession by the election of John Tonkin's Labor government in Perth in 1971 and Gough Whitlam's Labor government in Canberra in 1972.

As an insider in the property business, he must have seen the obvious signs of oversupply and overvaluation. There were also ominous omens of higher interest rates as the financiers bid up the cost of their borrowings in the capital markets to supply the money to meet the rising demand for their mortgage lending services.

He was not on his own in coming to the realisation that the land boom may be about to top and then slide — just as the share boom had done. Business cycles are as regular as the seasons. Dick Dusseldorp, founder and chairman of the highly successful Lend Lease Corporation, warned his shareholders as early as the 1971 annual meeting that the group was preparing for a downturn. 'The art is what not to be in,' he said presciently. 'The office property scene will be a buyers' market for some time to come. Undoubtedly some operators will go broke.' This opinion was reinforced in July 1972 when Mr R O Powys, the property investment manager of the AMP Society said: 'It seems clear that the market for office space in all major Australian cities is heading for a crisis of oversupply.'[89]

According to a contemporary competitor, 'Bond sensed that the property market was falling long before most of us. He was not able to make the best use of this foreknowledge, for a number of reasons, but he was adaptable enough to extricate himself and look for other opportunities.'[90]

So in early 1973 he knew the crash was coming, but that was only a small part of his problem. What he was going to do about it was the real issue. At a chance meeting five years after the event, Bond and his executives belatedly told Melbourne financial journalist Robert Gottliebsen the inside story of Bond-Corp's first major hand-to-hand battle with corporate death.

'It was decided to call in a couple of merchant banks to do some work on parts of the group and to map out a future strategy. The judgment of each of the merchant banks was the same — sell off land as hard as you can, and reduce borrowings, or you will hit a dreadful crisis. Bond's reaction as he read each report was that this was easier said than done. A major sell-out of property by Bond Corporation would turn the market. Moreover, the Bond people had faith in the long-term potential of their property — it was just the short term they were worried about. To meet maturing liabilities and to be cosy in the downturn they calculated they needed $30 million in cash. The Bond Group had five or six million; for most of 1973 they directed all their energy to gaining control of the $30 million. Bond set about trying to buy control of corporations which either had control of large amounts of cash or whose business generated large cash sums. His plan was that these businesses would buy out his assets and their cash would carry him through.'[91]

The 'Bond people' referred to here are the new management team that the chairman was putting in place to deal with these troubled and challenging times. As the basic core of this team features in many of the corporate manoeuvres that were to follow in 1973 and 1974, and indeed is still in place at BondCorp today, it is helpful to know the times of its members' arrivals and their appointed tasks. Like Bond, most of his senior staff were young. Unlike Bond, most of them had professional qualifications.

Peter Alexander Mitchell (also known as Black), who joined Bond's Progress Development Organisation in December 1966 as chief accountant, was made personal assistant to the chairman and managing director in July 1968, a director of BondCorp in February 1971, and finally deputy managing director in 1973 at age thirty-two. A Fellow of the Australian Society of Accountants, he is said to be a former trust manager in the UK and had the office nickname of 'Jeeves' on account of his accent and his follow-up activities. (Mitchell resigned from the BondCorp board on 2 August 1988, so that he could be appointed a director of The Bell Group Ltd. In the 1989 BondCorp accounts he is listed as one of the company's two senior executives.)

Peter George Beckwith joined BondCorp at age twenty-seven in June 1969 as group commercial manager. He was not appointed a director until June 1975 but became the managing director of BondCorp in July 1982. He had left two of the best schools in Australia (Hale in Perth and Carey Grammar in Melbourne) to become an office boy at sixteen. Beckwith had been a property developer in the East before joining Bond in the West. His father, Talbot Beckwith, was West Australian State manager of the English, Scottish & Australian Bank in the early 1950s before returning to Melbourne where he became chief manager, international, in 1965. In 1973 Talbot Beckwith retired from the then ANZ Banking Group after forty-seven years' service. He then became a director and deputy chairman of BondCorp.

Peter Charles Lucas was thirty-five when he joined Bond-Corp in 1970 by 'answering an ad. in the paper'.[92] At the time he was a legal officer with Western Mining Corporation. He was admitted as a solicitor in New South Wales in 1960 and spent some years in legal practice and commercial activity in that State. He became a director of BondCorp in November 1971 and was responsible for the corporate division as well as being group legal adviser. In April 1974 he moved back to Sydney 'to represent group interests in the Eastern States at board level.'[93] He resigned his BondCorp directorship in June 1976 to become managing director of Robe River Ltd. He remained chairman of Underwriting & Insurance Ltd. He rejoined the board in September 1985 as executive director in charge of the coal division. In March 1987 he became chief executive of Bond Corporation International Ltd in Hong Kong. He returned in November 1989 to become executive director in charge of public and investor relations, based in Sydney.

Warren Leslie Jones, an accountant by training, joined BondCorp in 1971 when Bond took over his plant hire business,

Mayday Hire Services Pty Ltd. Before setting up this business, in partnership, in 1968, Jones had been State accountant of a national neon display sign company and had worked as a marketing manager for another West Australian entrepreneur, Terry Crommelin.[94] He became an executive director of Bond's Amalgamated Industries Ltd and claims to have been appointed a director of BondCorp in 1973 but is not listed in the 1974 directorate. He is in the Summer 1975 directorate where his responsibility is given as managing director of the AMIN group, a position he held till he resigned in 1976. He went to the 1974 America's Cup challenge as an observer, was manager in 1977 and executive director of the 1980 and 1983 challenges and the 1987 defence. He resigned from the BondCorp board in February 1987 to become chairman of Bond Media Ltd. He was considered one of Bondy's main minders.

Antony Gordon Oates became BondCorp's legal officer in July 1974, having been head-hunted by Peter Lucas as his replacement when he moved back to Sydney in April 1974 to manage BondCorp's eastern States operations. Oates, a law graduate from the University of Western Australia and a partner in Perth legal firm Parker & Parker, had been doing a lot of work for BondCorp before he joined the company because he specialised in corporate and finance law. (Messrs Parker & Parker have been closely associated with BondCorp since its inception. Partner Henry Lodge was one of the original WAL and Bond Media directors. Alan's first son John practised as a solicitor with the firm from 1980 to 1982 and the managing director's executive assistant, Kenneth Judge, also practised as a solicitor with the firm from 1980 to January 1983.) Oates was appointed a BondCorp director in April 1975 with the title group general manager. He and Peter Mitchell resigned from the BondCorp board on 2 August 1988, when they were appointed directors of The Bell Group. Oates and Mitchell are the only two senior executives listed in the 1989 BondCorp annual report. The 1988 annual report carried six pages of executives' names and titles.

Noel Reed, the company secretary, had been there from the beginning. A qualified accountant, his nickname was 'Aunty'.

There were two other executive directors of BondCorp at the time: Ron 'Whipping Boy' White, the previous managing director, and Clive Hartz who held the job briefly in 1973. Both were from the new management team installed in 1968 to handle 'current group expansion', were without formal qualifications and appeared to be on the outer as the new team took up the running and the pressure increased. White and Hartz both left BondCorp in December 1974. Ron White suffered a serious back injury while on assignment for BondCorp in 1974. He underwent a series of operations and was off work for about two years, returning briefly in 1976. He is understood to have amassed many documents on the early growth of Lesmurdie Heights Pty Ltd and BondCorp but will not part with them.

There were also some interesting people on the sales team with Max Cunningham (the Yanchep manager) and Peter Beckwith. Dallas Dempster, promoter of the Burswood casino and vendor, along with Laurie Connell, of the Petrochemical Industries Company Ltd (PICL) idea, had spent two years selling land for Bond in the 1960s. 'I think the Bond experience brought out the entrepreneurial skills in me and put me on the path that I have followed since,' he says of that time.[95]

Another corporate tyro was Peter Laurance, now chairman of the Queensland-based Pivot Group Ltd which operates Sea World on the Gold Coast. He came to BondCorp as a finance journalist from the *West Australian* in the early 1970s and it is claimed he has the distinction of designing the three-piece, chain link corporate logo which is still used by the company. The logo is said to symbolise 'the joining of many parts' which in 1973 would have represented the company's property, industrial and mining interests.

But Bond's core team were well-rewarded entrepreneurs who acknowledged the leading role of the head entrepreneur and preferred to work creatively within the corporate structure which he had established. Laurie Connell has closely observed this special relationship since it was established: 'He's got a very good team of blokes that have been with him a long time. They do some very careful analytical work on whatever he's getting himself into.'[96] Connell says that, whenever you see Bond making a move, 'not too far behind is Mitchell, punching it out with a Hewlett Packard.'[97]

So it was the testy tycoon's new team that struck with a vengeance in the first week of April 1973, announcing four separate deals with a total face value of about $30 million.[98]

The largest of these was an outlandish proposal to buy a 43.7-per-cent interest in Robe River Ltd, which held a 35-per-cent interest in Cliffs Robe River Iron Associates (it diluted down to about 15 per cent of the consortium), the latest $275-million Pilbara iron ore mining project based at Pannawonica and linked to the port at Wickham by a 101-mile-long private railroad.

Literally, the initial Robe deal was only a cheap $50,000 thirty-day option to buy the parcel of shares from a company liquidator at a fixed price of $17.4 million on special terms staggered over twelve months from the exercise date of the option. But it also included a pre-emptive right to buy the shares at any time over the next three months (until 5 July). Naturally, Bond didn't have the cash but he seemed to know exactly what he was doing in this roll of the dice. The only way Bond could get his hands on that sort of money was by selling BondCorp's inflated land assets to Robe before the property market turned down. But the figurative reality was that Bond had pulled off a masterstroke despite some suggestions from contemporary cynics that the Robe deal was merely a publicity stunt.

BondCorp appeared to have taken an overnight quantum leap from small-town property developer to world-ranking mining giant. The Robe project partners held sales contracts to deliver eighty-six million tons of high-grade iron ore pellets to Japanese steel mills over a twenty-one year period and a further 71.8 million tons of prepared sinter fines over fifteen years. It was the world's largest iron export contract at that time.

But this time, Peter Mitchell's Hewlett Packard calculator was working overtime ahead of the deal and to a carefully conceived plan. In early 1973, while Lucas was putting the finishing touches on the Savoy deal in Melbourne, Mitchell was in Perth preparing a fifty-page analysis of Robe River's prospects and likely cash flow. 'Although they wanted access to Robe cash, they also wanted the investment to stand up in its own right,' they later told Gottliebsen.[99] Robe River would prove to be the single most important investment that the old BondCorp would ever make, and was to be crucial to its survival.

There is circumstantial evidence to suggest that the inspiration for Bond's plunge into the iron ore business came from his local MP and Dalkeith neighbour, Sir Charles Court, who lived in Waratah Avenue, around the corner from Bond's Victoria Avenue home.

Like Bond, Court came to Perth from England as a boy. He was a successful businessman and chartered accountant before entering State Parliament as the Liberal Member for Nedlands in 1953. Between 1959 and 1971 he was the minister for Industrial Development and the North West and, as such, was credited with laying the foundations for the exploitation of the State's massive mineral wealth during those years.

Court also claims the credit for having the Federal government's embargo on the export of iron ore lifted in 1960: 'When developing WA's iron ore mines we said to Menzies "You'll never know how much iron ore we've got unless you let us exploit it. We'll do a deal with you. We'll put a circle around each of the deposits that your experts and our experts have identified and they remain untouchable. Our deal is that for every three million tons of new iron ore we find outside those areas, we want the right to export one million and you get two million under your reserve." I remember saying to the old boy this means that we get one million tons of nothing and you get two million tons of something. He said that sounds a bit Irish but he agreed.'[100]

What followed was the development of ore bodies at Mount Tom Price (Hamersley Iron), Shay Gap (Mount Goldsworthy Mining Associates), Mount Whaleback (Mount Newman Mining) and eventually Mount Enid (Robe River Iron Associates). In Western Australia all deposits were reserved to the Crown. It was made of iron and it sat firmly on Charlie Court's head.

In 1972 Court was knighted and became Leader of the Opposition in Western Australia. In the same year Bond was elected to the Perth City Council and went on the town planning committee. While it would be wrong to suggest the two were close friends, Court is on record as saying 'I've got a soft spot for Alan. I've known him since his signwriting days ... He was always a fairly outgoing type of person. I knew his father-in-law particularly well. He gave me good advice on the politics of the Fremantle waterfront.'[101] There are suggestions that a company associated with Sir Charles may have, at some stage, been an indirect investor in WAL through Landall Holdings.

There is no doubt that Bond followed Court's business philosophy: 'If you are in business, you're in it to win. You might as well be in it boots and all. It's amazing how much fun you can get out of doing unpleasant things if you are in it up to your neck.'[102]

Bond's first venture into mining in the late sixties had been to search for iron ore in the Jack Hills area of the Murchison, well south of the Pilbara. Bond was working from reports that estimated the area contained 'more than 200 million tons of ore with an iron content of between 57 and 65 per cent'.[103] He never found it.

It was another Perth entrepreneur, Garrick Agnew, who conceived and prospected the Mount Enid (Robe River) ore body but it was Mines Minister Court who, in March 1970, announced the participation of Mineral Securities Australia Ltd (Minsec) — and not the underwriter, Darling & Co. — in the float of Robe River Ltd.[104]

The huge iron ore projects were structured in syndicates in order to meet their massive capital costs and political demands for local equity. Cleveland Cliffs Iron Co. of the US was project manager and had a 30-per-cent interest and Japanese trading giant Mitsui & Co. had another 30 per cent, which left 40 per cent available for Australian equity participation. Garrick Agnew's Mount Enid Iron Co. Pty Ltd picked up 5 per cent, leaving Robe River Ltd with 35 per cent. It was the first opportunity Australians were given to invest directly in a big iron ore project.

Despite this, Darling & Co. were having trouble getting the $29.2-million Robe River float off the ground until Minsec came to the party and subscribed for 14.4 million $1 shares and made a $3.6-million interest-free convertible loan to the company. Minsec, an ephemeral mining share trader and investor, took off like a rocket in 1967 during the Poseidon boom and came crashing down, just as spectacularly but with an enormous thud, on 3 February 1971.

Robe's public debut was anything but inauspicious. The $1 shares came on at $1.60 when first listed on the stock exchange on 16 August 1970 at the end of the Poseidon boom. Minsec was the sort of company that couldn't resist taking profits, so it dumped some 400,000 shares on the market on 20 and 21 August, which helped reduce its holding in Robe to 40 per cent.

Acting on bullish information received, Minsec had had a change of mind by 9 September and decided to buy another 10 per cent of Robe on-market and make the company a subsidiary. Its buying pushed the market for Robe shares to the giddy heights of $2.35 at the end of December 1970 (it had yet to produce, let alone export, any iron ore). Then Minsec did something seemingly inexplicable, even by yesterday's standards. Trevor Sykes relates the episode in his book *Two Centuries of Panic*:

> During the buying of Robe, someone thought of a way to repaint the accounts by what became known as 'the Robe shuffle'. Mineral Securities Australia Ltd still held millions of Robe shares that had been acquired in the float at $1. If these could be sold to another group member at, say, $2.30, a profit of $1.30 a share could be recorded. So Mineral Securities Australia Ltd began selling Robe shares to the broking firm, Hattersley & Maxwell, who sold them to Minsec Pty Ltd, a wholly owned subsidiary of Mineral Securities Australia Ltd. A total of 5.5 million shares were shuffled from Mineral Securities Australia Ltd to Minsec Pty Ltd through Hattersleys over three months. The total value of the sales was $13.5 million on which Mineral Securities claimed a profit of $5.5 million. This wiped out Minsec's share trading losses and gave the group a book profit for the December half of 1970–71, but commonsense dictates that the 'profit' was bogus. It is as though a man has a $5 note in his left-hand pocket and a handkerchief which cost $1 in his right-hand pocket. If the right-hand pocket sells the handkerchief to the left for $5, it has made a $4 profit and the left has an asset which cost $5, but the man is no richer at all.[105]

However strange it may seem, it was not Robe that caused Minsec's downfall in the end but a deadly flirtation with two uranium stocks called Kathleen Investments and Queensland Mines. What the episode illustrates, though, is how desperate the Minsec management was to remain in business as a share trader on the stock exchange and a heavy borrower on the unofficial short-term money market.

As the noose tightened around Minsec's neck (it crashed on 3 February 1971), many unsecured creditors got themselves last-minute security over Minsec's Robe shares to cover their exposure to the teetering giant. 'Nine major creditors had been granted security between 21 January and 3 February. The validity of such late security is always open to challenge,' says Sykes.[106]

When Jim Jamison of accountants Coopers was appointed provisional liquidator of Minsec on 11 February, one of the first things he did was go to the ANZ Bank where the scrip was held and ensure that none of it was sold. The crash of Minsec had caused such a panic both on the share market, where Minsec was a big trader and investor, and on the money market, where Minsec had borrowed $70 million, that he was fearful of the consequences of a legal challenge to the validity of the security. He told creditors — both secured or unsecured — that the only way they had any chance of getting their money back was to go along with his plans for an orderly liquidation of assets. 'A conspiracy of silence developed on the grounds that it was better if the whole rats' nest were left undisturbed,' says Sykes.[107]

It was bluff by Jamison but it bought him time and eventually paid off for both sets of creditors. He was gambling that he could raise enough cash from the asset sales to eventually pay them all off in full. It was the unsecured creditors who were most likely to cause trouble. Jamison had made the bet and now he had to cover it or the whole house of cards would tumble down. 'The repercussions of such a fight would be serious to most of the Sydney financial community and a large part of Melbourne's,' says Gottliebsen.[108] This fascinating situation was to provide Alan Bond with his trump card for survival. The information was common knowledge in financial circles and would certainly have been available to Mitchell.

Jamison managed to sell off all of Minsec's investments except the 43-per-cent controlling stake in Robe River Ltd, which, although saleable, required the right buyer at the right price. He approached BHP, who had the bordering Deepdale deposit in the lower Robe River valley, but they were not interested. A German company toyed with the idea but went no further. (Most of Minsec's other assets had gone offshore.) Garrick Agnew was interested in increasing his stake in Robe but didn't like the price. Lang Hancock scoffed that he was the only one who could save Robe but he would not move 'until the vultures clear[ed] from the Minsec carcass.'[109]

At that stage Jamison was saying he needed $1.15 per Robe share for the liquidation to break even. He was to spend two years looking for it but his real break-even price had fallen to 93 cents (the market price was closer to 60 cents); and, when Alan Bond was prepared to offer him that on 5 April 1973,

he took it. It was the first firm offer he had received. Jamison
needed Bond just as much as Bond needed Robe.

The Mitchell report on Robe had picked it perfectly, so his
information must have been good. The week the option deal
was signed, Robe announced a maiden profit of $83,231 from
the start of production in September to 31 December 1972. By
May the project was benefiting from the announcement of
higher prices negotiated for Pilbara iron with the Japanese
steel mills. Mitchell's information was that the project had
become less marginal with the addition of the pelletising plant
at Wickham and more profitable thanks to better-than-expected
production from the mine, and that the long-term outlook was
sound. (He didn't pick the Arab oil embargo, though.) It also
had some cream. Under the Robe partnership agreement,
excess production over contract could be sold by the partners
on a pro-rata basis. Bond talked of using his 'connections in the
shipping trade' to export this surplus. It was Bond's job to talk
up the investment; it was Mitchell's to iron out the details.

At first, Bond just laughed off the obvious question about
where the money was going to come from. He told the April
press conference that it had been 'tentatively arranged. It
would come from within Australia and be guaranteed by overseas banks. The Bond Group would pledge its substantial land
holdings to borrow the money needed ... We obviously need
considerable State and Federal government support. However,
it is in the interest of WA that control of this company should
be based here,' he said.[110] In May he was to say that the
financing was the least of his worries. 'It will be provided by me
in association with long-term financiers within Australia.' He
did stress that he was in a strong position to seek some finance
from the Minsec creditors who, of course, were now dependent
on him for their settlement. He hinted that the deal had 'several
prospective side benefits'.[111]

Now came the rub. As the full details of the deal Jamison
had done with Bond slowly became public, it was obvious that
Bond's men had held the whipping hand during the three-
month-long negotiations. He had won the money, the box and
vendor finance terms that stretched over nearly four years
instead of the initially agreed twelve months. He certainly
would appear to have exerted quite a lot of pressure and
leverage on the liquidator and the creditors to get them to
agree to his terms.

When Bond paid his $150,000 deposit and signed the BondCorp/Minsec/Robe share purchase agreement by 5 July 1973, he was on a hiding to nothing. 'Bond can't lose in Robe share deal', screamed a headline in the *West Australian*. One of the side benefits was that, if the whole deal fell though on 5 September, the deadline Bond had set for Minsec to meet certain conditions he had layed down (any or all of which he could waive at will), then Bond lost that deposit but gained the right to buy Minsec's interest in the Minpeto Pastoral Partnership, which owned three pastoral properties in the NT, for $100,000. He would not even lose his deposit, as the agreed purchase price for the three farms was $250,000.

However, there were a few major complications to this dream deal. They would cause him to change Mitchell's strategy slightly, but quickly, in order to meet his objectives within his rather limited time frame. The time he had before the credit squeeze began and the property market crashed was rapidly running out. By 5 July 1973 the long-term bond rate had risen a point to 7 per cent and debenture rates had jumped to 9 per cent. 'By September of that year, long bonds had reached 8.5 per cent and debentures had blown out to 11, the highest they had been in two generations.'[112] Poignantly, the *West Australian* pointed out on 26 May that 'Mr Bond's whole package deal has a shrewd sense of business timing about it.'[113]

The main stumbling block to the other (minority) Robe shareholders was his condition that Robe buy BondCorp for $25 million in a reverse takeover as part of the deal. That way he got to control both Robe and its access to funds and BondCorp with its inflated property values locked in. In essence, Robe would both pay for its own acquisition and give Bond a $25-million kitty to tide him over through the property downturn. The money and the box.

'The plan was first negotiated in May 1973, when the property market boom was still in full flight. Bond offered to have Price Waterhouse value BondCorp assets and to have the sale price determined on their valuation. He was confident that the final sale price of BondCorp to Robe would be around $25 million because of the high property values then in the market,' says Gottliebsen.[114]

When Bond first announced this aspect of the deal on May 22 (the deal was reached on May 16) he said a balance sheet for BondCorp was not available, but the assets included land held in Queensland, Victoria and at Yanchep, and appeared in the balance sheet at sworn valuations.[115]

The Robe board were hostile to the BondCorp approach from the start. They wanted to be in the iron ore mining business and not the property market. They put every obstacle they could in the path of BondCorp. There were suggestions that the reverse takeover contravened Section 67 (1) of the Companies Act which prohibited companies from giving financial assistance for the purchase of its own shares. Bond and Jamison stood side by side to refute the attacks on their plan. Jamison claimed that Robe was buying the shares in BondCorp not from Mr Bond but from the shareholders of Bond Corporation: 'Alan Bond advised me he was not a shareholder in Bond Corporation. Bond Corporation was not buying Minsec's 16.22 million Robe shares from the liquidator. Alan Bond was,' Mr Jamison said.[116]

Plan one actually had a new company being floated off, with Alan Bond owning 76 per cent of it and the other ordinary Robe shareholders 24 per cent. To get this they would have to subscribe cash to a non-assignable rights issue in the new company at par. This company would hold Bond's/Minsec's 16.22 million Robe shares (this represented about 43 per cent of Robe's ordinary capital. They already owned the other 57 per cent.) This company would control both Robe and Bond-Corp and all three would be listing on the stock exchange.

It is not surprising that there was little Robe shareholder interest in this proposal. Shareholders were resentful of the fact that the market for their shares had tumbled from $2.35 to 60–70 cents thanks to Minsec and the Minsec parcel hanging over the market, but Minsec was getting out at 93 cents and putting them into a new risky business that they didn't want to be in. At the same time they were also being asked to subscribe new money to buy a small stake in the old business they already owned. The largest minority shareholders, Elder Smith and Burns Philp, were conservatively run and opposed the deal. They didn't see $25 million for BondCorp as money well spent, especially considering its sky-rocketing debt.

The BondCorp/Robe reverse takeover also required the approval of Robe's long-term debenture holders who were being asked to remove 'certain restrictions' in the trust deed between Robe and the trustee for the debenture holders. This was to allow another condition of the bid to proceed. Bond wanted to roll over (extend) the debenture interest repayments 'to ease the demands on liquidity'.

As this group comprised merchant banks who had lent Robe $54 million and included the Australian Resources Development Bank ($25 million), Partnership Pacific ($15 million), AEFC ($7.8 million) and the US Export-Import Bank ($7.2 million), they began to wonder what was going on. He was not dealing with a suburban credit union or hire purchase financier here but some of the Western world's more sophisticated financial players. This money was Robe's working capital. It was required to fund Robe's $60-million share in the Wickham pelletising plant. If the cost of servicing the debt capital was not met, it would not be there. That was the purpose of the trust deed. It ranked above the equity capital of the ordinary shareholders.

But Bond was faced with the problem that the only way Robe could afford to buy BondCorp for $25 million was by a successful re-negotiation of the debenture repayments. With a clean slate, Robe could be re-geared to raise both the BondCorp $25 million and the Wickham $60 million. Bond worked long and hard on the banks within this group. He wanted their support. He wanted the Minsec creditors to meet the interest payments for him. He wanted to arrange other finance to buy them out.

His sales pitch went something like this: 'Assuming Robe successfully raises these funds on its re-negotiated debentures, the Yanchep borrowings could be repaid easily over ten years or less. Yanchep Estates, which comprises almost 20,000 acres, could be divided into quarter-acre sites and developed and sold over a twenty-year period. The 80,000-odd sites could then be sold for an average $5000 a site over the development period, resulting in a gross profit of $400 million. Development costs would probably account for half this figure, but a net profit of $200 million before tax would then be derived from the project. Assuming tax takes a maximum 50 cents in the dollar, annual net profit over the twenty-year period would be $5 million. This should be ample to satisfy funders of the proposed reverse takeover of Bond Corporation.'[117]

With a hostile board and no likelihood of shareholder or debenture-holder approval Bond was forced to abandon the reverse takeover scheme in August. He would have to find another buyer for BondCorp and its property assets ...

Meanwhile, he still wanted Robe, but now he would have to pay for the Minsec shares another way. He still had Jamison's backing and an agreement that allowed for the gradual release of Robe scrip to BondCorp for every time payment he made. They could still be made to pay for themselves through new borrowings once he got his hands on them. But before he could finally bed down the Robe stake and take control of the board, he had to face several more challenges.

Garrick Agnew of Agnew Clough, and Mount Enid Iron Co., who had a direct 5 per cent of Robe River Iron Associates, decided to make a play for Robe's 35-per-cent interest. Jamison stuck by Bond but he later had to put up the price to match that offered by Agnew. Bond made his first payment of $1,582,013 and the sale contract was finally signed on 4 September 1973.

The Robe board challenged the sale contract in the New South Wales Equity Court, seeking to have it set aside on the grounds that it was illegal. Their counsel argued that the agreement was *ultra vires* (outside the powers of) the liquidator, in that it involved time payments. They also argued that 93 cents undervalued the shares and that the sale to BondCorp was negotiated in haste and improvidently. Mr Justice Street ruled in favour of Jim Jamison, saying 'an assumption of illegality could be made but this was based on a technical breach in the extreme and therefore he found that there was no illegality.'[118]

When their court challenge was dismissed, the Robe directors resigned en masse and Bond and his merry men took control of the board at the annual general meeting in Sydney on 13 December. Mr Jamison attended the meeting and moved the bulk of the motions for election of new directors. In his chairman's address, Bond talked of new lines of credit.

During the court case Mr Justice Street, who was the Chief Justice in Equity, ordered that confidential documents handed to the court by BondCorp would be available only to legal advisers and the court itself. He also ordered that cross-examination or evidence-in-chief in relation to the documents be held in closed court. 'He said the reason for this was that information from the documents could be taken out of context and a "disturbed pattern may be revealed." He said there was no question as to the soundness of Bond Corporation.'[119]

In fact, there was some very real questioning to be done as to the soundness of BondCorp, its level of debt and the value of its properties in September 1973. On 9 September Prime Minister Gough Whitlam rose in the House to announce the credit squeeze, which declared monetary policy war on all property developers:

> Subsequent increases in other interest rates will follow as effects of the operations (on bond rates) spread throughout other markets for funds. If, as a consequence, the higher interest rates have the effect of curbing the speculative rush into land and property, that would be all to the good.

Bond's time had run out. He had to act now. On 8 October he announced that the Japanese Tokyu Corporation would buy a half share in Yanchep for $26.5 million. On 17 December he announced that WAL would buy BondCorp for $17.5 million. Both deals had their problems, but at least they were made before the bottom really dropped out of the market.

Back in April, when the Bond team were stitching together a deal a week in order to save the empire from the fast-approaching brick wall, Yanchep Sun City was on the market. Bond had wanted to delay the announcement of a new joint-venture deal for his cornerstone project until as close as possible to the sail-off for the America's Cup, then set for September 1973. He was seeking maximum impact. Yanchep's marketing pivoted on his Cup challenge and he wanted the whole world watching when this dream came true. But events overtook his plans. First the America's Cup regatta was put back a year until 1974 then the credit squeeze was standing there right in front of him.

Tokyu Corporation, a Japanese conglomerate which had developed Tama Garden City outside Tokyo, had been listening to Bond's sales pitch on Yanchep since at least October 1972, when an initial agreement was evidently entered into. By 30 June 1973, BondCorp had paid out $410,000 to buy back a half interest in the development of a section of 1450 Yanchep lots which it had sold to WAL the year previously for $1.05 million. According to Bond this was done to tidy up the estate into one block so the Tokyu deal could go through,[120] but it does not sound like a very good deal for WAL shareholders.

Yanchep, or at least part of it, had to be off-loaded for two reasons. It was now carrying at least $10 million worth of short-term debt (roughly one third of the lots were house and land packages but only 350 people were living there in June, so the borrowing level must have been based on the future value of the land) and the John Tonkin State Labor government was planning to nationalise a five-mile-wide strip of coastal land up to the Moore River, including Yanchep.

Tonkin wanted the 80,000 acres for a new satellite city to be called Salvado. He wanted the new Federal Labor govern-ment to pay for it and he wanted to peg land prices at the levels prevailing before 1 January 1973. Naturally, Bond wanted to stop the Salvado scheme at any cost. Even if the Labor govern-ments didn't take his Yanchep land (he was threatening them with a 'colossal' compensation claim, saying that his develop-ment agreements dated back to 1960), their cheap land would destroy his market for more expensive Yanchep lots. By taking a major Japanese partner into Yanchep, he thought he could forestall their scheme by raising fears of Japanese government and corporate retribution. With the Japanese, he turned the Salvado negative into a positive. This land was so good that even the government wanted it . . .

It was essential for Bond to keep 'talking up' Yanchep. Land sales (his basic income) depended on it, the borrowings in the balance sheet depended on the highest possible valua-tion, the 'colossal' Salvado compensation depended on it and now the joint venture entry price depended on it. Hence the constant sales pitch which talked of gross profits of $400 million that would come from selling 80,000 blocks at $5000 each. 'Twice in 1973 Bond sent Mitchell back to Japan to negotiate a higher price before the letter of intent was signed.'[121]

In the Perth *Sunday Times* of 5 August 1973, Bond said from London (he was there to compete in the Admiral's Cup yacht races) that 'he might have a major statement within 14 days which would surprise a lot of people.'[122] It took a bit longer but it certainly was a surprise. In September, the Reserve Bank of Australia approved the capital transfer (its two stipulations were that the land could only be sold to Australian residents and that majority control remain in Australian hands) and in mid-October the Japanese government followed suit.

When the deal finally came to fruition on 18 October there were two versions — the one given at a Tokyo hotel press conference by Ryuhei Kojima, a vice president of the Tokyu Corporation, and the concurrent one given in Perth by Alan Bond, the chairman and (once again) managing director of BondCorp.

Bond's version was that Tokyu would outlay $26.5 million for a 49-per-cent interest in Yanchep. Kojima insisted that Tokyu's direct commitment was $4.9 million for the same 49 per cent, a discrepancy that required some explaining.

Bond had in fact said that the acquisition price (book value on directors' valuation) of the total project was to be $23,355,000 (a figure that would prove significant in later life) and that Tokyu would provide $3,145,000 to reimburse Bond-Corp for capital improvement costs (what he had spent to date) to make up the difference.

A new company called Yanchep Sun City Pty Ltd (YSC) was to be formed with a paid capital of $10 million. BondCorp would pay $5.1 million and Tokyu, $4.9 million for their equity in YSC. YSC would acquire Yanchep Estates Pty Ltd and The Wydgee Pastoral Co. Pty Ltd — the two subsidiaries owning the Yanchep land – from BondCorp for $23,355,000.

But where would YSC get the $23 million to pay Bond-Corp? It would borrow $13,355,000 with a floating-rate commercial bill, dated 3 September, secured on Yanchep and drawn on 'various Australian banks who were guaranteed by the Industrial Bank of Japan (IBJ),'[123] and it would add to that $10 million in promised subscriber capital. QED.

BondCorp would trouser a net $21.4 million in cash and the Yanchep land valuation would be set in concrete in the BondCorp balance sheet. Of course, the $23,355,000 figure for Yanchep was one the directors made up. It was not a sworn independent valuation. But it was the best figure they could extract from Tokyu at the time. It became a real book figure when the transaction took place at that price. The cash in BondCorp's trouser pocket was real enough, and just as readily anticipated, although half of it would go quickly in retiring previous short-term debt that had been called upon as the credit crisis set in. The new debt, having been arranged by Tokyu and secured separately by YSC, was effectively off-balance-sheet.

Tokyu Corp's pockets were looking decidedly emptier although it did have a piece of paper saying it owned nearly half of another piece of paper which said it was worth $23,355,000. It had paid out $8,045,000 ($4.9 million and $3.1 million) in cash and it obligated itself to arrange and service $13,355,000 in new debt. A total liability of $21.4 million. The Japanese smiled, but not as much as Bond.

According to the later Gottliebsen executive confessional, 'The Bond camp was cock-a-hoop. In 1973, Yanchep land was selling rapidly; the Bond crew had buoyant projections as they negotiated with the Japanese.' It later came to light that Tokyu Corporation might have been unwittingly led down the garden path on its way to take the plunge and dive head first into the Indian Ocean beachfront at Yanchep during that crucial negotiating time between 30 June and the announcement of the marriage on 19 October 1973.

At that time, according to a later report to the Perth Stock Exchange, Shield Enterprises Pty Ltd, one of Alan Bond's two totally controlled family companies, had entered into 'contracts for the purchase of 46 developed lots at Yanchep for a total consideration of $345,693.'[124] It probably wasn't enough blocks in terms of the total Yanchep sales contracts (about 1250) to unduly influence Tokyu's investment decision, but it wouldn't have harmed the 'buoyant projections' on which Tokyu had based its buy decision.

The Japanese did drive their bargain as hard as they could. YSC was not registered as a company until 24 January 1974. Gottliebsen explains: 'When the Japanese came out to Australia it was clear the parties had different ideas on what had been agreed on. Tony Oates, then at Parker & Parker, spent six weeks in Japan sorting it out, and the deal was not consummated until February 1974 — almost five months from the original intention.'

But if Robe was Bond's security blanket, Yanchep was still his bread and butter. The jam, selling BondCorp before the time ran out, depended on the same $23-million Yanchep value being true and fair.

The sale of BondCorp to West Australian Land Holdings Ltd (WAL) was probably inevitable but still a major turning point. It was this back-door listing that gave the Australian securities industry its first look at the accounts of the private

developer that had grown from nothing to gross assets of
$104.3 million in just twelve years. And what a strange animal it
turned out to be.

The publicly listed WAL was the vehicle chosen to be the
receptacle for his private BondCorp interests because it was a
59.6-per-cent-owned subsidiary. Once Robe had knocked it
back at $25 million, it was always going to be difficult to find an
outside buyer for the property assets. Floating off BondCorp as
a separate company was considered but abandoned because of
the prevailing economic conditions. There would be no premium in a BondCorp float and the assets would have to be
sworn to by an independent valuer. It was a big move for Bond
because he was giving up his privacy and his 100-per-cent
control of BondCorp for public scrutiny and only 59.6 per cent
of WAL. But these were desperate times and he needed access
to the financial respectability of a public company to increase
his borrowing power even further.

WAL was floated in 1969 to acquire the Santa Maria land in
Perth and had since gone on to acquire the Savoy Corporation
which owned land in Victoria and in Queensland. In the first
week of April 1973, WAL sold Santa Maria for $4.6 million to a
new company called East West Holdings Pty Ltd (EWH) which
was jointly owned by WAL and the Melbourne-based developer
Hanover Holdings Ltd. In the same week it also sold Exchange
House to the MLC Assurance Co. Ltd for $2,564,000.

WAL was now all dressed up with nowhere to go. On
27 November it told the Perth exchange it was having talks
on 'a major acquisition by the company' which could lead
to increased asset backing and diversification.[125] In a brief
announcement late on 17 December, WAL directors said they
had agreed to buy BondCorp from Bond's main family company, Dallhold Investments Pty Ltd, for $17.5 million.

The terms were $3 million cash down and the balance
over ten years of time payments. Perhaps Bond was trying to
marry his Robe repayments with his Dallhold receivables from
WAL. If so, the balance was certainly skewed in his favour. It
was now WAL's responsibility to repay both the Minsec liquidator for the Robe shares and Dallhold for the BondCorp
shares. The 'shareholders' friend' appeared to have got all of
the direct care and none of the direct responsibility.

In another statement released the same evening, an

unnamed spokesman for WAL described the agreement as 'a red letter day for the company.' Red ink might have been more appropriate. On 19 December WAL asked the exchange to suspend trading in its shares until the effects of the takeover could be made public. (It was to remain suspended for five months.)

The next day, 20 December, was the annual general meeting of WAL in Perth and the shareholders had plenty of questions to ask about the deal. In answer to one of these questions to non-BondCorp directors, WAL deputy chairman Don Clark said the board was quite sure of the investment. 'A lot of time had been taken looking at the purchase.' He said that chairman Bond and Mr Hartz, the two BondCorp members of the board, 'did not take part in the discussions leading to the acquisition of the corporation.'[126] The WAL side may well have been so, but it was unlikely for Bond not to be involved in the talks on the BondCorp side.

Chairman Bond stressed the benefits. He said the merger was designed to eliminate a conflict of interest that might exist between the two property companies. It would prevent fragmentation of management between competing interests, it would generate more profit centres, it would generate more borrowings.

How would it be paid for? 'The acquisition will be financed by loans through the group's current lenders ... I'm absolutely confident that WA Land can meet its obligations in the purchase,' he said. But in this case, Bond was his own banker and Dallhold his hire purchase financier. He had set himself terms for the $14.5 million he was still owed by WAL. 'The balance of the purchase price will be paid in one payment of 10 per cent on 2 January 1975, and 18 equal half-yearly instalments.' Dallhold would charge WAL 7 per cent on the outstanding and only gradually reducing balance. These were tough terms and included penalty rates for late payment. Applied at a flat rate it would cost WAL an extra $1 million in the first year. The terms were remarkably similar in their structure to those he had forced on Jim Jamison for Minsec's Robe shares: vendor finance with time payment. In Australia at that time it was known as hire purchase and considered a dirty word, akin to usury.

But was BondCorp worth $17.5 million? This would turn out to be the 23-million-dollar question. In September, after

Robe had knocked back his bid to sell them his company for $25 million, he said BondCorp had net assets of $25.58 million. Since then he had done the deal with Tokyu. Was not WAL getting a bargain at $17.5 million? That depended on the value of Yanchep, its major asset, and that in turn depended on the price that Tokyu was prepared to pay for it. WAL's independent directors were of the opinion that the $23-million value put on Yanchep by the Tokyu deal was a fair valuation and justification for the $17.5-million payment to Dallhold. It was a circuitous argument but who was there to argue with them?

They had overlooked another asset of BondCorp's and this was to cause Bond considerable embarrassment. At the time of its proposed takeover by WAL, BondCorp owned 59.6 per cent of WAL's issued capital, a technical breach of the Companies Act prohibition on subsidiaries owning shares in its parent which was resolved only when Dallhold bought BondCorp's 59.6 per cent of WAL before the takeover went through. This was to cost Bond/Dallhold $3 million and effectively cancel the $3-million down-payment due from WAL on settlement date, 2 January 1974. This made little difference to Bond's now 60.5-per-cent control of WAL but it marked the emergence of the private Dallhold Investments as the new ultimate holding company for Alan Bond's business interests.

The Bondification of West Australian Land Holdings Ltd's name into Bond Corporation Holdings Ltd (the new BondCorp) took six months to complete, the title changing on 12 June 1974. The Bondification of the WAL balance sheet became apparent as soon as it was put together with that of the old BondCorp.

In May, after a request from the Perth Stock Exchange, WAL produced a seventy-page 'special report' on its new financial position. It was as close as we were going to get to a prospectus for the back-door listing of BondCorp. On page sixty-two was the revelation that secured advances stood at $81.6 million at 31 December 1973 — information which hit both the money market and the stockmarket with a short, sharp shock. The *Australian Financial Review* said: 'It must be the largest amount ever borrowed by companies with such poor profit records.'

The vast majority of this extraordinary level of indebtedness ($51 million) had been generated by the old BondCorp in the six months to 31 December 1973. It included the $15.6

million he still owed on the Robe shares and the $14.5 million he still owed himself for selling BondCorp to himself. It included the two large floating-rate commercial bills, issued by Savoy ($5.7 million net at 31 December but potentially $12.6 million and secured over Taylors Lakes) and YSC ($13.35 million and secured over Yanchep). These notes were drawn mainly on Tokyu/IBJ, IAC/Citibank and CAGA.

In the pro forma consolidated accounts drawn up to represent what WAL and BondCorp would have looked like together back on 30 June 1973, it was patently obvious that the new merged company was in deep debt. Secured advances at this stage had more than doubled from $23.4 million to $58.3 million over the previous year. Total liabilities had nearly quadrupled to $94.2 million. It left net tangible assets for the combined group of only $800,000 and even this paltry figure was propped up by $95 million worth of total assets, most with dubious authenticity.

It got worse as more analysts read the fine print of the May report. Of the $81.6 million owing at 31 December, $12.6 million was due to be repaid the next month (30 June 1974), another $19.8 million by June 1975, another $7.8 million in 1976 and a whopping $17.7 million by 1977. That still left $23.7 million of longer-dated debt outstanding. These were just the amounts of principal due for repayment and took no account of the interest accruing. It was estimated that the interest payments alone would cost him about $10 million a year for the next couple of years. This was big-time gambling. He had surely gone too far this time.

Alan Bond's companies had entered 1973 in search of a $30-million kitty to help them ride a temporary correction to the property market. They exited the year nearly $100 million in the red. The fan was about to be hit by excreta and Bond was still positioned directly in front of it.

It began to happen in April 1974: 'As the June quarter started and tax payments began to flow out of the system, call rates jumped from 10 to 12 per cent. Then, in a squeeze of unprecedented severity, bank bill rates soared from 10 to 17.5 per cent in the first three weeks of April. Banks were hard pressed to maintain their LGS (liquidity and government securities) ratios and by mid-May, bank certificate of deposit (CD) rates had gone as high as 20 per cent. The squeeze on financiers was extreme. By the end of May, FNCB-Waltons was seeking private debenture money at the astounding rate of 22 per cent.'[127]

There was no mistake that Whitlam was determined to get the snail crushers who made money out of property speculation. He told the June 1974 premiers' conference: 'We must show that those who bank on double-figure inflation continuing will be proved wrong and see that they find the lesson an expensive one,' he said. 'It has for some time been easy to borrow money, invest in real assets such as property, and emerge with a handsome profit arising not from productive effort but from inflation. When, as we will, we hear of some such ventures going badly wrong in the period ahead, we will know that the risk element has been reintroduced into such forms of investment.'

That time had come for both Whitlam and Bond. In April the Melbourne-based developer Leighton Holdings Ltd was having liquidity problems. Christopher Skase, then a journalist with the *Australian Financial Review*, reported Leighton's management saying its liquidity was 'tight but not bad.'[128] Leighton survived with the help of the AMP Society. Less fortunate was Sidney King's Home Units of Australia Ltd (HUA), a man and a company with many similarities to Alan Bond and BondCorp. HUA fell over in July 1974.

King was an English migrant who had arrived in Australia penniless in the 1950s and began building and selling own-your-own flats (high-rise apartments) in Sydney's inner and western suburbs. These he called home units and sold in great numbers. In 1973 he was even planning a home-unit block above Perth's King's Park where Bond had a development. 'King had a fast and flamboyant lifestyle, flying his own plane and living lavishly. King, it has been said by people who worked for him, had all the classic traits of entrepreneurs, being ambitious, ruthless and vain. A small man physically, who had always wanted to be rich and influential, he followed a Bernie Cornfield jet-set style of life,' according to a later description in the *Australian Financial Review*.[129]

In July 1973 King sold a half interest in HUA to the large industrial concern CSR for $4 million and also borrowed $2.1 million from CSR. 'The 1973 balance sheet showed assets of $24.6 million, of which $22 million was held in trading properties. A quarter of the value of these properties was accounted for by capitalised development costs and holding charges, including interest. The assets were funded by $27 million worth of borrowings, a substantial proportion of which had been raised by revaluing properties well above their original cost.'[130]

Within a year CSR would come to regret the decision to inject equity and liquidity into HUA. When CSR got the audited accounts of the developer for the year to 30 June 1974, they showed HUA had lost $8.5 million (a trading loss of $1.9 million and $6.6 million written off the value of its trading properties). CSR decided to cut its losses before things got much worse. On 24 July HUA was 'reconstructed', King sold his interest for a nominal amount, CSR wrote off its entire $6.1-million investment and retired to the sidelines as a passive investor with 25 per cent. HUA's major creditor, IAC/Citibank, took 50 per cent and agreed to provide funds to keep it going. Another creditor, CAGA, took possession of HUA properties on which it held mortgages. Another property developer, Hooker Corporation, took 25 per cent and agreed to provide management services but it was all to no avail.

The liquidity squeeze had set in and HUA had collapsed. King went to Monaco and was never heard of again. Keith Campbell, the chief executive of Hooker, survived the crisis and five years later was asked to head a significant committee of inquiry into the Australian financial system which produced wide-ranging reforms. (Hooker itself, having survived credit squeezes in the early 1960s and the mid-1970s, finally succumbed to the one that hit in the late 1980s.)

On 19 August Mainline Corporation Ltd collapsed. It, too, was a highly geared property developer and paid the ultimate corporate penalty for its over-exposure to debt when interest rates and the market turned. 'Mainline's plight was simple. Its cash flow dried up because it could not sell projects. Simultaneously it had to meet financing commitments on projects it was still building. If times had been normal, it could have bridged the gap by borrowing. But times were not normal and Mainline had stretched its borrowing capacity past its limits already.'[131]

The word quickly got out. Mainline's shares, which had peaked at $7.26 in 1973, fell as low as 23 cents in trading on 19 August when the company asked the ANZ Bank to appoint a receiver manager. Bondy's new mate Jim Jamison, the Minsec liquidator, got the job. He found that Mainline had total debts of $57 million. The directors claimed the assets were worth nearly $100 million and secured advances against them only $48 million but Jamison did not think a surplus could be realised. This set of figures was broadly similar to those facing BondCorp at the same time, yet Mainline couldn't survive on them.

Jamison asked Whitlam for assistance for a reconstruction on the grounds that the Mainline board had done nothing illegal but had merely been victims of changed economic circumstances. Whitlam said no because it would establish a precedent. At the time of its collapse, Mainline was building the huge Collins Place project in Melbourne where an industrial relations record of thirty-nine strikes in the last three months of 1973 was set. Builders' labourers boss, Norm Gallagher, said the Mainline collapse 'couldn't have happened to a greater pack of prize bastards.'

Sykes says that August and September 1974 saw the worst financial panic Australia had experienced since the 1930s. 'Everybody feared a domino effect spreading through other property companies to topple financiers and ultimately perhaps even the banks.'[132]

On 30 September financier and property developer, Cambridge Credit Corporation Ltd, went down the gurgler. It had announced a profit of $3 million for the year to 30 June 1974 but this figure appeared to have been overstated by some $3.7 million. It went into receivership two weeks after the profit announcement. Its largest creditor was IAC/Citibank which had advanced $35 million secured on property.

'Spot the lame duck' became a national pastime, with many fingers pointing in Alan Bond's direction. On 17 October the Perth Stock Exchange queried both BondCorp and Landall Holdings (his original WAL partner) about their financial situation in these times of stress. Landall responded next day by appointing a receiver and manager. Bond replied with a broadside: 'The sensational reportage accorded in recent months to our company and generally to the Australian business community has created a lack of confidence. We believe that if continued this will undermine the very basis of private enterprise in the Australian economy.' His answer to the question was 'naturally we have experienced the effects of the credit squeeze and the downturn of the property market. We have the confidence and support of our financiers and once through this difficult period we see a sound long-term future.'[133]

In a 1974 promotional brochure, Bond explained to the rest of the world just how he gets that 'confidence and support', given that the High Street bankers wouldn't touch him: 'The group has obtained finance from many sources within Australia, both private and institutional. It maintains a close association with lending institutions and government bodies. It is experienced in floating public companies in the industrial and mining fields and has successfully raised finance by way of share issues to the public. Equity in loan capital for property development can be arranged and the group is experienced in the planning and financing of takeovers and acquisitions. It organises and executes all aspects of financial planning, including the reorganisation of capital structure and existing borrowing arrangements either to raise additional funds or to reduce interest costs.'[134]

These were all skills that BondCorp had rehearsed on itself, but being self-financing was only a temporary buffer to rising costs and falling income. He raised some equity and debt from sources in the Middle East and the Far East and had re-negotiated the Tokyu agreement to cut $5.8 million off the $12.6 million he had to' repay by 30 June. Bond also gave personal guarantees to his many lenders.

BondCorp belatedly declared a consolidated net profit of $1.37 million for 1973–74, its first year as a public company. Total liabilities had increased slightly from the shock $81.6-million figure at 31 December to $82.9 million at 30 June. Total assets were listed at $92.9 million.[135]

The profit, no matter how constructed, would mean he would see out Christmas. On paper he had net tangible assets of $10 million, which was a vast improvement on the 1973 pro forma figure of $800,000, and his borrowing binge appeared to have been brought under control by the liquidity squeeze. The rubbery figure was of course the total assets. If push came to shove during a property crash they were not worth a fraction of that amount, assuming you could find a buyer in the first place.

On this asset figure rested the security of his creditors and on the security of his creditors rested his survival. What was more than interesting here was the number of American banks holding Bond paper. According to Gottliebsen, BondCorp's largest creditor in 1974 was IAC/Citibank which was in for about $35 million. Next in line was CAGA (20 per cent owned by the Bank of America) which was owed $10 million. Intermarine (a consortium of the Marine Midland Bank of the US and the Tokai Bank of Japan) was down for $5 million. The Australian money came from the Commonwealth Superannuation Fund Investment Trust (SFIT) and the Wales (Westpac). They had $5 million and $3 million respectively.[136]

So of the $58 million secured but outstanding, $50 million could be sourced indirectly to American connections. There were more. Bankers Trust of NY, through Ord BT, was owed $1.7 million as an unsecured creditor of Minsec and the US Export-Import Bank had $7.2 million worth of Minsec debentures. The point was not lost on Bond and it gave added poignancy to his America's Cup bid.

In late August his major creditors held a secret meeting at the IAC offices in Sydney.[137] IAC/Citibank had been heavily exposed to the HUA, Mainline and Cambridge Credit collapses and needed another one like a hole in the head. Two schools of thought contended. The first, motivated by self-interest, argued that BondCorp's going to the wall would flood the market with worthless property and mean mutually assured destruction for the property industry. The second argued the cleansing effect of a BondCorp failure. Sweeps were being run in Melbourne, Perth and Sydney on the date of BondCorp's demise. Its certain death would clean up the uncertainty and let things get back to normal.

Bond didn't know about the meeting. He was at sea two oceans away trying to win the America's Cup in a twelve-metre yacht called *Southern Cross*. By September Yanchep had almost ceased selling and interest payments for his financially strapped corporation were running out at about $100,000 a week, but the executive chairman was away playing boats. 'If you are the sort of person that unduly worries about things like that you don't progress,' he said of his predicament.

Bond had to progress because if he stood still he would be wiped out. The future of BondCorp may have been in the hands of his creditors back home but the future of Yanchep and his own credibility was wedded to this challenge for the America's Cup. This was something only he could do. It was his idea, it was four years and several millions of dollars in the planning and it was, in his parlance, a 'magnificent opportunity' to display his wares to the world. This was a job for the salesman.

For Yanchep to be a success he didn't need to actually win the Cup, although that would have been nice. He just needed a forum to promote the property and himself. The 1974 annual report would point out that the chairman's Cup campaign was accorded 'world-wide coverage in the Press, on television and [on] radio', and this had resulted in 'Yanchep and the name Bond Corporation being known throughout the world ... benefits will flow from this effort to our group in the coming years.'

No expense was spared in getting the message across. A book was commissioned about the 1974 campaign and $150,000 budgeted for a documentary. It was reported that Bond wired Noboru Gotoh, president of the Tokyu Corporation, an invitation to the event: 'An airline seat, he said, had been reserved for Mr Gotoh; and quarters made ready at Newport; and would Mr Gotoh do Mr Bond the pleasure of watching the America's Cup challenge with him? He would and did.'[138]

It was all to do with perceptions. If he was seen to be rich and successful and mixing with those who were rich and successful then his personal guarantees would carry some weight. How would it look if his creditors (foreigners at that) pulled the pin on him while he was over there competing in an international sporting event for his country (it is believed that he became an Australian citizen in 1974)? The argument now went: What was bad for Alan Bond and BondCorp would be bad for Australia in the world's eyes.

Bond left for Newport, Rhode Island, in June but three times he was called back for urgent business discussions. He told a press conference at Sydney Airport on 3 September that he had the same confidence in the future of BondCorp as he had in *Southern Cross*'s chances in the Cup. He said of his company: 'Its future is as golden as that of Australia.' Suggestions that there was 'trouble at the mill' were rumours put about by people who wanted to see his corporation go to the wall. And there were such people, he said: 'The "have-nots" always like to see the "haves" go broke. But we won't founder, I can assure you.'[139]

In the four years since he had announced the Cup bid, Bond had had himself elected to the Perth City Council, moved into an office at the top of Perth's most modern skyscraper, bought the most expensive home building block on the Swan and placed an order for a personal jet aircraft from the US. 'He has to keep running — to put on a bold front — just to stay alive,' said a Perth businessman. 'If the order for the jet was cancelled, the Bond bubble would collapse overnight.'[140]

But the America's Cup was no flight to fancy and fantasy. This was serious business for Yanchep. His big Ben Lexcen-designed aluminium twelve-metre, *Southern Cross*, was painted banana yellow and carried the name Yanchep Sun City on its transom like a real estate advertising hoarding. Bond shocked the genteel and mock-Corinthian America's Cup community with this bold statement of his intentions: 'Anyone who pretends that racing for the Cup isn't a business proposition is just a bloody fool. There's no justification for spending six million unless you're going to get more out of it than a silver cup. Let's see what they say about commercialism and sports-manship after we win.' The statement was designed to win headlines, not friends. It did, but the transom still had to be changed to read Royal Perth Yacht Club, Fremantle. He knew he couldn't get away with it, but by forcing the New York Yacht Club to order the change, he drew the world's attention to it. The desired effect was achieved.

At thirty-six Alan Bond was the youngest and the feistiest contender the America's Cup had seen. He was a huge and exotic media talent because he just kept the bellicose quotes coming and all his press releases mentioned Yanchep Sun City. (The nautical scribes referred to it disparagingly as Ratshit Fly City.) 'It's all very well for the "old money" people in London and New York to look down their noses at my challenge,' he said. 'They're the very people who wouldn't hesitate to change the rules if they thought it might help them. The good old days when gentlemen could say, "Jolly good show, sir, well done" are gone forever. America's Cup racing is far too competitive for that sort of sentimental nonsense today.'[141]

What the world didn't know, but suspected, was that Bond was fighting for corporate survival as well as the America's Cup. In that light, his words as he went into battle are particu-larly poignant: 'I'm going to keep belting away at whoever and whatever stands between us and the Cup. The Yanks are whingeing because, for the first time, they've got to face a bloke prepared to fight the way they do.'

The contest itself had to be an anticlimax. There had been only one real chance to win the Cup, and that had been 123 years ago in 1851 when New York won it. Bondy was also up against a thoroughbred aluminium defender called *Courageous*, designed by the legendary Olin Stephens, and regarded by the doyen as the ultimate twelve-metre boat. New York had recruited Ted Hood as skipper. An aggressive 31-year-old Californian was to be starting helmsman. His name was Dennis Conner.

Bondy's designer, Ben Lexcen (he was called Bob Miller then), had never done this sort of thing before. His twelve was too long and his sail plan too small to compete with the power of *Courageous*. His tank tests had shown the *Cross* to be faster than boat X, but *Courageous* did not turn out to be boat X. Then Bond sacked John Cuneo, his original choice as skipper, and replaced him with Jim Hardy.

In the first race of the best-of-seven series, the *Cross* went down by 4 minutes and 54 seconds and tactical errors were blamed. Syndicate boss Bond put himself aboard as winch-grinder for the second race (not a common thing for owners to do) and they lost by only 1 minute 11 seconds, her best effort. Then panic seems to have set in. Bond was to make several abrupt switches in crew, sails and gear and these only added to her problems in the third and fourth races, which were lost by 5:27 and 7:19.[142]

It was Australia's worst ever defeat in four attempts to win the Cup. 'In those four races she lost to America's *Courageous* by a total of 18 minutes 51 seconds. She was spared the humiliation of a thrashing worse than the 15-minute beating *Constellation* gave the British entry, *Sovereign*, a decade earlier, only because time ran out in the one abandoned race.'[143]

But Bond entered the post-match press conference at the National Guard Armory in Thames Street with his fists in the air 'like a prize fighter accepting applause'. He told the world it was not necessary to have won but it was necessary to have competed. He said that if anyone watching his challenge had learned a little bit more about Western Australia, 'and a little bit more about Yanchep Sun City', then he felt *Southern Cross* had won anyway. 'It's very hard to come to a foreign country and take away something that has been here for 123 years. We were outsailed. We'll learn by our mistakes. We'll be back.'

He announced a $25,000 world cup for twelve-metre yachts off his Yanchep Sun City development for 1976. YSC had paid for *Southern Cross* and now *Southern Cross* was paying YSC back.

CHAPTER NINE

1977: Courageous vs. Australia, Courageous, *4–0*

From where Alan Bond was standing in September 1974, after he had lost the America's Cup for the first time, the world had a slightly jaundiced look about it. He kept up a brave face, because it was his job and because he saw as temporary the severity of the liquidity squeeze that was gripping the economy back home and the property crash that was devastating his industry. But he would not even be standing where he was had he not taken precautions to save his empire in the knick of time in 1973 with the Robe, Tokyu and BondCorp/WAL deals.

But all around him were doom, gloom and corporate financial destruction of a like that had not been seen since the Great Depression of the 1930s. He faced a concurrence of misfortune that would have dimmed the ardour and increased the angst of lesser visionary entrepreneurs. This was no temporary aberration but a full-on recession that was to last four years in the glutted and overvalued property market from which he gained his bread and butter. We are entering the BondCorp Dark Age where there would be no growth through acquisition but only survival through disposal. Stout hearts, silver tongues and deep pockets would be needed to avoid the same fate as Home Units of Australia, Mainline and Cambridge Credit.

In the next six months Alan Bond would go through excruciating private negotiations with his anxious creditors under the full glare of public scrutiny. He would be put through hoops, frowned upon from on high and forced to grovel for a quid.

> At least three times he had no money to pay senior staff wages and he had to go to one of the major creditors (who never seemed to be in the best mood) for a loan. Each creditor required personal guarantees from Bond and when all these were added they came to $50 million. Most of the creditors were unsure how much a Bond guarantee was worth; not all may have realised that a majority had such guarantees and that their monetary backing was therefore very thin. The guarantees were only to be effective after the lender had called in and sold the security — and this in itself would be no easy task. Bond's guarantees reflected his strong personal faith in his property and were a very important factor in seeing him through.[144]

This was the lowest point reached, so far, in the BondCorp chronology and it took its toll. Bondy looked a mess in the newspaper photographs of the day. The sidelevers extended in a dishevelled manner below his ears and the kiss curl tucked around to overscore his left eyebrow after the fashion of the day, but his lifeless face was a dead giveaway. Bondy looked exhausted — his jowls flaccid, his eyes red and his voice harsh.

Fifteen years later, in 1989, when BondCorp would go through a crisis of similar proportion but greater dimension, he would not look as bad as this. On Friday 11 January 1975, Alan Bond was admitted to St John of God Hospital, in the Perth suburb of Subiaco, for a rest. On Saturday the hospital said he was 'fairly well' and on Sunday the Perth *Sunday Times* reported a member of his family saying he was not seriously ill and that his condition was not the cause of any great anxiety. He was back on his feet and fighting fit within a week.[145]

'The Cup losses and the appalling publicity were devastating to even such a sturdy ego as Alan Bond's, for the whole operation was carried on his bluster,' said Perth journalist Don Lipscombe in a *Bulletin* article that Bond took great exception to.[146] But Peter Beckwith, whose own health was to suffer in the 1989 crisis while he was managing director of BondCorp, tends to look back on those days with slight nostalgia: 'Even in the 1970s we never doubted our future, so we continued to do things like the Cup campaign that would benefit our future. The bad times are the right time to get ready for the good times and Alan Bond is wonderful at stiffening the back of anyone in doubt.'[147]

When the penny dropped after he failed to take the America's Cup in September 1974, there were many in the West who couldn't or wouldn't believe it. A slightly dazed Perth businessman told Sydney journalist Ron Saw: 'I simply cannot conceive how Bondy failed to win the America's Cup. Bondy said, quite unequivocally, that he was going to win the America's Cup. What Bondy says he'll do he does. That's all there is to it.'[148]

But BondCorp shares, which had peaked at 56 cents earlier in 1974, sold at 27 cents before the yacht races then dropped with each loss to reach a low of 9 cents in an isolated sale after the mismatch in September. Bond even had trouble scraping the money together to keep the challenge going at the end of August. For the sake of image, he spoke often about it being a $6-million campaign, but that figure included all the money he had spent on developing the boat harbour and marina at Yanchep Sun City, for which BondCorp had been compensated by the Tokyu Corporation. Some Newporters actually thought he had spent $9 million, which was what he wanted them to think.

The actual cost of the 1974 challenge was around $1.75 million to $2 million. About $1 million of this was spent before 30 June 1973, on buying *Gretel* and *Gretel II* as trial horses and on the design and construction of *Southern Cross*. Another $270,000 went on miscellaneous expenses up to the end of 1973 and they budgeted $500,000 for the campaign in 1974. YSC seems to have picked up about $1.25 million of this and sponsors had kicked in about $300,000, leaving BondCorp about $200,000 short at a time when BondCorp was lucky if it had two $1 notes to rub together.

Help came in the form of his friend and neighbour, Sir Charles Court, whose Liberal Party was returned to power in the March State election with the active assistance of Bond-Corp and a $20,000 donation.[149] Sir Charles put together a syndicate to raise $250,000 to save the challenge. According to Gottliebsen, the syndicate was to include Rod Carnegie, the chairman and managing director of mining giant, CRA Ltd.

In September, when the heat was really on BondCorp in Perth, and on Bond in Newport, 'Court phoned the managing directors of major creditors and pointed out that it would be a very serious blow to Western Australia if Bond went under because it would affect confidence in the State. Bond, through one of his subsidiaries, was a brick producer in Perth and his collapse would affect employment. Court's action would have had a major effect at a crucial time. If any financial institution wanted to do business with the WA government in the future, it did not really want to be known as the institution that pulled the plug on Bond in September 1974.'[150]

Court admits he 'put in a few good words' for Alan with the big international banks but gave them no government guarantees: 'We talked to them about Alan Bond, we told them we'd like to see this fellow succeed and survive.'[151]

Bond was not idle in Newport either. His three major creditors all had American parents. 'Bond took time off from the Cup to visit the top people at Citibank and the Bank of America, as well as the Marine Midland Bank, which had an interest in Intermarine. The US banks had a bizarre decision to make — should they send Australia's challenger for the America's Cup to the wall? America is known for playing a tough game in America's Cup races but surely this would be hailed as the worst dirty trick of them all — even if it were done after the Cup,' says Gottliebsen.

It was always helpful to be rich and famous in Newport, Rhode Island, but it was essential to be influential. In its mansions and at the Ida Lewis Yacht Club, a sub-station of the New York Yacht Club from Manhattan on Narragansett Bay, would gather the Western world's money magnates for the Summer season. Far from being away from the action, Bond was at the centre of it and pumping it for all it was worth. Once the races were over, he jet-frogged from New York, London, Tokyo and back to London again, looking for plums to pick.

'He first met Texas oilman, Perry Bass, one of the supporters of US helmsman Ted Turner, in Newport that summer and after the Cup races were over, Bond visited Bass, the head of the Bass Oil Company, at his home on a private island off Corpus Christi, in the Gulf of Mexico. "We became very good friends and he started my education in the energy field," said Bond. "He advised me to get some proven reserves somewhere because he said there would be a major upsurge in oil and gas and a huge demand for energy. It took me a little while to learn about the business, but I did." Bond also visited Baron Marcel Bich, the French plastics tycoon, at his home before returning to Australia. "The flow of information among people who are doing things, world leaders is fantastic. You learn to see the patterns. These people were not just business contacts, they became good friends."'[152]

But in Newport, behind his back, he was ridiculed for his lack of substance and nous: 'All sorts of people were chortling over the fact that stock in Bond's development company had plummeted,' said a local.[153] Bondy would have hated it. He hated to lose but what he hated more was being seen to loose, be it on the land or on the water. Sir James (Jim) Hardy, then his skipper, remembers being summoned by Bond, in front of the crew, after losing one of the races: 'Bond told the story of Napoleon calling in front of his troops a popular general who had lost a few battles — and having him shot. This action did not please the troops, but they started to win battles. "Are you trying to tell me something?" asked Hardy. "No," said Bond, "but you had better get back there and win something."'[154]

Bond did not return to Perth empty-handed. He had won millions of dollars worth of free publicity for Yanchep Sun City. He had established a valuable contact with Citibank (then the First National City Bank of New York) and Perry Bass had given him the drum on energy reserves. These intangibles were not physical proof of success but all would be valuable in his survival and give him the enthusiasm to fight for it.

His nervous and impatient creditors were waiting for him. 'He wrote personally to every director of the Bank of NSW and CBC Bank (parent to CAGA) to plead his case for more time to ride through the slump. He had long talks with the senior executives of each of the major creditors,' says Gottliebsen.

While he was away, Mitchell, new boy Oates, Lucas and Beckwith drew up detailed plans for a gradual reduction of assets to satisfy the creditors but they required the continuing support of his financiers and the confidence of the markets. Neither was forthcoming.

Bondy's hand wasn't just empty, it was outstretched. In one of his meetings with creditors in Sydney (he flew back from Newport for it) he asked for between $5 million and $10 million to tide him over. Gottliebsen comments of that meeting: 'Many of the creditors thought Bond was just too highly geared and had little chance of survival. They were not about to put good money after bad. Those who saw some hope would not give ground in front of the others. Bond learned a lesson most other corporate entrepreneurs in trouble have discovered — Australian institutions very rarely put rescue money in when a ship flounders.'[155]

While none of his major creditors (IAC, CAGA, Intermarine, Westpac, SFIT) wanted to lend BondCorp fresh money, they also seemed reluctant to pull the pin for fear of losing the lot. By asking for more, Bond had bought time and exposed the serious weakness in the position of his lenders. He now had two sets of creditors over a barrel, the Minsec creditors and the BondCorp creditors. Both depended on his survival rather than downfall.

A typical, and pressing, example was CAGA. It had lent BondCorp/YSC $13.35 million in September 1973 as part of the Tokyu deal. Like the IAC deal with Savoy, this money was raised by way of commercial bill finance on the short-term money market. CAGA would endorse the bill (with the backing of the Commercial Banking Company of Sydney, the Bank of America and, in this case, the Industrial Bank of Japan), then either hold the paper or trade it on the rediscount market.

The coupon, or interest rate, that BondCorp was to pay for the facility, was set for a year. When this fell due on 3 September 1974 — a week before the Cup races — it was rolled over (period extended and coupon increased) for two months. The bill, somewhat reluctantly, was rolled over again on 3 November, this time for three months. Each time the bill rolled, it added to its cost as the coupon rate was re-struck.

Lindsay Fox, head of the Linfox transport group, recalls

seeing Bond at breakfast in Sydney's then Wentworth Hotel in 1974: 'He had a meeting at 10 a.m. with the CAGA finance people. He told me he would be in all sorts of trouble if they didn't support him. But he expected their support. He said, "If they don't back me, they will lose money and so will I." He came out of the meeting with CAGA's support. The key to his success is that he does not accept defeat. There is probably no one in Australia who has lost so much money and is still ahead. He's just so tenacious.'[156] Another story about the same incident has Bond's first words on entering the CAGA boardroom as: 'Right, now what's this I hear about YOU having a problem with a bill?'

In early October, when Sir Charles let slip in State parliament that Bondy had liquidity problems, the heavens broke open. The eastern media rediscovered the May special report, the flies, the white elephants and the empty blocks at Yanchep. Then the Wilbinga Pastoral Co., which was next-door to Yanchep, began offering acre lots at $500 on terms — four times as much sand for less than a twentieth of Yanchep's asking price. Then Landalls collapsed and the stock exchange queried his position and Bondy lashed out.

He said at the end of his reply to the stock exchange on 18 October that no more statements or comments would be issued. The press, it seemed, were responsible for creating the 'lack of confidence' in BondCorp. Gottliebsen says his creditors were amused by this as they thought the press had 'grossly understated his real problems.' Although a useful whipping boy for those refusing to face economic reality, Bondy's Bad Press jibe reflected more his current image problem generally. Losers lacked credibility.

To his many admirers in the West he could now add a whole host of national and international enemies. These malefactors seemed to take inordinate delight in the prospect of Bond falling flat on his face. And, to a certain extent, Bondy, 'the well-known yachting and property identity and clever millionaire', had become a victim of his own social positioning, a 'tall irises' syndrome, if you will. He didn't complain when the national print media dubbed him the 'King of the West'. He could have turned his back on the door to the hot kitchen, but he didn't. It was his decision to adopt a high profile in international yachting, to turn his private company into a public company, to seek election to the Perth City Council and to live in ostentatious wealth way beyond his then-known means. The 'envy of the have-nots' and the 'sensational reportage' as he called it, enraged him until he finally won that Cup.

'Media criticism,' says his journalist friend Bruce Stannard, 'particularly of his financial activities, invariably hurts a great deal. When that happens, the old Bondy is likely to lash out. According to Warren Jones (his minder) "he can be very, very tough. I've seen him come down hard on people who have abused his trust," says Jones. "But he's got to be like that. People can't use him up or lean on him otherwise he bites back."'157

But in Newport it was Bondy's public relations machine that was doing the using, churning out dozens of press releases that pushed the product on the back of the Bond bombast. It was run by Brian Leary and Robert Hemery and its relations with journalists were so abysmal that they were referred to as Haldeman and Ehrlichman: 'Leary and Hemery were in constant communication with Australia so they could be briefed about what journalists were writing about Bond, and they often knew before the reporters themselves what had been printed. After an Australian Associated Press reporter, Richard Sleeman, had written a critical piece about the Bond effort, Hemery telephoned the editor of the [Sydney] Sun, where it appeared, to complain. And when Robert Pullen of the [Melbourne] Herald wrote an unfavourable review of the book "Southern Cross", Hemery told him by phone it would be pointless his travelling from New York to Newport to cover the races because he was on the black list.'158

It was dollars, not spleen, that were needed at this time. He began various manoeuvres to get cash into his companies, including 'putting in $4 million of his own money,' according to Lipscombe. In November, he announced a $4.7-million preference share issue. 'All that was needed was an underwriter to underwrite Bond shares. Not surprisingly, none could be found. But the creditors at least looked at the proposal, and all the considerations took a long time,' says Gottliebsen.

Bond was eventually forced into the arms of Mother Government in October, the same month he denounced the press attacks for undermining 'the very basis of private enterprise in Australia.' He was interested in 'what the Government

can do for me, he who has done so much for the Government.'
BondCorp's 1974 promotional brochure boasts that the group
'has had considerable experience in negotiations with government and semi-government authorities.' It also claimed a close
association with government bodies. BondCorp's 'close association' with Court's Liberal State government was to be the
embryo of what later became known as WA Inc.

The first to attack the closeness of the relationship was
the opposition Labor Party which would benefit so much by it
in the next decade. On 22 November 1974 Colin Jamieson, the
Deputy Leader of the Opposition, who had recently returned
from a trip to the US himself, started a vigorous debate on the
benefits of Bond's links with the Court government, during a
Legislative Assembly Budget debate at 4.15 a.m. He was pro-
voked by an interjection from Premier Court.

Jamieson had previously asked Court a simple question
about government assistance to Bond's challenge syndicate.
He was seeking details of concessions granted to the syndicate
by the Fremantle Port Authority, Harbour and Light Department and the Harbour and Rivers Department. Perhaps sensing
Jamieson's intent, Court reacted sharply. He accused Jamieson
of adopting a mean attitude over a Cabinet lunch held for
members of the *Southern Cross* syndicate on their return. Sir
Charles said he had personally paid for the lunch. He said
limited assistance was given to the syndicate by way of the use
of some government facilities but no direct expenditure was
involved.

In that early morning Budget debate, Jamieson had been
complaining about the way in which Sir Charles had replied to
the question about government expenditure involved in the
challenge when Sir Charles interjected that Jamieson only
wanted to criticise Mr Bond. Jamieson took his cue: 'He didn't
do us any good at all. These people who have big mouths have
to be able to produce the goods. Cassius Clay and the people
who can fight back and produce the goods can get away with it.
But some people who get downed in their efforts are not
thought much of, particularly by the Americans. Alan Bond is
regarded in the same way as Frank Sinatra — rude and rich.
Bond had his chance; he took it and entered a bigger league
than he could possibly handle. That is his business — I don't
object to it.'[159]

Court replied that he was entitled to react sharply to
Jamieson's barbs as the challengers had returned to WA without a civic reception or public recognition and that he had paid
for the lunch. 'I felt the least we owed them was to say thank
you for some mighty dedicated work.' As for the government
assistance, he said he had been advised that the amount
involved was so small that it was not worth costing.

Bond denied the allegation, claiming Jamieson must have
heard an isolated comment. He demanded an apology and
challenged Jamieson to repeat the statement outside parliament. He also produced a scroll signed by the mayor of the City
of Newport saying the City Council had passed a resolution
commending Bond and his syndicate for the 'sportsmanship,
enthusiasm and good fellowship' that prevailed during the
contest and praising them for their goodwill and friendship.
'One of our aims was to get people to know about Western
Australia,' said Bond. 'At least they have now heard of us.'

Although the incident appears trifling, it exposed sen-
sitivities about State government assistance to BondCorp, and
BondCorp assistance to the State government, that were close
to the mark. Since the Court Liberal government had come to
power, in March of that year with the active assistance of
BondCorp, it had been constantly lobbied by BondCorp to help
it resolve the zoning problem it had with the Santa Maria land
near the suburb of Hamersley on the northern outskirts of
town. West Australian Land Holdings Ltd (now BondCorp) had
sought funds from the public in 1969 on the strength of the
Santa Maria estate being eventually re-zoned from rural to
urban land. It had been a constant source of friction with the
previous Tonkin Labor government which backed the Metropolitan Regional Planning Authority's decision that the land
would remain open space under its corridor growth plan.

At one stage in this conflict, Bond, no doubt experiencing
déjà vu from the humble origins of his business empire,
erected a large, bogus land-for-sale sign on the cattle property
estate extolling BondCorp's belief that urban blocks could be
developed there for less than $4000 a block. It advised those
interested in living in that desirable location at that price to
contact Premier Tonkin. Ron Davies, Labor's Town Planning
Minister, suggested in parliament that people sue Bond for false
pretences as the land would never be subdivided or built on.

Santa Maria's re-zoning also cut across the Tonkin government's own joint venture with the Whitlam government to build Salvado City, a $10-billion satellite city in the northern growth corridor. Funds for this were to be provided by the Federal Department of Urban and Regional Development through new State-run Urban Land Councils. This attempt by Canberra socialists to seize West Australian land and put it on leasehold was equally detested by both Bond and Court as an affront to free enterprise and private ownership.

As premier, Court wanted to help Bond, but he wasn't about to change the planning code to underwrite his business risk. Court's particular brand of State capitalism involved getting money from entrepreneurs, not giving it to them. His public view, like Whitlam's at the time, was that not a cent of (WA) taxpayers' money would be used to bail out troubled property developers. The practical consideration in this stance was that if he helped one, he would have to help the lot. The huge Hooker Corporation, as well as Landalls parent, Hanover Holdings, were under just as much pressure as BondCorp at that time.

(Sir Charles Court may have had private reasons for not wishing to act unilaterally on the Santa Maria zoning. A Curtin University BA (Hons) thesis by Michael Rafferty of October 1989 claims that Court's family company, Cheratah Holdings Pty Ltd, had a large shareholding in Landalls. Rafferty says this association was revealed when Landalls went into receivership in October 1974. Landalls, with BondCorp Pty Ltd, were the sponsors of the WAL Santa Maria float and its largest shareholders when it was admitted to the official lists of the Perth Stock Exchange on 19 February 1970. Landalls' chairman, Don Clark, became deputy chairman of BondCorp when it merged with WAL. The suggestion is that Sir Charles may have had a conflict of interest if he had acted unilaterally to change the Santa Maria zoning.)[160]

To recapitulate: Alan Bond had bought the 5080-acre Santa Maria estate in 1969 off three old ladies for $700 an acre, or $3.55 million. He had put down $615,000, had the property valued at $4.6 million, then borrowed $750,000 from CAGA on the strength of his equity in the new valuation to cover the deposit. That same year he sold the estate to WAL for $4.1 million (roughly $800 an acre). In April 1973, WAL sold it to

East West Holdings Pty Ltd, a joint venture with Hanover Holdings Ltd, for $4.6 million, or just over $900 an acre.

Under Bond's deal with Hanover, he (WAL) would retain a half interest in any future development without incurring further holding charges. The advantages of these syndications, or joint ventures, to BondCorp were twofold. The property's borrowings were kept off-balance-sheet and could be geared separately (Yanchep wasn't because it was 51 per cent owned), and it was a way of unlocking pre-crash land values and retiring expensive debt.

However, the Melbourne-based Hanover's interest in the Santa Maria development is slightly more difficult to fathom. Hanover had strong links with the Landall Construction and Development Co., which initially picked up 20 per cent of WAL when the Santa Maria property was floated, so it would have been aware of the blanket ban on re-zoning the land. Hanover also had land near Taylors Lakes in Victoria. East West Holdings then, seems to have been a marriage of convenience, a financing technique for both companies, much like the relationship with Landalls had been in the 1969 WAL float.

Landalls' going into receivership on 18 October 1974 would have galvanised the squeeze on both BondCorp and Hanover. IAC/Citibank was a major lender to the East West joint venture, according to Gottliebsen, so it probably had some exposure to Landalls as well. The ANZ Bank was a major lender to Hanover but had sold its 21-per-cent interest in IAC to Citibank in May 1971 following its merger with the ES&A Bank in 1969. In his book *Two Centuries of Panic* Sykes says IAC at this stage had about $25.8 million tied up in Home Units, $7.6 million in Mainline and $32.6 million in Cambridge Credit. All of it, plus the $35 million it had riding on BondCorp, was at serious risk.

IAC then, was apprehensive about all its outstanding risks. It would have been particularly anxious for a resolution of the five-year-old Santa Maria zoning stalemate. At $4.6 million, Santa Maria was a very expensive, near-city cattle farm that could not pay its way. The Hanover people also made representations to Court but the State government said its hands were tied by the planning code. It appears strange that Bond does not seem to have attacked the Court government publicly on the issue. Perhaps the two friends knew something the market didn't.

But the Santa Maria deal had to be picked over just one more time, as BondCorp's need was great. This was potentially his second biggest subdivision after Yanchep as it was twice as big as Taylors Lakes in size. Bondy's patois of potentiality was brought into play to sooth the creditors: 5000 acres = 20,000 quarter-acre blocks @ say $4000 a block = $16,000 an acre = $80 million gross. Half share = $40 million. QED. The equation could just as easily been read as half of nothing = nothing.

Finally, an indication of the source of some real money which might save his bacon was delivered at the 1974 annual general meeting in December. Here chairman Bond forecast the sale of $16 million worth of land in the current year to retire debt. Only a government body with bulging pockets would be silly enough to be the buyer at BondCorp's top prices. The question was, which one? 'Bond evidently had wind that large government sums might be available in June 1975,' says Gottliebsen.

In BondCorp, it was the job of Peter Beckwith to make sure the company received its share of government land purchases. In Canberra, it was the job of Tom Uren's Department of Urban and Regional Development (DURD) to allocate interest-free urban development funds to the States under the Urban Land Councils scheme. Fast-growing Western Australia had been allocated $13 million. The money had to be spent before the end of the financial year so large chunks of land were purchased usually on or just before 30 June.

Court took the Federal money and purchased Santa Maria from East West for about $4.6 million ($900 an acre) on 18 June. BondCorp got $2.3 million and Hanover $2.3 million and the valuation that Bond had put on the property back in 1969 became self-fulfilling. IAC was well pleased because it could now call in at least some of its credit. Tom Uren and the Whitlam government were furious because they had been dudded. Court said his Urban Land Council planned to use the land as a green area to preserve underground water supplies. This fitted in with the State's planning code but was a long way off the Federal government's intention when it extended its easy money for State-run housing developments. Court later admitted that he gambled on the Whitlam government not being there twelve months later. He gambled correctly.

Court also denied any collusion with Bond: 'Bond wanted it at residential values [$16,000 an acre at $4000 a block]. Alan was never happy about it. He held it against me for a long time.'[161] Uren said he wrote to the West Australian government questioning the propriety of the deal: 'The conservative government there used our money to buy out their friend Bond.'[162] Ron Davies, the former Labor Minister for Town Planning, described it as a scandal involving the old pea-and-thimble trick: 'It is unthinkable that a Federally funded, State-run land council should buy, for open space, land that was already open space. Bond must believe he has found a fairy godmother at last and Sir Charles Court must think Gough Whitlam is a fairy godmother.'[163]

Court said it wasn't taxpayers' money because the WA Urban Land Council wasn't a statutory authority. But he also granted East West continued development rights over the Santa Maria land in the event of a future government agreeing to release the land for urban development. The West-Australian-government-controlled ULC also bought 1500 acres of slow-moving Yanchep land from BondCorp for $1.95 million ($1300 an acre). In Victoria, BondCorp sold the local ULC land held by the Savoy subsidiary, Gisborne Views Pty Ltd, at Ballarat. It was claimed at the time that the sale price was above the Valuer-General's valuation.[164] Hanover's land near Bond's Taylors Lakes project also went to the Victorian Liberal government's ULC.

Taking government money didn't seem to bother Alan Bond's capitalist conscience in the slightest. He was selling land and they were buying it. Most things were as simple as that with Bondy. He had told the Federal government's Land Tenure Inquiry in July 1973 that the government should provide subsidies, or tax incentives, to developers to provide essential services to prevent an imbalance of supply and demand. 'Insurance companies could provide the essential services if the government hasn't the money now to do so,' he said.[165]

On 15 October 1974, soon after his return from Newport and just before the BondCorp bubble burst, he made a 'secret' visit to Canberra to enlist government aid to save his empire. The irony was that it was this Labor government that had deliberately brought on the recession (an act of 'economic sabotage', according to Sykes), to cripple the boom and destroy speculators of Bond's ilk. It had also turned its back as the Home Units, Mainline, Cambridge Credit and Landalls dominoes collapsed, so was deemed unlikely to fall for his gift of the gab.

Bond, game as Ned Kelly and as desperate as Buckley, approached Whitlam, the developer's Antichrist, and got a polite referral to Treasurer Frank Crean and DURD Minister Uren. Bond had come well prepared with a two-level line of attack in his submission.

The first of these, which could be termed the 'hand-out' approach, sought direct government investment, in the form of grants and long-term loans, in his resources and property portfolio. Bond played the patriot game to perfection, offering his stake in Robe to the government's investment bank, the Australian Industry Development Corporation (AIDC), so as to keep up the Australian equity in the foreign-dominated resources boom. He 'discussed the operations of a possible lands commission in WA' with DURD officials, poignantly pointing out 'that the operations of land commissions were a State matter' and making 'several suggestions'.[166] He also proposed the establishment of a new joint venture organisation with the Federal government, to be called the Bond Foundation, and to which he would personally contribute $500,000. This body would jointly develop land held by him in Melbourne (Taylors Lakes) and Perth (Santa Maria) but not Sun City. The Bond Foundation would of course be a charity, and charities could import overseas funds.

Bond's second line of attack, which could be termed the 'hands-off' approach, involved his gaining Foreign Investment Review Board (FIRB) blind-eye approval to import a large swag of short-term funds from his Newport friends, the First National City Bank of New York (Citibank), comptrollers of his major creditor, IAC Holdings Ltd, itself a basket case. Foreign investment was anathema to the Whitlam Labor government, and short-term foreign investment was akin to treason. To discourage its spread, the Reserve Bank of Australia (the central bank) imposed variable deposit ratio requirements on overseas borrowings. A proportion of the borrowings had to be lodged, interest free, with the Reserve Bank. This effectively pushed up the cost of foreign capital. When it came to power in 1972 the Whitlam government had set the proportion at 25 per cent, then raised it to a peak 33.3 per cent in early 1974. They got it down to 5 per cent as the recession bit and they realised the economic folly in their ideological stance. Bond wanted Crean to waive the deposit on the Citibank funds altogether.

Bond got only 30 minutes with Treasurer Crean, nothing more. He did come away with a consolation prize of sorts, though. Because IAC was under so much pressure, it had called in its generous ten-year advances to the Savoy Taylors Lakes project, on which the first sod was yet to be turned. Bond wanted to give IAC additional security to cover its $35-million exposure to BondCorp, but needed FIRB approval because Citibank owned 40 per cent of IAC. It is said that Crean gave no assurances but suggested the government would be 'favour-ably disposed' to Bond's proposal, which was to give IAC options over Taylors Lakes and a 'special sort of ownership security over parts of Yanchep.'[167]

But by going cap-in-hand to Canberra on 15 October 1974, Bond had entered a media shooting gallery. The queue of ailing developers offering land and assets to the Federal government was conspicuous by its presence. (A desperate Landalls had been there the day before trying to sell 500 units to the Department of Housing — it was not to last out the week.) In his *National Times* series on Bond in 1978 Gottliebsen says of this day trip: 'The first purpose of Bond's visit — that he'd asked the government for help — was leaked to the press, and there were headlines about his liquidity problems. It was the first time his difficulties were detailed in the press. This was a tribute to the effectiveness of his secrecy. It was also an illustration of lack of vigilance by reporters.'[168]

This is not strictly correct. Trevor Sykes, then Melbourne editor of the *Australian Financial Review*, had been sent to Perth in early 1974 by editor Vic Carroll to examine the Bond phenomenon. His four-part series 'Alan Bond's Sunshine Empire', published in the *AFR* in February that year, was the first serious assessment of the BondCorp balance sheet, the part property revaluations had played in its growth and the dangers of its high gearing level overbalancing.[169] When WAL lobbed its Special Report to the stock exchange in May, several journal-ists, including the *National Times*'s Malcolm Wilson, were highly critical of the BondCorp accounts and the dangers faced by investors in the company.

It is true that the Canberra visit opened the floodgates and that the provincial Perth press seemed either sycophantic or reticent in their reporting of BondCorp's problems. He was, after all, a local boy who had achieved a great deal of international recognition in a very short time and cut a very powerful figure in his home town. Bond's constant obfuscation and obscurant nature did not make him an easy person to interview. Witness this exchange the day of his Canberra visit: 'Asked whether his business empire was in trouble, he said: "That is an absolutely rude question which I am not going to answer. We are a public company ... I don't see why there should be any speculation about the future of the company or my reasons for talking to Mr Crean. I don't really see why I should say anything about it. What took place in Canberra is purely a private business matter."'[170]

What Bond fails to comprehend here is that it was precisely because BondCorp was now a public company that these questions had to be asked and answers given. The market in the company's listed securities was not fully informed at this stage. He was yet to produce audited profit figures for the year to June 1974, and the company was the subject of intense market speculation. It was queried by the Perth Stock Exchange two days later.

When the results for the year to 30 June 1974 were finally tabled, they showed, surprisingly, a nearly-fifty-per-cent boost in profit from $747,450 to $1.37 million. A year earlier, when Bond was selling the private BondCorp to WAL for $17.5 million, he claimed it had earned a net profit of $1,725,000 in the year to 30 June 1973. The 1975 results were to show a loss of $8.95 million, 'one of the biggest ever reported by a local company', according to the *AFR*. The 1975 figure is the first full year since the merger of WAL and BondCorp and made the $17.5-million acquisition price hard to justify.

As 1974 turned into 1975, Bondwatchers closely monitored the money markets for signs of debt default. Interest payments on mortgage loans due on 14 October were met. CAGA rolled over its facility on 3 November. At the December AGM, Bond assured shareholders that all was well: 'The economic climate continued its worsening trend but the diversified interest of our group cushioned the impact to some extent.' The good news was the forecast $16 million in land sales, the bad news was that Yanchep, despite the huge hype, produced only satisfactory results.

Gottliebsen observes: 'Christmas and early January, 1975, was spent in the sure knowledge that when the clock struck midnight on February 5, Bond needed $2.2 million to pay Minsec liquidator [Jim] Jamison [for the Robe shares]. There were even larger sums required for other creditors. It seemed Bond would be lucky to raise two bob, let alone two million.'

Bond was yet to get the DURD money for Santa Maria and had failed to convince the AIDC to buy or fund his Robe River stake. This was the third time payment due to Jamison for the Robe shares and if BondCorp defaulted, the consequences would have been disastrous for three interlocking reasons. Firstly, Jamison wouldn't be able to pay the Minsec creditors; and this, in turn, would have led to a court battle over the assets, which, we are led to believe, could have brought down the whole eastern States financial Establishment. Secondly, BondCorp would have been put into receivership by its own creditors, who would view the default as inability to service their credit. Thirdly, BondCorp wouldn't be able to meet its liabilities to repay Dallhold, which had sold the Robe debt to WAL a year earlier for $17.5 million.

The 5 February deadline, then, was exactly that — except that this time the whole world would be watching. Bond's tactic was to weave a web around all the creditors, and their backing banks, in such a way that his downfall would have meant all their downfalls. It was a hair-raising game of brinkmanship that he only just managed to pull off.

Robert Gottliebsen, who was given the inside story a few years later by Bond, Oates and Mitchell, tells how it was almost achieved on the day before the 5 February deadline:

Bond's creditors [and Minsec's unsecured creditors] met in a room in Jamison's Sydney office. There was an air of tension as the scheme was announced to them. The plan was that the Bank of NSW [the Wales, or Westpac as it is now] would advance BondCorp $2.2 million. BondCorp would then pay the $2.2 million to Jamison, liquidator of Minsec. Jamison would keep $500,000 for part of his liquidator's fee. Jamison would pass the remaining $1.7 million on to the Minsec creditors.

However, the Bank of NSW would not lend the $2.2 million without security. Bond's search for suitable security started with Robe River shares themselves. Under the original agreement for the purchase of Robe River shares by BondCorp, Jamison released shares as payments were made. For every 93 cents of principal paid, BondCorp received one share. The 1975 payment involved $1.4 million of principal, for which Jamison would release 1.5 million Robe shares. To these, Bond was able to add one million Robe shares which he had not previously mortgaged to make a total of 2.5 million Robe shares available as security for the Wales.

With a then market value of 47 cents, these shares were worth $1.2 million — $1 million short of the $2.2 million Bond had to find. There was no way the Wales would accept the shares as full security for the loan. The Wales was prepared to take some risk, but insisted that it would only make the $2.2-million loan to Bond if the bulk of the Mineral Securities creditors would agree to buy back the Robe shares at 93 cents each should Bond default on his repayment of his loan. The hope was that eventually Bond fortunes would improve or the Robe shares would go up. However, what creditors were in fact being asked to do was guarantee part of the money they would receive from the Minsec liquidation.

Would [unsecured] creditors buy it or would they be prepared to take the chance of a domino-style collapse and let the whole thing slide? Alan Bond waited outside while it was explained to the creditors, who did not all take kindly to the scheme, including the size of Jamison's fee. Among the opponents were George Carmany of Ord BT, one of the merchant banks claiming security, and Partnership Pacific. The Partnership Pacific opposition appeared strange in view of the fact that it was one-third owned by the Bank of NSW and the Wales man handling the deal, Bill De Boos, was a former chief executive of Partnership Pacific ... The stance of the other partners in Partnership Pacific — the Bank of America and the Bank of Tokyo — may also have been important.

In making the proposal, the Bank of NSW was aware of the wider ramifications of the Minsec affair and the implications of a Bond collapse. In addition it was involved as a Bond creditor for around $3 million because it had provided a credit facility for acquisitions which had become largely unsecured as result of a fall in asset values. To help close the gap between the current value of the 2.5 million Robe shares and the $2.2-million payment, Bond gave the Wales a first charge over its shares in Yanchep. This was an important security because of Bond's Japanese partners, Tokyu Corporation, who appeared likely to buy out the Bond share altogether.

Intermarine, a creditor of Bond for about $5 million, agreed to guarantee 10 per cent of the $2.2 million. Like the Wales, Intermarine also lacked full security on its Bond loans. It had an additional reason. One of its shareholders, the Tokai Bank (of Japan), was banker to the Tokyu Corporation, Bond's partner in Yanchep. Intermarine agreed to receive a second charge over Bond's Yanchep shares. This move, along with the Wales proposal, substantially reduced the gap left by the refusal of some Minsec creditors to guarantee repurchase of the Robe shares in the event of a Bond default. But it was not enough. George Carmany would not budge. Nor would Partnership Pacific. As Alan Bond, Peter Mitchell and Tony Oates turned in for the night on February 4, it seemed that only a miracle could save the group the next day, for they were still $500,000 short.

That miracle came in the form of Rex Davidson of the ANZ Bank, who agreed to join as a late guarantor. The ANZ was not a security holder in Minsec but would have assessed that the effect of a Bond collapse on the property market would be dramatic. In particular, the ANZ Bank had been a large lender to the Hanover group, who would have been put under severe pressure by a Bond collapse. Hanover had a big joint venture with Bond at Santa Maria in WA and had land near Taylors Lakes, Melbourne. Rex Davidson knew the Hanover situation intimately. He also was aware that the ANZ Bank had lent Bond $600,000 unsecured through Savoy. A little security was found for the ANZ who found themselves better off.

The ANZ did not bridge the gap but made it close; and at 10.55 p.m., with sixty-five minutes to spare, Jim Jamison gave Bond another week. In that vital week, the *National Times* ran an article by Malcolm Wilson setting out many of the details of the meetings. The article made some of the bankers a little twitchy. Bankers and merchant bankers don't like to be seen in public doing deals like the Bond-Robe one. Bond whipped in a writ against the *National Times* which he now admits was a 'stop writ'. It prevented further articles and this made the bankers sleep a little better at night (whether the writ would have succeeded in court or not is a separate question).

A lot of work was required in those seven days to bridge the remaining gap. Finally at 10.20 p.m. on 12 February the cheques changed hands and the immediate crisis was over. It could be said that Rex Davidson saved Alan Bond. In reality, he provided just that stiffening of backbone that was needed. It would never have been put together without Bill De Boos, Jim Jamison and Tony McGrath of Intermarine. Bond and his crew went to the Wentworth Hotel to celebrate. But Tony Oates could manage only a few sips of beer before retiring, exhausted.

The next day, 13 February 1975, dawned and Bond's problems were far from over. The Minsec deal effectively meant that the Bank of NSW and Intermarine would not insist that the amounts due to them in February from the Bond group must be paid. Instead they would be deferred or 'rolled-over'. But what about IAC and CAGA which played no part in the Minsec deal? Moreover, Bank of America, which was taking a large hand in CAGA affairs, was also a one-third stakeholder in Partnership Pacific, whose Minsec attitude had almost destroyed Bond. There were many negotiations and further plans were put forward. In the end no one called in their security and Bond had passed through February.[171]

In 1980, two years after the Gottliebsen account, Bond was the subject of a *Playboy* interview in which he gave Russell Deiley a slightly different version of the ten days that shook BondCorp, but by then he was coming from a much-improved vantage point:

During that period, we could quite clearly show that we had the resources to liquidate those loans over a very short period — maybe not there and then, but we only needed time. There was a lot of publicity associated with our acquisition of the Robe River company — Bond had not paid on a certain date or Bond had paid the day before an instalment was due. Although it was never reported properly, we did, in fact have a clause in our Robe River contract that permitted us to extend the repayments beyond the prescribed date if we so wished. The clause gave me the option to extend the repayment instalment for six months at an interest rate of 2 per cent. It may well have been cheaper for me to use that extension period in the contract in preference to arranging alternative financing.

The misreporting at that time did us tremendous harm. Because of the wide publicity given to the fact that we had large repayments to make on certain dates, people wouldn't lend us money in the normal course of business. Yet we were in a similar position to the individual whose collateral is his home and who borrows against that asset. Our collateral was $20 million worth of business assets. You can imagine the reaction to the publicity — loan sources were saying: 'We had better wait and see if Bond makes the Robe payment before we lend against his collateral.' My ability to borrow against my collateral was taken away from me because of the publicity. As a matter of fact, we took action because the misleading publicity did us tremendous harm.[172]

If this is correct, that Bond's Robe contract with Jamison had an option clause allowing him to extend the February repayment for six months at an additional 2 per cent penalty interest rate, then he would have indeed been wiser to take it up. For, with hindsight, the publicity that was the inevitable consequence of his convoluted 'arranging alternative financing' could have been avoided and the DURD money for Santa Maria would have been through by then and his bacon saved.

There seem to be two reasons for the fact that this extension was never invoked. Firstly, the Minsec creditors wouldn't wear it and neither would Jamison, who could have turned his back on Bond and sold the remaining Robe shares to Garrick Agnew or Lang Hancock, who were still keen. Secondly, if he lost his hold over the Minsec creditors and their backing in the eastern and international banking community, then he lost his insurance policy against going under. With three years of the property crash yet to come and two more February payments to make to Jamison (the last a whopping $11.7 million in February 1977), there could still be another rainy day out there like 5 February 1975, and he might need dry powder for one of them. Jamison doesn't appear to have ever mentioned this option and neither does Gottliebsen's semi-official version of the truth.

The second point Bond makes is that the 'misreporting' denied him access to his $20 million worth of business assets by scaring off his normal business bankers. In fact, all the bankers and financiers were already scared of BondCorp, and for good reason. Still, they went ahead and arranged the 'alternative financing' anyway and BondCorp stayed in business. BondCorp didn't have $20 million worth of business assets, according to the market and his own balance sheet. At 10 cents a share, BondCorp's 9.46 million listed shares were worth less than $1 million on the stock exchange. Even at their par (issue price) value of 50 cents, the company's issued capital was worth only $4.73 million. The latest accounts to June 1974 showed BondCorp with net tangible assets of only $10 million based on total assets of $82.9 million, a figure which incorporated many assets at either dubious valuation or valuations which were not realistic in terms of reigning market values.

A continuation of the *Playboy* interview reveals other home truths scattered among the flights of fancy but confirms that even Bond viewed the first week in February 1975 to be absolutely paramount to his survival: 'What I did in 1974 was put a lot of my own money on the line. And the funny thing is that we didn't owe any money to creditors. We had some major bank loans. We have never been in the credit business and we have always paid everybody. All we were doing at the time was rescheduling some loans ... It was a time of decisions and I was prepared to work hard. I was prepared to talk to the people with whom the company was involved and to keep them informed on what we were doing. Because of the state of the economy, it wasn't simply a matter of selling off assets. It wasn't a matter of not having any money. We had a mass of wealth in assets, but we just couldn't move them. It was a matter of waiting for the market to settle down and rescheduling loans and that's what we did. It took a lot of talking to convince the board and bankers with whom we were involved that we had the capability.'

Little by little, the truth about the devastation the crash had wreaked on BondCorp eventually came to light. Bond was always playing for time by delaying bad news for as long as possible and exuding confidence in his company and its paper at all times. He needed to radiate this confidence in his own abilities and capabilities because, without it, he could not expect to maintain the confidence and support of his financiers on whom he now depended for his daily survival. In May 1975 BondCorp disclosed a loss of $2.87 million for the six months to 31 December 1974. It was BondCorp's (as distinct from WAL's) first-ever loss as a public company and twice the size of the profit reported for all of 1973–74. It would have diminished Bond's credibility and shot confidence in BondCorp to pieces had it not already been anticipated by the market. It was the ultimate horror of the full year's results for 1974–75 that the market was now hanging out for.

To regain control of the agenda again and boost confidence, Bond needed to announce something positive and something big, and to do it quickly. He needed to pull a rabbit from his hat to prove he still had that old magical charm which allowed him to attract capital with ease. He needed to give creditors hard evidence that he had the wherewithal to survive. So, soon after the half-year loss was announced in May, Bond disclosed that in America he had been offered a mammoth US$100-million letter of credit, which wasn't repayable until the mid-1980s, and wasn't it a shame that Australian financiers had no faith in him but American ones did.

It was a masterstroke. Here was tangible evidence of the America's Cup connection. It was, we presume, initially arranged in talks he held with the First National City Bank (Citibank) in New York and Newport in September 1974. He had sat on it since then because its major stumbling block was that he needed approval from the Whitlam government to bring it in and that presented great difficulties.

It appears Bond went to see Citibank to get them to call off their IAC dogs, who were barking at his heels back in Australia, and in the course of his presentation spiel, put the hard word on the parent bank to directly back his entrepreneurial zeal and vision splendid. The FNCB people must have been impressed with his potential to move mountains. Who else but a mountain-mover would be plucky enough to attempt to remove the America's Cup from the New York Yacht Club after 123 years? But then, Citibank seemed to be a sucker for worthy causes. A decade later they were to write off billions of dollars worth of bad debts to Latin American dictatorships.

Inevitably, the plan to import the Yankee dollars was knocked back by the Whitlam government as an attempt to circumvent the government's amorphous foreign investment guidelines and as a currency speculation, but not before Bondy had full use of its potential benefits. With it, he argued, he could not only weather the present storm but be in a good position to take advantage of the coming recovery. He continued to pursue the deal until August, trading off it where he could, and was eventually to blame its lack of success as the main reason for his being forced to sell the other half of Yanchep to the Japanese. He was to hold this against the Whitlam government and actively campaign for its downfall. The antipathy was mutual.

Temporary relief came in June with the sale of the Santa Maria estate. The agenda now was to dispose of, in as orderly a manner as possible, properties which 'may be of sound potential in the long term but are not suitable for immediate requirements as they do not provide a positive cash flow initially.' The words come from a confidential document dated 23 February 1978, given to Bond's bankers and financiers as evidence of his good stewardship in debt reduction since the crisis of confidence had begun. It shows his eagerness to keep his creditors informed and to be seen to be doing something about his mountain of debt.[173]

Two of the quixotic assets disposed of in 1975 were his ill-conceived adventures into the insurance and the unit trust businesses. That a property developer had gone into the financial services industry in the first place is intriguing. That he had such diversified interests to dispose of at this time was a godsend as every little bit counted in the battle to impress creditors and maintain that illusive confidence.

Bond bought his first insurance company, Transport and General Life, from Westpac-associated financier, Australian Guarantee Corporation, in July 1972 and renamed it Shield Life Assurance Ltd (the name came easily as he had a private family company called Shield Enterprises Pty Ltd which held 10,000 shares in his major family holding company, Dallhold Investments Pty Ltd). He purchased his second insurance company, Underwriting and Insurance Ltd (U&I), through his listed Amalgamated Industries Ltd (AMIN) from the Warner family and public shareholders in April 1973.

In 1974 Bond boasted that the businesses were doing brilliantly, with annual premium income of $2.8 million and total assets of nearly $20 million. But the net income was not all that special once you took into account their high acquisition costs, and he could not access the assets as they were life assurance statutory fund assets. Worse still, these assets were balanced by equal amounts of liabilities which served only to weigh down his balance sheet position at a time when he needed to lighten it considerably.

As both takeovers were made in the 1972–73 financial year, it is possible to calculate their purchase price by reference to the increase in the value of goodwill items in the accounts of both BondCorp Pty Ltd and AMIN for that year. Shield appears to have cost BondCorp $4.7 million and U&I set AMIN back $4,135,187. Of this latter figure, $4,061,504 is represented as a goodwill item, meaning that U&I had net tangible assets of only $73,683 on acquisition.

Lipscombe quotes an unnamed Bond banker as saying the U&I deal was Bond's earliest and costliest mistake but one that he was unable to talk him out of. One can only imagine what

Bond had in mind with his determined thrust into the insurance business. Life assurance companies, the major ones, exercised enormous influence over investment decision-making because of their vast pooled resources. Perhaps it was this prestige and backing that Bond was seeking. Perhaps it was an impulse purchase, an opportunity too good to miss in an industry where his marketing skills could be put to good use (Shield claimed to be the first to offer reduced-rate life policies for non-smokers). Whatever it was, his timing this time could not have been worse. In December 1974 Cyclone Tracy hit Darwin and his insurance companies had become more of a hindrance than a help. It was time to cut his losses. The 1975 annual meeting was told that BondCorp had contracted to sell the U&I subsidiary and that a partial float of Shield Life was being considered.

There seemed more method in the madness with a scheme to sidestream funds from Universal Flexible Trusts Ltd (UFT), Australia's third-largest equities unit trust company, with $45 million under management and a good investment record. BondCorp even had some experience in this area, with Peter Mitchell having been a trust manager in the UK before being recruited by Bond in 1966.

The scheme was approached cautiously at first. Bond teamed up with another corporate raider, Ian Murray's Reinvestment Australia Ltd, to offer the Parker family $1 million for the business on 25 January 1974. By June 28 Bond's private company, Dallhold Investments (it always seemed to have more money than BondCorp), bought Murray's half interest for $500,000 and the BondCorp/Dallhold partnership assumed liabilities of about $2 million on top of its $1-million entry price.

There doesn't seem to be much doubt about BondCorp's motivations for seeking absolute control of the unit trust company and its intention to direct UFT funds toward Bond-Corp properties: 'In the property market, Universal will gain valuable added experience from their recent acquisition by the Bond Corporation group through the group's wide knowledge in this area and in the finance sphere of operations,' said a BondCorp promotional brochure in 1974.

Gottliebsen says the redirection was prevented by the intervention of the cautious UFT investment manager, Hans de

Lange, who blew the whistle on Bond's plans and aroused the suspicions of Eagle Star Insurance, trustee for the Universal unit holders, and an opponent of UFT going into the softening property market.[174] Bond backed off. He had failed to change the trust deed covering the Robe River debenture holders and he looked like running into similar difficulties here. If the unit holders were stampeded into cashing in their units, the purpose of the exercise would have been defeated. In October 1975 Bond and BondCorp sold out at a loss. Serge De Kantzow, the NSW State manager of BondCorp, got 25 per cent of the business with the rest going to QBE Insurance Ltd.

One of the fascinating things about BondCorp in the early 1970s was its predilection for unusual businesses that were often quite unrelated to its core business of property development. If there was a quid in it, then Bond would have a go at it. Sometimes there wasn't but he'd still have a go anyway. It provided some interesting challenges for his management team. The first issue of BondCorp's quarterly house journal, *Enterprise*, in Autumn 1974 explained the phenomenon this way: 'The group actively seeks business opportunities in other fields of activity. It has shown great success in recognising, assessing and exploiting a variety of projects not directly linked with property development. Put briefly, the group's business is to look for new business.'

Several of the opportunities involved his in-laws, the Hughes family. His business association with his father-in-law, Doozer Hughes, dated back to the Nu-Signs and Lesmurdie Heights days, and one of their businesses involved the export of live sheep to the Middle East. In 1972 when AMIN acquired Skipper Holdings, Bond sold seventy-five per cent of the car dealership to his wife's cousin, John Hughes. Skipper Mitsubishi is now one of the largest car dealerships in Australia and John Hughes still has links to Bond Motor Corporation. In 1975 his brother-in-law, Bill Hughes of Westwools, financed a Perth property deal that Bond regarded as a certainty but couldn't get backing for.

Savoy had a thirty-per-cent interest in Northern Wood-chips Pty Ltd which had plans to set up a paper-making plant at Vanimo in Papua New Guinea and big contracts to sell the output to Korea. The interest was sold to the AIDC at a distress price after the PNG government pulled out of the agreement.

Another AMIN subsidiary was involved in wholesaling imported furniture and light fittings. There were plans to form a joint
venture with no less a person than the Shah of Iran, and
another with 'Tom the Cheap', a grocery chain run by former
Perth lord mayor Sir Thomas Wardle, which was going through
hard times. Bond had attempted to take over the Great Boulder
nickel mine. There were also forestry plantations, an ice works
and a ten-pin bowling alley in the group.

However diverse, disposal of these peripheral businesses
could not get BondCorp the reduction in liabilities that it
required to survive. Bond's initial instinct, to just trade out of
trouble with his non-property assets, was still predicated on
his belief that the property downturn was only a temporary
correction that time would cure. But the 1974–75 annual
report, released in October, was evidence that he would have
to take more drastic action. During the year he had managed to
reduce assets from $92.86 million to $87.78 million (he wrote
off the holding costs for the investment in Robe) but liabilities
actually increased from $82.89 million to $83.37 million. It was
becoming obvious that he would have to sell his three jewels
— Robe, Yanchep and International House — if he expected to
be taken seriously on his promise to reduce the debt burden.

The result for the year to 30 June 1975 was an earth-
shattering loss of at least $8.95 million — a $10.3-million
turnaround on the previous year's profit of $1.37 million. Bond
commented: 'I can't say it's been a successful year but it's had
its highlights.' The *AFR* described it as 'one of the biggest ever
reported by a local company.' A sombre chairman Bond told
shareholders at the December 1975 AGM in Perth that the
assistance of the group's bankers 'was of paramount importance to our continued operation.' He said the group had
incurred extraordinary losses on the realisation of several
assets, and efforts to issue equity had been frustrated by 'the
steady deterioration in the market, plus the short supply of
money and the lack of confidence.' He said there was no
chance of recouping the losses in the current year but the
group was 'containing the situation and re-establishing
profitability.'

Fortunately, BondCorp's effectively 43.3-per-cent-owned
iron ore miner, Robe River Ltd, had a much better year to 30
June 1975. Robe announced a maiden profit of $4,059,288 and a

cheerier chairman Bond told the shareholders at the AGM in Sydney that the mine had managed to sell all of the project partners' record annual production of iron ore to the Japanese. He said Robe has not, at present, been adversely affected by the world economic slowdown and the consequent reduction in demand for steel products.

Was the fatted lamb being dressed for the kill? He even told the BondCorp AGM that the market value of the Robe shares had gone up in the last six months, justifying the deal. The Robe result and rising share price were Bond's first major victory since his troubles began. He wanted to show that he got the sums right in the first place. In particular he wanted to convince WAL/BondCorp shareholders that the $17.5 million they had agreed to pay Dallhold for assuming the $19.6-million debt to the Minsec liquidator for the Robe stake was somehow justified.

Another Robe payment of $2.15 million was due on Jim Jamison's desk at midnight on 4 February 1976, and everyone knew it. Could BondCorp, which had just lost $9 million, do it? This was the question being asked in boardrooms and newspaper offices across the nation. Bond wasn't keen to have the press peering over his shoulder and 'misconstruing his position' again. He had had enough of that pain and trauma from the probings the previous year. It was decided — reluctantly, we are told — to dump the Robe stake while the market was rising because it was not producing desperately needed cash flow.

The decision was really forced on Bondy by the logic of his balance sheet, and the anxiety of his creditors and his shareholders. Even if BondCorp could scrape together another deal like last year (with different bankers) and make the $2.15-million February 1976 payment, an $11.7-million final pay-out would still be hanging over its head in February 1977. The decision was a difficult one for Bond, who liked the prestige that went with being chairman of a successful international mining company after so many years of trying to become one, and was uneasy with the thought that the end of the deal with Jim Jamison would mean the end of his Minsec security blanket. Bond also had a personal shareholding in Robe. The decision was further pushed by outside interest in the Robe shares.

According to Lipscombe, who interviewed Bond for the *Bulletin* in February 1976, Garrick Agnew and Lang Hancock had put up a joint proposal to him late in 1975 which he rejected.[175] Bond also claimed to have had six other offers for the Robe shares — one, it appears, from the Hancock family acting alone. Hancock had been approached by Jamison, but did not join in the original bidding for the Minsec shares in 1973 because he was 'waiting for the vultures to clear from the Minsec carcass.' He did, however, declare: 'we are the only people who can save Robe.' He was to show how in early 1976.

Hancock's bid for Bond's Robe shares was worth $27 million but it was complicated and highly conditional. Bond would have loved it because it gave him a handsome profit and was structured very much like his own attempt in 1973 to get Robe to buy BondCorp for $25 million so that he could then afford to pay Jamison for the Robe shares. Hancock would pay Bond the $27 million for his Robe stake, provided that Robe paid him $22.4 million for one third of his Hamersley Iron royalties plus a one-quarter interest in another iron project at Marandoo, so that he could, in turn, pay Bond.

It was to be another busy February but this time Bond-Corp was selling, not buying, Robe shares. It was planning to sell a lot of Robe shares that it didn't yet own to a man who would pay for them only if the Robe shareholders footed the bill. It sounded like a great deal for Bond and Hancock but not so good for the Robe shareholders who owned the other 57 per cent of the company.

When the clock struck midnight on 4 February 1976, and yet again Bondy hadn't fronted with the Minsec money, Jamison gave him an extension. But in effect, Bond was now exercising his option to extend the payment date for six months at the penalty rate of interest (up from 6 per cent to 8 per cent). He maintained that he would not be in default until midnight on 4 August, by which time he hoped to have disposed of the Robe stake and fully settled the outstanding $13.85 million with the Minsec creditors.

The Perth Stock Exchange got wind of the Hancock-Bond talks (the two men lived five doors away from each other in Dalkeith but conducted their negotiations in the city) and queried BondCorp that day (5 February). Bond confirmed that he had signed a letter of intent for the Hancock family to buy

Bond's Robe stake. Preliminary heads of agreement were signed on the following Monday (9 February) and more details given. But on Wednesday 11 February the exchange again queried the Hancock-Bond deal. It noted that the proposed sale was contingent on 'a number of conditions and consents' and asked for speedy advice when the conditions and consents were obtained. What the exchange wanted to know was, would the deal be put to Robe shareholders for their approval?

The Hancock deal seemed to be on the nose. The Sydney Stock Exchange intervened and laid down the law on 18 February. It told Hancock that unless he could demonstrate 'special circumstances', he would (quite rightly) have to extend the $1.38 a share he had offered Bond to the other Robe shareholders who were missing out. With the Hancock deal fast running out of legs, Bond tried to whip up enthusiasm among the other bidders for his Robe stake for a less conditional bid that would get him out of this mess with as little pain, and as much profit, as was possible in the circumstances. 'I put it to you this way,' Bond told Lipscombe, 'should a buyer come along — at a price — then we would be a seller.'[176]

Re-enter, stage left, Garrick Agnew, whose interest in Minsec's Robe stake had three times been shunned. He is said to have organised a counter proposal in March involving Burns Philp & Co., one of the original shareholders in the Robe float, and the US-based Engelhard Minerals and Chemicals Inc., which had links with the giant South-African-based mining house, Anglo American Corporation. This consortium was offering only $1.15 a Robe share. It was cash on a take-it-or-leave-it basis.

BondCorp accepted the $22.05-million bid on 31 March. Many Robe shareholders seemed pleased to see the back of him, for in May they cleared the transfer without demanding that the offer price be extended to them. However, BondCorp executive Peter Lucas was asked to stay on as managing director of Robe when all the other Bond directors resigned.

Jamison, who had extended Bond's deadline again on 5 May, eventually got the outstanding $13.85 million for the Minsec creditors on about 26 May and settled. The Minsec liquidation was completed ahead of schedule and Jamison's original vendor-finance, time-payment scheme with Bond was vindicated. 'If we'd failed, the whole liquidation would have come undone. We trebled our money on that deal,' Bond was to later boast.[177]

After paying Jamison, Bond was left with about $8.22 million in hand. Westpac and Intermarine relieved him of the $2.2 million he had borrowed from them to make his February 1975 payment and the Robe book was squared with Bond looking at a $6-million capital gain for his efforts over the past three years.

However, the smoke never seemed to clear on the ultimate destination of this profit. Did Bond or BondCorp own it? Jamison had said quite categorically on 13 June 1973 that BondCorp was not buying Minsec's Robe shares, 'Alan Bond was.' Maybe Dallhold had held on to some Robe shares when BondCorp Pty Ltd was sold to WAL. BondCorp/WAL certainly had use of the Robe profit. When its results for the year to 30 June 1976 were released, BondCorp reported an operating loss of $4.4 million for the period but posted a net profit of $630,579 after booking a profit of about $5 million on its Robe stake.

Gottliebsen says the $6-million profit 'went to Bond's family company, Dallhold, as part of its first charge. In the Robe crisis a year earlier, no one had insisted on a charge on the Robe profits, probably because they seemed unlikely. Bond could have walked away a millionaire, although Dallhold itself had given one or two guarantees.'[178] The discrepancy could relate to Bond's acknowledged personal shareholding in Robe. It would also have been consistent with an arrangement whereby $5 million went to BondCorp, for making the time payments, and $1 million to Dallhold, for arranging the deal in the first place. If so, it would not be the last time that Dallhold would take a free ride and fee from BondCorp for providing management services. Dallhold also had a floating charge over all of BondCorp's assets relating to the reverse takeover of WAL in December 1973. What BondCorp owned was Dallhold's anyway so the argument was semantic.

Two days after the Robe deal was signed, liquidators moved in on eight wholly owned BondCorp group companies. Dudley Allan of D N Allan & Co. got the job of winding up the non-operating subsidiaries from the Savoy group to save on administration costs. They had no assets or liabilities.

The first great BondCorp liquidation sale was now well under way. It would not be completed until early 1978, when he finally parted with Yanchep and International House, but the unloading of Santa Maria and Robe was a significant start. All that his bankers and financiers were looking for (besides their money back in tight times) was tangible evidence that Bond recognised the seriousness of his problem and was prepared to rectify it. He had shocked the West (and eastern) Australian financial world by running up a debt of $81.6 million in double-quick time and then backing it into a listed company with almost a devil-may-care attitude. He had hung on stubbornly for a while, playing games and stalling for time, hoping against hope that his ship would right itself and liquidity and confidence (the two ingredients in land sales) would once again flow smoothly under his keel.

Bond, scoffed at sarcastically as 'the shareholders' friend', had become 'the bankers' friend'. For them, it seemed, he was prepared to bend over backwards. He had to. In the three and a half years between 31 December 1973 and 30 June 1977, Bond reduced the level of unsecured creditors in BondCorp by 40 per cent from $81.6 million to $48.5 million. It had taken a long time and he still had a fair way to go but Bond, the eternal optimist, was beginning to see light at the ends of tunnels.

He told Lipscombe in February 1976: 'This time last year we had to raise $10 million to see us completely through, make all the payments, and give us enough liquidity. We couldn't raise the $10 million at that time. Today, this year's program entails a total of $3.25 million, including the sum of money necessary for Jamison. That's all our funding requirements are. Any one of a number of property sales would give us that amount of liquidity.' But could he make it without having to get over another hump of creditors? asked Lipscombe, the cynic. 'No, that's it. We're out of the hump area. We believe that everything that's going to come out of the woodwork has come out of the woodwork, everyone who could call us has called us. We've survived and there's no question we'll stay up,' replied Bond, the optimist.

Of course, there was one creditor — his largest — which temporarily emerged from the woodwork and attempted to make its voice heard, then disappeared back into the woodwork again. Its name was IAC, it was owed $35 million and it was not without troubles of its own. But because bankers don't like to admit they make mistakes, IAC's downfall, and subsequent rescue by Citibank, did more to save Bond in the 1970s that any other single factor. It was more important than Sir

Charles Court buying Santa Maria and the Robe time-payment deal with Jim Jamison. 'If IAC had gone, they'd probably have taken me with them,' Bond told Lipscombe in his only recorded admission of defeat.

IAC had crashed from a $16-million profit in 1975 to a half-million loss in 1976 and a whopping $32-million loss in the first half of 1977.[179] 'They themselves were in financial trouble,' said Bond later, 'when I say that I mean real financial trouble. Citicorp came and took that over. Took control of that. And that was exactly the same time as we had our problem. They couldn't continue the advances on the Taylors Lakes project.'[180]

IAC was Bond's financier and profit-sharing partner in the Taylors Lakes development in the outer western suburbs of Melbourne. On 11 September 1975 Bond, wearing a garish blue pinstriped suit and a yellow hard hat, had turned the first sod on what his people were curiously calling 'a $100-million development'. So far, IAC had put down about $15 million and it had stalled on the $5 million required for the next stage. 'A representative of IAC was at the opening ceremony. He was smiling as the first earth was turned.'[181] He shouldn't have been. Under the ten-year deal that the financier had signed with BondCorp/Savoy in early 1973, IAC had to provide all the finance yet get no repayment of principal or interest for three years.

If IAC had called BondCorp, thereby causing it to fail, it would get no interest, no profit and would be left with dubious security over the suburban heartland because its parent company was foreign owned. It had what had become known as a 'non-accrual' exposure to BondCorp. In effect, it was a no-win situation. And a very expensive one, as IAC had to rely on high-cost public subscriptions to its debenture issues to fund its operations. BondCorp was getting a free ride and sitting in the driver's seat. IAC had bought the car, was making all the payments and could get only a tenuous grip on the bumper bar.

Citibank had paid about $36.5 million for 40 per cent of IAC in May 1971, when times were good. With IAC's troubles mounting it had moved to 51 per cent, then in April 1977 launched a bid for the outstanding shares at 70 cents each. 'From New York, Citicorp (the holding company) helped prod shareholders into acceptance by describing the Australian property market as being "in a state of collapse". One evening during this time, Citibank managing director John Thom was at a university delivering a speech on an unrelated subject. When he finished, the first question — quite out of the blue — was: "Is 70 cents a good price for IAC?" Thom, not expecting the question, answered by reflex. "If Citicorp buys IAC for 70 cents it is a steal. But if Citicorp does not buy, the shares aren't worth two cents."[182]

Thom later told Trevor Sykes: 'When a property company got into trouble, we would ask ourselves: "Who is the best receiver we could appoint?" The answer was usually the borrower.' This was IAC's attitude towards its BondCorp exposure. It did the minimum necessary to hold on to the property and waited for the market to recover. It adopted a similar attitude toward Sir Paul Strasser, allowing him to run his own liquidation in the Parkes Development group for years.

The other factor influencing IAC's attitude to Bond was his yacht-induced friendship with the Citibank parent board in New York and Newport. They liked him so much they were prepared to lend him $100 million. They were hardly likely to send him down the tube. He was a good god-damn friend and he was gearing up for his second tilt at the Auld Mug — wasn't he?

A different man might have let the 1977 America's Cup challenge pass, but not Alan Bond. However, there was serious doubt for a while as to whether he would go ahead. BondCorp had sponsored a new Sun City Yacht Club to make a fresh challenge after 1974 but with Yanchep now on the block, there didn't seem to be the same urgency to promote sales at the Indian Ocean estate: 'Last time we were here to promote Yanchep. We achieved that purpose and now we're here to sail ... I'll enjoy it much more this time. There was too much tension before. And we didn't think we could lose,' Bond said on his arrival.[183]

In the middle of a serious self-liquidation of his assets to placate anxious creditors, this hardly seemed the appropriate time to be squandering money on an expensive yacht race on the other side of the earth. But Bond had friends there in high places who would become most concerned if he didn't front. It was expected of him. He had promised them last time he would return and now he had to deliver the goods. In the end, he did it to maintain the 'confidence and support' of his ultimate backers — those upon whom the very survival of BondCorp ultimately depended.

America's Cup yachting was held to be above business and above board by people in high places. It was something you did for your country upon attaining great personal wealth. A sort of *noblesse oblige* for bored businessmen and the patriotic inheritors of massive wealth. Somehow, Alan Bond didn't seem to quite fit that description. He had secretly become an Australian citizen only on 1 May 1974, just before he lead his crack Australian troops to the Newport beaches for the first time. In the fourteen-plus years he had so far spent in Australia he had never before felt inclined to renounce his British nationality and take Australian citizenship.

This seems odd as the Australian Nationality and Citizenship Act came into force on 26 January 1949 — a year and a week before he arrived on the *Himalaya*. As a British subject, all he had to do was register to become an Australian citizen. Non-British 'aliens', on the other hand, had to go through a naturalisation period before being granted citizenship. This discrimination between British subjects and aliens was stopped in 1973, allowing all migrants to become Australians after three years' residence. Although he spoke often of his pride in being an Australian, he was a belated convert. However, he called his new challenger *Australia*, so there would be no doubt about where he was coming from.

Bond set up a new company, America's Cup Challenge 1977 Ltd, to manage his involvement this time. The last campaign had been funded off the back of Yanchep Sun City Pty Ltd. As advertising promotional expenditure it was possibly tax effective to that company. This time he had nothing to sell, but his very presence was certainly advertising to the big bankers that he and his corporation had survived the rigours of the economic storm and were a good bet for the future.

Unfortunately, BondCorp was now awfully short of a quid. The 1977 campaign would require contributions from other Australian corporations despite its greatly reduced budget. This was set at $1.4 million for the 1977 challenge but Dallhold had to pick up at least half of that amount when the sponsorship money fell short. This was because a Royal Sydney Yacht

Squadron syndicate had entered against him with his old trial horse, *Gretel II*, and the corporate sponsorship dollars had to be split. A 'people's boat' syndicate, led by Sir James Hardy, also foundered through lack of finance. In late August, Bond's syndicate was to run out of cash: 'Frantic calls were placed to 150 companies in Western Australia. The syndicate was looking for an additional $220,000 just to complete the match and get *Australia* shipped home.'[184]

It was even harder on the water where he had to race against three other challengers just to get to the American defender. In his previous outing his only obstacle had been the eccentric Frenchman, Baron Bich. Bich was back again but his *France I* and Gordon Ingate's *Gretel II* were the first boats eliminated. On 29 August *Australia* defeated *Sverige*, the first Swedish entry, backed by a US$2-million contribution from Volvo, and Bond became the official challenger again. This time there was no gloating over the body of the victim. 'We just bought one boat this time, and all we want to do is win some races,' said a mellower Bond.

That he had got this far was an achievement in itself. Only fourteen months earlier his challenge had lain in tatters when his two designers — Ben Lexcen and John Valentijn — resigned their commission to build the new twelve-metre yacht for Bond. Valentijn said from London: 'We do not believe Mr Bond's challenge has a realistic chance of success, so we are not putting in any more time or effort.'[185] They were talked around in the end but Valentijn's assessment was to remain correct.

Australia was slaughtered four straight by 'Terrible' Ted Turner at the helm of second-time defender *Courageous*. The margins were 1:48, 1:03, 2:32, and 2:25. At no stage of any of the races was *Australia* in front. Turner, the flamboyant owner of a TV network and a football team, had become an overnight sensation and one of the most famous men in the US. At the post-race press conference, Turner said his Aussie friends were the 'best of the best ... the best of the best', but he was drunk at the time.[186]

CHAPTER TEN

1980: Freedom vs. Australia, Freedom, *4–1*

Next to Ted Turner at Newport in 1977, Bond looked like a quiet achiever. He had not achieved anything on the water, mind you, but he had done so on land and had been relatively quiet about it. There were no accusations in parliament this time about him being 'rude and rich', for they would have been hard to justify on both counts. Neither was there much in the way of sabre rattling at the 'old money' people from the New York Yacht Club, even though this was generally considered an allowable part of the Auld Mug's psychological warfare. Bond was on his best behaviour for he was out to impress. He even managed to sound altruistic and sportsmanlike: 'There is a great fascination about competing for and winning such an old sporting event that has never been won by anyone but the Americans. It's like climbing a great mountain,' he said on his arrival.

Of course, one of the reasons the Americans liked young Bondy so much was that he was absolutely no threat to their yachting supremacy. He had failed to take even a single race in eight outings. But like good old Sir Thomas Lipton and Baron Marcel Bich, he kept coming back to take American stick. This was the sort of worthy opponent the Yanks loved to beat and back. He spoke English, knew the pointy end of a gentleman's boat from the blunt end, and he was no damn Commie.

He got on well with the swashbuckling Turner and his wealthy Texan oilman mate, Perry Bass. Bond had encountered Turner on various world yacht race tracks. They sailed against each other in the 1972 Sydney-Hobart, which Turner won outright and on handicap with the twelve-metre *American Eagle*. Hugh Whall says of the relationship: 'They are alike in many respects. They are both in their thirties. They share an aggressive, hold-on-tight, never-say-die, go-for-broke attitude towards winning. And they are close enough that at one point Bond agreed to exchange a piece of property at Yanchep Sun City for shares in one of Turner's Atlanta television stations.'[187]

Turner, Bond and Bass were also members of the Young Presidents Organisation, a sort of junior entrepreneurs group-therapy and self-help club. There is a certain camaraderie that exists among self-made men who have the ability to tackle, with equal aplomb, the sorts of challenges presented in life by the Establishment and the high seas. They tend to enjoy life, and the fruits of their labours, to the fullest. Usually, after one of their latest conquests, they liked nothing better than to wind down away from the office and in the close company of like-minded spirits. There they would brag, party and swap insights and information.

Ever since the 1973 Arab-Israeli war and the resulting oil embargo, the energy crisis had remained a fashionable topic of conversation among those most affected by it and those who saw it not as a problem but as a new business opportunity, part and parcel of the ever-changing world markets. Initially, Bond would have been among the former group. He had been immediately hit by it in 1973 because the sums Mitchell had done on the Robe acquisition made no allowance for a hike in the international oil price. Robe was a big user of oil but, more importantly, so were its main customers — the Japanese steel mills. They were cutting back on their steel production and hence demand for iron ore as a consequence of the oil price spiral.

Bond confirmed this on 13 December 1973, the day he was first elected chairman of Robe River Ltd. Typically, he wanted the Australian government to solve the problem by making special arrangements to supply the Japanese steel mills with oil. But he made an important contribution to the debate: 'One lesson Australia should learn from this embargo is that we should seek to refine our own natural resources, utilising our own fuel and gas resources so that tonnages shipped ex Australia are less, and furthermore so that we are less dependent on the manufacturing process of other countries.' It was prophetic stuff but it sat uneasily with his demand that the government send limited Australian oil reserves to the Japanese mills.

Bass had been in Bond's ear about the need to get some proven energy reserves 'somewhere' since he visited Bass's private island off the coast of Texas after the 1974 challenge. Bond was now a believer. Since dumping Robe the previous year he had had Mitchell working on finding him an energy play 'somewhere' in Australia. The closest thing Australia had to on-shore, oil-gushing Texas was South Australia's Cooper Basin. What Bond needed was money. What Bass had were contacts. Bass gave him an introduction to Republic National Bank of Dallas, which proved fruitful. He met other bankers at Newport and some would later be drawn into his web.

Bond did his now-usual international zig-zag through bankers' haunts for a month before finally arriving home in Perth from the Cup campaign in early October. 'You have to be able to perceive things ahead of other people. Part of this is being in with world trends, which is why I travel a lot, both interstate and overseas,' he was to later say.[188] One of the first people he arranged to see after stepping off the plane was the WA Premier, Sir Charles Court. Bond was prepared to have a third tilt at the Auld Mug but he didn't want to be placed in the embarrassing situation of having to beg for money during the race finals again: 'We will be having a meeting of the fund-raising executive next Tuesday and expect to make an announcement on Wednesday. We will then know where we stand and can say what our program is,' he said in an airport interview.[189]

Bond probably expected to be pilloried on his return in October 1977. His financial situation at that stage was still desperate. BondCorp had lost $942,000 for the year, taking accumulated losses to $8.2 million. The accounts showed that the company was still sitting on secured advances totalling $48.5 million. This was eating its head off in interest charges of about $100,000 a week. On top of all that he had just lost four inglorious boat races for his adopted country. But, no, his worst fears did not materialise. Losers, it seems, are forgotten far more quickly than winners.

Quite the opposite occurred. On Australia Day, 26 January 1978, Alan Bond was named Australian of the Year by the Canberra Australia Day Council. The award went to the person the council believed had brought the 'greatest honour to Australia in 1977'. His citation was for 'outstanding personal achievement and endeavour in the field of Australian sport.' Surely this was the reverse of the 'tall irises' syndrome; this was more like the real Australian battler egalitarianism at work. Were the Australian 'have-nots' backing the time-honoured national ethos of the game, but vanquished, under-dog? The inglorious slaughter of Australian and New Zealand troops on the beaches at Gallipoli during the Great War had been turned into a magnificent victory in the minds of those who were not there.

The award was to provide an enormous personal and corporate fillip for Alan Bond. He had been an Australian for only three years and eight months, he had done his best to minimise the effects of Australian taxation for eighteen years, he had recently tried to settle a thousand white Rhodesians at Yanchep, he had just sold the other half of the Yanchep resort to the Japanese and he couldn't take a trick off the Americans — and he was loved for all of it. Bond, in Melbourne, said he was honoured and thrilled: 'It's hard to say if I deserved it or not, there were a lot of people to choose from. Of course I told my wife about the title and she was thrilled too. She has supported me through all the difficult times and it is just as much her honour as mine.'[190]

Court, in Perth, said it was good to see a West Australian win it. Though a controversial figure, he had been prepared to 'give it a go' and his efforts on behalf of Australia had been rightly recognised. Malcolm Fraser's Liberal Party had won another Federal election in December 1977, with BondCorp support, and Bond's nemesis, Gough Whitlam, had retired from politics as a consequence. The only hiccup in the run-up to the election had been when Fraser's deputy and Treasurer, Phillip Lynch, was implicated in the Victorian land deals affair. Lynch had a pecuniary interest in the Stumpy Gully estate which was sold to the Victorian Liberal government for housing based on a now-disputed valuation.

There were no Foreign Investment Review Board hassles when Bond announced on 28 December 1977 that BondCorp was selling the controlling 51-per-cent interest in Yanchep Sun City to Tokyu Corp and other Japanese investors for $7.1 million. The nearly ten-year-long odyssey to sell the distant fly-infested sandhills to suburban punters had come to an end. To some extent, Yanchep too had fallen victim to the oil crisis. The sixty-kilometre drive up the coast was thirsty work for cars and drivers alike. Bond normally travelled there in an air-conditioned Rolls Royce.

'It was a great shame,' he later reflected. 'We really had a big development going when the whole market turned down. I was offered a US$100-million letter of credit in America but the Whitlam government would not give me permission to import the money. I then approached both State and Federal govern-ments and invited them to put money into it or buy a half share, but they were not interested. I had no alternative to selling to the Japanese, who waited till we were really short of money. If I had been able to hang on to it, the America's Cup would be sailed off Yanchep in 1987, because I would have challenged from the Sun City Yacht Club as I did in 1977 ... I have had some big disappointments, but that was the biggest. Not all bad came out of it, however. It made people aware of what could be done in development.'[191]

Bond's crocodile tears for Yanchep should be put in some perspective. The sale of the entire Yanchep estate was no failure for Bond but a raging financial success. Like the sale of the Santa Maria estate to the ULC three years previously, it had eventually justified the high directors' valuation placed on the project at the outset. For face-saving reasons, Tokyu Corpora-tion had confessed to putting down only $4.9 million for its first half of the project; for similar reasons, the final down-payment for the second half was recorded at $7.1 million. This gave the impression that the market value of the project was some $14 million. But it was later revealed that debt of some $32 million was retired as a result of the transaction, at least $12 million of this (the CAGA commercial bill) was assumed by Tokyu. Taking this into account, the total value of the Yanchep exercise to BondCorp was much closer to $50 million, the figure that Alan Bond had said it was worth at the outset.

Also, according to the Gottliebsen version, Bond had put the squeeze on the Japanese: 'Throughout the crisis, the Japanese group had been concerned, because if Bond had failed much of their earlier investment would have been scattered in the Yanchep sands. They were under some pressure to buy out Bond Corporation and secure their position. Such thinking would not have been discouraged by the Bank of NSW and Intermarine, who held the Yanchep shares as security. Bond did not go cap-in-hand to the Japanese. Instead he told them the project needed a heavy injection of funds. The Japanese, in contrast, wanted to sit tight. Bond, despite his problems, wanted to buy them out. Just how he would do this remains obscure but involved unconventional financing. Alternatively, the Japanese could buy him out — at a price. Out of this situation evolved the $7.1-million deal. And so in March 1978 he finally made it. Accordingly, Bond Corporation was able to pay out the Bank of NSW and Intermarine. Alan Bond now carries around his 1978 annual report as a priest carries his Bible. It shows a big reduction in debt.'[192]

The liquidation sale reached its climax with the sale of International House, the BondCorp corporate headquarters, also in March 1978. After the sale, Bond estimated his borrowings from external sources had fallen to $15 million — a sixth of the peak. International House, and the adjoining Ansett Gateway Hotel on the old Celtic club site, had originally been a joint venture with Taylor Woodrow, the British construction company and developer which had been BondCorp's first partner in Yanchep. It was owned by a company called TWB Pty Ltd, which at the time had an issued capital of $200,000. Bond had had it on the market for at least two years with an asking price of $10 million.

The starkly white, clean-lined, eighteen-storey office tower in St Georges Terrace stands overlooking Government House and the Perth Concert Hall, to the blue pond of Perth Water, and beyond to smoky Fremantle on the horizon. Dallhold and BondCorp had the top four floors. Just underneath them, on the fourteenth floor, resided the WA State Development Office (later the WA Development Corporation) — WA Inc. in its earliest and most visible form. The building featured on the cover of most BondCorp documents at the time and marks the beginning of Bond's edifice complex.

Sykes was struck by its 'garish opulence' on his assignment to discover BondCorp for the *Australian Financial Review* in February 1974: 'Instead of the traditional sombre mahogany trappings, the decor of the Bond headquarters verges on the psychedelic. As a visitor steps out of the lifts he is struck by the colour scheme. A long curved seat of shocking pink is in vivid contrast to the deep blue of the carpet and ceiling. The reception area is behind a long curved desk, also in shocking pink and topped with a transparent black screen.'[193] Two years later, Lipscombe would describe the building's executive suite as having 'steel mirror doors, red upholstered armchairs and lavish spaciousness.' He was told the building had a valuation of $10.5 million, a replacement cost of $12 million and debts of $6.5 million.[194] It was eventually sold for $9 million.

All up, the great 1970s BondCorp liquidation sale settled $51,740,671 on the anxious creditors in just over eighteen months. The three key sales that went to make up this figure were $22 million for the Robe stake, $19 million for the YSC shares ($7 million in equity and $12 million in debt) and $9 million for International House. Veteran Perth journalist John McIlwraith, who sighted the confidential document given to BondCorp's bankers and financiers on 23 February 1978 to proclaim the miracle, says it listed 'scores of sales, the prices received and the institutions holding mortgages, as if to give those houses fresh heart.'[195]

Bond had told Sykes back in February 1974 that he had 'a substantial reduction in borrowings going on' so the clean-out took a lot longer than expected and was reported to be worth between $60 million and $70 million all up. It was, however, a significant turning point. 'We exposed ourselves greater than we should have done and to some extent we were lucky to survive,' he told Lipscombe. 'Notwithstanding that, we have. That's the name of the game. There's those that do and there's those that don't. Having succeeded in that, we certainly won't make the same mistakes twice.'[196]

But Bond proceeded to do exactly that. For no sooner had

he emerged from his contraction phase than he was expanding again with borrowed money. His target this time was to buy his way into energy projects. His starting point, identified by strategist Mitchell, was a small listed mining company called Endeavour Resources Ltd. Endeavour had oil exploration interests as well as control of another miner, Leighton Mining. On 15 February 1978 BondCorp took up a 25-per-cent stake in a complicated restructuring of Endeavour's capital. The interest was to cost $2.5 million but Bond was given time to pay.

Time payments were becoming a hallmark of his financing arrangements. Basically they reflected his inability to obtain finance from the major Australian banks. They had lent him money for his property developments, indirectly, through their finance company arms which charged higher rates of interest and gained security of sorts, but generally they didn't want on their books someone with his high-risk profile and unorthodox methods. Bond loathed them for this attitude: 'We weren't part of the establishment. We weren't a Western Mining, we weren't a Fairfax or a Herald & Weekly Times. They would lend to those. As much as they wanted. But they wouldn't look at the new people coming in.'[197] Bond banked with the National but they wouldn't give him credit.

Endeavour quickly came under BondCorp influence. On 30 May the exploration company announced it was spending $1.06 million to buy a tin mine at Moolyella in Western Australia. The deal was arranged for it by BondCorp and the mine was supposedly grossing $700,000 a year. The lesson Bond did learn from the mid-1970s property crash was the need to get hold of businesses that generated cash flow.

Bond had declared on his return from Newport that at least a third of his funds would henceforth be devoted to resource investments, with energy stocks the highest priority. Was this intuition or was he acting on information received? The Perry Bass broadsides in 1974 and 1977 tend to indicate the latter but there was also a touch of the former. At that time the Australian mining industry was still in recession. 'We like to buy in depressed times when others are not buying. So we are often criticised for being the odd man out. The unfashionable things are the ones we look at,' he said later.[198]

But how could the unrenewable natural energy resources — oil, gas and coal — possibly be considered unfashionable post-December 1973 when the Arab oil crisis hit? Well, the embargo imposed by the Organisation of Petroleum Exporting Countries (OPEC) producers' cartel had the effect of quadrupling oil prices, and world demand slumped. Consumers simply cut back or switched to alternatives. Oil exploration was a high-risk, high-cost and long-term business. It was not the place for a little Perth property company that had just been taken to the cleaners. Attaining proven reserves, the stuff Bass told Bond to go after, seemed an impossible task for any local company, let alone one with BondCorp's slender financial resources.

Australia was not self-sufficient in oil and was considered never likely to be so because the age of the continent's rock formations seemed to preclude it. The first strike at Rough Range off the West Australian coast in 1953 was too small to be commercial. The first commercial discovery at Moonie in Queensland in 1961 was tiny by world standards. In 1964 a field of some small substance was found at Barrow Island off the north-west coast but the ninety-five wells sunk in search of it had cost $85 million. It took the resources of oil giant Esso and Australia's largest company BHP to bring the Bass Strait oil and gas field off Victoria on stream in 1967. Although still small by world standards, Bass Strait enabled Australia to shelter from the worst of the OPEC price hike.

Big gas finds were to follow at Gidgealpa-Moomba in the Cooper Basin of South Australia and at North Rankin on the North-West Shelf off the West Australian coast, and a British company called Burmah Oil was behind both of them. Burmah, then Britain's third-largest oil company, owned 22 per cent of British Petroleum. It also owned about 42 per cent of Woodside-Burmah Oil NL, the operator of the North-West Shelf development and 37.5 per cent of Santos Ltd, the operator of the Cooper Basin gas field project in northern South Australia, which had plans to pipe natural gas to Brisbane and Sydney as well as Adelaide.

Unfortunately for Burmah, the OPEC imbroglio brought the great oil company to its knees. In the early 1970s the company began amassing a huge fleet of supertankers to carry crude oil and liquefied natural gas (LNG) to waiting world markets. It had forty-two tankers on its books in 1974 when both supply and demand dried up and the oil bubble burst.[199]

On the verge of bankruptcy, Burmah began a billion-dollar liquidation sale. In 1976 BHP bought Burmah out of Woodside and the North-West Shelf. In 1978 Bond bought Burmah out of Santos and the Cooper Basin in what still ranks as one of the best buys in modern mining history.

Why he did it is no mystery. He wanted the property, any energy property, desperately. The timing was right. Burmah was ripe for the plucking. The place was right. Mitchell had done the sums. It was the only energy play still available in Australia and potentially the cheapest in terms of entry price as the gas field and the supply pipelines were yet to be developed.

How he did it remains one of the great mysteries of Australian corporate achievement. Basically Bond pitted his abilities as a super salesman against the Burmah board's reluctance to part with a prime property at a fire-sale price, and won. 'Get me inside any boardroom and I'll get the decision I want,' Bond bragged to his in-law and good mate John Hughes.[200]

On a wing and a prayer, Bond flew off 'home' to London to beseech the Burmah board to part with its bouncing baby. Amazingly, a deal was struck and he returned in triumph at the end of August 1978 to announce he was 'buying back the farm' for Australians. Bond had got hold of nearly 50 per cent of the huge Cooper Basin oil and gas field by backing his judgment and playing a hunch.[201] 'His real pleasure in life is to do a deal,' says his former mate Laurie Connell. 'He has this irresistible bug to jump on a plane and do a deal. He can't stand to think that somebody else is doing a deal and he is missing out.'[202]

Bond got 37.5 per cent of Santos, plus 66.96 per cent of Reef Oil NL and 30.86 per cent of Basin Oil NL (two bit players in the Cooper consortium) for $36 million. He won these controlling interests without making takeover offers for any of the companies or extending the offer to the balance of the shareholdings. Burmah had sold him its wholly owned sub-sidiary, Burmah Australia Exploration Pty Ltd, which owned the stakes. This gave him rights to 46 per cent of the gas reserves and 60 per cent of the gas condensate (liquid hydrocarbons) of the Cooper Basin fields.

Yes, he got time payments. The deal was $11 million down, $5 million on 30 May 1979, and the balance by 30

November 1979. The buyer was a consortium in which Bond-
Corp held 50 per cent, Endeavour 30 per cent, Dallhold 10 per
cent, AMIN 5 per cent and Leighton Mining 5 per cent. The
others were brought in to help fund the down-payment,
with BondCorp's contribution coming from a combination of
asset sales revenue and a Dallhold advance. A $3,363,637
subordinated loan from Dallhold Investments was converted
into BondCorp equity (6,727,273 shares) in 1978.

An exuberant Bond waxed lyrical about his Santos coup,
telling anyone who would listen that the shares he had bought
from Burmah for $1.75 each where worth at least $10. Australia's Texas in the Cooper Basin matched his grand vision of
owning proven reserves in an energy-starved world. He pre-
dicted a vast future for natural gas saying Australia's energy
needs would accelerate faster than in other parts of the world
because of Australia's limited resources. He said the investment was made because Santos was a going concern with
established cash flow and because the known reserves 'were
capable of considerable expansion — sufficient possibly to
meet the needs of the majority of Australia's population on the
eastern seaboard.'[203]

Bond's excitement over his good fortune was not shared
by the Adelaide-based board of Santos, which correctly pre-
dicted that the King of the West would not be a passive player
in the eastern seaboard gas game. On 24 September Santos
took Burmah to court to dispute the sale to BondCorp on the
grounds that it was not consulted about the deal. The Adelaide
Stock Exchange also attempted to get the offer extended to the
minority shareholders in Santos, Reef and Basin but it was too
late. On 26 September a major oil strike in the Cooper Basin
was confirmed and shares in all stocks associated with the area
shot up. Bond was born again. By mid-October Bond had
secured a peace deal with the belligerent Santos board and was
appointed deputy chairman.

As the year drew to a close his attention was focused on
the related problems of meeting the two instalment payments
due in the coming year and exploiting the value he had added
to his energy investment. On 3 November 1978 BondCorp
announced a 1-for-3 rights issue at par to help finance the
Santos purchase. It was to successfully raise $2.85 million from
his long-suffering shareholders and it was the first time he had

been game enough to approach the equity markets since the West Australian Land (WAL) float in 1969.

His shareholders had not had a dividend since 1973 but they would have been heartened by the recovery from the brink and the new-found energy wealth. A net profit of $1.4 million was declared for the year to 30 June 1978. It was struck after deducting $3.2 million for interest charges. It was a good year for shareholders because accumulated losses had been reduced from $8.2 million to $2.5 million. A further profit of $1.48 million was posted for the six months to 31 December 1978, but, even annualising this earning rate and projecting it forward, BondCorp would take more than eight years to earn enough to make the residual $25 million in payments due to Burmah in the coming year.

In December Bond took a fast plane to China where he was to spend three weeks negotiating a new source of finance. This turned out to be the most pivotal deal in Alan Bond's long and eventful career as a businessman and a borrower par excellence. One can point to the involvement of Finance Corporation of Australia (FCA) in the initial Lesmurdie Heights development in the early 1960s or the deal with IAC/Citibank to fund land purchases in the early 1970s as being critical in the development of the Bond deep-debt profile, but none can compare with the deal he was to strike during this brief visit with the venerable Hongkong and Shanghai Banking Corporation, for the relationship with this bank was to carry him right through the heady 1980s.

There was a dual purpose to his initial approach to the Hongkong Bank (HKB). As part of his peace settlement with the Santos board, he said he would help them to raise the $600 million in long-term finance the Cooper Basin consortium needed to fund pipeline development. He also needed backing for his own Santos play and he hoped to piggyback his personal needs on the monster credit facility he hoped to arrange for the consortium. One of the extraordinary things about Alan Bond's personality make-up is that whereas ordinary people suffer enormous anxiety owing a bank $60,000 for a modest home mortgage, he seemed unperturbed about knocking on a banker's door with a demand for ten thousand times this amount ($600 million).

To the amazement and astonishment of all and sundry, he

achieved both of his objectives. His success in this fund-raising exercise was to give him a terminal addiction to big licks of deep debt but for the moment he savoured his moment of gratuitous glory. The money was not his but someone else's. The debt was not his but someone else's. The anxiety, likewise, seems to have been transfered to other shoulders: 'He is one of those almost unique fellows who measure wealth in the amount they can borrow rather than the amount they have,' according to merchant banker Geoff Hill, who eventually replaced Bond as chairman of Bell Resources.[204]

'In the Santos deal,' he told Hugh Schmitt years later, 'I had to raise $600 million overseas and people told me I could not get it, but we did. We got $200 million from each of three banks, one American, one Canadian and one English and they have done very well by it.'[205] The American bank was the Republic National Bank of Dallas, Texas, the one he had been introduced to by Perry Bass after the America's Cup races in 1977. The Canadian bank was the Canadian Imperial Bank of Commerce, another Newport devotee. The 'English' bank actually has Scottish origins but had been domicile in the Crown Colony of Hong Kong since 1866 — the HKB. It had connections with the Marine Midland Bank of the US, another Newport connection and a parent of Intermarine Australia which had been so important in the success of the Minsec arrangement of the mid-1970s.

Another member of the syndicate was the Australian Resources Development Bank (a consortium of the big four Australian banks established under Federal legislation and backed by the Reserve Bank of Australia). The ARDB was also an old acquaintance. It had had $25 million invested in Robe River debentures.

An establishment fee of $3 million was paid to Wardley Holdings Ltd (HKB's merchant bank in which the Tokai Bank of Japan also had an interest), for setting up the facility. Two others who helped organise this deal were Talbot Beckwith, the former ANZ Bank chief manager for international business who had now joined his son Peter on the board of BondCorp and Bond's good friend the Perth merchant banker Laurie Connell, a former employee of the Martin Corporation which was owned by the Canadian Imperial Bank of Commerce. Connell once described the Santos funding package as 'most unorthodox' and for that reason terribly significant in the development of BondCorp.[206] 'We never feel bad about paying big money to people with skill at putting deals together. We pay the best for success,' Bond told Schmitt.

Needless to say, BondCorp also got the backing it required to make the final two payments to Burmah Oil, although Bond was fairly coy about it when he gave an interview to Geraldine Doogue of the *Australian* on his return from Hong Kong in early January 1979: 'There's no problems there. Absolutely none. We had stand-by facilities available last time and we didn't have to use them. We have several options open to us now and we are ascertaining what is the best course of action. Frankly, we are more concerned with the funds the other consortium members have got to find for the development of those liquids.' Doogue then asked him directly whether the remaining Burmah payments would be underwritten by overseas backing capital. 'Ah, now . . . I didn't say where it was coming from,' came Bond's cryptic reply.[207]

Bond was also asked in this interview whether he had any plans to take full control of Santos. His 'no comment' reply struck fear and trepidation into the heart of the Adelaide Establishment. South Australians have no monopoly on parochialism but the State's central location on the island continent makes its inhabitants particularly paranoid about corporate raiders from both the East and the West. This small-town phobia is soundly based. Most of the corporate giants thrown up by the city of churches have indeed fallen victim to cross-border raiders. They were used to it from the East but Bond's attack from the West on their major energy company stirred them into a frenzy of provincialism.

In late April the Don Dunstan/Des Corcoran State Labor government decided to act to protect Santos from interstate market forces — particularly BondCorp. Mines and Energy Minister Hugh Hudson foreshadowed legislation that would limit individual ownership in the locally registered energy company to 15 per cent. Initially, the State government itself had offered to buy Bond's stake at a 10-per-cent premium to his entry price and, when he refused, it enacted the draconian legislation which is still in force.

Once again Bond was in conflict with a Labor government. During debate on the Bill in the South Australian parliament on

27 May, Hudson and other ministers criticised the BondCorp accounts, alleging that the Perth company was using Santos to solve its financial problems. Hudson also argued that Bond's strategic holding in Santos would enable him to 'threaten and attempt to govern by fear'.[208]

Bond appealed to the Federal Liberal government for intervention to override the South Australian legislation but none was forthcoming. By July he had reluctantly started selling down his Santos stake but, where possible, he retained an option to buy the shares back at a later date. He was hoping against hope that a change of government would lead to the legislation being reversed. The government did change later that year but the legislation remained in place.

During the second half of 1979, Bond reduced his Santos holding to just below the prescribed 15 per cent. But in the meantime, the Santos share price had more than doubled. Bond claimed a profit of $100 million on the investment and cried all the way to the bank. It was the quickest and easiest money he ever made and it gave him a strong taste for the windfall profits that can flow from clever stock exchange position-taking and trading. This would be the direction on which his corporate brains trust would now concentrate.

But while Bond took to the stock exchange with great glee, the feeling was not totally reciprocal. He had received support from the chairman of the Australian Associated Stock Exchanges when the South Australian government had taken its precipitous action, but the burghers of the quaint little Adelaide bourse took exception to his touting of the Santos share price. On 22 May they queried the company when deputy chairman Bond repeated his claim that the shares were worth $10 each.

But Bond's exuberance knew no bounds. In the 1979 BondCorp annual report he spoke of the Cooper Basin having the potential to contain two or three times the already discovered 350 million barrels of liquid hydrocarbons. 'I've sometimes been accused of being a visionary because I've sometimes been too far ahead only because I did the right things . . . I was ahead of the timing of it. I could not have done some of the things I did later without causing any ripples on the water,' he once opined.[209]

One of his forward plans related to the Cooper Basin was

for a petrochemical plant based at Redcliff in South Australia. Dow Chemicals were commissioned by Santos to do a $3-million feasibility study. Nothing came of it at the time but ten years later he was to return to the same idea, although it was to be based in WA and use liquids from the North-West Shelf gas field.

Bond never forgave the South Australians for mucking up his plans to take Santos, even though he made a fortune as a result of the government's action. Although he hung on to his remaining Santos, Reef and Basin shares for a few more years and used the assets as a bankable base, he claims to have never invested another dollar in South Australia. However, his hatred of Labor governments was to prove a passing passion.

BondCorp probably ended up with more than enough profits from its Santos play to meet the final Burmah payments without drawing down its new HKB facility. But even before the Santos spoils began to flow into its coffers, the company had finally staged a recovery from the dark days of the mid-1970s, when nothing seemed to go right in the property markets. For the year to 30 June 1979, profit was up 73.5 per cent to a record $2.52 million, just enough to clear the backlog of accumulated losses. Shareholders also got their first dividend for six years — a frugal $800,000 to be split among the 22.4 million shares on issue. The bad news was that total liabilities were on the increase again. At balance date they stood at $59.6 million, which represented a gross debt of $2.66 per ordinary share.

However, there was no sign of the massive profits in the following accounts for the six months to 31 December 1979, an indication that some of the booty had gone to settle the Burmah account or had been ploughed into other sharemarket ventures. In this period a net profit of $2.36 million was posted and extraordinary profits of $5.2 million were declared. Shareholders were also rewarded with a 1-for-3 bonus issue when these half-yearly results came out in February 1980. Chief among the beneficiaries were Alan Bond and his Dallhold Investments, which would have picked up at least 4 million free Bondcorp shares based on his combined holding of about 12 million shares (5.3 million in Bond's name and 6.7 million in Dallhold's) at 30 June 1979.

Based on these figures, neither Bond nor Dallhold seems to have taken up entitlements to the rights issue made to all

shareholders in November 1978 to help fund the Santos purchase. Indeed, had Dallhold not been given the 6.7 million
shares in exchange for clearing a subordinated loan to Bond-
Corp in 1978, it would have cost Bond dearly, both on the share
register and in the trouser pocket. BondCorp's share price ran
up from 47 cents at 30 June 1979 to $1.45 at the beginning of
November, when the annual report was posted.[210] At that stage
the 12 million shares that Bond controlled had a current
market value of $17.4 million. And for some strange reason a
placement of 405,000 shares was made at 65 cents in 1979 to
raise 'working capital' at a time when the company appeared
flush with funds for the first time in years.

September 1979 was again a time for navel gazing, when
management consultants Price Waterhouse (PW) were flown in
from Sydney to prepare a ten-year corporate plan to take the
group through the 1980s. The last time Bond had called in
management consultants was during the last days of the property boom in 1973, when he was looking for an escape plan
from the coming property crash. This one was more positive
and came up with a series of 'development options' designed to
take BondCorp through the then strongly running resources
boom and beyond.

That Bond felt the need for such a document reflects in
part the loose end he was at as a result of his failure to gain
absolute control of the management and cash flow of Santos.
Even people with loads of intuition need reassurance from time
to time that they are heading in the right direction. But as is the
nature of these things, what you pay for is what you get. Bond
knew exactly what he wanted. He wanted to keep his core
property and industrial businesses and build on his energy and
mining interests. He also was acutely aware of the need to
develop a regular source of recession-proof cash flow so that
he would never have to go through the horrors he had just
experienced and he figured he was now smart enough to make
a packet as a sharemarket trader.

The first stage of the PW report was presented to a
BondCorp board meeting on 3 December 1979 and, as it
seemed to confirm the chief executive's basic prejudices, the
firm was commissioned to proceed to stage two. The final
report was dated 31 January 1980 and was delivered soon
after. Basically, it recommended that BondCorp clean up its

corporate act by bringing the core property, industrial and energy divisions in-house while keeping the more risky mineral exploration and property deals off-balance-sheet. It stressed that the group needed to develop a strong cash-flow base to support its entrepreneurial activities.

Savoy Corporation had already been fully integrated into the property division and the Shield Life assurance company sold off in August, so a full takeover of the 64-per-cent-owned Amalgamated Industries Ltd (AMIN) listed subsidiary was recommended. Endeavour Resources was already targeted as the group's risk-taker so it was up the deal-doers of the corporate finance division to come up with the strategic cash-flow base and to provide income from investment activities until it came along.

Cashed up on Santos and the HKB line of credit, and just ahead of the PW report that was to sanction their activities, Bond's corporate cowboys hit the takeover trail with a vengeance. They figured that if they could turn $11 million into $100 million without even trying, they would make killing after killing with some serious application. The pent-up executive energy that had been constrained for years by the liquidation straightjacket was given vent. In September a $20-million bid was made for the Beverley uranium trio of Oilmin, Petromin and Transoil. Bond's bid was blocked by directors so he sold out and settled for a $3.1-million profit. In October he got 26 per cent of Hampton Gold Mining Areas from Colonial Mutual for $5.76 million. He retreated five months later with a profit of $3.2 million. Attempts were made on Broken Hill South, Ampol Petroleum and H C Sleigh, but nothing came of them.

By 1980 the appearance of Bond's name on a share register was enough to strike fear and panic in boardrooms across the country. 'Those were the days,' says Laurie Connell, 'when we got the balance sheet and put it in the bottom drawer and said, "We've got to do this on a deal-by-deal basis." I knew the bloke. I knew he was right. I knew he was a survivor, a man with enormous capacity and ability. I have faith in that sort of individual. We've seen the good, the bad and the ugly together but one thing about Bondy you can count on is that if he's with you, he's with you 100 per cent. He sticks. He never backs away from a deal.'[211]

Bond was still looking for an energy project where he

Chilean dictator Augusto Pinochet and Alan Bond shake hands after the Chile Telephone Company deal. (Photo courtesy of *Reuters*.)

Van Gogh's 'Irises' became the world's most expensive painting when Bond bought it in November 1987 for $69.5 million. It was repossessed in 1989.

This house at 75 Mclville Beach Road, Applecross, was Bond's last on the south side of the Swan River. In 1968 he moved to the more exclusive Dalkeith on the north side of the river.

Bond's Boxing Kangaroo battle flag became a marketing tool after the Cup win. Here it holds a can of Swan lager on the side of a pub in Fremantle.

Alan and Eileen at the christening of Dallhold's maxi yacht *Drumbeat* in May 1989. *Drumbeat* won line honours in the 1989 Sydney-to-Hobart yacht race.

Bond in Napoleonic guise for *Drumbeat*'s christening.

Bond's gift to the nation is a recreation of Captain Cook's *Endeavour*. It was being constructed on the site of his America's Cup challenge headquarters in Mews Road, Fremantle.

In September 1988, Bond paid $22 million for the Glympton Park estate in Oxfordshire. Bond, the son of a Welsh coalminer, bought the manor built by a 19th-century colliery owner. A Feudal village with sixty inhabitants went with it. (Photo courtesy of *News Limited*.)

Mark Knight (Courtesy of the *Sunday Herald*)

John Spooner (Courtesy of the *Age*)

could control the management and the cash flow. In January he set his sights on New South Wales coalmining and construction group, White Industries Ltd, buying about 5 per cent of the capital on the market. Kerry Packer's Consolidated Press Holdings group had been there before him and built up a substantial stake before splitting with the White directors when his overtures were rejected. The two entrepreneurs never admitted a pact to warehouse the ConsPress stake but Packer remained faithful to Bond. The White board and Bond then entered a desperate seven-month battle for control of the company.

White's chairman, Geoffrey White, and his associates were thought to control close to 50 per cent of the company. From this position of strength they probably thought they had seen off the raiders. However, White was to find it was foolish to under-estimate Alan Bond's deep pockets and commercial aggression. In April BondCorp snapped up 5 per cent of Mareeba Mining NL which also held about 5 per cent of White Industries. By May, Bond was ready to reveal his hand. Endeavour Resources disclosed that it had bought the BondCorp, ConsPress and Mareeba interests in White and now held 43.5 per cent of the capital and was prepared to bid $18 a share for the balance, thereby placing a value of $169 million on White.

As part of the deal, BondCorp also sold its Bond Mining and Exploration Pty Ltd subsidiary to Endeavour for $16.3 million and received a share placement from Endeavour that took BondCorp to nearly forty per cent of Endeavour's capital ... White still rejects the takeover bid and a stalemate is reached. This is broken when BondCorp executives fly to Japan for talks with Mitsubishi Corporation, another White shareholder with an interest in gaining control of White's black gold. Another deal is struck. John McGuigan, a Sydney solicitor and White director, agrees to act as an agent for Mitsubishi and a go-between with BondCorp/Endeavour. In August, Bond accepts $78 million for his interests in White Industries. Once again he has lost an energy play but his consolation prize is a cash profit of at least $45 million ...

While the White saga was being played out, Bond made two other bids related to the PW corporate plan — both closer to home and both fraught with controversy. The first was for TVW Enterprises Ltd, owner of one of the only two commercial television licences in Perth and a steady cash earner. In 1978–

79, TVW earned 37.9 cents a share, which fitted the PW directive to find a proven cash producer with little risk to its income stream. 'It didn't have to be the highest, just regular and steady,' Bond said of his search for the elusive cash cow.[212]

In December 1979 Bond commissioned Perth stockbroker Patersons to comb the TVW share register and quietly assemble him a parcel large enough to get him in the front door of the television station. Money was to be no obstacle but secrecy was. Perth being the small town that it is, with a would-be entrepreneur on every corner, this second stipulation was a tall order for Patersons to fill. Laurie Connell maintains that in Perth every deal is picked over again and again by business rivals who would 'eat your arm off for a dollar'.

The business rival that Alan Bond was seeking to avoid — at least until he could see the whites of his eyes — was Robert Holmes à Court, whose Bell Group Ltd had also been quietly soaking up TVW shares. Bell and Bond were the Perth business world's pepper and salt, except these two never mixed. They had first clashed in December 1971 when Holmes à Court's Stanford Securities made a bid for the car dealer, Skipper Holdings. This brought him into conflict with Denis Horgan's Metro Industries which also had an interest in the company. In this particular battle, Bond's Amalgamated Industries (AMIN) came in over the top and won the prize. The 'tall man' and the 'fat man' had given each other a wide berth since then and concentrated their takeover spleen on interstate victims.

Holmes à Court, who at the time was attempting a take-over of the Melbourne-based Ansett Transport Industries, got to hear of Bond's interest and no doubt brought it to the attention of the TVW board. Bell itself had 9.45 per cent of TVW and the grateful board appointed Holmes à Court a director and a protector. Bond was forced to play his hand. On 14 December he revealed that his family company, Dallhold, had snapped up 15.4 per cent of the capital for $7.54 million. Bond was now the largest shareholder on the books but the board was not impressed. They immediately made a placement of 240,000 shares to Holmes à Court which had the effect of boosting Bell's holding to 11.4 per cent and reducing Bond's to 15 per cent.

Ron White, who was now Dallhold's managing director, pleaded that Bond's only interest in the company was as a long-term investor who would restrict his ambitions to a maximum 20-per-cent holding. He would not comment on suggestions that the purchase agreements organised by Patersons contained an escalator clause for the sellers and had been bought on a deposit of 10 per cent with the balance in thirty days. He said Dallhold had not made overtures for a board seat but 'it would obviously be nice if we were invited.'[213]

White was whistling Dixie. The reality was that Bond had been gazumped by Holmes à Court and this game was over almost before it started. Dallhold could not afford to hold $7.5 million worth of TVW dead wood indefinitely so the stake was quickly passed on to AMIN, which had been accepting dead wood from BondCorp for ten years. The Perth Stock Exchange thought this was a bit rough on the minority AMIN shareholders, especially as the market value of the parcel had declined by some $800,000 since the shares had been transfered and the takeover premium had come off. On 19 February the exchange queried BondCorp over the deal and suggested that the AMIN shareholders be given the opportunity to vote on the transaction.

Bond disposed of the TVW shares on 18 April and a matter of days later, on Thursday, 24 April, the BondCorp board resolved to bid for all the outstanding shares in AMIN at $1.35 a share. BondCorp did not inform the Perth exchange about the bid until Monday 28 April, following the Anzac Day long weekend. The bid was announced to the public at the end of the first trading session that morning. But 14,000 AMIN shares were traded in that morning session at prices ranging from 97 cents to $1.05. On 30 April the West Australian Corporate Affairs Office was asked by the Perth Stock Exchange to investigate possible insider trading in the AMIN securities on the twenty-eighth.

The report of the inspector appointed to investigate those dealings, Mr R G Hamilton, makes interesting reading.[214] It reveals that Mr Russell Hawkins, a managing director of Kimberly NZI Finance Ltd, had placed an order to buy 12,000 AMIN shares at $1 in the name of Chippenham Nominees Pty Ltd at 8.30 a.m. on the twenty-eighth. In an interview with the inspector, Hawkins said he had 'never dealt in AMIN shares before but that he had some spare funds and thought AMIN was a good investment at the time.' He stated that through his employment he knew some of the members of the board of directors of BondCorp.

The next day, 29 April, Hawkins sold 12,000 AMIN shares

at $1.25 to merchant bank L R Connell & Partners 'to make a quick profit rather than wait for the takeover bid to be finalised.' Laurie Connell told the inspector that his purchase of the shares 'was basically a banking exercise,' as they were at least guaranteed to receive $1.35 by accepting the BondCorp offer. A month later, on 29 May, BondCorp varied its bid and lifted the AMIN offer price to $1.50 after AMIN received an independent report from merchant bank Schroder Darling & Co. that on a break-up basis, the AMIN assets were worth $1.75 a share. No action was taken against Connell as he had bought the 12,000 shares after the initial bid was announced.

The AMIN bid was a key recommendation in the 31 January PW report but the BondCorp board had procrastinated over the bid until apparently spurred into action by the stock exchange's reaction to the TVW transaction. Inspector Hamilton said the existence of the report was generally known.

Apart from his moving to 39 per cent and hence control of Endeavour Resources in 1980, Amalgamated Industries was Bond's first successful stockmarket takeover since the Savoy Corporation move in late 1972. But winning is not everything in the world of high finance. In the year to 30 June 1980, BondCorp's profit rocketed from $2.5 million to $6.33 million. The profit on extraordinary items was an extraordinary $64 million, and that's not counting BondCorp's share of the White greenmail profits in Endeavour. Total assets more than doubled to $182.4 million and dividend doubled to 7.5 cents on the capital increased by the 1-for-3 bonus issue.

With such a spectacular performance in the profit and loss statement, no one noticed that the red ink on the balance sheet (total liabilities) had jumped to $97.3 million — the highest it had been since the $94.2 million revealed in the 30 June 1973 pro forma accounts that consolidated WAL and BondCorp Pty Ltd for the first time.

Alan Bond's third tilt at the America's Cup in August and September of 1980 should have been his luckiest and his last. It was neither. Since the dead-serious 1974 *Southern Cross* challenge (he had land to sell), the 1977 and 1980 campaigns gave the impression that he was simply going through the motions — using them as training runs where he could gain experience and show the flag. The real business in 1974 and 1977 had taken place behind the scenes.

The true test of Bondy's seriousness about the America's Cup was always the amount of money that was actually outlaid on the sailboats. The budgets for the second and third campaigns were roughly $1.5 million apiece. If we allow $3 million for the first Yanchep effort, it shows he was in a holding pattern — making contacts, learning skills and waiting for a technological advantage over, or a sign of weakness in, the old enemy.

Meanwhile, the Cup contest itself had gone through fundamental changes. It was no longer an exercise of individual *noblesse oblige*. It was not even a sporting event any more, but a contest of national management styles and technological resources. With the notable exception of Baron Bich, there were no more 'robber' barons with bottomless pockets. They had been replaced by tax-effective syndicates which drew on commercial sponsorship and were run on efficient business lines. The amateur weekend sailors had been replaced by hardened professionals, such as Dennis Conner, who saw absolutely no excuse to lose. Sport and friendly competition were out the window.

Bondy did not instigate this evolution with his crass commercialism in 1974 but was merely a stark by-product of its inevitable development. His blunt words about its being a 'business proposition' simply articulated the new reality. The turning point came when an American defence syndicate calling itself the California International Sailing Foundation gained tax-exempt status with the US Internal Revenue Service (IRS) in mid-1971. The IRS had previously argued that syndicate contributions were no more tax deductible than the costs of a garden party. This ruling allowed contributors to deduct donations from their income tax and changed the nature of the game.[215]

In Australia the Yanchep 'home of the twelves' publicity stunt had been a variation on the same theme. Bond explains how it worked: 'In 1974 we were trying to develop Yanchep Sun City, and in order to get a tax deduction for the America's Cup expenditure, it was necessary to prove that the development of the estate was part of the challenge. It was necessary to demonstrate to the Tax Department that we really thought we could win the Cup.'[216] Yanchep Sun City Pty Ltd and BondCorp would not have been the only beneficiaries of this Australian Taxation Office largesse. The 1974 campaign included $50,000 donations from both Comalco and Amatil. According to Bond 'they had gone into the sponsorship on the understanding that they derived some promotional spin-off from the challenge. And they got that — international publicity.'[217]

Bond had proposed a Bond Foundation to Whitlam in 1974 but the plea fell on deaf ears. The company he set up to run the subsequent campaign, America's Cup Challenge 1977 Ltd, rolled over into America's Cup Challenge 1980 Ltd. It owned the boat and incurred the expenditure. The latest challenge was also being sponsored by Qantas, Channel 7 and Old Spice, among others. Although he was now dealing with a more sympathetic Fraser Liberal government, it was never clearly stated how the tax benefits were distributed between ACC and the individual sponsors, but Bond was not heard complaining publicly about the arrangement he had reached. He could argue, of course, that the expenditure was incurred in the national interest and that, as the US government was indirectly supporting the defence syndicates, an unfavourable ruling from the Australian Taxation Office would disadvantage the Australian effort.

The most likely scenario is that ACC gained stamp duty, sales tax, import duty and other concessions from both the State and Federal governments and that donations to ACC were tax deductible to the sponsors who made the contributions. The major contributors would have been Dallhold and/or BondCorp and, given the windfall profits they were making from sharemarket raids, the tax relief would have been most welcome.

Bond supposedly made his first million when he was twenty-one. Now that he had turned forty-two he was presumedly working on his first billion (crew members were paid $15 a day). He was chairman of ACC and the syndicate boss but the executive director of the challenge campaign was Warren Jones, a BondCorp director, a former Fremantle boy and Bond's minder. 'One of his main duties is to tame Bondy, to keep the boss on a tight leash until he has fed him all the facts,' says sailor-turned-real-estate-developer John Bertrand in his best-selling book *Born to Win*. 'At least then, Alan knows the arguments that will be flying back at him. Warren has become a master at this, and as we left the 1970s and moved into a new decade, Bondy never came out swinging at the New York Yacht Club until he had a meticulously prepared case, beautifully put together by the very, very meticulous Warren Jones.'[218]

But Bondy was not a man easily muzzled. Fellow property developer and yachtsman, Syd Fisher, who had captained Australia's victorious Admiral's Cup team with *Ragamuffin* in 1979, popped in to Newport for a look-see in 1980 and was spotted by Bond. The two had a long-standing and often bitter feud that flared on sight. According to reports, 'Bond ordered Fisher from the *Australia* dock and later from a press conference he was giving.'[219]

Public interest in the America's Cup had reached an all-time high in 1977 — the previous peak being reached in 1962 when the Australians first arrived on the scene — and even more tourists were expected to crowd the tiny town of Newport (population 30,000) in 1980.[220] This was to be Baron Bich's, Ted Turner's and Jim Hardy's last hurrah. But when acceptances closed in May 1978, Bond's name was not among the challengers listed by the NYYC. Royal Perth and Royal Sydney were there but there was no sign of an entry from the Sun City Yacht Club.

At that time, things were still crook in the BondCorp household. The garage sale was in progress and the stork bringing Santos was a distant dream. An ACC 1977 spokesman said the company would not be challenging 'because of the huge cost involved'.[221] Worse still, its two boats, *Southern Cross* and *Australia*, were up for sale. The Americans were reported to be astonished that Bond had failed to make a third challenge and no doubt conveyed that message to him. Bond had been in deeper debt in 1974 and in 1977 but he still turned up for the party.

By September 1978 there had been a change of fortune (Santos shares were soaring) and a change of heart. Warren Jones spoke about Bond being part of a 'WA-based people's boat syndicate'.[222] In October ACC 1980 was reformed and in November Keith Turner, the Bunbury businessman who had issued the earlier challenge in the name of the Royal Perth Yacht Club 'to promote the cause of autistic children' wisely decided there were more direct ways he could help his cause. Bond's ACC 1980 replaced him as the RPYC entry. There would be no new boat, however. *Australia* would be revamped by Lexcen, who would also be tactician, and Hardy would once more take the wheel. First base was reached when Royal Sydney's *Gretel II* syndicate also pulled out.

The Swedes and the British were first eliminated. Bondy's boys came up against the bizarre biro baron and won four out of five races in the final series to become the official challenger. Bich bowed out after squandering millions of dollars on four attempts stretching over ten years. Dennis Conner's *Freedom* ruthlessly eliminated Ted Turner and Russell Long (who had the backing of PanAm and Bacardi Rum) to become the defender. The San Diego draper had been practising full-time for nearly a year for this very moment. It is said that the main thrill in his life came from beating a Space Invaders video slot machine.

Attempting to defy the inevitable with a technological advantage, *Australia* stole the new bendy mast idea from the Poms, but it was too little, too late. Conner won the twenty-fourth defence of the Cup 4–1 but the series did have its moments. *Australia* won race two by 28 seconds in what was described as the best match in the history of the event and the first Australian victory since Hardy's last one on *Gretel II* in 1970. Conner didn't see it that way. He lodged a protest on the grounds that *Australia* didn't have its navigation lights on when it crossed the line after sunset. He was that sort of competitor. To his credit, the protest was later withdrawn. His four victories were by 1:52, 0:53, 3:48 and 3:38.

According to Bertrand, Bondy raced on board his boat at the end of the last race 'full of vim and smiles: "Don't worry, boys," he yelled. "That was great, we gave it our best shot." He didn't seem to give a damn whether we had won or not ... "I have decided," he said, "that we are coming back in 1983 with a major challenge. We'll have the budget and the boat. And we are going to win the America's Cup. Right?"'

CHAPTER ELEVEN

1983: Liberty vs. Australia II, Australia II, *3–4*

Looking back on the three-year lead-up to Alan Bond's final voyage to Newport in search of the Holy Grail, one is struck more by the great helmsman's gross ineptitude than by any pursuit of excellence in the conduct of his affairs. Even with the blinkered benefit of hindsight, it seems almost incomprehensible how a man who had narrowly survived the 1961 credit squeeze and the 1974 property crash — and swore that it would never happen again — could so quickly, and so imprudently, forget those lessons and once again court jeopardy by over-extending limited resources.

Given his erratic circumstances at the time, some of his actions during this period display symptoms which would indicate delusions of grandeur in lesser mortals. But perhaps self-styled 'visionaries' should be judged by different criteria.

There had been no legal instrument governing the sale of strata titles for home units in WA until BondCorp started to sell them in the late 1960s. The law eventually caught up to the reality forced on it by these actions. But corporate law also caught up with some of Alan Bond's sharper business practices in the early 1980s. In 1981 one of the companies in which he was a director suffered the ignominy of receiving the new National Companies and Securities Commission's first 'unacceptable conduct' declaration — the nation's first corporate black mark. In 1983 there was a conviction for breaches of the Companies Act in the Victorian Supreme Court.

He did have some great successes, which went some way toward counterbalancing the notable failures; and he obviously survived this era of ignoble risk-taking, which was a feat in itself. In the end, winning the Cup covered the cracks and the tracks — but close examination of the lead-up leaves one pondering the air of unreality that surrounded much of the preparation for that fateful event. The story of the yellow 'Rose of Texas' gold nugget and its intended home, the Palace Hotel in St Georges Terrace, is a prime example.

In June 1978 BondCorp paid $5.5 million for the Palace Hotel, a wonderful piece of resplendent gold rush architecture, erected in 1896 and classified by the National Trust, as the site for its new corporate headquarters to replace the recently sold International House. This in itself was a controversial move as five years earlier Councillor Bond, then a member of Perth City Council's town planning committee, had fought tooth and nail to stop the Commonwealth Bank from demolishing the hotel in order to build a new high-rise office on the site. At the time it was suggested that Bond's opposition to the Commonwealth Bank's plans related to an option he once held on the building before its purchase by the bank. 'Asked if this influenced his stand, Cr Bond said he regarded the question as impertinent,' a newspaper reported at the time.[223]

In March 1979 Bond paid $18,500 for a fifty-six ounce gold nugget, appropriately named 'Kalgoorlie's Pride', which had been eureka-ed in the goldfields in February by two part-time prospectors. It was thought to be the biggest nugget found in WA for forty years. The plan was for 'Kalgoorlie's Pride' to take pride of place in Bond's Palace Hotel, which continued to trade as such while Bond awaited development approval for the construction of Perth's tallest tower behind it. The pub was patronised by stockbrokers, lawyers and journalists who had organised themselves into a group called the Palace Guard to protect their watering hole.

Then, lo and behold, another nugget (this one maliciously named 'The Rose of Texas'), eight times as big at 419 ounces, turned up on the market on 5 November 1980, just after our boy Bond returned from another post-Cup visit to the Lone Star State to see Perry Bass et al. Of course he just had to have it for the Palace. This one cost him $350,000 and according to Stewart Graham, the metals broker who sold it to him, had been found by 'an anonymous couple' somewhere east of Kalgoorlie in July. Graham was acting for the retired Perth couple, who had informed him that they wanted their identity kept secret for security reasons and vanished back into the bush. But, as it turned out, a rose by any other name would have at least had some smell. This one was a fake. A clever fake, but a fake nonetheless. Salesmen are supposed to be the most gullible of people but that didn't lessen the embarrassment.

The 'Rose of Texas' saga was to jinx the Palace site. A few years later Bond, Beckwith, Mitchell and Oates went to the WA Supreme Court in a vain bid to block publication in Holmes à Court's *Western Mail* newspaper of an allegation that the four had made a personal profit of $3.5 million at the expense of their shareholders through the later on-sale of the site to BondCorp. The magnificent slope-headed edifice, now the R&I tower and BondCorp group world headquarters, was not completed in time for Australia's America's Cup defence, and the lavish Dallhold atrium eyrie at its summit was where the chickens came home to roost when the Tiny (Rowland) pressure was applied to BondCorp in 1989.

Bond can be forgiven for being preoccupied with more weighty matters on his return from Newport in November 1980. In his absence, the BondCorp management triumvirate of Beckwith, Mitchell and Oates had been diligently searching for the fervently required cash cow and had come up with a prime milker in the Swan Brewery Co. Ltd. Mitchell calculated that the brewery was capable of earning $50 million a year in recession-proof cash. Hanging around the sacred cow's neck was a garland of forty-six hotels on freehold land, 10 per cent of the Australian Bank and 49.9 per cent of the Darwin Brewery.

However, there was some urgency concerning this target as it was also in Holmes à Court's sights. The Swan board, fearful that their independence would vanish if the tall one achieved his aim, were seeking friendly 'white knights' to protect them from their perception of Holmes à Court's intentions as a marauding 'black knight'.

But the Swan Brewery was to be a pawn rather than a king-maker in this game. It was very much a victim of its own success, in that it ran Australia's most modern and efficient brewery which had a monopoly in its home market in WA and exported its thirst-quenching Swan and Emu products to over fifty countries. Naturally, its profitability and cash flow made it an object of corporate desire. It was a 'situation' stock because it was in a situation where everyone wanted it.

Swan had board links with Carlton & United Breweries (CUB) in Melbourne through the Cohen family (Montague Cohen, who had masterminded the amalgamation of six Melbourne brewers into CUB in 1907, had founded the Swan Brewery Co. in Melbourne in 1887) and the two brewers jointly owned Northern Territory Breweries. It also had a thoroughly modern management headed by Lloyd Zampatti, who was in Perth Modern School's famous class of 1946 along with Bob Hawke and a host of other notables. Zampatti was so relaxed during his time at the helm that his chauffeur would drive him home for lunch every day.

This meeting between Bond and Holmes à Court was destined to be vastly different from their last encounter on the steps of TVW Enterprises. This time it was Bond who had the inside running with the board and Holmes à Court who was the rank outsider. The Bond interest in Swan was welcomed if not encouraged by Zampatti because the Bond 'Beagle' Boys had assured him they were long-term investors with no predatory designs on the management and the assets of the local brewer. Their primary motive, they assured him, was making money out of trading minerals and energy stocks and property development. The comparatively staid world of running an industrial company was not for them. They merely sought for some of their Santos booty a safe haven which would return steady dividend income.

Zampatti's big mistake was not in believing them but in believing that the Swan Brewery could not be taken over. Their story was certainly plausible and, with the resources boom bubbling away, BondCorp seemed to have its plate full. But Zampatti's defence strategy was not totally reliant on Bond-Corp's stated good intentions. His agenda was to set a thief to catch a thief and to have a policeman standing by in case the victor became unruly. The policeman in this case was to be the Singapore-based Overseas Chinese Banking Corporation (OCBC) and its interlocking network of related companies and 'a staunch friend of the Swan Brewery, having held shares in the group for a least 15 years.'[224]

It should be remembered here that Singapore is closer to Perth than Perth is to Sydney and that the two Indian Ocean cities lie in the same time zone. OCBC and its wily autocrat, Tan Sri Tan Chin Tuan, were long-term thinkers and short-term players in the Australian sharemarkets. OCBC interests had been prominent in the float of Bond's West Australian Land and when the BondCorp Top 20 Shareholders list was first published in May 1974, no fewer than eighteen of them had addresses in Singapore and Malaysia. Bond was proud of this link and obviously thought it would prove useful in the coming battle for Swan: 'We have a long-term relationship with OCBC and I have a personal relationship ... I've been to lunch and dinner at the boardroom there with Tan Chin Tuan since 1974. He was a shareholder in BondCorp and my personal relationship with the bank goes back to the 1970s ... So, when we bought the shares in Swan Brewery, even though the board then ... and certainly he had a visit from a well-known chief executive ... the relationship was such that it was stronger,' he said in his own inimitable manner.[225]

Swan chief executive Zampatti knew the tall man and the fat man loathed each other and he assumed they would each dissipate energy pursuing the other's demise to their mutual destruction. He figured there could be no winner as Swan's monopoly could not be acquired without reference to the Trade Practices Commission. The Singapore bank was to be his defence of last resort, as he figured no one would attempt to outbid a bank.

As the saga developed just before Christmas 1980, Bond-Corp and Holmes à Court's Western Mail Ltd each gained a 10-per-cent foothold in the brewery. Bond jumped to 19.9 per cent when Holmes à Court took a profit and ran away. Bond was still categorically denying any intention of making a bid but Laurie Connell recalls the historic moment when Bond first became a power in the brewing industry: 'I can remember sitting down with him in his study on Christmas eve, scheming out what we were going to do with it and how we had to raise the money by Boxing Day to get the whole thing worked up.'[226]

This took a lot longer than expected. Swan was one of many irons BondCorp had placed in fires around the nation. The seeing off of Holmes à Court had removed the urgency, but without full ownership and management control Bond could not get his hands on Swan's fistful of dollars. Zampatti and OCBC became truculent and were determined to frustrate BondCorp's naked, but not stated, ambition to tap the cash flow. At directors' meetings Bond openly disagreed with Zampatti's investment decisions (the half interest in NT Breweries was sold to CUB in 1981). OCBC were upset because Bond was doing business with the rival Hongkong Bank. 'When you do business with an Asian bank it is done for the long term. They really are looking to be your long-term banker,' said Bond.[227]

Nine months later a full bid was born. Bond made out it was from him, personally, but that was to frustrate the letter of the Trade Practices Act which prohibited corporations, but not explicitly an individual, from acquiring a monopoly without TPC approval. Jaws dropped on trading floors on 1 September 1981 when the $130-million personal bid for the brewery was announced. It was the greatest piece of one-upmanship Australia had witnessed since Captain Francis de Groot had bolted forth from the crowd to cut the ribbon at the Sydney Harbour Bridge opening ceremony in 1932. Jokes flew around about Bond having a big drinking problem. But Bond had made personal bids before. In 1969 he made a direct offer for all the shares in Metro Industries Ltd; and at one stage in 1973, Minsec liquidator Jim Jamison was convinced he was to sell Robe shares to Alan Bond and not to BondCorp.

The bid was for the 80 per cent of Swan not already owned by BondCorp. The document said BondCorp shareholders would be asked to approve a loan of $120 million to Mr Bond in exchange for Mr Bond giving them an option over his 80 per cent. There was little Zampatti could do. Swan's assets were valued in the books at only $78 million and Holmes à Court could not be enticed back into the fray. Talks were held with Castlemaine-Tooheys, the other big eastern seaboard brewer. It started buying but it was swimming against a pro-Bond tide as well as the Trade Practices Act.

However, a stubborn OCBC was determined to spoil Bond's party. It knew the money for the bid was coming from the HKB and it went into the market to build its Swan stake close to 10 per cent so that it could frustrate compulsory acquisition and access to the cash flow. OCBC now had Bond stretched over the barrel. If he wanted the Singapore bank's shares, the Hongkong Bank would have to cough up more money. In October it did just that and on 25 October Bond claimed total victory. Zampatti was gone within a week, crossing the Nullarbor to join rival brewer Castlemaine-Tooheys after ten years at Swan.

The money had come from the HKB but it had been arranged by its new local merchant banking arm Wardley Australia Ltd, which was fast becoming an important conduit in the transfer of Asian money to Australia.[228] It had turned a $1-million commission by acting for Adnan Khashoggi's Southern Pacific Hotel Corporation when it sold the Travelodge motel chain to Singapore businessman Tan Sri Khoo Tek Puat for $98 million. It also acted for the Ho family when they bought Sydney's Hyatt Kingsgate and the Birkenhead Point shopping centre. Its head office had of course funded Bond's Santos play and participated in the syndicate that raised $600 million for the Cooper pipeline development.

Wardley Australia had been formed in 1979 with a paid capital of $20 million and the backing of the HKB and the Tokai Bank of Japan (13 per cent). Within two years it had expanded its asset base from $62 million to $400 million by first merging with Intermarine Australia and then taking over John D G Robinson & Associates. It had two people dealing with the BondCorp relationship: James Yonge from corporate finance and Tony McGrath from corporate lending. While working for Intermarine, McGrath had been one of Bond's saviours in 1974. Yonge had arrived from Hambro Australia just as Bond was plunging into Swan shares. The promissory note discount facility that was offered was short term and would need to be replaced within five years. Security for the Swan loan was by way of a charge over the brewery assets and a personal guarantee from Alan Bond. It was a profitable arrangement for both sides and cemented a firm relationship that had been anointed by the head office in Hong Kong. (HKB chief executive Michael Sandberg and BondCorp chief executive Alan Bond often lunched at the top of the HKB building overlooking Hong Kong Harbour.)

Brilliant though the acquisition was, it immediately added $160 million to BondCorp's debt profile of about $100 million at 30 June 1981. No matter how clever you are, it is difficult to imagine how a quarter of a billion dollars worth of debt can be carried when you are earning profits of less than $10 million a year. And interest rates, which had already climbed from 10 per cent to 15 per cent since January 1980, were heading towards 20 per cent. Alas, the question seems never to have been asked, although Bond did say he had plans to raise $120 million from share and option issues in the near future. Instead all eyes were glued to BondCorp's dazzling displays on the floor of the stock exchange.

Back around the same time as the 'Rose of Texas' gold nugget scam and at the outset of the Swan move, Bond's 'Beagle' Boys were putting on a great floor show. On 3 November 1980, Endeavour outlaid $17.5 million for the Rhondda Colliery near Ipswich in southern Queensland. The coalminer's son had finally become a colliery owner. Would his uncles and cousins in Monmouthshire have been proud of him? It is doubtful that they ever heard about it. His mother was, though; but then she always knew he would rise above his station. Rhondda was followed by the acquisition of the Great Greta open-cut coalmine at Singleton in New South Wales. They were both part of his energy push and proved that the move on White Industries was genuine and not a greenmail attempt. BondCorp also had about 10 per cent of Griffin Coal Mining Co., which had a mine at Collie in the West.

More fanciful and, as it turned out, just as foolish as the 'Rose' purchase was Endeavour's plunge into the aptly named Rabbit Warren gold prospect near Leonora in WA. Nearly $8 million disappeared down this hole with nothing of substance ever coming to the surface. But some gold plays were profitable, notably Nannine and Ingliston near Meekatharra. These mines were said to return a profit of $5 million in little over a year. Bond's fascination with goldmines later became an obsession and he collected them the way little boys collected swap cards.

But it was the pursuit of diamonds that was to get Alan Bond into more trouble than he could ever have imagined. There was nothing wrong with the desire — but the way he went about satisfying it was found wanting and landed him in the courts, where he received a heavy admonishment. Like diamonds, the tarnish on his reputation from that court appearance would last forever.

In December 1969, at the peak of the Poseidon share boom, Northern Mining Corporation NL (NMC) listed on the stock exchange as an iron ore explorer. By 1978 it had become famous and desirable for its diamond interests in the Kimberleys. NMC had a 5 per cent stake in a consortium that had found the fabulously rich AK-1 pipe near Lake Argyle on the WA-Northern Territory border. It was one of the world's most extensive diamond deposits, capable of producing up to 25 million carats a year when fully developed and impacting on the South African-controlled cartel's Central Selling Organisation which had a monopoly on the world marketing of the 'girl's best friend'. Endeavour Resources had 20 per cent of NMC but as the two other Argyle joint venturers were foreign controlled there was a strong possibility that foreign investment guidelines would force up the NMC stake in the project.

Bond was keen to get a major cash producer into Endeavour so that it could pay its own way within the Bond-Corp group and so a decision was made in 1981 to acquire all of NMC and consolidate some sparkle in Endeavour. But a full bid for NMC would cost in the order of $50 million cash and both BondCorp and Endeavour were absolutely strapped for cash at the time, as every cent they had was tied-up in various market plays. It was pointless putting the hard word on his bankers as they were loath to lend at the speculative end of the mining market — even for something as hard as diamonds.

On 29 May Bond sent this fascinating communication to the National Mutual Life Association: 'This is to confirm my company's guarantee for a client which is not known to you, the following purchases: 1: 3,000,082 shares in Northern Mining, partly and fully paid shares. 2: The purchase price is A$3.50 per share. 3: The date of settlement is 7 July 1981 in Melbourne, Australia.'[229]

The buyer of this $10.5-million 20-per-cent stake in NMC may have been a mystery but the seller was quite clearly the National Mutual Life Association. As is required by the Companies Act, the seller notified NMC within fourteen days of a change in its substantial shareholding. NML's notice went to NMC on 10 June. There was not a peep from the mystery buyer who was also required by law to send a substantial shareholder notice. NML was acting under legal advice that, following the Bond letter, it had sold the NMC shares even though settlement would not take place for another five weeks. This timing is important.

If BondCorp had been acting as principal, rather than agent for the mystery buyer, it would have a deemed interest in 40 per cent of NMC's capital and therefore have exceeded the 20 per cent takeover threshold and so be required to make an immediate full bid for NMC. That would have cost an extra $35 million on top of the $10.5 million and Endeavour didn't have it. NMC waited five days — till 15 June — before informing the stock exchange about the NML disposal notice. When the news hit the market it inevitably led to speculation that the parcel had gone to a BondCorp associate or had been parked in a friendly warehouse. This was strenuously denied by a BondCorp spokesman who said he knew of no recent purchase of NMC shares 'by the Bond Corporation or any of its associates'.[230]

Meanwhile, BondCorp had come up with $30 million from a property deal. On 25 June, Bond went to an Endeavour board meeting and offered them the NML parcel on behalf of an unidentified offshore purchaser and it was accepted. On 7 July, Endeavour told the stock exchange it had bought the controversial stake and would be launching a full bid for NMC at $3.64 a share. When Endeavour's Part A statement relating to the takeover was released on 27 August 1981, it listed BondCorp and the ANZ Bank as the source of its funds for the takeover.

But the Melbourne Stock Exchange was not happy about the lack of disclosure relating to movement of the mystery parcel from NML to Endeavour on 7 July. For more than a month the market in NMC shares had been seriously uninformed about a potential takeover offer. During that period nearly 200,000 NMC shares had traded on the Melbourne and Sydney stock exchanges at $3 or less. On 29 May, the date of Bond's confirmation letter to NML, NMC shares were selling at $2.60 — a substantial discount to the eventual bid price of $3.64 a share.[231] The Victorian Corporate Affairs Commission suspected that a breach of the Companies Code had occurred and launched an official inquiry into the transaction. This led to a conviction in 1983 for failure to issue substantial shareholding notices covering the acquisition. A subsequent appeal against the conviction was lost on 27 June 1984.

In early September 1981 Endeavour withdrew its bid for NMC, citing delays in the start-up of the Argyle diamond mine as a change in circumstance. But Bondy could not take a trick with this ploy either. On 7 September the National Companies and Securities Commission used its influence to get the bid reinstated. But the new offer was conditional on litigation over cross claims to the Argyle deposit being satisfactorily resolved. On 9 September NMC went to court in an attempt to get the original unconditional Endeavour offer reinstated. The next day the NCSC publicly declared the revised offer to be 'unacceptable'.

It was the first time the regulatory body that grew out of the abuses of the Poseidon share boom had made an 'unacceptable conduct' declaration. The NCSC was operating in uncharted waters, unsure of its powers, but when it threw down the gauntlet at Endeavour's feet, Bond backed away. By late September, Endeavour had not only agreed effectively to reinstate its original offer for NMC but to raise the offer price slightly to compensate shareholders for lost time. The takeover was successful but had proved more costly that first thought and didn't provide Endeavour with the immediate cash producer it now desperately needed to service its heavy debt burden.

On 29 June 1983, NMC's 5-per-cent interest in the Argyle diamond mine was transferred to BondCorp for $43 million with a more tarnished image. It was essential to preserve the remaining value in the investment and the only way to do that was to realise the asset. As its real market value was probably closer to $23 million at the time, a friendly buyer had to be found. Four months later it would be on-sold to Brian Burke's new Labor State government for $42 million and WA Inc., mark 2, was open for business. The government's financial adviser in the deal was Laurie Connell. The corporate shell of Northern Mining Corporation NL would become WA Government Holdings Ltd. Sir Charles Court's Liberal State Development Office would be replaced on the fourteenth floor of BondCorp head office at International House with Brian Burke's Labor West Australian Development Corporation (WADC).

The new WA Inc. relationship between government and business was slightly more 'interventionist' than Charlie Court's had been but also more 'corporatist' in its approach to making money. Burkie and his mates ended up making a packet out of Bondy's troublesome Argyle diamonds — first by screwing the Argyle joint venturers for $50 million in return for not forcing them to build a $70-million company town at the mine site in the Kimberleys. The first $42 million of this went to BondCorp for all the issued capital of NMC.

Then the WADC created the $65-million WA Diamond Trust which bought the Argyle diamond interest from the government for $45 million. It then turned around and flogged off sixty million $1 units to the public and gave the WADC $5 million worth of units for arranging the deal and making it bankable. It did this by undertaking a contingent liability to guarantee a synthetic income for the trust for seven years. Then a temporary loophole in the tax laws of the Hawke Labor government in Canberra was exploited to allow investment in the units to be tax effective.

The special arrangement between the Burke government and his 'four-on-the-floor entrepreneur' mates was formalised in the public announcement of the establishment of the John Curtin Foundation on 12 September 1984. Its patrons were Burke and three former Labor premiers, John Tonkin, Bert Hawke and Frank Wise. 'The vice patrons are drawn from the biggest and the richest of Perth's magnates, developers and businessmen,' said the advertisement. It named Alan Bond, Mick Michael, Sir Ernest Lee-Steere, Laurie Connell, John Roberts, Sir James McCusker, John Horgan, Dennis Cullity, Rod Evans, Kevin Parry and Rick Stowe. The foundation was to be a $5-million ALP slush fund with a minimum entry fee of $100,000. The tax deductibility of donations was also being examined. In an historic compromise between the forces of capital and the forces of labour, a 'sweetheart' deal had been set up and Alan Bond was out of diamonds and into politicians again.

He lost money on diamonds because he had paid too much and the investment turned sour. It had become more a sacred cow than a cash cow and he was lucky to escape in the way he did. His flirtation with the stones had also been very damaging to his reputation because of his regular run-ins with the regulatory authorities. That was ultimately bad for business. Conservative bankers don't like to see that sort of thing at the best of times, let alone when interest rates on 90-day bills are up over 20 per cent as they were in early 1982.

Bond also spent two years trying to turn a quid in the retail industry from early 1981 but his efforts here turned into another management disaster. In accordance with the Price Waterhouse corporate plan, he was seeking a steady income stream of cash sufficient to service both debt and equity, much like the brewery business promised to be. But Bond never seemed to have the patience required to handle these two slow-moving, but cash-generating core commercial businesses and he bungled them both, through a combination of wilful interference in their workings, over-ambitious expansion and bad timing. In the property and resources fields he could do million-dollar deals at the stroke of a pen. But running a shop required the mundane cutting of costs and counting of cents and therefore lacked entrepreneurial appeal. He was psychologically more suited to being a buyer than a seller — despite his reputation as a super salesman.

He wanted to add value to the retail business by becoming big in the industry fast and then participating in the rationalisation of its assets and the monopoly of its cash flows. But he got ahead of himself and was caught when economic conditions changed and he couldn't afford to hang on any longer. In trying to do too much too soon he was driven further into the arms and the control of the moneylenders. In the end Bond was forced by his bankers to make a choice between being a retailer and being a brewer. He chose the latter but his reputation as a picker of winners and a solid industrialist was severely dented by the experience.

The saga of Bond the shopkeeper began innocently enough in 1981 and ran concurrently with his moves on the Swan Brewery and Northern Mining. An optimistic Bond had begun the year in high spirits, sending his shareholders 'warm greetings for the year ahead ... another year of sharing with you the benefits of our corporate progress.'

The thing that Bond liked about retailers was not just the cash in their tills but the prime real estate their department stores sat on. BondCorp had not had a decent injection of new assets into its property portfolio since the Savoy takeover in the early 1970s. It also had a load of slow-moving residential

developments, such as Taylors Lakes in Victoria and the Gold
Coast land in Queensland, which it wanted to dump or joint
venture because of their high carrying costs. By tying property
development to the retail industry, Bond saw major financing
benefits. Not only would the money from the cash registers
service the interest on old and new borrowings but the
interest bill could be offset by making it deductible from the
retailing profits.

Housing starts, retail sales and interest rates are three key
economic indicators of the health of an economy. At the
beginning of 1981, Waltons Ltd, the Sydney-based retail chain,
couldn't see the direct connection between them but it would
soon learn. Waltons began as Cash Orders (Amalgamated) Ltd
in 1926. After surviving the Depression years it bought a
furniture store in Sydney's Haymarket. After World War II, it
expanded rapidly through its association with the giant Sears
Roebuck & Co. of the USA. The partnership ended in 1959 but
the relationship endured, with the Sears buying offices in New
York supplying Waltons stores with imports. By 1968 the
company had fifty-three homeware stores and twelve department stores in New South Wales, Victoria and Queensland.

In 1966 the First National City Bank of New York (Citibank), Bondy's old friends from Newport and the eventual
controllers of IAC, bought a half share in Waltons Credit
Corporation Ltd, renamed it FNCB-Waltons Corporation Ltd
and began a rapid expansion of its credit facilities. Aspects of
this business would later be criticised by consumer affairs
groups for alleged loan sharking and other acts of usury.
Waltons also formed an insurance subsidiary.

By the early 1980s the retailer had lost its direction and
much of its panache. The recession, unemployment and the big
drought had hit the group harder than other retailers.
Waltons' traditional customers were down-market, mostly in
the middle- to lower middle-income bracket and sensitive to
changes in economic conditions. There was also a heavy
reliance on the level of rural income, with 50 per cent of retail
sales coming from country areas in New South Wales and
Queensland. Retail sales had turned around briefly in 1980 and
the company had reorganised its operations by closing down
non-profitable ventures and selling the insurance company to
gain liquidity.

Bond could have met chairman John Stuart Walton, the son of Sir John Walton and the holder of a Master of Business Administration degree from Stanford, at the Cruising Yacht Club in Sydney. Waltons' adviser was Mark Johnson, who also knew Bond because he had been on the Robe River board. When Sydney broker Bain & Co. put a proposition to BondCorp to assist Waltons to fend off takeover moves, Bond was immediately interested. The rag trade had been first to spot the break-up potential in Waltons when Abe Goldberg and John Gandel bought in. They sold to Melbourne's Liberman family in late 1980. From a base of 20 per cent, the Libermans launched a $1-a-share takeover offer on 23 February 1981, which valued the company at $37 million. The asset backing of the shares was $1.80. As if on impulse, Bond began buying Waltons shares.

Within three days he had wrapped up 30 per cent of the capital and launched a $1.10 on-market bid for the rest. The Libermans capitulated in March and Bond was left holding 76 per cent of the capital. The defence had been too successful. Bond wanted Waltons as an associate, not as a subsidiary. He announced he was selling down his interest to a maximum 49 per cent but not before Narcissus had renamed the company Waltons Bond. Wardleys had arranged the finance for the takeover and introduced Bond to the big Hong Kong property developer, Carrian Investments Ltd, which eventually took 14.9 per cent of the Waltons Bond equity.

Alan Bond's quid pro quo for rescuing John Walton soon became apparent. On 12 May, Waltons Bond announced it was paying $30.3 million cash for the BondCorp property portfolio in New South Wales and Queensland. Waltons Bond would borrow $25 million in new debt and take on BondCorp's existing property debt. It was an extremely good deal for BondCorp and could not have come at a more fortuitous time. The deal was approved by Waltons Bond shareholders on 12 June and the funds were immediately available to finance Endeavour's takeover of Northern Mining, which was launched within two weeks. In early August, Waltons Bond announced a share issue to raise $11.6 million. On 11 November, Waltons Bond paid BondCorp $27 million for the Taylors Lakes development in Melbourne.

Bond had now recouped all the money he had outlaid on Waltons, had shifted the property debt off-balance-sheet and still had control of the assets. Carrian latter formed a joint-venture company with Waltons Bond to purchase the Park Street, Sydney, site of Waltons' major store for $30 million and the Taylors Lakes shopping centre development site for $20 million. A vigorous sale-and-lease-back program was undertaken, with plans to raise $85 million by selling the freehold to the company's sixty stores.

The property deals aside, Bond's management contribution to solving Waltons Bond's retailing nightmare was a simple one. Bond wanted either to be big in retailing or to be out of it. He figured that retailers obviously didn't know anything about the business because they didn't make enough money out of it. The visionary helmsman wanted to put Sydney's up-market Grace Bros Holdings chain together with Waltons and dominate the market from top to bottom. Bond's strategy toward the industry's rationalisation was essentially correct — Myer would later get together with Coles, and David Jones with Woolworths — but he was way ahead of his time and there were too many big names standing in front of him.

The battle for Grace Brothers (GBs) got under way in June 1982, with Bond cashed up on new Santos profits. He quickly moved to 20 per cent, where he was opposed by John Spalvins's Adsteam group (which owns David Jones) and the Grace family, both also on 20 per cent, and Tan Sri Khoo Tek Puat on 18 per cent. Woolworths attempted to break the stalemate by making a $196-million share-swap bid for GBs. Bond became momentarily distracted from the task at hand in July when he bought the controlling interest in ailing down-market retailer, Norman Ross Discounts Ltd, from GBs for about $13 million. It was a bad buy.

In August the GBs board recommended the Woolworths offer but also disclosed a much lower profit than was anticipated. Woolworths withdrew the offer and legal attempts to get it reinstated failed in December. Bond was locked in, with nowhere to go. In February 1983 Bond attempted to sell his retailing interests to GBs but they were not interested. Then Myer Emporium entered the fray by buying Tan Sri Khoo Tek Puat's interest. Although a late starter, Myer was as keen to get GBs as BondCorp was and it had support from the Grace family.

On 30 March, BondCorp decided to go the whole hog. It

launched an all-paper bid which valued GBs at $235.9 million.
BondCorp planned to issue 8 per cent cumulative redeemable
preference shares to pay for the takeover. Only John Spalvins
was interested in Bond's paper. The rest of the GBs shareholders rushed to accept Myer's lower, but cash-based, counter offer when it was made on 6 May. BondCorp capitulated and
sold its 40 per cent to Myer just before the 30 June 1983
balance date. This freed up $80 million but left Bond with two
retailing dogs — Waltons Bond and Norman Ross — and a $38-
million debt to John Spalvins's Adsteam which had to be
serviced and repaid. Waltons Bond's property interests were
sold back to BondCorp in 1986 and the retailing operations
were finally sold to Venture Stores in 1987.

Numerous other money-making schemes were attempted
and deals done in the early 1980s but none was as fundamental
as the moves into brewing, diamonds and retailing. One of
them, the attempted takeover of the US company, Simplicity
Patterns Inc., in late 1981, pointed to BondCorp's future global
direction. It also involved a grab for $169 million in surplus
cash, the side-streaming of funds from the associate company,
Waltons Bond, and a string of hopeful bankers led by Wardleys/
HKB, and was accident prone — ending in May 1982 with a
$7.3-million loss.

Another scheme, the bail-out of Western Continental Corporation Ltd in December 1981, involved Bond's two close
friends Laurie Connell and Joseph Maxim (Yosse) Goldberg
and is also instructive. Goldberg and his partner Ron Wise
controlled Western Continental, which had got into difficulties
as the resources boom petered out and the recession rushed
forward. This gung-ho pair of stock exchange entrepreneurs
had survived the Poseidon nickel boom in the late 1960s and
emerged in the late 1970s as deal-doers and money miners in
the archetypal Perth tradition. They bought several moribund
companies at share prices of one or two cents and husbanded
capital appreciations of at least 20 or 30 times their initial
investment. In the process, they accumulated some promising
assets, but without cash flow they could not service the high
interest rates on their borrowings.

When liquidity haemorrhaged, most of their friends deserted them. 'It was a classic problem of borrowing short on the
expectation of long-term gain,' said one. 'It is one talent to

make money in a boom. Survival is another,' said another.[232] In December 1980, Goldberg and Wise had bought the old Swan Brewery site on the river in Mounts Bay Road from Lloyd Zampatti of the Swan Brewery Co. Western Continental paid $4 million for the site in the expectation that it could get planning approval for a high-rise office/restaurant complex. It couldn't. But a year later Alan Bond and Laurie Connell would help them out by becoming owners of the old brewery for a day (by now, Bond owned the new brewery at Canning Vale as well). Goldberg and Wise were later to claim that they lost $900,000 in the buy-back on the twenty-four hour Swan brewery deal. It was eventually sold to the Burke government for $5 million.

Bond was competing in the 1981 Sydney-to-Hobart when BondCorp led the $65-million rescue of Western Continental. Its most valuable asset was its controlling interest in Eastern Petroleum Australia Ltd, which had rights to the Woodada gas field in the Perth Basin. Bond and Connell also took on the 2450-hectare Brigadoon estate on the upper Swan as a joint venture. This is still in the BondCorp accounts and was where Bond planned to build his National Equestrian Centre. Some CBD properties were also acquired from Western Continental. In October 1982 BondCorp also bailed out Austmark International Ltd, another property developer, by underwriting a $35-million share issue which left BondCorp with about 31 per cent of the company. Austmark owned the land at Scarborough Beach where Observation City would be built. It also bought the Palace Tower from BondCorp.

The up-streaming of management fees, royalty rights, commissions and other considerations from BondCorp and Endeavour to Dallhold Investments Pty Ltd became prevalent in the early 1980s. When Endeavour bought the Rhondda Colliery for $17.5 million in November 1980, Dallhold got the royalty rights to the coal. In September 1982 it offered to sell these royalty rights to the shareholders of Pacific Copper Ltd for $6 million. They were eventually sold to BondCorp for $5 million on 29 June 1983. The Rhondda mine site was sold at the same time (and, thankfully, to the same buyer) for $28 million.

Despite its name, which is a legacy from the nickel boom, Pacific Copper Ltd was a substantial coal producer in the lower Hunter Valley, New South Wales, and owned the Great Greta Colliery. In 1982 Endeavour had 20 per cent of the company but wanted more. It gained board control in December but the NCSC stepped in and suspended trading in Endeavour shares on 14 January 1983, after examining recent trade in Pacific shares. The NCSC claimed that Endeavour shareholders were not adequately informed about loans of almost $8 million from Endeavour to two small private companies which held about 19 per cent of Pacific's capital. The commission said the shares were sold by the borrowers in November 1982 at a 'substantial loss'. It queried the chances that the loans would be repaid.[233]

The suspension was lifted on 19 January when Endeavour convinced the NCSC that BondCorp had guaranteed to make good any losses that Endeavour incurred on the loans. On 5 May, BondCorp bid for Pacific Copper on-market and immediately gained the 19 per cent parcel that had been owned by the companies supported by the Endeavour loans. The NCSC re-opened its investigation into Pacific share trading but Bond-Corp had moved to 63 per cent of the capital and wrote off a $7.5-million provision against loans to an 'external party' as a non-recurring, extraordinary cost. Pacific Copper's Great Greta Colliery finally joined Rhondda in BondCorp's coal division just as Alan Bond was sailing to victory in the America's Cup in September 1983.

A plan for a casino licence at Hope Island on the Gold Coast never got the go-ahead but Skipper Caravans Pty Ltd was sold for a $1.2-million profit on 7 October 1982 and sent to the 'bottom of the harbour' in what appeared to be a tax avoidance scheme. In March 1981 BondCorp invested $300,000 in a three-year sponsorship of the South Melbourne Football Club for 'commercial and other reasons'. South Melbourne would become the Sydney Swans Australian Football League team. The deal resulted from a chance remark to new Federal MP and the Swans number-one ticket holder, Mr Bob Hawke, that Bond 'would like to involve himself' with a Melbourne football club.[234] Bond would later become president of the Richmond Football Club but would resign ten days after taking office.

Despite, or because of, all this frantic concurrent activity, BondCorp managed to find itself facing a $250-million debt crisis in February 1982. The dimensions of this crisis were twice as large as the one that nearly brought it down in 1974. Like in the 1970s, Bond claimed that he had plenty of assets to meet the deficiency but his new bankers were convinced that

Bond had gone 'over the top' and would have to be brought to ground. No exceptions could be made for him this time as the whole economy was in recession. Interest rates were peaking at 22 per cent, commodity prices had plunged and company profits were falling over like nine pins. The onslaught of the worst drought this century didn't help. Even beer sales were down.

The Hongkong and Shanghai Bank considered BondCorp's debt-to-equity ratio simply outrageous, given the troubled times. BondCorp was paying out much more in interest than it was earning in real profits. The interest bill had doubled from $7.1 million to $14.9 million in 1980–81. In the December half-year it had risen from $6.8 million to $11 million. The bill would double again in 1981–82 from $14.9 million to $31.5 million. This was not considered prudent. The Taipan in Hongkong ordered BondCorp to reduce its debt by $200 million by selling assets. It was time to pay for the lunches with Sandberg atop the HKB.

The brewery had only just been acquired, there were no liquids flowing yet from Santos, the diamond carats had not filtered down from Argyle, the Waltons cash registers were empty and property was selling only to Waltons Bond. More than half of BondCorp's 1980–81 profit of $10.8 million had come from the sale of property to Waltons Bond. The 1981–82 profit figure would be down to $4.3 million. Bond's situation was serious but he didn't see it that way or necessarily agree with the way the bank chose to interpret the figures.

He said in an press interview at the time that the Swan Brewery was sitting on an enormous cash flow 'averaging $50 million to $60 million annually. To a group of our size that is particularly important.' He also said Waltons was 'under-understood'. Bond claimed that Waltons Bond 'currently held more than $200 million of property assets with not more than a 10 per cent mortgage on all of them.' He attempted to minimise the impact of the increasing interest rates on the company: 'If you take our total corporate borrowings, which are in the order of $250 million, a 5 per cent increase (in interest rates from 15 to 20 per cent) means that over 12 months you have got to find an extra $12 million. And $12 million, while it is important, is not hugely significant even if it's compared with just the Swan Brewery's expected cash flow. People just haven't done their sums,' said Bond.[235]

But the market had. The crunch came on 25 February 1982, when BondCorp's share price collapsed to $1.50 in what the *Financial Review* called a 'savage selling attack'. In January the shares had been selling at $2.50 and Bond's broker, Jacksons, was maintaining that they were worth $7.40 a share. In the week before the bear attack they had been trading at $2.15. The frantic selling that week wiped more than $30 million off BondCorp's market capitalisation and would have cost Bond and Dallhold more than $15 million in lost paper profits.

The run on BondCorp scrip was based on widespread and intense market rumours that the company was 'sliding into a financial abyss'. Although this view could be supported by a cursory glance at the figures in the balance sheet and a quick comparison with the ruling interest rate for 90-day bills in late February, the *Financial Review* reported that 'some had heard it from London, some from Hong Kong. One punter even based the rumour on a suggestion that backers of Bond's latest quixotic tilt at the America's Cup were getting cold feet.'[236] Bond had been in Hong Kong the previous week and, no doubt, had talks with the HKB about reducing his debt levels. That much was common knowledge. He had then gone on to New York and London, where he was on the twenty-fifth, the day the scrip hit the fan. But the purpose of these visits related to the $200-million takeover that BondCorp and its British associate NCC Energy Ltd had launched for Simplicity Patterns Inc.

Bond later claimed that the panic selling had been inspired by a misdirected telex which had created a peculiar situation: 'It was based on a telex that was sent incorrectly, he said. The telex was background information on interest payments on Waltons Bond's purchase of a 13.3 per cent interest in Simplicity Patterns Inc. of New York. Mr Bond was negotiating the deal in New York at the time and the telex was wrongly sent to a media service. By the time Mr Bond realised what had happened the information had filtered back to Australia and the rumours which precipitated the spectacular price slide had started.'[237]

This 'background information' on Waltons Bond's debt scheduling must have been dynamite to cause the implosion in the BondCorp share price that it did. Wardleys had organised Waltons Bond's $27-million acquisition of the 13.3-per-cent stake in Simplicity. The other bankers to Waltons Bond were the Commonwealth Bank and the French merchant bank,

Société Générale Australia Holdings Ltd. There were some market doubts about Bond's partner in the Simplicity play, the mysterious NCC Energy Ltd. NCC held another 15.4 per cent of Simplicity and Waltons Bond may have been financing that stake as well. By coincidence, in December 1981, NCC had purchased from Bond a 40-per-cent interest in two goldmines for $20 million. Simplicity had about 55 per cent of the world market for paper dressmaking patterns but that was not Bond's reason for buying. The US company was rudderless but was sitting on $169 million worth of surplus cash. Bond and NCC had 'plans to introduce new activities to revitalise the company.'[238] Perhaps the scare was somewhere in here and involved the sale of BondCorp's energy interests in the Cooper Basin to an offshore group. When the deal fell over two months later Bond had to write off a loss of $7.3 million on the play.

With Bond on the first plane back from London, Bond-Corp's number-two head-kicker, Peter Beckwith, was left to halt the slide and field the Perth Stock Exchange's customary query to directors as to the reason for the shake-out. In particular, Perth had wanted to know whether there were any matters of importance that the board was about to announce to the exchange and, if there were, could it do so immediately? Beckwith's answer was No. He was obviously in possession of information which was not generally available to the public but he didn't consider that responsible for a market slide of this proportion. Beckwith denied the market rumours that the sell-off was related to the group's financial position: 'We have heard a number of rumours and there is no substance to them. I can therefore only wonder and speculate as to the motivation of anyone spreading those rumours. There is no reason of any substance for the fall in the price of the company's shares. Our security position is absolutely intact,' he said.[239]

When Bond returned, he was unruffled by the run that had just cost him $15 million: 'We do not have any exposure to problems whatsoever. The rise in interest rates was well budgeted for. Anyone who did not budget for high interest rates is dumb,' he said.[240] While he spoke, Beckwith was putting the finishing touches on a deal which would not only halt the market slide but go some way to solve the company's deep-seated debt problem. On 2 March, BondCorp launched a $43-million cash bid for the outstanding capital in Reef Oil and

Basin Oil, the two junior partners in the Cooper Basin project. Bond may have been restricted to 15 per cent of Santos but there was nothing stopping him swallowing these minnows, provided the price was right and he had the money.

BondCorp had arranged a short-term Wardleys/HKB facility to cover the cash bids but his bankers knew what his game plan was. The object of the exercise was to restore market confidence by showing that the company still had enough money to splash about and the support of its bankers. The hidden agenda was that Bond was not buying deeper into the Cooper Basin but selling out altogether so that he could reduce his debt to the HKB. It was a bluff and a blind but it worked. Had the market known that BondCorp was about to lose its most valuable asset, the share price may have come down sooner and further. A negative had been turned into a positive.

BondCorp sold its major interests in Reef and Basin for about $53 million on 1 June after its bids were rejected as being too low. The buyers were National Mutual Life (which twelve months earlier had sold/not sold Bond the crucial 20-per-cent mystery stake in Northern Mining) and the Australian arm of the Bankers Trust of New York. On 2 June the Santos parcel also went to National Mutual, for $137 million. Those two sales in early June 1982 totalled $190 million, which was close to the figure that the HKB had been looking for in the controlled liquidation. In theory, the big debt reduction should have been evident in the 30 June 1982 accounts. It wasn't. They showed that total debt had risen from $140.7 million to $170.8 million and total liabilities were up from $156 million to $237 million. Trading profit was down from $10.8 million to $4.3 million, but Bond was able to book a profit of $47 million on extraordinary items (the Cooper profits minus the Simplicity losses).

Western Australia's biggest company had survived another crisis by selling the family silver at the last moment, but it was far from being out of the woods. Luckily for Bond, the 1983 results did not come out until after he won the America's Cup. They were extremely disappointing. There was no big boost to revenue, operating profit edged up only slightly to $6.8 million, there was a loss of $12.2 million on extraordinaries and the interest bill hit a new high of $40.4 million. Total liabilities were up to $276.6 million. But by the time he'd won the Cup nobody cared about the red ink, the danger signals and the poor performance written in the 1983 balance sheet. The cover of the 1982–83 annual report has a full-colour picture of *Australia II* flying down-wind under spinnaker off Newport. There were plenty of pretty pictures inside, too, but the accounts were tucked away inside the back cover.

Given that the balance sheet was still in tatters in 1983, it is hard to say how Bond survived the 1982 crisis. The assets-and-cash-flow argument looks pathetic next to the reality of the indebtedness and the profit performance. But the HKB was happy and that was the main thing. It can't have been easy for him to dump the Santos stock, but then he hadn't wanted to sell the Robe parcel either. He grossed about $250 million out of the Cooper Basin experience and it allowed him to ride free into new industries and to keep the HKB wolf from the door. If he hadn't had it to fall back on, we may never have heard of him again. He was not responsible for the skyrocketing interest rates, but he was responsible for the debt build-up which was subject to them. The 1982 crisis had not been helped by his regular run-ins with the regulatory authorities. He made himself a prime target, in that, according to the responses of the NCSC and the Victorian Corporate Affairs Commission to his actions, he appeared to be engaging in sharp practices and much bending of the rules.

It is no coincidence that Alan Bond stepped down as chief executive of BondCorp on 20 July 1982, just after the immediate crisis had passed. Peter Beckwith got the nod (over Mitchell, Oates, Jones and new boy Alan Birchmore) to become managing director. Bond remained executive chairman but was relieved of many day-to-day management tasks. There would be no change of style, as his frontline men were fashioned in the same mould as the great helmsman. Bond could now concentrate on the thing he did best — looking for new business opportunities and doing deals. He could also concentrate full-time on winning the America's Cup.

The 1982 crash was essentially a crisis of confidence in BondCorp by the sharemarket. The market could not bring Bond down because he was not dependent on equity capital to survive. Thanks to the existence of the entrepreneurial Dallhold, he was not dependent on the BondCorp dividends either. He needed the goodwill of his bankers for the debt capital that he ran off much more than he needed the goodwill of his shareholders for the equity capital. More than half of it was his anyway. Bond thought the market was dumb: 'We have a philosophy that the market doesn't necessarily record the value of anything other than what people are prepared to pay on the day. It can be over-priced or under-priced,' said Bond, and he should know.[241]

In the end, Alan Bond survived his third corporate crisis because he won the America's Cup.

It was Ben Lexcen who took the Cup from the New York Yacht Club on 26 September 1983, with his brilliant winged-keel design for *Australia II*, but it was Alan Bond who accepted the trophy. Who knows what would have happened had this victory not taken place. It was extremely doubtful that Baron Bond would have continued his quixotic quest for the Auld Mug. But in some ways Bond had already extracted maximum value from his involvement in the competition. It had brought him social positioning, valuable contacts and great wealth, even though he had won only one race in his thirteen encounters in 1974, 1977 and 1980. Winning in 1983 was the cream but it was to be oh so close. Without that win, BondCorp definitely faced a black hole. He may have been sucked in but he might just as easily have pole-vaulted it and come up somewhere else with a huge grin on his face.

I have fond memories of that last Newport summer. As a schoolboy I had followed the fortunes of Frank Packer's *Gretel* with a Boys' Own sense of adventure and excitement. Being there for the big one was the thrill of a lifetime for this enamoured amateur. It was magnificent theatre but it was the theatre of the absurd. Here were grown men going down to the sea to play in boats, with no purpose other than to win a baroque silver ewer. The tangible prize contained 134 ounces of silver. The intangible prize is incalculable. The magic was not in the Cup but in doing something that hadn't been done for 132 years. And Bond did it.

Probability theory has it that the odds improve with every challenge. If that is the case, Sir Thomas Lipton and Baron Bich set the stage for Bond's victory. Business theory has it that to win the prize you must simply be in the right place at the right time. Bond's pugnacity was undeniably a big factor. He virtually talked the New York Yacht Club into handing it over. The salesman's guile combined with the designer's technological breakthrough won the day and the twenty-fifth defence was lost.

Daring to win is probably another ingredient worth exploring. Had Bond lost again in 1983, he would have been crucified for the extravagant waste of time and money and labelled a born loser. The epitaph would have been anathema to the 45-year-old wheeler-dealer from Perth, who had been called many things in his thirty years in business, but never a loser. Bond's companies had always played for high stakes on borrowed money and with the cards held very close to the chest. Three times in his bewildering career, the established players and the banker had called his bluff in an attempt to force him from the table. But each time he came up with the goods. He hadn't played according to Hoyle but he had won.[242]

The risk he took in going to Newport for the fourth time was real enough but it was inconsequential when compared with the risks he was taking every day in his office above Perth. Bond thrived on challenges. During the 1981 Admiral's Cup series at Cowes, Bond was challenged by Peter de Savary, a British property developer with a thirst for the limelight, to a match race in their boats the next day. As the dare was delivered over dinner and much wine in an Isle of Wight restaurant, a wager of 10,000 pounds in Krugerand gold coins was put on the outcome. There was no winner in the race as the three-and-a-half-hour time limit elapsed with Bond's boat twelve minutes from the finish line. Bond's response was to count the cost of the lost minutes in Krugerands per minute.

Bond seemed to enjoy the diversion that he got from sailing and running a yacht syndicate but it was still a business proposition and he played it hard. Horror stories abound about what a poor loser he was and how this led to outbursts of foul temper. When Sir Tommy Sopwith gave the game away he said in his autobiography:'The America's Cup has been my principal recreation for over 30 years. It has kept me young, eager, buoyant and hopeful. It has brought me health and splendid friends.' Bond has never considered the America's Cup a recreation but it did keep him eager and bring him wealth and splendid friends.

Waiting at New York's JFK Airport for the Pilgrim Airlines commuter shuttle flight to Newport, Rhode Island, I had a strange feeling that the dapper New England businessman pacing up and down in the lounge as he waited for the same flight looked familiar. It was Federal Treasurer Paul Keating, taking a break from an International Monetary Fund meeting in Washington to drop in on the Bonds in their moment of triumph. Keating was one of many thousands of Australians who flocked to the little town on Narragansett Bay that summer. I didn't see international media magnate Rupert Murdoch burst into tears at the end of the last race but I did see Bondy vouch for his credentials and drag him past the security guards who had barred his entrance to a press conference. 'I think it's absolutely fantastic,' he told me. 'What Alan has achieved from his humble beginnings should be an inspiration to all Australians.'[243] Murdoch had dropped in for the day but got caught up in the euphoria and stayed till the end. John Spalvins, on the other hand, thought the polite thing to do after *Australia II* had lost the first two races was to exit town.

As my knowledge of yachts was restricted to a nodding acknowledgment of the difference between the pointy end and the blunt end, I stationed myself one morning on the jetty leading to Bond's thirty-metre motor launch *Southern Cross II* to watch his personal entourage remove their footwear and scramble on board with as much dignity as they could muster. Bondy certainly looked after those who have looked after him. His mother, Kathleen, came first, followed by his banker, James Yonge from Wardleys, his broker, Bruce Jackson from Jacksons, his lawyer, Henry Lodge from Parker & Parker and Geoff Summerhayes, the architect of his Dalkeith mansion. Angus Johnson, chief general manager of the Swan Brewery, was there in his capacity as chief sponsor of the *Australia II* challenge. Brian Coppin from Western Underwriters was there in his role as a friend and financier. No one was sure whether Laurie Connell was there or not.

There were many more. As *Southern Cross II* carried only fifty life jackets, Bond hired two other boats to carry the overflow. The *Curt C* carried the chosen few from the Royal Perth Yacht Club and the *Taurus* carried lesser lights from the *Australia II* challenge syndicate.

The crossover between yachting and business came in the competition and the tactics Bond once claimed: 'There is no second place, only a winner. Match racing is different from any other form of competition in that the time is not important. It doesn't matter how long it takes you to get round the course as long as you finish in front. Tactics are of primary importance. Once you get in front, you do all you can to make sure you stay there. And to do this you use all the foul means available to you within the rules of racing. When I say "foul", I am talking in terms of ensuring that the yacht you are leading is sailing in your foul air.'[244]

Controversy had raged all summer over Lexcen's secret winged keel, its psychological effect maximised by the canvas skirt modestly hiding it when the yacht was out of the water. Lexcen said the paranoia this engendered was worth a minute a mile. The New York Yacht Club had repeatedly tried to have the keel outlawed on the grounds that it gave the Australians an unfair advantage. Warren Jones responded that the only unfair advantage was that 'we thought of it first'.

The advantage was not apparent in the first two races, which were won by Dennis Conner's *Liberty* by 1:10 and 1:33 respectively. The Australian boat had suffered equipment failures in both races. The 'little white pointer', as *Australia II* became affectionately known, romped home in the third race by 3:14 — which is akin to a thrashing in America's Cup competition. Bond told the press conference that evening: 'I feel with great, great optimism that we have a real chance of going on to win the Cup. I couldn't say that on the last occasion I was here.'

The optimism was short-lived. Conner jumped Aussie skipper John Bertrand at the start of the fourth race and hung on to cross the finish line forty-three seconds in front. Being 3–1 down in a best-of-seven series looked like curtains for the Australians but Alan Bond was used to going to the brink. (He was certainly more familiar with that than with Australian history. In an attempt to drum up some ANZAC fighting spirit, he told that evening's press conference: 'We had our backs to the wall at Gallipoli and we won that one. So you can't count us out yet.' There was stunned silence. The foreign journalists didn't know what he was talking about and the Australians were almost too embarrassed to speak. Pat Burgess finally reminded him that we had been driven into the sea by the Turks in that battle. Bond said he had meant to emphasise that Australians hate to give up. But many of us felt like it that night.)

A new day brought a new victory to *Aussie II* by 1:47. This was the first time a challenger had won two races since Tommy Sopwith in 1934. Back at the dock, Bond's battle flag, a boxing kangaroo, was rampant. His battle theme, Men at Work's top-40 hit song 'Downunder', was blasting forth over PA systems to tantalise the opposition and, overriding all of this was a huge 20- × 12-metre Australian flag flying from the mast of sister yacht, *Challenge 12*. Even cynical journalists were moved. Race six was a pushover, with the Australians winning by 3:25. Everything was a new record now but a 3–3 tie had set the stage for what Conner called 'the race of the century'. The whole world would be watching but Bond said he wasn't worried about the outcome.

I saw race seven on 26 September from the Coast Guard cutter *Point Turner* which followed the Jury boat behind *Liberty* and *Australia*. If I hadn't seen it I wouldn't have believed it. The course length was 4.5 nautical miles and it had taken 132 years to travel it. *Liberty* tacked 47 times on the last leg and *Australia II* won by 41 seconds.

Bond still has the telegram from Prime Minister Bob Hawke that was waiting for him when he got back to the dock. It reads: 'Congratulations on your historic achievement in becoming the first to climb yachting's Everest. It was a stunning victory and a magnificent team effort which turned Australia into a nation of proud insomniacs. We said we could do it and our word was as good as our Bond. Our Cup now runneth over.'

Bond had reached the pinnacle. From here on, he could do no wrong.

CHAPTER TWELVE

20 October 1987: Luck's a fortune and a curse

'If I could give back to Australia some pride in itself and have all the people moulded together in one cause, that will mean I've given back something for what the country has given me,' successful migrant Alan Bond said in Newport on the eve of his historic victory. 'The Cup is worth a huge sum. They'll have to build ten new hotels in Perth. *We* might not build them but we'll supply the beer,' added the home-town brewer.

The altruistic graciousness of the first statement and the commercial hopefulness of the second did not prepare the world at large for the BondCorp onslaught that was about to hit. Engorged on new bank credit lines and sure of his own ability to pull off the impossible, Bond went on a four-year, $5-billion takeover binge that made BondCorp an international

BOND 236

conglomerate and Dallhold a personal treasure chest. The scale was grand and the ambitions unrestrained. Such was the awe in which the Cup-winner was held that few even questioned his ability to manage and run a global enterprise. The empire developed empires and growth was exponential. The great sharemarket crash on 20 October 1987 dealt BondCorp a mortal blow for which it was ill-prepared — but still the monolith ploughed on, with the momentum it had picked up during this purple patch.

That this was achieved on a balance sheet which, in 1983, had been stretched to near breaking point indicates either the extraordinary pulling power of the America's Cup or the patriotic gullibility of the bankers who fed Bond's ego and his wallet rather than examine his financial fundamentals with 'due diligence'. But as one Perth businessman said on V-NYYC day: 'It's about to become un-Australian not to invest in Bond and his Cup.'[245] Prime Minister Hawke had told the frenzied mob at the Royal Perth Yacht Club that morning that it was to be an unofficial national holiday: 'Any boss who sacks anyone for not turning up today is a bum!' Premier Burke started counting the money. His first 'guesstimate' was that the America's Cup would introduce $500 million to the State economy. Of course, he and many other Australians were hallucinating about the benefits of the Auld Mug to Young Australia. But Alan Bond wasn't. The Newport win would turn out to be worth more than ten times that amount to him and BondCorp in the form of access to assets through debt and equity raisings. While Men at Work sang endlessly but fortuitously:

> Do you come from a land down under,
> Where women glow and men plunder?
> Can you hear, can you hear the thunder?
> You better run, you better take cover,

Australians heard a catchy tune rather than the cryptic irony of the words. Half Perth's population of around one million turned up on the Esplanade for the homecoming parade. 'Bondy! Bondy! Bondy!' they chanted. John Bertrand says 'It might have been the most exuberant welcome home since Julius Caesar re-entered Rome forty-seven years Before Christ.'[246] The 'land shark' had become the queen bee.

Even Donald Horne, author of *The Lucky Country*, confessed that he had celebrated *Australia II*'s win 'with typical

[Australian] spontaneous mayhem.' Horne said he was reminded of the improvised 'VJ' celebrations that followed the
announcement in 1945 of the Japanese surrender. 'Why,' he
asked, 'do we behave like that? The answer ... [is that] the two
ways Australians can least anxiously proclaim themselves as a
nation are through international victories in sport and war ...
The America's Cup becomes not only a celebration of wealth in
a millionaire's sport: bizarrely, it also becomes a symbol of
"free enterprise", so ... we can dream again of pioneers and
battlers and little men in corner stores.'[247]

The dream-like idolatry in which Bond was held post-Cup
hid a multitude of corporate and financial sins. Bond had
always been more an astute asset-dealer than a successful
business manager and this had already started to show. But
Bond was now to be entrusted with unlimited, unsecured
(negative pledge) credit which allowed him to become the
major player in the Australian brewing, media and debt industries. He was not only to become the biggest player on the
Australian block but to take his ambitions global. Aussie
Bondy, 'the winner', became an international celebrity and
flavour of the month. It was an opportunity he was to capitalise
on but it was also an opportunity that was thrust on him freely.

Within weeks of the win, Bond announced from New York
that he had registered Swan Brewery with the US Securities and
Exchange Commission and intended to raise US$125 million
with a long-term (junk) bond issue. He then moved on to
London where he announced that BondCorp had acquired 49
per cent of the Canadian oil and gas group Sulpetro Ltd for
C$150 million, and that he was prepared to spend a similar
amount buying other international oil and gas producers. Back
home, the Burke government in Western Australia bought out
his 5-per-cent holding in the Argyle diamond mine for $42
million (he'd paid over $50 million for it) and announced that
it would provide financial assistance for the 1987 Cup defence
off Perth.[248]

But while everything was going right for hero Bondy on
the public relations front, there was 'trouble at the mill' as
Bond's wrecked retailing springboards (Waltons Bond and
Norman Ross) racked up monstrous losses which tortured the
BondCorp profit and loss statement. New chief executive officer Peter Beckwith had special responsibility for the retailing
arm but was reluctant to discuss the messy details: 'We have

BOND 238

never been in the habit of doing things we don't have to,' said the corporate clone.[249] Bond was above it all. The chairman was now statesman and sportsman. He had moved out of BondCorp HQ at International House and into new Dallhold digs three hundred metres away at 44 St Georges Terrace. By freeing Bond from day-to-day responsibility for his entrepreneurial decisions, BondCorp had set up a loose cannon on its foredeck.

Beer-making, shop-keeping and media ownership were the three areas of relevant cash revenue generation identified by Price Waterhouse in the 1979 corporate plan that BondCorp was working to until it won the Cup. But in Waltons Bond and Norman Ross he had picked two dogs (bad losers) in the retailing stakes and the problem was compounded by his failure to get hold of Grace Brothers and become a major player in the industry. When the distressing 1982–83 results were released after the Cup win, Beckwith said that the $80-million proceeds from the exit from GBs had improved BondCorp's prospects for 1983–84. It had not.

Norman Ross (NR), the whitegoods and electrical discounter purchased from GBs and others for $22 million all up, went from bad to worse and became a black hole in the accounts. It was jointly owned by BondCorp and Waltons Bond through Waltons Bond (ACT) Pty Ltd, which kept its losses off-balance-sheet and its performance out of sight. NR had made a pre-tax profit of $5.2 million in 1980–81 but lost $468,000 in the year to 31 July 1982, which was about the time when Bond bought it. In 1982–83, NR parent Waltons Bond ACT (WBA) had a trading loss of $10.5 million but the information had to be dragged out of BondCorp by a stock exchange request on 26 March 1984. In the same period it also lost $8.6 million in extraordinaries but this was not revealed until later.

At 31 January 1984, WBA had a $26,296,000 deficiency on assets over liabilities of which $14.6 million was an advance from Waltons Bond. In the first eleven months of 1983–84, NR lost $11.8 million on a turnover of $141.5 million. In the full year to 31 July 1984 the trading loss was $13.3 million and another $2 million went down the drain in extraordinaries. Norman Ross therefore chalked up losses totalling $34.5 million in the two years to July 1984 — its first two years under BondCorp ownership and management. The deficiency on assets by 31 July had grown to $34 million and advances from BondCorp were worth $20.7 million of the outstanding money.

Two days before its 1985 balance date, BondCorp sold its half share of WBA to Waltons Bond, effectively lowering the impact of NR's results on BondCorp and taking the figures out of view. But the 1985 BondCorp accounts did show that NR losses continued in the six months to January 1985, albeit at a slower rate, with a trading loss of $2.1 million and another $3.7-million loss on extraordinaries. Later entries in BondCorp accounts show a continuation of the losses even after the business was sold on 26 March 1987. WBA lost $2.646 million in 1987–88 and a further $16.7 million in 1988–89. This is an inglorious record of management and financial failure, even taking into account the difficult trading conditions that existed in the early part of BondCorp's control of the assets and the cash flow of the business.

Shortly after the initial BondCorp Norman Ross takeover, New South Wales managers were called to a meeting at the Parramatta store: 'We were told Alan Bond had said we didn't know anything about retailing because we didn't make enough money out of it,' said an NR manager at the meeting. 'If we couldn't manage the business profitably, Waltons Bond would move in someone who could,' the managers were told.[250] Responsibility for that job eventually went to Beckwith and, given the results down the track, Alan Bond and BondCorp didn't know much about retailing either. Sheer willpower and hard work (considered Bond's saving graces at the time) are not always enough to turn a sow's ear into a silk purse. But what BondCorp managed to achieve on its own at Norman Ross was the reverse of the process. Many of the managers at that meeting had left the company by then.

What then was the situation on the retailing side of the Waltons Bond operation? Was that any different from the Norman Ross experience? Were the banks who were lending him money hand over fist on negative-pledge/cash-flow-service terms for other diversified ventures watching these retail developments with due diligence? Surely they provided a pointer to how BondCorp might run the big global brewing, media and mining interests he was assembling with the debt financing at the same time?

Waltons had made a net profit of $4.498 million on sales of $352 million (the trading margin over costs was $14.8 million) in the year to 31 July 1981, which was the year in which BondCorp took it over/came to its rescue with a 76-per-cent holding in the issued capital in late March. Because of the extant recession (which retailers are always the first to feel because of the drop in expectations and hence sales) this had been Waltons's first profit since a similar profit of $4.34 million in 1977–78, when the trading margin was only $10.6 million and the sales were $296 million.

By the time BondCorp's direct preferred position of 42.3 per cent of Waltons Bond was attained, the cost of this controlling stake had set back BondCorp no more than about $21.5 million, or the same as the outlay on Norman Ross.[251] The rest of the surplus holding went to: Carrian of Hong Kong, 15 per cent (with an option to go to 20 percent with 5 per cent possibly held for it by Dallhold); Endeavour Resources, 10 per cent; and Leighton Mining, 4.3 per cent — all presumedly at BondCorp's entry price, if not better.

But Waltons Bond had been purchased by BondCorp less for its retail profit recovery potential and more for its surplus unencumbered real estate values. At the time of purchase, BondCorp was working on projections of net available profits of $11.3 million for 1981–82, $21.1 million for 1982–83, $13 million for 1983–84 and $15 million for 1984–85 — but most, if not all, of this profit growth was slated to come from property sales rather than merchandising and credit sales.[252]

Whatever cash was in the Waltons tills when BondCorp took over soon went to BondCorp, depleting working capital and raising borrowings for the retailer. Waltons paid out at least $30 million almost immediately for the first tranche of Bond-Corp's unwanted property interests in New South Wales and Queensland and followed it up with a $27-million outlay for the unsold and unwanted Taylors Lakes estate in Melbourne. These deals, in June and November of 1981, were great for BondCorp's balance sheet but not so good for Waltons Bond's.

The 1981–82 Waltons Bond profit is not even hinted at in the BondCorp report of the same year, which indicates that there wasn't one on trading. However, notes to the accounts do show a $1.8-million gain on the sale of property. As this was the first full year under BondCorp tutelage a good result would have been expected. Sales had increased by $48 million to a new record level of $400 million, which is a nice cash flow. In the six months to 31 January 1983, a disappointing trading profit of $410,000 was revealed on a turnover of over $200 million. With extraordinaries, the half-year profit could rise to $1.38 million but it would still be down from the $6.5 million earned in the previous corresponding period.

In the full year to 31 July 1983, the situation deteriorated, with Waltons Bond losing $21 million all up ($10.3 million on trading and $10.7 million on extraordinaries). Turnover was down to $343.6 million. The main Melbourne store was closed in February 1983. Bond spoke of Waltons Bond's retailing being 'a most unrewarding investment' in the 1983–84 annual report. Turnover was down to $303.9 million and losses totalled $19.8 million ($17.6 million on trading and $2.2 million on extraordinaries). BondCorp was forced to inject $35 million into the business to keep it solvent.

But Waltons Bond and subsidiaries lost a further $34 million in 1984–85. At 31 July 1986 BondCorp was able to boast that Waltons Bond had carried forward tax benefits of some $63 million. In August of that year it sold its property interests back to BondCorp and there was an immediate improvement — losses for 1986–87 were only $16 million. On 26 March 1987 what was left of the retailing business was sold to Venture Stores for $53 million. So keen did Bond seem to off-load it that he took $33 million as a cash down-payment and the balance in equal amounts over four years. The six-year retailing nightmare was finally over. It had brought no glory to BondCorp — worse, it had taken cash out of the company. In the 1985 annual report Bond spoke of a 'light appearing at the end of a costly and exasperating tunnel.' He was right. But the tangled wreckage he was left with was never recognised as management failure and soon forgotten by a world that only wanted to see Bondy as a winner.

With hindsight, one could readily assemble a portfolio of Bond's other business disasters, projects which for one reason or another never lived up to the group's high expectations for them and so became losers in terms of those standards. They covered many different fields of activity but they were consistently incapable of producing high earnings before interest and tax. There was the original Mayday plant hire business that Warren Jones brought to the group in the early 1970s. Even when combined with the Skipper operations and the Whitemans Brickworks under the Amalgamated Industries umbrella, the business failed to prosper and was eventually sold.

Mineral exploration had dealt Alan Bond's ego huge blows when he was starting out on the stock exchange. The Durack Mines hot rocks shambles has already been mentioned but Pacific Island Mines Ltd (PIM), which he chaired in 1969–70, had the misfortune to miss one of the Pacific Rim's largest goldmines. PIM had spent years searching Misima Island in Papua New Guinea for a pot of gold. When Placer Pacific Ltd found it more than a decade later it contained 56 million tonnes of gold-bearing ore, enough to produce 220,000 ounces of gold a year and make its owner considerably rich. During Bond's chairmanship of PIM, the company spent $2 million buying Dalston Developments Pty Ltd (which owned the Greenwood Forest development in Perth) and other suburban real estate from BondCorp Pty Ltd, instead of using the money to explore for gold.

Insurance was another business that Bond should never have gotten into. He was advised not to, he ignored the advice and he failed to make it pay handsome dividends. Acts of God in the form of Cyclone Tracy and the Brisbane floods didn't help his ability to withstand the financial risks that he had undertaken. There were other failures of expectations and fulfilment in the transport, quarrying and brick-making industries and these interests were subsequently sold after the Cup win. Airship Industries Ltd, an ailing British blimp maker, is an enduring folly that dates from this era of post-Cup euphoria.

One of the reasons Australian institutional investors would not touch BondCorp stock was because of the erratic performance in profit generation. Non-disclosure of the loss-making contributions from various associates, and group cross-company deal-making, left the major life offices with a cynical view of the statements and accounts as presented every year by the BondCorp whiz kids. Before winning the Cup, Bond told shareholders (in the 1982 annual report): 'Our growing cash flow and substantial income from the retail sector and the brewing division will now give us a capacity to invest in other resource development projects, severely undervalued by market and credit conditions.' As we have just demonstrated, retailing was not to become the source of the 'substantial income' spoken of here. Would it come, then, from the Swan Brewery?

Alas, even the Swan Brewery, with its modern equipment and market monopoly, did not live up to its promise of fabulous wealth for BondCorp shareholders. In the dying days of Lloyd Zampatti's defence of the brewery against the encroaching BondCorp, before Christmas 1981, the board released profit and cash flow projections out to 1988. These showed profits averaging about $20 million a year and cash flow totalling about $200 million over the seven-year period. In 1982–83, BondCorp's first in full control and the year Zampatti said the company would earn a net profit of $14.2 million, it in fact returned a loss of $5.3 million according to the breakdown of results by subsidiaries in the annual accounts.

In 1983–84, the Swan brewery profit was $4.2 million against a projected $17 million. It dropped to a little over $1 million in 1984–85 (projection = $19.8 million), rose to $15.1 million in 1985–86 ($23 million), dropped to $4.9 million in 1986–87 ($26.6 million) and finally established itself as a solid contributor in 1988 with a $39.5-million profit that was well above the projected $30.4 million. Now the 1983 and 1984 figures may have been affected by the Swan brewery's contribution to the $6–8 million spent on the successful Cup challenge at Newport. If the major cost of the Cup could be written off against real beer profits and even losses, then this could be tax effective for the group as a whole. It is not known what effect internal transfers or cost attributions had on the Swan brewery results as published but the figures should have reflected the bottom line for the business as a going concern.

As the Swan brewery was to be the basis for the impending Bond Brewing empire and many substantial loans would be raised both in Australia and internationally to fund that rapid growth, a more diligent appraisal of Swan's profit figures would have revealed this inconsistency in performance under Bond-Corp's tutelage. And the Swan brewery was not the only loss maker revealed in the 1982–83 annual accounts when they were posted to shareholders after the America's Cup win. Amalgamated Industries lost $4.2 million and Northern Mining was down $2 million.

That BondCorp itself had been able to post an operating profit at all in Cup year 1983 was due almost entirely to its corporate finance activities rather than its core trading subsidiaries. Turnover was $308 million and the figure given for operating profit was $6.8 million, although a good deal of this came from tax credits. But once extraordinary profits ($15.3 million) were piled on top of it and even more extraordinary losses ($27.5 million) were written off against it, the net profit came down to a loss of $5.4 million.

Using conventional accounting on the following 1983–84 year, when turnover was up to $392 million, produced a less than brilliant but at least respectable net operating profit of $9.3 million. Even with net extraordinaries off, it still stood up at $8.9 million. But if the same figures are done on a consolidated equity accounting basis (BondCorp did them in supplementary accounts that year) the result is a disastrous loss of $14 million before extraordinaries, which would take it to $16 million down. The reason for the dramatic turnaround was because conventional accounting, as applied by BondCorp, excluded the group's $22.3-million equity share in losses racked up by BondCorp associates Waltons Bond, Norman Ross/WBA, Austmark International and Endeavour Resources in the same year.

The 1984–85 accounts, the ones on which Bond based his first billion-dollar bid, contained an equally unconvincing argument that the group had cast-iron, sustainable earning power (or, for that matter, cover for exposure to foreign exchange fluctuations that would result from major offshore loans). Turnover that year was worth $517 million. On it, BondCorp claimed a conventional profit of $20.5 million (with one-quarter of the earnings coming from transfer pricing sales to associates). Equity-accounted, it was a loss of $5.7 million.

The addition of net extraordinaries took the conventional profit to $26.1 million while it raised the equity-accounted loss to a profit of $10.2 million. Extraordinary items of income and expense are normally excluded from trading results on the grounds that the sale of a major asset is an exceptional event. This was not the case with BondCorp. 'As Alan Bond has made his fortune dealing in such assets, however, it seems more realistic to include them,' argued Trevor Sykes at the time. 'Indeed, "extraordinaries trader" would not be an inaccurate description for the Bond group,' he said.[253]

The 1984–85 accounts are tendentious for another reason. They show how creative accounting techniques can accentuate the positives and eliminate the negatives for a company frozen at a point in time. At 30 June investments in listed associate companies were costed in the books at $126 million, whereas their market value at the time was only $62 million. If the accounts had been drawn up on the basis of the market value of these investments, an additional extraordinary loss of more than $64 million could have been written off against the profit and loss statement. Unrealised losses of $48 million caused by fluctuations in the foreign exchange rate on overseas borrowings could also have been written off but weren't. A change in these two items could have turned the conventional $20.5-million profit into a whopping $92-million loss after extraordinaries.

So, the first three annual results issued by BondCorp after winning the Cup, but before the quantum leap into mega-debt, show a company devoid of a consistently strong source of earnings derived from a trading operation under its direct control. On the contrary, if there was any real net revenue, it would have provided barely enough to cover the $10 million or so pay-out due each year to preference (John Spalvins) and ordinary shareholders.

But it was the ability to service debt capital that should have been the primary concern of the banking syndicates about to lend the company big licks of fresh debt. BondCorp's interest payments had grown like topsy in the years to 30 June 1985. Between 30 June 1982 and the same date in 1985, BondCorp's annual interest pay-outs doubled from more than $30 million to more than $60 million. This was six times as much as the cost of servicing the equity capital, and that wasn't all of it. A change in accounting policy was notified in the 1982 annual report which allowed BondCorp to capitalise interest-paid holding costs on certain investments as a $14.7-million extraordinary profit in that year.

Was this rapid growth in debt capital over equity capital of concern to post-Cup chairman Bond? In the 1984 annual report he appeared to take great pride in the extra $172 million in term borrowings that he had achieved in 1983–84 because it was part of his strategy. Listen while he talks: 'Reliance on borrowings supports our firm policy not to use equity financing while the market value of Bond shares is around half their asset values.' It is the unrealised prospective value of the assets that is Bond's only concern. Interest payments, profits, dividends and the like have become minor intrusions into his grand plan. The fact that Alan Bond's Dallhold Investments owned over half the BondCorp stock probably contributed to the preference for debt financing. Equity issues would involve Dallhold giving money to BondCorp, not the other way around. The alternative was to be watered down to less than 50 per cent control, and that was totally unacceptable.

'The development strategy of Bond Corporation has been modified as the group has grown,' Bond told shareholders. 'Our early strategy of growth through acquisition of substantially undervalued assets was moved towards a preference for businesses with strong cash flow ... (to this) we have added the requirements of strong proven management and a major if not dominant market position. We intend to consolidate the progress of the several separate segments within Bond Corporation, each of which warrant appropriate recognition from the investment and financial community,' he said. The gist of this statement is that new little BondCorps were about to be brought into being. These spin-offs would be listed and able to raise their own debt based on market monopolies and good management — the two being equated. The significance was in the need for 'appropriate recognition' by brokers and bankers.

In January 1984, he successfully bid $50 million for Swan Television and Radio Broadcasters Ltd, licence holder of STW Channel 9 in Perth, and tiptoed into the electronic media business. The only connection between the Swan Brewery and Swan Broadcasters was a chronic lack of imagination which afflicted nomenclature in the West. Bond would later solve the problem by renaming the former, Bond Brewing (WA) and the latter, Bond Media. They were not to be Bond's only obsessions but they were his latest and most exciting technological toys.

The media had long held a special appeal for Bond, and they for him, which was good for his ego. Appearing in front of cameras created no fear in him. He even thought aloud in ten-second grabs, which is about as deep as the electronic media ever get. He was a natural talent, presentable and provocative, and his rich-and-famous lifestyle provided the perfect backdrop. To the salesman the electronic media also provided the perfect audience — captive and receptive. He had used it to sell land in the days when he styled himself the Progress Development Organisation and it was his chief weapon in the battle with the New York Yacht Club, which had a complete and utter aversion to publicity. His Newport friend, Ted Turner, had given him the message about the medium. Turner bled heavily when setting up the new Cable News Network (CNN) in the US from his regional base in Atlanta, which Bond was supposed to have shares in.

Bond was not going to make the same mistake as friend Turner. Turner might have had a bigger market to aim for in the States but Bond could deliver established market reach in Perth for a fraction of Turner's CNN establishment costs. STW commanded more than 50 per cent of the fast-growing Perth commercial viewing audience — the widest metropolitan reach in the country. Bond became the biggest and the best media mogul in town by snapping up the market leader in a closed commercial duopoly. There were two government clouds on its horizon, but for the moment it was a licence to print money and contributed $11.2 million to group profits in 1984–85. This was a damn sight more than Swan Brewery and Waltons Bond contributed.

Media was on BondCorp's 1979 Price Waterhouse cash cow shopping list and the company undertook a study that year to see whether they should seek a licence to operate a new station in WA. Dallhold had made a desperate lunge for control of TVW7, the other commercial channel, in December 1979. His nemesis here had been Perth's other crown prince of commerce, Michael Robert Hamilton Holmes à Court (Hacca for short). Bond had seethed at the lost opportunity at the time and was forced to wait four years for his ever-so-sweet revenge. What Bondy could offer STW and what Hacca couldn't give TVW were world rights to the exclusive coverage of the next America's Cup to be staged off Fremantle in 1987.

Grencol Holdings Pty Ltd, the BondCorp subsidiary that acquired control of the listed STW, would change its name to Bond Media Ltd (Australian Stock Exchange code: BOM) in 1987 and take control of Kerry Packer's National Nine Network in a billion-dollar deal. But Bond's earliest television adventures provide theatrical insights into later doings and have led to questions being asked about his fitness and propriety to own a TV licence.

At $49.5 million, STW was a good investment in January 1984, though the price paid was considered far too high for a provincial station at the time. In two years, Bond would double its value; but in the meantime, the ground rules for TV broadcasting were changing at a rapid rate. On 7 May 1984 Federal Communications Minister Michael Duffey invited applications for a third commercial television licence in Perth and the initial value of Bond's TV investment was looking to be under threat. Bondy and Hacca would now have to share their advertising revenue with a third player and a dogfight for the dollars would ensue. The Kerry Stokes-controlled West Coast Telecasters Ltd won the third licence on 31 July 1986. It was the first metropolitan licence to be granted since 1966 and the first to be issued by the Australian Broadcasting Tribunal since it was formed in January 1977.

The fifteen-month ABT inquiry hearings into the new licence applications revealed fascinating details about the relationship between BondCorp and the Burke government, between those in the John Curtin Foundation and WA Inc. and those not, and between Bond and Holmes à Court. The bombshell was dropped in October 1985 when one of the applicants, the Western Television consortium, told a private session of the tribunal hearings that Hacca, who owned the *Western Mail* newspaper as well as TVW7, had threatened to bring down the Burke Labor government.

The claim was made by Darcy Farrell, a former TVW journalist colleague of Burke's and a former adviser to the Burke government. He was now chairman of the Western Television consortium in which Laurie Connell was a major shareholder, and his application was being opposed by both Bondy and Hacca, who for the first time were on the same side. The two proprietors were jointly arguing before the inquiry that Perth was too small a market for a third licence to be granted. Farrell had made the allegation in response to a statement to the tribunal by TVW concerning a 1975 racing inquiry which had resulted in Connell being found guilty of a 'dishonourable action' by the WA Turf Club stewards.[254]

In evidence, Farrell alleged that Holmes à Court had made public his antagonism towards Connell through the *Western Mail* newspaper and had singled out Connell for attack because the latter had given financial advice to the Burke government several times since its election in 1983. (Holmes à Court had made no public contribution to the ALP's John Curtin Foundation slush fund and his name was conspicuous by its absence from the list of foundation supporters.) Farrell told the tribunal that an 'impeccable source' had told him of Holmes à Court's threat to bring down the government. The sensational allegation was, of course, hotly denied by Hacca but the headlines screamed 'Tycoons' Collision Course' when it was later revealed that the 'impeccable source' was Brian Burke and he had been told by Alan Bond. Dallas-on-the-Swan came alive.

Burke went public on 28 October when he entered the ABT witness box and confirmed that he had told Farrell about the alleged Hacca plot to unseat him and that his trusted informant was Bond. Burke had asked for a meeting with Bond 'following reports that had come to my ears of things that Mr Bond had said to two or three other people.' At that meeting, which had taken place about six months previously, Bond told Burke that Hacca had recently told him in conversation that they 'should jointly press the State Government to take a position in opposition to the granting of a third commercial television licence for Perth,' Burke said that Bond said that Hacca said!

'I also told Farrell [that] Bond had said that, failing compliance with the request, Holmes à Court had proposed to Bond that they should combine their efforts to strongly oppose the Government at the next election. I told Farrell that the phrase "cut the Government's throat collectively" was used, but I cannot recall now whether it was Bond's phrase or a phrase I put to him and with which he agreed. I told Farrell that Bond made it quite clear that he would have nothing to do with such suggestions ... I was very concerned about the report.' [255]

BOM/STW9 then issued an eighteen-point statement putting forth Bond's recollections of the event. It claimed that Bond had met Holmes à Court about once every six months over recent years. The meetings took place at one or the other's home or office, even Bond's London office 'if appropriate'. They were informal and discussions centred on the economy, the operations of their respective interests, and other matters. Bond said that the two had met at one of Holmes à Court's offices and talked about the proposed third television station for about fifteen minutes. Holmes à Court or he (Bond) had said: 'We should make the Premier aware we are not happy about the third licence.'

According to the Bond statement, they had then stood up to shake hands and 'Holmes à Court said to me words to the effect that "the Government should realise that if we were to combine our efforts we could probably change the Government".' Bond had replied with words to the effect 'I don't think we have to go to that extent'. Bondy then subsequently dobbed Hacca in to Burkie for what he was alleged to have said and wore his heart proudly on his sleeve: 'I wouldn't have a bar of that, and I want you to know that,' Bond says he told Burke.

Having been slandered before the ABT and in public as a manipulator of governments by Farrell, Burke and now Bond, Holmes à Court took action in the West Australian Supreme Court. Late on 28 October writs were issued against all three men claiming unspecified damages for defamation and injunctions were sought restraining them from repeating the claims. 'These allegations,' said Holmes à Court, 'are without foundation and there is no evidence to support them. They represent a series of rumours originally transmitted among the defendants.'

The fight was on, WA Inc. *vs* the stand-offish tall man ... Bond said he would 'vigorously' defend the action, then Burke told parliament 'the State Government refuses to be stood over by anyone, regardless of their financial resources or influence', which is an interesting statement in itself. Then Hacca burst into print on the dust-up in the *National Times* on 1 November: 'The plot's weak but the casting's good,' he said of the situation. 'I don't believe that I could bring down or contribute to the bringing down of a government.' Hacca denied that he held regular meetings with Bond. He could not recall seeking a meeting with Bond in the past ten years and he was unaware of where his office was. 'Burke asked me whether I was opposed to the Government or whether he was being paranoid. I told him he was being paranoid. I spent the rest of the lunch expressing my view that government should not have a close association with business people. I have a view that no politician anywhere should be close to any sectional interest, including business,' said Holmes à Court.[256]

The matter was eventually resolved and the writs were withdrawn on 15 November, but not before the attendant publicity had given the world a glimpse of realpolitik WA-style. Holmes à Court never forgave Bond for dobbing him in and Bond never forgave Hacca for telling the world that he didn't know where the BondCorp office was. What is amazing about the incident is that the ABT licence application hearing had nothing directly to do with the West Australian State government. Darcy Farrell and Laurie Connell missed out on the third licence but Hacca and Bondy were forced to share the airwaves and the profits with a new competitor: Kerry Stokes, who, having won the lucky dip, on-sold the licence company to another party before the station went to air.

STW's profits to BondCorp were never the same after the first good year to 30 June 1985, when the station returned $11.2 million. According to the accounts, profit in 1985–86 was $1.3 million and a loss of $1.08 million was incurred in 1986–87, the period covering the Fremantle America's Cup telecasts. A profit of only $268,000 was evident in 1987–88. But if STW was doing little for the BondCorp bottom line it was doing heaps for the asset side of the balance sheet. BOM/STW had cost just under $50 million to purchase but the value ascribed to it in the books grew steadily to $80 million and then $100 million in a very short time.

But Bond was certainly no dilettante when it came to media ownership. Not for him the cheap thrills of being a big fish in a small sea. He would settle for nothing less than access to the entire world — but he would start with Brisbane. Exactly a year after buying STW9, Bond lashed out $65 million for Queensland Television Ltd, which owned QTQ9 in Brisbane. The bidding vehicle was Fairlanes Pty Ltd, an Amalgamated Industries subsidiary better known for its ten-pin bowling alley in Perth. The price paid was a new Australian record for a metropolitan TV station but it was to lead to more dealings with a State premier and more troubles before the ABT.

When Bond gained control of QTQ in January 1985, the company had an outstanding defamation action against the previous management from Queensland Premier Sir Joh Bjelke-Petersen. Bond, who was keen to do more business in Queensland, wanted the business resolved and herein was to lie the root of the problem. Bond was used to dealing with Liberal and Labor premiers who, with the notable exception of the South Australians, were as flexible as eucalyptus saplings.

But in the Queensland National Party's Bjelke-Petersen, Bond found an ironbark stumbling block.

Bjelke-Petersen had raised the issue with Bond executives the month they took over. Apart from a reference at a board meeting the following month, the claim appeared to have been treated like a routine defamation claim until the following October, when Bjelke-Petersen again raised the matter during a meeting with Alan Bond. 'He wanted a fertiliser plant in Gladstone with cheap gas and tried to buy shares in the Greenvale nickel plant but he got absolutely nothing from my government,' said honest Joh.

Bjelke-Petersen told Bond he was suing for $1 million, which was a bit over the top considering the going rate for settling out of court a slander against Joh's business-like government was around $50,000. As is the nature of these ambit claims, there was room for negotiation. It has been suggested as a result of the findings of the recent Fitzgerald inquiry into police corruption that, in Queensland, 'honour had a price like every other commodity'. Bond did well in negotiating the settlement figure down to $400,000 but he appears to have had some difficulty selling the deal to his BondCorp executives and his insurer, Brian Coppin, who, according to Joh, were on his back because they thought the figure was too high. BOM/QTQ's insurers denied liability on 28 November because Bond had negotiated directly with Sir Joh. In December, the ABT held a public inquiry into the acquisition of the whole of the issued capital of Queensland Television Ltd by Fairlanes (WA) Pty Ltd. No mention was made at this inquiry of any settlement being reached with Joh.

Enter the corpulent BOM/STW boss David Aspinall on a bread queue behind Alan Bond on Rottnest Island during the 1985 Christmas holidays. We are told that Bond tells Aspinall to 'attend to the particulars' of the Joh settlement but also to emphasise the vital nature of confidentiality. Aspinall, breadstick in hand, 'misinterprets' the executive chairman's command and fires off a telex to Joh on 2 January, offering a settlement based on the $400,000 but conditional on a confidentiality agreement and a restructuring in some way. Aspinall also requested a meeting with Joh on 17 February to resolve the matter finally.

Evidence was presented that from about mid-February

Warren Jones, the BondCorp executive director in charge of
BOM media operations, and managing director Peter Beckwith
were active in seeking to have Mr Bond attempt to persuade Sir
Joh that it was in the interests of neither party that Sir Joh
should require a direct payment of $400,000. According to later
testimony by Joh, at that 17 February 1986 meeting Bond had
attempted to restructure the deal so that the pay-out was
$50,000 in cash and the other $350,000 through either an
overseas payment, a non-repayable loan or a property transaction. Honest Joh, as was his wont, rejected these alternatives
and insisted on receiving the $400,000 in cash. This payment
was approved by a BondCorp board meeting on 24 March.

It has been unjustly suggested that the payment was a
secret commission or an out-and-out bribe. It was in fact
a pretty straightforward commercial settlement arranged
between two skilled negotiators capable of protecting their
own interests. If Bond wanted to bribe Joh there was a more
established route to follow. According to evidence presented
to the later Fitzgerald inquiry into corruption in Queensland,
the way to win friends and influence National Party politicians
was through donations to the Bjelke-Petersen Foundation. This
long-established political slush fund provided the role model
for the ALP's John Curtin Foundation in Perth.

Bond could be forgiven for having a fairly cynical attitude
towards politicians. But he was a businessman first and foremost and he was just trying to get on with his business of
turning a quid without undue government interference. The
ABT would later rule that Bond dealt personally with Sir Joh
Bjelke-Petersen because he 'believed that Sir Joh was in a
position to affect his group's interests and Mr Bond believed
that failure to settle the defamation action might result in Sir
Joh causing adverse consequences to his group in their
commercial activities.'

This brings us to Queensland and those commercial
interests. Bond had, of course, been in Queensland since the
1970 takeover of the Savoy Corporation, which gave him real
estate interests on the Gold Coast. Dallhold was to gain control
of the Greenvale nickel project, too. Walton's Bond also had a
strong retailing representation in the north-eastern State on
the opposite side of the continent to Perth. West Australians
and Queenslanders were considered to be of similar frontier

stock, despite the fact that they drank different beer and played different codes of football. Bond was to make it his major beachfront on the eastern seaboard.

The biggest thing since beer in Queensland was the Castlemaine Perkins brewery, and Bond decided he would make it his in June 1985. The degree of difficulty in this takeover was immense but, at $1.2 billion, the price was astronomical — no one had ever attempted such a large cash takeover in Australia before. Castlemaine, whose origins, like Swan's, were in Victoria, had merged with the Tooheys brewery in New South Wales in late 1979 as a defensive move against acquisitive acquisitionists. Castlemaine Tooheys Ltd had a market capitalisation more than five times the size of Bond-Corp's. Its chief executive, Lloyd Zampatti, was familiar with the BondCorp stalking tactics but he once again underestimated BondCorp's ability to bite off a lot more than it could possibly chew. History, for Lloyd Zampatti, was about to repeat itself.

Takeovers as big as Castlemaine Tooheys (CaTs) don't just happen on impulse, though Bond did have a strong tendency to act precipitously. This one had been on the boil since the Cup win in 1983. Without the Cup win, the funding for the CaTs tilt would have been hard to come by. Even with the funding lined up, there were many impediments to success. It was imperative that BondCorp have the element of surprise on its side in this battle if it was to avoid a Dutch auction. Not only was Zampatti, the old Swan boss, now the boss of CaTs, but some world majors were as interested in the CaTs business as CaTs was in staying out of their clutches.

The business strategy was pretty simple. By putting Swan together with Castlemaine and Tooheys you got geographical spread and could achieve critical mass in the national beer market. It would make Bond Brewing about the same size as CUB, which, having bought the Tooth NSW brewing assets from John Spalvins in August 1983, was presently the largest in the land, with 45 per cent of national beer sales. Swan's 10 per cent would combine with CaTs's 34 per cent to create a national beer war ball game.

The architect of this scheme was Lloyd Zampatti. He was also twice its victim. Zampatti had proposed the same idea to CaTs as part of his last-ditch attempt to ward off Bond from the Swan vats in 1981. When CUB snapped up Tooth's Sydney assets for $160 million in August 1983, Zampatti felt compelled to give it another whirl. This CUB move signalled the death-knell for regional brewers as it effectively opened the flood-gates to national competition for the $5-billion beer-drinking market by removing the protection afforded for so long by State boundaries. Zampatti knew he would be on a hiding to nothing in a national beer war unless he could attain critical mass and develop a national and international brand to go up against CUB's Foster's. He had two regional market leaderships to protect and nowhere to expand. He could not expand Castlemaine's XXXX (Fourex) into New South Wales because the Castlemaine-Tooheys merger was basically a non-aggression pact. And Melbourne drinkers would rather cut their throats than drink a draught of Tooheys. They were slightly more receptive to Fourex as a national brand name and taste.

Zampatti was uniquely placed to see both the problem and the solution. With Swan, he had commissioned the thoroughly modern Canning Vale brewery and was pushing the product in London (through Courage) and on the eastern seaboard by back-loading. With CaTs, he got the benefit of seeing how Tooheys had destroyed Tooth's dominance in New South Wales with a better product and clever marketing. He was also in charge at Castlemaine as Fourex was developing a national profile and successfully pushing into the UK market through its tie-up with Allied-Lyons. Having run three out of the five remaining mainland brewers, he knew what was coming long before Alan Bond and John Elliott.

To buy Swan in September 1983, Zampatti had to talk BondCorp into selling it. This meant flying to Newport, Rhode Island, where Bondy was in the countdown to the big one, and there dealing with his nemesis. There were delicious ironies in this but none more so for Bond than someone flying to Newport to put a deal to him. It was usually Bond who went to Newport to do business, with the yachting a mere sideline. Zampatti told him of the cost benefits of amalgamating Swan with CaTs and offered him a handsome profit on what was then only a peripheral investment for BondCorp.

Bond was flattered but wasn't interested in selling. He did, however, take the idea on board. He was always prepared to listen to a deal that offered him a profit or the prospect of a bigger profit. Interestingly, Bond would now rely on the TPC ruling that Swan's monopoly in the WA market prevented other majors from buying it. It was because of this restriction that he had made a personal bid for Swan and then transferred it to BondCorp. The monopoly ruling did not work the other way. Swan had the potential to move on CaTs and become a major player, perhaps the largest, in the cash-flow beer industry. Bond thanked Zampatti for his kind offer and then handed the subversion of CaTs over to Peter Mitchell to work on.

Zampatti returned disappointed, only to find his beer war nightmare coming true. In December, John Elliott's Elders IXL team borrowed $750 million in forty-eight hours and launched an audacious $1-billion bid for CUB, which owned 49 per cent of Elders. Elliott was 'saving' CUB from takeover merchant Sir Ronald Brierley's speculative partial bid for CUB in late November. In just two days the largest brewer in the land fell to a man who knew all about marketing products and had plans to 'Fosterise' the world. Foster's was already being produced under licence in England by Watneys and from the new CUB Kent brewery in Sydney. The front line of the beer war had shifted to Sydney and CaTs was already feeling the pressure of a CUB onslaught. Desperately seeking to avoid the inevitable, Zampatti launched into a series of diversifications to shore up CaTs's defences. He made an unsuccessful $307-million bid for Nicholas Kiwi Ltd and bought a series of Coca-Cola franchises.

The two keys to the CaTs treasure chest were the British brewer and tea merchant, Allied-Lyons Plc, which was CaTs's largest shareholder at 20.9 per cent, and the Australian Trade Practices Commission (TPC), a trust buster capable of raising its finger at the slightest appeal. As it was, the TPC had no objection to a Swan-Castlemaine-Tooheys combine. Swan had 96 per cent of its market, Castlemaine 73 per cent of its and Tooheys 55 per cent of the New South Wales market — the largest of all. But three market leaderships did not a monopoly make in the TPC's eyes. Combined they could match CUB's strength and enhance competition.

In his post-Cup 'royal tour' at the end of 1983, Bond had gone courtesy calling on Allied-Lyons and lunched with the board. 'I'd had talks. I'd had two or three lunches with the Allied board in London ... It was openly said — it really didn't matter who — that someone would have to put the two brewers (CaTs and Swan) together. One of us would have to move,' Bond said later.[257] Allied-Lyons were aware of CaTs's interest in Swan. They were now also aware of Swan's interest in CaTs and it added to the value of their investment. But they were not yet prepared to dump Zampatti, who seemed to know what he was doing downunder. Zampatti didn't need to be warned about Bond's London lunches. He had seen Bond fly to London and buy Santos from Burmah and he had personal experience of Bond's visits to Singapore to see the OCBC about its Swan holding.

Beckwith signalled the start of the great CaTs kidnap late in 1984 when he said BondCorp had lined up finance for another major acquisition. Statements like this were two a penny from post-Cup BondCorp and the confusion they caused in boardrooms across the country was extremely effective. In 1985 BondCorp was in and out of Hooker Corp, Arnotts and Wormald, among others. No one ever knew what their real target was and consequently no one took its stated intentions seriously. This worked strategically in BondCorp's favour, as Laurie Connell, an adviser to Bond on the CaTs raid, was to later testify: 'People never took him seriously. The board of Castlemaine can only be considered inept because for a long time all the signals were there that he was marshalling his resources to have a go.'[258]

Bond quietly entered the CaTs market in April, picking up 97,000 shares at $4.80 through Sydney broker Rene Rivkin. Asset backing of the shares was only $3.40 and the lowest they had traded in 1985 was $4.25. On 5 and 7 June, BondCorp placed orders with brokers for 10 per cent of CaTs. By mid-June he was paying $6 a share and had moved to 6 per cent of the capital. Zampatti responded by buying half of the Britvic soft drink operation in the UK from Allied-Lyons for $37 million. This was satisfied by the issue of new CaTs shares to Allied at $6.10, which took the British brewer's stake in the Australian brewer to a commanding 24.9 per cent and watered Bond down. Bond took legal action to stop the placement but failed.

The defensive placement gave CaTs only a temporary respite but it stiffened the BondCorp resolve: 'The (Britvic) placement ... showed us Allied's interest [in doing a deal with Bond] had also waned. We would have to go it alone ... we'd have to be the catalyst. And once we'd moved we were never going to be sellers ... we were prepared for the long haul. We were prepared to take two or three years,' said Bond.[259] Twenty-one days later he had lined up all the finance required for a full bid.

Then, in an amazing coincidence, John Elliott came to Alan Bond's aid in July 1985. Elliott was squeezed into paying the OCBC an extra $34 million profit for the last 9.3 per cent of CUB in June 1984. Without that blocking stake he could not fully access CUB's massive cash flow. OCBC had pulled the same sort of trick on Bond at Swan in late 1981 and so the two men had more than one banker in common. (The Hongkong Bank had backed Elders' move on CUB and was also backing BondCorp's move on CaTs.) But Elliott was two steps ahead of Bond. He had already tied up Australia's biggest and best brewery group and now he was taking on the world by buying 10 per cent of Allied-Lyons, preparatory to making a full bid for the English brewer. Elliott's Elders was helping itself but, in the process, the pressure it was applying to the Allied board was helping BondCorp.

On 4 July, BondCorp responded to a formal CaTs disclosure notice with perfunctory disdain. But before trading began on 12 July, the Perth minnow launched a $500-million bid for 50 per cent of CaTs at $7.10 a share. The *coup de théâtre* was delivered by flamboyant Sydney stockbroker Rene Rivkin who walked onto the floor of the Sydney Stock Exchange and charged into the CaTs market with orders of 'buy, buy' on behalf of BondCorp. The share price rocketed to $7.74. 'By the end of the day he had taken most of the ten million shares traded for more than $77 million.'[260] BondCorp went from 14 per cent to 20 per cent and then the buying stopped and the share price dropped back to $7. Sceptics suggested that Bond-Corp wasn't fair dinkum in going for 50 per cent. They thought Bond was just trying to flush out another buyer and, having done so, would retire with a handsome profit. That was his usual modus operandi. CaTs rejected the BondCorp offer as 'nowhere near adequate'. These are believed to be the same words Bond had used in response to Zampatti's bid for Swan in Newport in 1983.

Enter Philip Morris, the US giant which owns the Millers brewery in the States ... It is interested in acquiring CaTs and it holds talks with Zampatti in Brisbane and Allied in London. Beckwith is sent to London to 'babysit' the Allied board which is now under more pressure than it can handle. Everything is working to plan. Back in Sydney, Bond turns up the pressure on Zampatti and Allied by going the whole hog and bidding $1.2 billion for the lot at $7.50 a share on 25 August. Beckwith soothes the anxious Allied directors. If they accept the now-generous BondCorp terms, they can have both Elders IXL and Philip Morris off their backs and still get to brew and sell Castlemaine's Fourex under licence in Europe. The Allied board accepts a new Bond offer of $8.25 a share which gives them a capital gain of $150 million. Philip Morris was offering $9 a share but they are not interested. Zampatti is sold down the river by the Poms. Jerry Holden-Brown, son of Allied chairman, Sir Derrick Holden-Brown, gets a job as a 'brands manager' with Bond Brewing in London. In Brisbane, Zampatti plunges into his own heart the double-edged sword which he had fashioned, and which had cut him twice ...

CaTs directors recommended the BondCorp bid on 27 August after talks with Bond. Bond Brewing is born when a victorious Bond emerges from the talks and tells reporters: 'You can now say BondCorp owns Castlemaine Tooheys.' When asked about Zampatti's future Bond replied, 'He will leave.' Bondy had done it again and once again punters were left stunned in the aisles. Writing in the *Age* the next day, Terry McCrann said it was 'without doubt the most amazing takeover in corporate history. Indeed the exercise in which — figuratively speaking — a $200-million corporate mouse was able to persuade a group of bankers to lend it a billion dollars in order to swallow a $1200-million elephant could well be the most amazing financial coup seen anywhere in the Western corporate world.'

Elliott was pleased because Bond had paid twice as much for 34 per cent of the market as he paid for 45 per cent. The higher capital costs would make competition on the margin that much tougher for Bond Brewing in the coming war with Carlton. It was Bond's biggest thrill since winning the Cup. That night he and twenty revellers invaded Mario's restaurant in East Sydney after winning the directors' recommendation and they celebrated till the early hours of the morning. Bond had ordered two cases of Fourex and plenty of Bollinger.

The next day Bond confessed to Tony Grant-Taylor of the *Australian Financial Review* that CaTs's attempt to block his 1981 bid for Swan had been the genesis of the victory but he had decided after the London lunch with Allied in 1983 that CaTs would be his next big target: 'The bid for 50 per cent was part of the bid tactics. It aimed at seeing who would sell early, believing a full bid wasn't on. But we knew a full bid, and one that was basically unconditional, had to be made. We didn't know Allied would come in. But we knew we'd need that sort of bid to get control over their 25 per cent start,' Bond said. He modestly down-played his role in the incredible feat: 'I played a very small role, really, except for the funding and consultation. The architect of the bid was Peter Mitchell. He's responsible for our twenty-year plan for our business development. Peter Beckwith brought home the Allied bacon. We figured Peter should be in London, and he was there once our bid was fully on the table, for that purpose.'[261] The only person who didn't get a mention was Lloyd Zampatti who had put the concept forward four years earlier. Zampatti left CaTs within a week, and a month later became chief executive of Brett & Co., a small Queensland timber, hardware and stevedoring business which Alan Bond couldn't or wouldn't take over.

With time, Bond would learn to crow about the victory and show his intentions towards the vanquished CaTs. In the process he would reveal a flaw in his business practices that would later worry his bankers: 'It [CaTs] should have been using its cash flow to do things. It wasn't doing that. And therefore it had nowhere to go. So it made sense to put the two businesses together. One that had surplus cash together with the growth company. They're an ideal fit. A cash cow. Better it go to us than to anyone else, that's all I can say,' he told the *National Times* in September.[262]

But if the big CaTs cow was to be milked with the same ferocity as the small Swan cow had been, would there be any cream left over to pay the kind men who lent BondCorp the shiny penny to buy the creature in the first place? Did the men providing the shiny penny worry about BondCorp's propensity to drink milk or its skills in animal husbandry? What would happen if the 'growth company' stopped growing or started 'doing things' that didn't work? Rather than giving BondCorp the third degree in 1985, bankers were tripping over themselves to load it down with as much money as it could carry away.

BondCorp took immense pride in its ability to get into debt. It equated debt with assets and it appeared to measure wealth by the amount it could borrow rather than the amount it had in hand. This was because the company was driven by a desire to achieve its corporate objectives at all costs. Debt capital was a means to that end. In the period between the Cup and the Crash (1983 to 1988 accounts), BondCorp's total liabilities grew from $275 million to $6387 million. If you add in $707 million worth of convertible notes in 1988, total indebtedness exceeded $7 billion. Equity capital in the same period increased only about ten-fold, from roughly $20 million to roughly $200 million. This is an unenviable record of growth which exposed the company to substantial risks in liability management that would eventually lead to its downfall.

This is how Beckwith described BondCorp's finance and liability management strategy in 1987: 'At Bond we have been extremely innovative in our financing techniques and were the first Australian company to take advantage of the US bond market to provide long-term subordinated unsecured debt, unavailable to us in Australia. We believe that good liability management is just as important as good asset management. Our total Group financings are almost all borrowed on an unsecured basis, clearly supported by the Group's strong, reliable cash flows. Because of our attention to key personnel in Treasury and liability management, we are able to borrow in currencies which produce the lowest cost to the Group.'

The theory was fine but look at its practice. Alan Bond had personally borrowed $120 million from BondCorp to buy the Swan Brewery in 1981. BondCorp raised the money with access to bill lines of finance totalling $125.9 million. These were extinguished before 30 June 1982, with the substitution of 'cash deposits for original collateral'. Merchant bank Wardley Australia arranged to replace the bill finance with a 'promissory note discount facility' backed by the Hongkong Bank and secured against the assets. But no matter what you would call it, debt is debt and it has a cost which cuts into the bottom line, especially when interest more than doubles to about $32 million in one year.

When Mr Bond sold his eighty per cent of Swan Brewery to

BondCorp subsidiary Residential Developments Pty Ltd in the same year, the total consideration was given in the books at $163 million. Dallhold usually charged BondCorp a fee for services rendered and this was possibly included in the price, which is said to be 'equal to cost'.

Bond's winning of the America's Cup in 1983 coincided with considerable liquidity in the US banking system. To mobilise these funds, New York investment bank Drexel Burnham Lambert Inc. had invented a new synthetic security which it colloquially but aptly termed 'junk bonds'. These subordinated debentures carried a high rate of interest to compensate for the high-risk nature of the funding and the lack of security. It was an implicit assumption with junk bonds that if the businesses issuing them were more soundly based they would not have to pay the higher interest which reflected the risk attached to them. They were medium to long term and unsecured. Provided you were prepared to wear the price, the money was available in large licks.

Junk bonds were designed with long-sighted and short-funded entrepreneurs like Bond in mind. He was introduced to them in Newport when he met Barrie Lepley, who with his partner Andy Decker controlled the New York boutique investment bank Ocean Securities Corporation, Inc. (OSC). There must have been many private bankers who wanted to act for Bond once he had won the Cup, but Lepley made an impression because he was discreet and had good contacts. Lepley ushered Bond into the Hall of the Junk Bond King, Drexel's dealing room at Beverley Hills in California, where sat Michael Milken at his infamous black X-shaped dealing desk. It was a marriage made in mammon.

Bond would pay Drexel's (later disgraced) Milken a staggering $3.75-million fee for providing Swan Brewery with a US$135-million junk bond facility. They were called 'limited subordination debentures', they paid 14.875 per cent interest and they were not due until 15 December 1998. The issue was announced in October 1983, straight after the Cup (it was only going to be US$125 million then). The prospectus wasn't registered with the US Securities and Exchange Commission until 15 December, when it was fully subscribed through the Drexel network. On 9 December 1983, Treasurer Paul Keating announced the floating of the Aussie dollar. This meant that the exchange rate with other currencies was not fixed by the government but was set by market forces. When Bond made the Swan junk bond issue the Australian dollar was worth US 88.27 cents. In two years it would drop about 20 cents in value, leaving Bond with an unrealised foreign exchange loss of $48.4 million at 30 June 1985.

BondCorp also made its debut in the highly fashionable, offshore Eurobond markets in March 1984 with a Swiss Franc (Sfr) 125-million issue of 10-year 'straight bonds', lead-managed by Soditic. But, though the interest cost on these bonds was relatively inexpensive, the A$/Sfr exchange rate was about to go through convulsions with the floating of the Australian dollar and the issue would expose BondCorp to heavy losses as the A$ plunged because its risk management skills were extremely deficient at the time.

A wise person would assume that the new debt would be used to retire the old debt but this does not appear to have been the case. Long-term secured advances did drop by about $25 million in 1983–84 but that seems to have been about the extent of it. The rest of the $172-million rise in unsecured term borrowings (the junk bonds) was used to provide working capital to BondCorp which was the stated intent of the issue. Waltons Bond got $35 million of it ($25 million in loans and $10 million in preference capital), $20 million went on oil explora-tion, the Swan TV takeover took $50 million the Winthrop Investments takeover another $30 million, Swan Brewery got $12.5 million for expansion and the rest went on new invest-ments in associates Pacific Copper and Airship Industries. If Swan Brewery was having to pay interest on two lots of debt related to its purchase, it is no wonder its profits were so far below expectations in the early 1980s.

The great advantage to Bond of the Swan junk bonds was that they were secured only on the cash flow and not the assets. Bond's preference for unsecured, or negative-pledge, debt was because it left the assets unencumbered and capable of supporting more debt. No principal repayments were due on the bonds until December 1989 'under normal circumstances'. The US debenture holders were entitled to exercise a put option which would require Bond to pay US$13.5 million of principal if it was demanded. It wasn't, in the first six years.

BondCorp's interest bill, which had doubled to almost

$32 million in 1981–82, grew to $40 million in 1982–83 and then dropped to $34.6 million in 1983–84. Had Bond changed his habits and reduced debt that year? On the contrary, term advances (borrowings) increased from $214 million to $386 million; but the cost of funds was cheaper, as interest rates on 90-day bank bills bottomed at 8.6 per cent on 16 December 1983. Also, $2.9 million in interest charges was capitalised that year and long-term secured debt had been lowered by $25 million.

In 1984–85 interest rates had resumed their inexorable climb and borrowings had increased from $386 million to $651 million. The result was a sharp increase in BondCorp's interest costs that year from $34.6 million to $60.9 million. This excluded $9.6 million in interest which had been capitalised. The effect of the new CaTs borrowings did not cut in until the half-year to 31 December 1985. Interest expense in this six-month period jumped to $79 million from the $26 million paid in the same period the previous year. Another $10.2 million worth of interest was capitalised. To be fair, revenue and profit had increased dramatically in the 1985 December half. But when the full 1985–86 figures were in, borrowings had gone through the roof to $1700 million and the annual interest charges were stratospheric at $209.4 million. This was twice BondCorp's operating profit for that year.

Having lost his fear of debt way back in 1974 when he owed $100 million and didn't have a brass razoo, Bond considered himself blessed to be in such a fortunate situation. The $1 billion required for the CaTs takeover was raised with consummate ease by the super salesman: 'Fortunately, I was able to get early finance,' he said the day after the event. 'Standard Chartered in London came in, then the Hongkong & Shanghai Bank, and Nick Whitlam's State Bank [of New South Wales]. Nick had been with us in the Arnott's bid. We knew the players. I got it all lined up in 21 days.'[263] (Nick's father, Gough Whitlam, an implacable foe of Bond in the 1970s, would have blanched at the involvement. But then, Gough wasn't a banker.)

This instant financing package put together by Bond was extremely interesting to trained observers. Notable by their absence were the big American banks — Citibank, Chase Manhattan and Bank of America — who had experienced the BondCorp joy-ride in the late 1970s. But a late addition to the original syndicate was the Bank of Tokyo, which had burnt its fingers in the hot Yanchep sands but participated because it was involved in the separate $300-million financing of the Waltons Bond Park Street development in Sydney. The Industrial Bank of Japan (IBJ) also joined. There was no surprise in HKB's presence: it was clearly now BondCorp's lead banker, confidante and major supporter. Once again Wardley Australia arranged the details and participated in the syndicate.

Standard Chartered, the English bank which had heavy third-world connections and was much admired by Robert Holmes à Court (he had 15 per cent of the stock and a seat on the board), was a new catch and rightly mentioned first by Bond. Bond had a personal banking relationship with Standard Chartered who were funding Dallhold's rapid expansion of his private nickel and gold interests. Its participation, and the slim recognition of the big four Australian banks (Westpac was a big player in the original syndicate), can be directly attributed to the decision by the Federal government in February 1985 to grant banking licences to sixteen foreign banks. Standard Chartered, HKB, Bank of Tokyo and IBJ were on that list and were looking to build business in the new market. Bond could not have picked a better time to approach them.

To virtually cut the big Australian banks out of the financing of Australia's biggest takeover was a calculated insult to his past tormentors: 'They haven't changed a lot, the Australian banks. One of the principal banks we deal with, the National, just haven't changed at all! The glossy photographs have changed but they haven't changed at all ... I mean they're still talking about a sixty-per-cent mortgage on a piece of property. Now that banking is finished. You've got to be talking about cash flows ... They're just not up with it. And they're going to get slaughtered by these foreign banks coming in,' he said in September 1985.[264]

This statement was to have a galvanising effect on the Australian banks, notably the National Australia and Westpac, who were now clamouring to be part of the refinancing of Bond Brewing Holdings Ltd (BBH), having seen the money that was made out of the Swan adventure. The original syndicate had provided Bond only with a short-term blank cheque so that he could complete the CaTs takeover. Just under $1 billion was drawn down and US$700 million of this was imported, unhedged, by the foreign banks. Nick Whitlam was also risking the savings of widows and orphans on a corporate play that could come unstuck.

When the long-term refinancing of BBH debt was completed in November 1986, the lead Australian banker to the deal turned out to be the National Australia Bank (NAB). Bond had banked with the NAB since he was a schoolboy in East Fremantle but it had never felt inclined to lend his businesses money before. What was so different now? Was it the Cup? The advent of the foreign banks? Or was it just a good business proposition? BBH was now claiming to be Australia's largest brewer. Almost by definition, such a business could not possibly fail unless there was a radical change in Australian consumption patterns and folklore, it was argued with much conviction. It was probably a combination of these factors that drew NAB into Bond's debt web.

Wardley Australia put together the new $1.6-billion restructuring of BondCorp's principal lines of finance within twelve months. It was a complicated deal involving layers of international lenders who were secured only by the cash flow generated by the brewing business and not by the assets themselves. This was something Bond insisted on. To quarantine this flow of beer money away from BondCorp's other flights of fancy, a loan-and-credit agreement was signed on 21 November 1986 with the senior lenders. As the lead local, NAB was appointed their agent and the keeper of the covenants and 'negative pledges' given by BBH in regard to the conduct of its business and financial affairs.

NAB appears to have won this key role by default. It was the Westpac bank who had made all the fuss about its role in helping Bondy 'unbolt the Cup' in 1983. It had 'saved him' in the 1970s and been part of the original CaTs syndicate. In the face of the foreign onslaught, Westpac was looking to back winners in the 1980s. But Westpac baulked at the negative pledge. Keen as it was to be part of the beer syndicate and associate with the first Australian defence of the America's Cup in Fremantle later that year, it could not come at lending money with only a lick and a promise as collateral. Bond would not budge from his insistence that the brewing assets remain unencumbered and that, should anything happen to BBH, the parent company should not be held responsible for the debt. Westpac pulled out. The Bank of Tokyo and the IBJ also rejected the kind offer.

Reflect on this for a moment. The banks now needed Alan Bond more than Bond needed the banks. If they didn't lend him the money on his terms he would take his beer barrel and get it filled elsewhere. Such was the strength of his standing position that few of the timid bankers gathering around the money pot at his feet were prepared to call his bluff. They knew he was right about the alternatives. Either they wanted his business or they didn't. The choice was theirs, as was the chance. NAB and Nick Whitlam's State Bank of New South Wales took it.

Other participants in the senior facility were the HKB, Standard Chartered, the First National Bank of Boston (Newporters to a man), Société Générale (a Waltons Bond lender), the Toronto Dominion Bank, Pittsburgh National Bank (Bond had bought the local brewery there too), the Mitsubishi Trust and Banking Corporation and the Sumitomo Trust and Banking Co. Ltd. It was their job to come up with an $880-million 'revolving medium-term multi-optioned credit facility', which is bankerspeak for a big loan. The first $600 million was syndicated multi-currency cash repayable over seven years. The second $280 million was a US$175-million letter of credit facility backed by bank-backed 'zero coupon bonds', which are really quite good for you financially. It was handled by Drexel.

Underneath this upper layer of senior debt was a massive US$510-million (about A$750-million at the time) pile of junk bonds. These particular BBH 'extendable subordinated debentures' paid a cheaper interest rate of 12 and 5/8ths per cent than the Swan junks offered but that reflected the prevailing interest rate timing rather than the quality of the assets. Drexel arranged and placed the BBH junks among its American client base and created a secondary market in the debt. 'We managed to do that right in the middle of what was a fairly critical period for the subordinated debt markets and for Drexel, when the kitchen sink was being thrown at them,' BondCorp finance director Tony Oates admitted later.[265]

The senior debt was clearly superior to the subordinated junks bonds but then some of the deck chairs on the Titanic were more comfortable than others. Both facilities were unsecured and without recourse to the BondCorp lifeboats. The existing US$135-million Swan Brewing junk bond issue and the Sfr125-million Eurobond issue remained in place. Cheap offshore loans, particularly those denominated in Swiss Francs, were all the rage in the frenzied 1980s. The deeper the debt, the more excited and honoured the BondCorp chairman became: 'These new arrangements demonstrate the confidence of the world's capital markets in your company,' he told share-holders. The refinancing against 'the strong and consistent cash flows from brewing . . . has left the balance of the group's operations largely unencumbered and available to support debt required to grow our core businesses.'

Before the ink was dry on the $1.6-billion Bond Brewing cheque, Bond's troops were sailing triumphantly into Hong-kong Harbour and sizing up the New Territories of the Crown Colony. Some of the HKB's money came straight back to them. On 6 November 1986 BondCorp bought a controlling interest in Town and City International Co. Ltd, an ailing Hong Kong property developer operating under a Supreme Court scheme of arrangement because of a gaping hole in its profit and loss account. On 13 November, Narcissus changed the company's name to Bond Corporation International Ltd (BCIL) and waved his magic wand over its balance sheet.

He paid HK$1.3 billion for a bunch of high-rise residential properties in the Midlevels area, HK$1.5 billion for about 25 per cent of HK-TVB Ltd and HK$1.9 billion for a major futuristic twin-tower office development under construction downtown. It had been called Financial Square but it soon became the Bond Centre. When BCIL listed on the Hong Kong stock exchange on 5 January 1987 the shares were rushed. The prospectus offering the shares must have been very impressive as the small issue closed sixty-seven times oversubscribed in overcrowded Hong Kong. But even this wasn't enough for the ever-optimistic Bond.

He innocently gave the shares a bit of a boost by telling a local press conference that the asset backing of BCIL shares was much higher than the figure stated in the prospectus. It was the sort of enthusiastic statement you would expect from the great salesman in cynical Australia. But in the prim and proper British Crown Colony it caused corporate culture shock. The stock exchange were not impressed and considered charging our hero with the issuance of misleading information. He was saved in the end by a humble apology and his Hong Kong connections. Sir Run Run Shaw, the chairman of HK-TVB, was an old friend of BondCorp; and the HKB, listed as principal bankers to BCIL, were not without considerable influence.

From November 1986 Alan Bond lived in a blur of activity. Everything was happening to him at once that month. In the three years since his Newport victory the size of his company had grown six-fold and he was clearly only just beginning. Now the Cup had come around again and this time it was his Cup, and the regatta would be held off the Fremantle of his boyhood. But, frankly, at this time he needed the boat race like he needed a hole in the head. The Cup served only to remind him that he was falling behind in his timetable for world domination of the communications, brewing and gold industries. He had set this lavish target in 1983 and had 'Jeeves' Mitchell enshrine it in a twenty-to-fifty-year corporate plan.

Goal-setting was something Bond did instinctively. As a callow migrant youth he had promised himself to be a millionaire by his majority. He had turned forty-eight in 1986 and BondCorp's turnover had gone through the $1-billion mark. What else do you offer to inspire a man who has the America's Cup and a billion dollars? Winning the Cup had been a goal of sorts but its actualisation in 1983 could be turned into a windfall for Dallhold (and, to a lesser extent, BondCorp) only if he could capitalise on that fortuitous spin of the dice while the going was good.

Having been nearly put through three times before — in 1961, 1974 and 1982 — Bond should have been cautious about the future. It pays a man with pretensions to being seen as a visionary or seer to plan ahead to the next big turning point in the trade cycle. Bond had been obsessive in his desire to obtain recession-proof cash flow and unencumbered assets to ensure his continued survival. In November 1986 the biggest international sharemarket crash that BondCorp is ever likely to encounter was less than twelve months away; but he wasn't to know that, judging by his actions.

If there seemed to be a great urgency to dump Waltons Bond and bed down BBH and BCIL at that time it was because BondCorp was about to give birth to its most promising, yet explosive, child — Bond Media Ltd (BOM). 'On November 27, 1986, Federal Cabinet announced its intention to introduce changes to the law governing television ownership thereby permitting one person or group to own any number of television stations up to a point where that person or group would have access to no more than 75 per cent of the national viewing audience,' said the BOM prospectus.

The news would set a fire-cracker under Australia's old media moguls, Kerry Packer, Rupert Murdoch and the disparate Fairfax family, and allow a whole host of new players to enter the television industry. Until the Labor Party changed the rules, owners were restricted to two metropolitan stations. Kerry Packer had the Channel 9 stations in Sydney and Melbourne; Alan Bond had the Channel 9 stations in Perth and Brisbane.

Kerry Packer inherited the Nine Network from his father, Sir Frank Packer, Bond's mentor in the quest for the Cup. Bond had the Cup and wanted the Nines in Sydney and Melbourne. Kerry Packer had the Nine Network and didn't want the Cup because he had World Series cricket. He wanted to add Perth and Brisbane to his private TV interests now that he could. Bond and Packer had a history of successful negotiations and this one would be no different. Both men are big gamblers but Kerry Packer was better at the odds.

They had first got together in March 1980 when Packer's Consolidated Press (ConsPress) sold to BondCorp 18.7 per cent of Pacific Copper (the Maitland, New South Wales, coal-miner) for $10.2 million. At the time, both Packer and Bond were jousting for positions on the share register of another New South Wales coalminer, White Industries, and once again Bond ended up with Packer's stake. It was alleged that Cons-Press had 'warehoused' its 25-per-cent White stake for Bond-Corp for a period of time before the parcel changed hands on 12 May 1980. Bond never got control of White Industries but both he and Packer made a lot of money out of the deal. Bond did get control of Pacific Copper with Packer's help. The two men's companies were also joint owners of some forest land at Burleigh Heads, near Palm Beach on the Gold Coast, where re-zoning to residential was considered 'imminent'. When BondCorp sold its half interest to Waltons Bond in June 1981, the consideration was $7.7 million. ConsPress valued its 50 per cent at $11.7 million. .

Bond's corporate plan insisted that he grow his media and communications interests as quickly as possible because the future was in ownership of the airwaves and data communication. He had two provincial stations but it gave him no network hardware and no clout in the boardrooms of Sydney and Melbourne. To this end he was about to launch Sky Channel as a satellite broadcaster but he desperately wanted to be the biggest and the best in television in Australia. When Hawke bounced the ball on 27 November Bond was ready to fly into action.

The negotiations began in early December and continued right through the two months of challenger and defender elimination trials for the America's Cup in Perth. Packer had entered the negotiations as a buyer but when it became apparent that Bond was talking long-distance telephone numbers in his offer for the Nine Network, he traded positions and agreed to sell for $1,055,000,000. The deal was signed on 20 January 1987 and announced by Bond the day his *Australia IV* boat was eliminated from the America's Cup defence off Fremantle. Bond had won the Nines and lost the Cup all in the one day. Packer had lost the Nines but won a billion dollars for something that cost him nothing. An enlargement of the cheque for the cash component of $805 million, with Alan Bond's signature on it, is said to adorn a wall in his executive washroom.

Bond had of course borrowed the money for BOM from his new banking friends at NAB and was quick to offset some of the cost of the acquisition by immediately selling down Bond-Corp's stake to 50 per cent. Through a rights issue, BondCorp shareholders were made the unlucky recipients of roughly 25 per cent of the BOM capital at the grossly inflated price of $1.55 a share. The BOM issue was 40 per cent under-subscribed and the underwriters, NAB, had to pick up the shortfall. The shares listed on 4 June 1987, at a 27-cent discount to the issue price. Kerry Packer would later value the BOM shares at 10 cents.

Like BBH and BCIL, BOM would be loaded down with unsecured debt. BOM still owed Kerry Packer $200 million and it had a $385-million term facility from a bank consortium led by NAB. Bond would add to his media interests by picking up Robert Holmes à Court's Club Superstation satellite service for next to nothing on 20 May and paying $115 million for an initial 22.5-per-cent stake in British Satellite Broadcasting on 16 July.

At 30 June 1987 BondCorp would claim total assets of $4.1 billion and total liabilities of $2.6 billion. Borrowings would advance from $1.7 billion to $2.3 billion, with $2 billion being in foreign currencies. Net profit would rise from $104.4 million to $117.7 million but interest payments would go up from $209.4 million to $282 million with the BOM debt yet to cut in.

With national brewing, international investment and national media assets in place, Dallhold would add to its Bond International Gold (BIG) interest with the purchase of the St Joe Gold Corporation, one of the Western world's largest, for $700 million in August. Bond's mother, Kathleen, died that month. She was aged seventy-nine and Bond grieved. But, driven by its desire to achieve its corporate goals, his Bond-Corp empire marched on with relentless aggression. His trusted lieutenants set about the completion of the entrepreneur's fifty-year master plan. In October, finance director Oates, who has a law degree and no accounting qualifications, was working on a new A$500-million short-term debt facility that would not be guaranteed by BondCorp but which BondCorp would draw down and repay at its leisure. He was having difficulty getting it away.

On 12 October 1987 a BondCorp subsidiary, called the Amber Acquisition Corporation, agreed to pay US$1.28 billion (A$1.7 billion) for the G Heileman Brewing Company, Inc., based at La Crosse in Wisconsin, with money borrowed from a consortium of international banks. This was led by the Bank of Boston and also included the Bank of Nova Scotia, Wells Fargo and Continental Illinois. The 'dealer managers' of this exquisitely bad-timed tender deal were Barrie Lepley's Ocean Securities Corporation and the solid Wall Street investment banker, Salomon Brothers. (Laurie Connell was busy on the Fairfax takeover.)

A press release issued that day made this claim: 'The Heileman acquisition places BondCorp at the forefront of world brewing operations. The successful acquisition makes BondCorp the fourth largest brewer in the world, and continues Bond's global expansion, begun with its 1986 acquisition of the Pittsburgh Brewing Company in Pennsylvania. As the fourth-largest brewer in the US, Heileman produces approximately 18.7 million hectolitres of beer, an amount roughly equal to the total Australian beer market. As a joint force, Bond and Heileman are in a position to tackle markets previously beyond either's reach.'

According to Alan Kohler, who was editor of the *Austral-*

ian Financial Review at the time, Bond's 12 October US beer bid would qualify him as an entrant in the 'Last Dance on the Titanic' award: 'But he wasn't the only one still spinning around the streamer-strewn dance floor as the ship went down.'[266] Between 10 a.m. and 10.45 a.m. on Black Tuesday, 20 October 1987, the Australian Stock Exchange's All Ordinaries index dropped 516 points (25 per cent) to 1549, following, and exaggerating, a 20-per-cent fall in Wall Street overnight. 'While the entrepreneurs were all still on the dance floor, the fund managers had begun to saunter towards the lifeboats, trying to act nonchalant,' Kohler said.

BondCorp's share price fell $1 from $2.50 to $1.50, which represented a paper loss of about $220 million to Alan Bond and Dallhold Investments. For the next two years Bond would tread water.

CHAPTER THIRTEEN

December 29, 1989: 'They said you'd never make it'

On the last business day of the 1980s — Friday, 29 December 1989 — when the beginning of the end came for the company that had become known worldwide, the Bond Corporation still thought it was poised on the edge of greatness. On this fine line between great wealth and a financial holocaust, BondCorp ran out of credibility and people to do deals with. As Kerry Packer remarked, Bond had 'too many balls in the air'. They would crash to the ground as management fumbled the defence of Bond's now infamous juggling act. In the month-long court case that followed the appointment of receiver/managers to Bond Brewing Holdings (BBH) that day, Peter Mitchell would confess to being a director of no fewer than six hundred group companies. Few of these could have received his undivided attention as the countdown began to the demise of the ailing corporate monster that BondCorp had become. Unruly and unruleable, it had lost the confidence of its major bankers. The time had come to call in the massive debt that had been accumulated as if with gay abandon. Alan Bond had ceased to amaze.

Although the Bond Brewing arm was the first to be lopped from the BondCorp trunk, it was chopped as much for a property deal as for maladministration of the brewing assets. Property had been the basis of the growth of Lesmurdie Heights Pty Ltd from a company with a capital of $1000 in the late 1950s to the global BondCorp octopus with shareholders' funds of $891.3 million at its peak in 1988. Unlike Bond's attempts to gain cash flow from retailing, media and brewing businesses, property was the only business BondCorp could rely on to produce capital gains when they were needed. And there was heavy demand for capital gains to prop profits in the late 1980s.

The cover picture on the 1988 annual report shows the thrusting edifice of Perth's fifty-storey R&I Bank tower, built on the site of the old Palace Hotel and with its uppermost floors devoted to the delights of Dallhold and the chairman's price-less art collection. The 'prestigious offices' include a full board-room and a dining room with kitchen facilities that enabled the chairman 'to conduct his meetings as well as entertaining govern-ment heads, financiers, business people, etc. to the standard required having regard to his standing in the community.'[267]

The inner sanctum is guarded by vast expanses of black marble and huge gold-metal sliding doors. This eyrie faces Fremantle, where the fairytale rise of BondCorp began. But the building's journey through the balance sheets is more reveal-ing. Purchased from the Commonwealth Bank on or about 27 June 1978 for $5.5 million, the site was 'independently valued' at $10 million on 23 October 1980 and this figure was adopted in the 1981 accounts. The $4.5-million added value seems reasonable, considering that BondCorp was planning a $70-million landmark tower for the site.

Arkingdale Pty Ltd, and its wholly owned subsidiary Row-dore Pty Ltd, were the two BondCorp subsidiaries which ended up owning the Palace Hotel and the Terrace Arcade properties on which the tower was built. Both were sold to 37-per-cent-owned associate Austmark International during 1982–83 for what appears to be a consideration of $4.6 million. It is, of course, inconceivable that BondCorp would take a loss on any property deal, let alone a $5.4-million paper loss on a property that had a $10-million book value. The plot thickens when the same accounts reveal that the extraordinary profit on the sale of the two subsidiaries was $5.9 million. But Austmark appears to have picked up $18.5 million in debt associated with the site, and $13.6 million of this was an inter-company loan. To cover this large debt, the value of the land and improvements at the time of the sale is listed as $22.9 million. Austmark would have had to pay this figure just to clear the debt and leave BondCorp with its $4.6-million consideration.

But we know that BondCorp initially paid $5.5 million for the property and an extraordinary profit of $5.9 million was booked on its sale. Confused? So was the tax man who found that private interests associated with Bond, Beckwith, Oates and Mitchell had each made a profit of $900,000 by selling Rowdore to Arkingdale for $3.6 million on 29 June 1979.[268] Now, if the total cost of the property was $9.1 million ($5.5 million + $3.6 million for Rowdore) and a profit of $5.9 million was booked on the deal, then the property could have sold for about $15 million; but a shareholder cannot tell this by looking at the accounts.

What is interesting here (besides the profit-sharing arrangement offered to benefit the top four executives at BondCorp) is that the following year, 1983–84, Austmark incurred 'significant losses' as a result of this and other deals, straining stretched resources. It had heavy debts and little income while its projects were being developed. Believe it or not, BondCorp was attempting to help its associate Austmark at the time. BondCorp had taken part in a capital reconstruction of Austmark in December 1982 and had offered to support its future loan-raising activities. But who was Peter and who was Paul?

BondCorp had paid out $1.2 million in holding costs for Arkingdale's debt in 1981–82–83. (It had also paid out $89,000 for Rowdore's debt over the same period.) This debt was transferred to Austmark with the sale; and, as much of it was an inter-company loan, the payments presumedly came to Bond-Corp as interest earned. BondCorp also got an extraordinary book profit of $5.9 million on the sale of land. Without that bonus, the group's results for 1982–83 (Cup year) would have shown extraordinary losses of $18 million, dwarfing operating net profits of $6.8 million.

The tower was eventually completed as a joint venture with WA Inc. partner, the Rural and Industries Bank. When BondCorp took over Austmark it regained a direct 50 per cent of its head-office tower but soon sold it to the R&I for $108 million in the great BondCorp asset sale of 1989. The property was valued in the Austmark takeover documents at $97 million. The Palace Hotel is now an R&I banking chamber standing at the foot of the R&I stalagmite. The Palace/Bond/R&I tower was one of the few property assets not temporarily transferred to Waltons Bond to gain liquidity in late 1981. Another was the David Jones site, also in St Georges Terrace, where Bond's two partners were Laurie Connell from Rothwells and Brian Yuill from Spedley Securities Ltd. Rothwells and Spedley were to fall over after the crash and splatter the wider financial community, but not before BondCorp had done a few more excruciating last-minute deals with them.

Two other property transactions proved extremely useful in propping up the 1988 accounts — the Sydney Hilton Hotel sale and the Rome land deal — but they had a smell of desperation about them and they ended up creating more problems than they solved. The Hilton deal was described by Mr Justice Beach of the Victorian Supreme Court as

> one of the more mysterious transactions I have been called upon to investigate during the course of my legal career. In some respects it has been like dealing simultaneously with a slippery eel and a large and very active octopus. When one feels one is making headway towards gaining an understanding of the true nature of the transaction one suddenly finds oneself up a blind alley and obliged to start afresh. I fear that a full investigation of the transaction or multiplicity of transactions will ultimately take some unfortunate member of the judiciary a considerable period of time.

But Beach damns the Hilton transaction with faint praise. It was hailed as a brilliant financial coup at the time, and to some extent it was. As the 1987–88 balance date approached, Bond desperately needed such windfalls because the first accounts after the crash would be an acid test for BondCorp. Had he survived the 'sharequake' unscathed, as he had claimed? Were the brewing and media businesses bringing home the profits, dividends and debt servicing costs, as was expected?

Bond's ability to produce rabbits out of hats at the right moment was legendary, and one of his better rabbits was the one he pulled out in March 1986. Bond had bought the rights to the Screen Entertainments film library from Thorn EMI Ltd in the UK and sold them to the Cannon film group in the US five days later for what appeared to be a clear (untaxed) profit of $100 million in cash and Cannon shares. This figure roughly equates to BondCorp's net profit of $103 million in 1985–86. The Hilton deal took longer but was eventually to put the Cannon deal in the shade.

Bond bought the Hilton Hotel/Capital Centre complex from the Abbey Capital Group (AMP Society) for a reported $160 million in June 1987 — four months before the big 'sharequake'. Bond was craving high-profile landmark sky-scrapers at the time. This edifice complex had been com-pounded by having in his portfolio the tallest building on the Indian Ocean and the stunning twin towers of the Bond Centre in Hong Kong. A policy decision was taken early in 1987 to concentrate on these highly visible Central Business District (CBD) property activities, and the Hilton acquisition was part of that process but an adjunct to the main chance.

Undaunted by the massive obligations BondCorp had recently acquired with its thrusts into brewing and media, rampant optimism appeared to triumph in June 1987 when the company announced it would build 'one of the world's tallest buildings' on a Waltons department store site in the centre of Sydney and adjacent to the Hilton Hotel. It would be called 'Skytower' and its 102 levels were planned to rise 381 metres from the highest point in the CBD of Australia's largest city. The Hilton was acquired as part of the overall plan and provision was made in the planning to link its retail levels with those of the Skytower.

For the patriotic Mr Alan Bond, Skytower represented an 'opportunity to capture the symbolism of Australia's 200th birthday ... [with] a project that will transform the Sydney skyline and, in itself, represent a dramatic restatement of the energy, persistence and flair which have made our country so great. Skytower is also a practical expression of confidence in Sydney's commercial future,' he said. But the Manhattanesque project was knocked on the head by the powers that be in Sydney for being too grotesque, and Skytower went back to being a scaled-down Park Plaza which was sold for $278 million in 1988.

On 7 January 1988 Bond got a 'highly visible' replacement project for the Skytower in Sydney when the Hawke Labor government sold him the downtown Chifley Square site for $306 million (it was won at tender). On this site, John Bryan Bond, the eldest son, who was now a Sydney resident and a BondCorp director in charge of property development (like his father had been twenty years earlier), proposed a $1-billion, 43-level structure to be called 'The Bond Building'. (The project, half-completed, was for sale as this book went to press.)

Exactly one week later, on 14 January, the Sydney Hilton was 'sold' to an unnamed buyer for $300 million. This placed BondCorp in a wonderful financial position. With the defeat of the Skytower proposal, the Hilton had become surplus to group needs but very handy in meeting the bill for Chifley Square. It would also prove helpful in meeting a shortfall in Bond Brewing Holding's profits from brewing in 1987–88 and would keep the NAB-led bank-lending syndicate happy for another year at least.

On the surface (never a good vantage point from which to explore a complicated BondCorp property deal), BondCorp turned a $140-million profit on the sale of the Hilton in just seven months — $20 million a month for those as astute at mathematical progression as the Bonds were. The 1988 annual report confirmed that the sale 'was negotiated for a substantial profit over acquisition cost', but it didn't say to whom, at what price or under what terms. In the back of the book, a new subsidiary called Lawson Holdings Ltd, which had ultimately owned the property for the seven-month term of occupancy, reported a tax-free profit contribution to group results of $80.491 million. It was tax free because Lawson operated in the corporate tax-free enclave of the Cook Islands in the South Pacific. What happened to the other $60 million component of the Hilton 'profit'? As a shareholder, you could not tell from the annual report.

It is here that we get into the very complicated world of 'slippery eels' and a certain 'large and active octopus' of which Justice Beach spoke in February 1990 in the Victorian Supreme

Court. Suffice to say that it seems that BondCorp, through Bond Brewing Investments, funded a certain Mr Ong Beng Seng of Singapore and his aptly-named Noble Choice Corporation to complete the other half of the Hilton deal — thereby fulfilling all BondCorp's expectations of the event. (At the time of publication, the deal was still to be settled but Mr Ong had also purchased Bond Motor Corporation.) We will leave this part of the story here. Others may not ...

Another deal going on at the time was much more romantic but almost as profitable for book entry purposes in the 1987–88 accounts. It was dubbed 'the Rome land deal' (Porta di Roma was its handle) and the dry facts, as reported by the *Australian Financial Review*, are these: 'On October 3, 1987, BondCorp bought about 300 hectares of land outside Rome in Italy and plans to build Europe's largest shopping centre on the site. The land was purchased for about $60 million.'[269] The 1988 annual report, the last one with glossy colour plates, takes up the story. It says that early in 1988 (May), BCIL, the 66-per-cent-owned, tax-effective offshore international investment arm of BondCorp, acquired an option to take up a 49-per-cent interest in a company holding the Porta di Roma land parcel on the outskirts of the eternal city. 'The remaining 51 per cent is held by Bond Corporation Holdings Ltd.' Like Romulus and Remus, the Italo-Australian twins had intertwined to effect control of a *'centro ingrosso'* (wholesale distribution centre) where the road to Florence intersects the ring road, nine kilometres north of Rome.

This was a $1.2-billion project with potential for windfall profits but you had to be in the know to become a player and participate in them. Bond's inside information was said to have come from 'yachting contacts'. It was not only good, it was detailed. Bond promptly snapped up four farms on the crucial intersection: 'Holders of the farming blocks were having financial problems with their banks and the Bond group stepped in to buy in late 1987 at a reported price of A$73.6 million.'[270]

But how's a good old Freo boy (Italian though contemporary Fremantle has become) going to get to hear about a Rome land deal when he's living the jet-set life of a tall iris miles from the action? Why had the person who had done all the detailed groundwork and the discounted cash-flow projections on Porta di Roma give it away to Bond for nothing? Did the reticence of the original predator have anything to do with the fact that the great October-1987 international sharequake was less than two weeks away?

Years later, the answers are (still) blowing in the wind.

Bond and his now-Japanese-owned *Australia III* and *IV* boats had been competing in the world twelve-metre championships at Sardinia (Italy's Tasmania) when, according to local legend, Bond heard (the Aga Khan and Peter de Savary were members of the local yacht club) that the Porta di Roma was for purchase. It was destined, according to BondCorp market research, to be the greatest thing to happen to Rome since the postwar Marshall plan went into effect. Rome was a pure gushing spring for the thirsty BondCorp, which did not have to be forced to drink.

Even the tax-effective distribution of the profits was pre-planned. BondCorp had a Cook Islands company called Sphinx Holdings Ltd hold its parcel; while BCIL had plans to register a company in equally tax-effective Jersey, in the Channel Islands, to hold *its* half. BCIL had also entered into a joint-venture partnership agreement with an unnamed British developer on the Rome deal. This silent partner ended up owning the 49-per-cent BCIL stake. It operated through the Monaco-based group with the less-than-revealing name of Monaco Group SA. It is possible that the mysterious British entrepreneur and yachtsman Peter de Savary was both the source of the info and BCIL's silent partner in the Rome land deal; but, again, a shareholder simply cannot tell by looking at the relevant annual accounts. It is doubtful that the Aga Khan had need of a handy little earner at the time.

When BCIL bought half of the Rome project in May 1988, what they did was actualise a huge book profit for brother BondCorp in time for its 30-June balance date. BCIL had paid HK$112 million to BondCorp for an option to acquire half of the Rome land and the exercise price was US$120 million. Let us suppose that these two payments were worth A$175 million to BondCorp. That put a 'market' value of about $350 million on the four farms on the cloverleaf. If entry price was $74 million and commissions made up another $16 million, then Bond-Corp's paper profit on the entire investment was worth about $260 million already. Half of that was $130 million, nearly twice the entry price.

But in the 1987–88 BondCorp accounts Sphinx Holdings reported a more modest 100-per-cent profit of $73.759 million. It was off-balance-sheet and offshore, but a positive contributor to group profit nonetheless. A further $18.5 million followed in 1988–89 but by then BondCorp had sold its 51 per cent of Roma to a $2 company called Kitool Pty Ltd. This enterprising little shelf company was associated indirectly with Brian Yuill's Spedley Securities which, in turn, was owed money by Laurie Connell's Rothwells which by then was in deep post-crash trouble.

Now, Kitool agreed to purchase 51 per cent of the Rome land some time in September 1988 for $110 million, but this appears to be just a financing technique that was devised and supported by interests associated with BondCorp. The sale was fully reversible through put and call options at the same price which meant that the sale was not a sale at all but a market maker. This deal ultimately fell through and the 51-per-cent stake was purchased by BCIL, which was very handy for BondCorp as the group was under a lot of pressure over the deal. BCIL had on-sold its 49-per-cent stake before Christmas that year to a 'European company', presumedly Monaco Group SA.

BondCorp would later confess to the Australian Stock Exchange that a profit of $106.5 million on the sale of the first tranche of Rome land to BCIL was included in the BondCorp results for the six months to 31 December 1988. Indeed, a property segment EBIT (earnings before interest and tax) of $152.2 million was included in those figures without attribution. The source of this contribution appears to be the Jersey-based company Kerrison Ltd. For the full 1988–89 year, Kerrison contributed $193.8 million to the BondCorp bottom line and was its healthiest performer.

In the end, two profits worth $212 million (Kerrison and Sphinx) appear to have been booked by BondCorp on the complete sale of the Rome land to BCIL in 1988–89. Add in the $74-million Sphinx contribution of the previous year (which was never reversed in the accounts) and the grand *centro ingrosso* profit looks more like $286 million, and all of it tax effective.

In its essence, the Rome deal had been very much like the Palace deal in Perth, the Bond Centre deal in Hong Kong and the Hilton deal in Sydney. Indeed many BondCorp property deals had the same basic ingredients. They were leveraged purchases followed by a revaluation which would be subsequently confirmed by its 'sale' to an associate or friendly company, preferably with a put and call option. It was a sure-fire way of making money and few people in the world were as good at it as the BondCorp team.

The one apparent contradiction to this theory was the sale and subsequent repurchase of the Emu brewery site on the edge of the Perth CBD. Here BondCorp was caught on the horns of the put and call dilemma and lost on the call of the spinning coins. In his judgment, Mr Justice Beach described this deal as 'an extraordinary financial transaction and one which should cause any lender to the Bond Group the utmost concern.' But most of Bond's financial transactions over the years had been extraordinary ones. This had not stopped unconcerned lenders lending to him.

Some history: The Emu brewery had indeed operated from this site but it became redundant with the opening of the new Swan brewery at Canning Vale in the suburbs. The old Swan site further downriver had already turned into a profitable property plaything before being sold to WA Inc. An interest in both properties had originally come gratis with the brewing business in 1981. An entry in the 1981–82 accounts shows that, at that stage, the Emu site had been acquired for redevelopment in a joint venture with Lord McAlpine (owner of Broome, treasurer of the British Conservative Party and contributor to the ALP's John Curtin Foundation).

This deal apparently fell through 'because of the present low state of the property market in the central business district.' More details about later deals surfaced in the Victorian Supreme Court hearings into BBH's receivership and through a NCSC inquiry. They were not apparent to shareholders attempting to pursue the topic in the BondCorp annual reports. The Emu land was theoretically owned at some stage by Actraint No. 84 Pty Ltd, a subsidiary of Bond Brewing Investments, which was a subsidiary of BBH, which was a subsidiary of BondCorp. Actraint No. 84 first appeared in the 1987–88 annual report.

But the year before that, according to evidence presented in the Victorian Supreme Court, the site had been sold for $35 million, which represented a profit of $19.6 million to Bond-Corp. The buyer was not disclosed but it was believed to be Inkberry Pty Ltd, which is described in the 1987–88 accounts as 'an unrelated corporation' even though both Dallhold and BondCorp had rights to any profits it would generate on the sale of the Emu site.

But Bond must have thought the property was worth much more than the $35 million he had sold it for in 1986–87 because on 29 June 1988 — the last day before that all-important 1987–88 balance date — he appears to have bought it back and sold it again for $130 million and was offering to buy it back again for $130 million. The buyer this time was certainly Larry Adler's FAI Insurances Ltd. FAI was the sole institutional friend to BondCorp and an unsecured lender to the group. This deal is intricately related to that relationship (Larry's son Rodney Adler now runs FAI and is not as well disposed towards BondCorp as his late father had been). It has also been the subject of a long investigation by the NCSC.

The NCSC later declared on 21 December 1989 that the sale to FAI on 29 June 1988 was not a sale but only a 'financing arrangement' involving security for a loan of $130 million to BondCorp from FAI. It ordered Dallhold to return a $30-million fee it had obtained from BondCorp for arranging the deal. BondCorp had declared a profit of $45 million on the deal in its crucial 1987–88 accounts. This could not be taken away from it as it had already had the effect of making the BBH results look a lot better than they really were. But if the transfer of the land had been by way of providing security to FAI for its $130-million loan to BondCorp, what was BondCorp doing claiming the advance as a profit?

There was more. BondCorp had paid FAI $10 million for an option to call the property back at about $130 million and FAI had obtained a put option allowing it to sell the property back to BondCorp for a similar figure. The put and call options were originally exercisable by 30 June 1989. But in January 1989 the option term was extended by six months to January 1990 and the option exercise price was increased to $160 million. Bond-Corp had also added a $40-million deposit to its $10-million option fee. FAI exercised its put option against BondCorp's Actraint No. 84 Pty Ltd in January 1990. This left BondCorp holding a $200-million baby for whose delivery it still owed the stork $150 million. Surely this had not been the desired outcome when Inkberry and FAI's United Bodyworks (Queensland) Pty Ltd snuggled up together on the eve of the 1987–88 balance date.

In qualifying BondCorp's 1988–89 accounts, auditors Arthur Anderson & Co. pointed out this $150-million liability but were unable to give a certain opinion as to the value of the land and whether a provision for loss was required. BondCorp had it in its accounts as a capital commitment. FAI had it in its accounts as a overdue receivable, secured by title. The matter was still unresolved in February 1990.

While Justice Beach did not agree with NAB's submission that BBH/Actraint had made an improper transaction in breach of the loan and credit agreement with the bank syndicate by giving FAI the $40-million deposit for the Emu land as part of the put and call option, he said he understood the banks' concern over the transaction: 'A further matter of concern is that the decisions to enter into the transaction, make a payment and grant the charge, were not made by BBI or Actraint in the ordinary course of business; they were made by BCH (Bond Corporation Holdings).' Beach agreed with NAB that 'it was an extraordinary thing, to agree to accept being compelled to buy in three months' time for $160 million land one was entitled to buy for $130 million and to pay a fee for doing so.'

The NCSC had been much more harsh in its 22-December-1989 verdict on the original transaction of 29 June 1988, the one which gave BondCorp a $45-million profit and Dallhold a $30-million fee. Its damning declaration that the deal was a 'financing arrangement' was hotly contested by both BondCorp and Dallhold but in the end Alan Bond personally guaranteed Dallhold's performance of its obligations under the settlement and Dallhold agreed to meet the NCSC's $3-million investigation costs. Why?

The NCSC was reported to be considering legal action against BondCorp under the Companies Code. Section 542 enables the commission to seek orders where it is satisfied that a person is guilty of fraud, negligence, default, breach of trust or breach of duty to a company, and the company has, as a result, suffered, or is likely to suffer, loss or damage. This is not to suggest that BondCorp directors did anything wrong or improper. No charges were laid and the company strongly disagreed with the NCSC interpretation. However, the NCSC determination was extremely damaging to BondCorp's credibility and the award of $3 million in costs was widely interpreted as a fine. There seems little doubt that the timing of its release was a contributing factor in the NAB syndicate pulling the pin on BondCorp a week later.

Of interest in this exercise is the exponential growth in the reported value of a fairly ordinary piece of city-edge real estate (with a freeway running through the centre of it) in such a short space of time. It had been valued at $15.4 million, cost price, before it was sold to Inkberry for $35 million in 1986–87 and a profit was taken. Its value jumped to $130 million in 1987–88 and another profit was taken. In 1988–89 it was back in the Bond books with a $200-million value on its head. But now the profits had stopped and there was potential for a $120-million loss on a property deal. A loss such as this was not a usual occurrence in the Bond corporate culture.

Bond's $200-million valuation was not a fiction but an independent valuation provided by professional valuers Richard Ellis: 'Our opinion of value was based on certain assumptions,' said Richard Ellis WA manager, Gary Ryan, in a business magazine interview. 'We thought about it for a long time before we put our cock on the block. We knew where the valuation was going,' he concluded painfully.[271] The assumption that Ellis mentions probably refers to Bond's plans for a $700-million business park for the site. But the Ellis opinion was on the block against two other independent valuations which set the value of the land at $80 million and $120 million. These were available to the directors, the auditors, the NCSC, the ASX and FAI. FAI also had another one for $110 million and was planning to obtain yet another.

East coast valuers rushed to check out the local work. One valuer said: 'Major land and property valuation in Perth is called "Tiddly-winks on the Terrace". In a small market, players churn values to suit themselves. They set the levels without reference to the market. I would not value for the big groups. There is too much pressure to get optimistic figures. I feel sorry for the people who do the work. Even if nothing is said, there is pressure to maintain the big valuation portfolio and the property management work that can go with it.'[272]

The Bond University, Australia's first private university

opened by the self-educated chairman in May 1989, was itself a property deal. It started life as the Savoy Corporation's Burleigh Forest estate on the Gold Coast. The university idea was a guaranteed high-profile sales pitch to get people to buy into the business and technology park that surrounds it. Half of this estate, which was to be a 'silicon valley' in the suburbs, was sold to the Japanese developers EIE International Co. Ltd. EIE Development Corporation Ltd had also been joint owners of the Bond Centre in Hong Kong and eventually bought the lot.

There were other hotels, too. The Majestic on a headland in the Swan was going to be a major BondCorp development but it never got past first base with the local council. Austmark had more success with Observation City at Scarborough Beach, which was linked to the America's Cup but had a low occupancy rate. He bought the St Moritz on New York's Central Park from Donald Trump but was forced to sell it to Rodney Adler's FAI to settle a debt. He purchased the famous Melbourne watering hole and art gallery, Young & Jacksons, for $8 million and an American architectural masterpiece in San Diego called the Kona Kai Beach and Tennis Resort. He had plans for another hotel development on the St George's hospital site in London but was a forced seller. Now the international five-star hotel business seems a handy adjunct for an international brewer but it is a very expensive way of buying market share in the beer business. As real estate deals they were probably brilliant but Bond was beginning to run out of time and money and he was no Leona Helmsley in the hotel business.

It was hard for Bond, the businessman, not to think in terms of spectacular returns on spectacular property developments. This way of thinking was in his blood but it was a dangerously optimistic world view to bring to the brewing and media businesses, which where not in his blood. The upwardly mobile 'values' ascribed to real estate and mining ventures did not translate to more mature industries. When the big crash came to claim the Gordon Gekkos of high finance on 20 October 1987, all values — both real and imagined — nose-dived and BondCorp was left high and dry and breathless. It was a concept that Bond had difficulty coping with but it was reality nonetheless.

Naïvely, Bond saw the crash as a great opportunity to pick

up cheap assets. Somewhat perversely, he was right and way ahead of his time. But he was in no position to take advantage of it as his own assets had been thoroughly undermined by the very same process. He was also locked into his own single-minded determinism. His simple alternatives as he gazed out the window on 20 October were to either lie down and die like a dog or get up and bite the postman. 'Yes, I would say that I'm not prepared to accept defeat. I think that people do tend to give up too easily,' he was once to say with the dogged determination that so often masks the massive egos of both heroes and villains.

Bond began his chairman's review in the 1987–88 annual report with a cheery exhortation and a brutal admission: 'Record results were achieved in all divisions. But those figures tell only part of the real story of the group's performance in 1987–88.' These statements are true in every respect. What follows was a tragic misreading of an ebbing tide that had permanently changed the financial shoreline: 'The fact is that they [the record results] were achieved despite the most serious upheaval in the business environment worldwide in more than half a century. The downturn in global stockmarkets which commenced in October 1987 severely shook the confidence of investors and business managers and many companies of previous high repute faltered. However, BondCorp emerged from this period STRONGER THAN EVER [author's emphasis] and with its capacity for continued development unimpaired, ready to take advantage of the opportunities which would follow.'

He said this a year after the event (the 1986–87 report was at the printers when the index tumbled) and it could not possibly be true any more. Bond's assets were built on debt and his exposure to the 'serious upheaval' was heightened by this leverage, not lessened by it. His 'capacity for continued development' had been permanently impaired. Fuelled by the 1980s takeover boom in which he had been a major player, asset values had soared and the market had bid up price-earnings multiples to unsustainable levels. 'Almost overnight,' the *Financial Review* was to say, 'asset values were slashed and the supposed asset backing of much corporate paper simply no longer existed.'

But if Bond was right then the markets must have been

terribly wrong. Bond said as much in his chairman's address in the ballroom of his Observation City Hotel on 27 November 1987 — a good month after the impact of the event had hit home to the more pragmatic in the game of life. The meeting was beamed by satellite to BondCorp shareholders gathered in BOM's Channel 9 studios in Brisbane, Sydney and Melbourne. Tongue-tied by jet lag and unaccustomed nervousness, he gave the highest sources for his outlandish assessment of the world situation: 'I was recently at a major conference at the US State Department and the White House in Washington and let me say that America will bring its deficit under control and they will again become the great powerhouse of the world economy ... International markets which are making false judgments on the United States have also savagely down-graded Australia's prospects too. This is completely unjustified and also has no basis in reality,' he said.

Reality is relative. Bond seemed to see it as a perception that could be changed through the power of positive salesmanship: 'BondCorp's financial strategy is increasingly being recognised by the world's financial markets. That strategy is linked through strong and widening associations with leading financial institutions in Great Britain, the United States, Japan and Australia. That recognition of BondCorp's financial strength was highlighted in the past week with the news that your company's credit rating will remain unchanged, at a time when some other major companies are being down-graded,' he said.

So, the emperor did have clothes! Or was it that no one was game to call the situation for what it was? Bond and his executives were obviously convincing, for the front pages of Australian newspapers listed Bond among the great survivors of the great sharequake the day after the event. Bond, they said, was different because Bond had cash flow from solid assets, little money in the equity markets and little exposure to the debt markets in its own name. This false impression of BondCorp's changed status was successfully imparted. Managing Director Peter Beckwith said that 'brewing and media are reliable year in and year out, and that was the criterion in the original judgment to pursue those lines of business. That reliability is the base from which we will see the ability of the group to springboard to growth in other sectors.' The statements had a soothing effect on the market, halting the price slide, and allowing the bankers to sleep easier.

One of the documents distributed to shareholders at the 1987 AGM was a *Euroweek* interview with Finance Director Tony Oates dated 30 October 1987. It had been conducted soon after Black Tuesday (20 October) and was titled 'Bond dispels the myths about its finances'. In it Oates argued that Bond-Corp's investments were mostly in wholly owned subsidiaries 'resulting in quite a low exposure to the sharemarket', unlike other entrepreneurial companies (meaning Holmes à Court). He conceded that, on a consolidated basis, gearing might seem high with an overall debt–equity ratio of 1.1:1 before the crash but 'most of that debt is subordinated and in the name of wholly owned subsidiaries like Bond Brewing or 50-per-cent-owned Bond Media. Bond itself owes directly only A$200– A$300 million,' he said, apparently in all seriousness.

'This makes it very easy for us to go to the public markets and issue unsecured debt, because when people [read bankers] look at Bond they can see that as far as risk is concerned, IT IS IN A SUPERB POSITION [author's emphasis]. It has about $1.5 billion in assets that have no charge against them of any kind. The decision to structure debt in this way stems from a desire to maximise the rapidly expanding group's flexibility, and take advantage of the fact that brewing and media are not cyclical businesses ... Behind the rapid expansion that has seen the company swell its assets from A$1.3 billion in 1985 to more than $4 billion today has been a will to back its judgment by borrowing at a higher level than some other companies,' said Oates.

That judgment turned out to be incorrect. BondCorp was heavily exposed to the market through BCH, BCIL, BOM, and the junk and Eurobond issues and was about to increase that exposure dramatically through new takeovers and share raids. Oates's view that debt wasn't a problem because it didn't exist to any great extent was at odds with the cost of borrowings detailed in the annual report. BondCorp's interest bill jumped from $286 million to $505 million in 1987–88. That the company was planning to expand this debt even further was surprising, given that domestic interest rates had begun the long climb from 12 per cent to 18 per cent. That bankers were prepared to lend the company billions more was downright foolish.

That Alan Bond and the BondCorp inner circle of Peter Beckwith, Tony Oates and Peter Mitchell had failed to pick the crash before the event was self evident. They had agreed to pay out well over a billion dollars for a US asset that wouldn't be worth half that a week later. But BondCorp was not the only entrepreneurial company caught breathless in the world that week. It was a matter of mismanagement that the executives failed to recognise the crash for the fundamental correction that it was after the event, for now it appeared that they were borrowing short to lend long. At 30 June 1989 BondCorp had debts of \$9.25 billion, and \$3.63 billion was payable within a year.

But someone in BondCorp must have suspected something because a remarkable occurrence took place in the five weeks between the crash and the televised 1987 annual general meeting on 27 November. While the rest of the Western world reeled with post-crash trauma, BondCorp and its legal advisers came up with some cute 'compensation packages/restraint agreements' which would benefit its top executives (excluding Bond) to the tune of \$41.5 million 'upon termination of their association with the company'. The resolution was put to the meeting and lost on a show of hands but a subsequent poll, where Dallhold voted its controlling interest, saw it pass. Bond urged shareholders to approve the motion because 'without the commitment and dedication of the senior management . . . your company would not be the success it is today' (*sic*). Bond told shareholders that the resolution was 'an absolute necessity for the future of your company', which made it sound as though he was going to lose these executives within weeks.

'BondCorp is competitive in global markets not only with our products but also with our management talent, any of whom could command the same compensation packages, with the restrictive covenants, from other overseas corporations. One of the great strengths of BondCorp has always been the stability in the ranks of our senior management. In current markets, preserving that stability and talent pool is vital. It is intended that the \$41 million proposed will be paid out by instalments over five years,' Bond said. In the two years that followed the passing of that resolution \$18.3 million was paid out to Beckwith, Oates, Mitchell and others for the 'hard work, sound judgments and imaginative decision making of a small group of dedicated, talented and professional individuals' upon whom depended the future prospects and security of 21,000 employees, 12,000 shareholders and some of the world's biggest banks.

The executive agreements made Beckwith a $10-million man, with Oates and Mitchell worth $6 million a piece. They can be seen as both golden handcuffs and golden parachutes. Bond told the meeting that chief executives should not stay for more than four to five years. Beckwith had been appointed managing director in July 1982 but the new four-year contract at $2.5 million a year (on top of his other payments) would take him to 1991 — twice the length of time recommended by Bond. He would suffer a heart attack half-way through the new term and be forced to rest. While there is nothing wrong with compensation payments for key executives as such, they are usually performance-based and structured as a 'success' fee. There appeared to be no such requirement in the BondCorp executive agreements. Certain directors and principal executive officers walked away with restraint agreement payments totalling $10.65 million in 1988–89, despite the fact that BondCorp incurred a $1-billion loss and totally dissipated shareholders' funds that year.

But the year before that BondCorp had apparently performed miracles by snatching a huge profit increase in the year that included the crash. The executives were certainly worthy of a bonus that year for, had they failed in their appointed task, the bankers would have got nervous about the group's liquidity, and confidence in the non-cyclical cash cow strategy would have been seriously eroded. On paper, the result was fantastic. Turnover had nearly doubled to $4.6 billion and consolidated net profit trebled to $354.7 million. The revenue figure was up because the results included eight months of G Heileman Brewing's beer and asset sales and four months of Bond Media's full revenue.

But BondCorp's profit success in 1987–88 seems to have been an illusion designed to maintain confidence in the share price, the business plan and the management team. As it stands, the $354-million result looks like an improved rate of return on the additional revenue in the brewing and media businesses. For the shareholder, it certainly signified that. Earnings a share had increased from 25 cents to 80 cents and all looked well. But the profit was not all that it appeared to be. Extraordinary losses of $81.2 million reduced the profit to $273 million. Then there were the property profits — Rome brought in $74 million, the Hilton added $80 million and the Emu site contributed $45 million. Without those three windfalls, profits would have been a pathetic $74 million on assets of over $9 billion.

For the bankers, those unsecured creditors with more than thirty times the share capital invested and at risk in BondCorp, only the EBIT (earnings before interest and tax) figure counted. This rose from $342 million to $778 million, which is just as well as interest charges jumped from $286.7 million to $505.7 million. The amount of interest capitalised (not charged against the profit) was $35 million. BondCorp's gamble in borrowing heavily to build its asset base before the crash would come unstuck if ever the EBIT cash failed to cover the interest bill. This happened the following year, 1988–89, when interest charges rose to an incredible $1.064 billion ($58 million capitalised) and EBIT dried up altogether. At this stage the 'TILT' and 'GAME OVER' signs came up and the machine was switched off.

So where did the BondCorp strategy, which seemed so enlightened and soundly based, go so terribly wrong? Bond had set out to acquire global operating businesses 'with strong, recession-proof cash flows and quality assets', as these were to be the 'wellsprings' of his ongoing success. The obvious conclusion is that BondCorp had either exaggerated the strength of the cash flows or had paid too much for the quality assets. The property-propped profit in 1987–88 took attention away from Bond's actual performance as a manager of media and brewing assets. A breakdown of the BondCorp profit into industry segments shows that brewing earnings produced only 36 per cent of EBIT in 1987–88. The previous year it had been 57 per cent. Media's contribution to EBIT was a miserable 4 per cent.

Media was to be Bond's brave new world of technological toys and unspeakable wealth. It was low cost and high profit, or so he thought when he bought in. Its satellite-based technology enabled him to go global from his provincial base in Perth and this he proceeded to do. Inspiration for this move came years before from his friend Ted Turner who had eventually established the Cable News Network (CNN) in the States. Fellow Australian Rupert Murdoch was a latter-day role model here, too. He had started the Fox broadcasting network to compete with the TV network majors in the US following his US$575-million purchase of 20th Century-Fox Film Corp in 1985. Murdoch was spending $1 billion to set up the Sky Channel direct-broadcasting satellite service in Europe at the same time as Bond was cobbling together a pub-based narrowcasting Sky Channel in Australia. They were different kettles of fish but they both ended up with the same name.

In July 1987 BondCorp joined the British Satellite Broadcasting (BSB) consortium that was setting up in opposition to Murdoch's Sky TV in the UK. It cost $115 million for the initial 22.4-per-cent stake. Bond had moved to 37 per cent and was the largest shareholder by the time the first of BSB's two Hughes Aircraft Corporation satellites went into orbit on 29 August 1989. (This interest was also for sale by February 1990.) The move completed a ring of Bond satellite links which girdled Mother Earth and opened up possibilities for data communications, teleconferences and 'real-time' information systems on which the business world depends and where annual growth was running at 35 per cent. Global telecommunications was the buzz phrase for it and it was all the rage at the time, thanks to government deregulation of the airwaves.

BondCorp's first satellite interest came in October 1985 when it signed an agreement for the exclusive use of a 30-watt transponder on the first generation of Aussat domestic satellites. The Australian Sky Channel sports and entertainment network was launched on the back of this transponder on 20 October 1986 and soon swallowed its two rivals — Club Superstation and Sportsplay. It went to only about five thousand subscribers, pubs and clubs but according to management it managed to break even in 1988–89 and had plans to move into the Asian market. It is one of the few businesses that Bond has grown from the ground up, despite his constant claims to be a builder of businesses.

The $1-billion bid for Kerry Packer's National Nine Network in January 1987 brought a galaxy of new satellites into his firmament. BOM gained 85 per cent of a 12-watt Aussat transponder lease which was used for transmission and distribution of television programs. Packer's Nine Network had also been a pioneer in international satellite links. In the early 1980s it leased dedicated transponders on the Intelsat satellite in geostationary orbit over the Pacific Ocean and one over the Atlantic Ocean. The feed for these two links goes through a switching facility on the corner of Sunset and Vine in Hollywood.

Bond was invited to join the BSB consortium in England in July because of his Sky Channel experience, and his new BOM clout had made him an international player. BCIL had a slice of HK-TVB in Hong Kong and Packer had delivered 24.9 per cent of TV-am in the UK, 50 per cent of EM-TV in Papua New Guinea and 80 per cent of the Fiji Television Corporation.

Access to the Pan American satellite came in December 1987 with what must have been Bond's most controversial investment — Compania de Telefonos de Chile (CTC). Not all of Bond's sources of information were 'yachting contacts', as Porta di Roma had been. The Chileans have never entered a boat in the America's Cup; but in August 1987 Bond had snapped up 90 per cent of the US-based international miner, St Joe Gold Corp, for $700 million through his private company, Dallhold. St Joe had a big mine in Chile called El Indio. Bond wanted nickel feed stock from the El Indio mine for his/ Dallhold's Greenvale nickel smelter in Queensland, which was conveniently located on the opposite rim of the Pacific Ocean.

While he was there, he heard that the Chilean government had joined the deregulation kick and wanted to partially privatise CTC, the national phone company. Bond was to turn fifty in 1988 and he had thrown all his enthusiasm into a private gold rush and the public space race in the lead up to this momentous event. He wanted more direct involvement in the hardware of the communications industry to complement his existing electronic media interests. He had eyed off the Australian phone company, Telecom, but Prime Minister Hawke had made it clear that the telecommunications monopoly was not for sale to him or any other privateer at any price. So he tendered for the Chile Telephone Company and won.

At that time Chile was being run by the particularly nasty military dictator called Captain General Augusto Pinochet who had come to power in a bloody coup and ruled through authoritarian excesses. He had, however, got the trains to run on time, reduced the foreign debt, got inflation down and GDP growth up, and had half a phone company to sell. Bond and

Pinochet met and a deal was sealed. It would be political dynamite for BondCorp but for Bond it was just another business proposition. He would do a similar deal over cellular telephones with the reactionary Hungarian Communist Party regime in Budapest but there would be no political fallout from that encounter. Opponents of the Pinochet regime saw the telephone company as an instrument of political repression. Bond saw it as a tool for liberating the economy: 'We were convinced that an adequate telephone system would assist immeasurably in the rate of economic progress which could be achieved as Chile moved towards a democratic system of government ... our involvement with Chile is purely commercial,' he said.

Bond's political naïvety would cost him heavily in terms of lost image and credibility back in Australia but at the time he couldn't see what all the fuss was about. Bond had been photographed shaking hands with the despot Pinochet at the conclusion of the deal in Santiago and had made some mildly supportive comments about economic progress under the regime. The resulting impression would call for extensive damage control but few could grasp the peculiar nature of Bond's absolutely pragmatic value system which saw a quid as a quid regardless of its connections. 'Ideology is dead,' he would rant to his friendly soothsayer Bruce Stannard in the *Bulletin*. 'When I deal with people in Canberra, I don't stop to ask myself, "Are they Labor, are they Liberal?" I don't go there for political meetings. As far as I'm concerned they are businessmen like myself.'[273]

Bond never said Pinochet was a good bloke, or even just a bloke it was good to do business with, but the compromising radiogram picture of the two portly autocrats in hand-to-hand embrace caused a public outcry when it was flashed around the world, and Bond copped a bucketing. He was reportedly stung by the constant criticism he received from his former friends in the Federal Cabinet, particularly Prime Minister Hawke. In circumstances where Bond feels he has been betrayed he lashes out: 'The Prime Minister goes to Moscow and remains very friendly with the Russians and yet he says nothing about Siberia, the Gulag. If he had taken the trouble to inquire properly of our embassy in Santiago he would have discovered that dirty tricks and a campaign of disinformation were coming from our main corporate rival down there, the Spanish Telephone Company, which has been trying to buy us out. The Prime Minister and others have chosen to listen to the voice of the Chilean communists. We have a lot of Chilean communists here in Australia ... I would like to see these Chileans in Australia checked to see just where their loyalties lie.'[274]

This was a peculiar construct to put on events. Bond would have been better off arguing the investment merits of the deal and leaving the conspiracy theories alone. A democratically elected civilian government was due to take power in Chile in March 1990 and BCIL, who had owned the 48-per-cent stake in CTC, sold it to the same Spanish Telephone Company in February 1990. Bond knew exactly what he was doing when he did the deal with Pinochet at the end of 1987. Negotiations had started before the crash and, according to Beckwith in the annual report, had involved 'months of research using information supplied by the Chilean Government'. They were concluded not long after the crash because Pinochet was desperate for foreign investment and Bond wanted to get his hands on the El Indio mine, the phone company and access to the Pan American satellite.

The last link in the satellite chain came on 1 July 1988, when BondCorp picked up the Queensland government's private satellite communications network, Q-Net. This acquisition also had political implications because of Bond's close involvement with the Joh Bjelke-Petersen National Party government but it created far less of a stink than the tie-up with the Pinochet regime in Chile. Q-Net provides data, voice and video communications between the Queensland government in Brisbane and its public servants in regional and remote centres. It was set up to compete with more costly services provided to the State government by Telecom and it will eventually become a national network with both public and private clients using it. BondCorp set up a new operating division, Bond Communications (Australia) Pty Ltd, to operate Q-Net and pursue national expansion opportunities for Bondnet's private satellite in competition with Telecom. For this move it has approval from both the Queensland government and the Federal Department of Communications. Q-Net made a profit of $667,000 in 1988–89 but it is not clear from the accounts what the acquisition cost.

When BondCorp announced its record 1988–89 loss of $980 million on 20 October 1989, the company's directors expressed the hope that the remaining media and communications businesses would carry the group through into the next decade. But with HK-TVB, TV-am and CTC already sold and BSB on the market, the springboard to corporate survival had narrowed. Despite its glamour, Bond Media failed to produce a pot of gold at the end of its dazzling rainbow. This was because Bond had paid too much for the BOM television hardware before the crash and too much for the program software to run on it after the crash.

Squeezed by a heavy debt burden and a 6-per-cent hike in interest rates in its first two years, BOM floundered financially despite its clear market leadership in the ratings. BOM chairman Warren Jones put the problem expressly in the company's 1988–89 annual report: 'The net trading results we achieved are certainly unsatisfactory and shareholders have every right to be concerned. A turnover in excess of $500 million and a profit before tax of $2.5 million clearly demonstrates that costs are too high. Principally, these are the costs of programming and the costs of borrowed funds.'

Net interest expense for BOM went up from $41 million to $57.4 million in 1988–89. While nowhere near as extensive as the $1 billion in interest which its parent company paid out in the same year, combined with increased programming cost and a loss on extraordinary items of $46 million, BOM lost $44.1 million in the 1989 year compared with a profit of $30.6 million in the 1988 year. Auditors Price Waterhouse qualified the 1988–89 accounts because no provision had been made for the possible diminution in value of the TV and radio licences which were carried in the books at a value of $1055.511 million.

In February 1990 BOM's future was looking perilous. The Australian Broadcasting Tribunal had ruled on 26 June 1989 that Alan Bond was not a fit and proper person to hold a TV licence. This finding was set aside by the full Federal Court but the ABT had been granted leave to appeal the matter to the High Court. BOM was also subject to a takeover offer from Kerry Packer's Television Corporation of Australia Ltd, announced on 1 December 1989, which valued the share capital at $53 million or about 10 cents a share. The bid was being contested. Debts totalling $585 million to Kerry Packer and an NAB-led bank syndicate were deemed due and payable and awaiting repayment or refinancing.

Granted, Bond Media had some tough breaks and wasn't the licence to print money that it was expected to be but the National Nine Network was still the industry leader and still taking the largest slice of the advertising dollar. There was nothing wrong with the basic business. It was set up by Packer and Son and Bond didn't interfere (much) with the management. Bond Brewing, on the other hand, was Alan Bond's creation and he took a very hands-on approach to the management of this business. Under his control it took a spectacular dive from a claimed 50 per cent of the Australian beer market to an actual 38 per cent in the space of four years and ended up in the hands of receiver/managers. This cannot be attributed to bad luck. And as most of BondCorp's massive debt had been piggy-backed on a guaranteed flow of cash from the recession-proof beer business, it turned out to be his Achilles heel.

Aggressively fought beer wars between evenly matched competitors are, by their very nature, unique, heroic and popular contests where the consumer is rarely the victim and theatrical performances by the jousting 'beer barons' are guaranteed. They are much like general elections, in that everyone interested gets to participate in the outcome and the loser is put to the sword. They also have beneficial economic side-effects which are the very essence of the capitalist system. But with each percentage point of the Australian retail market share, won or lost, worth roughly $50–60 million in much-sought-after cash flow (based on an all-industry value of $5.5 billion) the outcome of an open beer war has a quantifiable truth value which can be catastrophic for the loser. As Queen Victoria was told when she asked who was coming second in the Cup won by *America* in 1851, 'Your Majesty, there is no second!'

Bond Brewing Holdings (BBH) failed the test against Carlton & United Breweries (CUB) decisively — both on the local front and on foreign fields. That this happened is a market indictment of the brewer in the loser's corner. Bond had successes, initially, with very low-alcohol White Swan, and later with Dry Swan/XXXX/Tooheys; but overall he copped a bath. A few of the many marketing and financial disasters serve to justify this assertion.

On 4 May 1987, over Charlotte, North Carolina, a Bond Airship (think of a Goodyear blimp) drifted into the hazy view of local media and government officials bearing an exhortation to drink 'American Beer' (a graphic of an eagle in stripes seeing stars was provided for the illiterate). This was not a xenophobic industry campaign against foreign imports but the national test launch of new Bond Brewing International brand label 'positioned to compete directly against Coors, Miller and Budweiser' in the US domestic market. Harvey Sandford, chief executive of Bond Brewing, Pittsburgh, and its subsidiary, the American Beer Company, did the honours: 'A year and a half of planning, research and development went into the American brand — the greatest beer ever brewed by an American brewer.'

Without going into the gory details, let it suffice to say that the new product failed to capture its target market and very quickly disappeared into the dustbin of brewing memorabilia. If this was good old Australian know-how tackling the world's largest and most competitive beer market, the campaign had two fundamental lacks — the financial resources and the production resources to back the marketing boast. The production resources were added four months later when Bond bought the G Heileman Brewing Co. Inc. (for a grossly overvalued pre-crash price). But for any sort of management realist, it would have taken at least US$700 million-plus in promotion funds to make a slight impression, let alone an impact, with American Beer against Budweiser — the world's volume leader. Naïvety like that is innate. It is impossible to learn from experience.

Bond practised the skill first in Australia in November 1985 when he decided, against advice to the contrary, to launch his new yuppy BBH flagship label, Black Swan (Swan Premium Export Lager), against CUB's Foster's Lager (Big Blue) — the runaway national market leader. Again the planning, market research and technical development were probably excellent but the strategic decision-making was the problem. As a new brand, Black Swan (it had the backing of the America's Cup and the National Nine Network) failed to score any marketing victories outside of its home State despite massive promotion. It was to be a beer for achievers and the slogan used to promote it was 'They said you'd never make it.'

The ads starred popular sportsmen and others who had defied the odds to become achievers in life. One of them featured Alan Bond as the hero. The label was discontinued as a national brand in November 1989 — four years after its brave-but-expensive launch in Melbourne, CUB's heartland. A marketing opportunity, a battle, and the beer war were over.

Bond's most publicised beer marketing blunder was when he changed the name on the Castlemaine Perkins brewery in Brisbane to Bond Brewing and the address on the Fourex labels to Perth, WA. This riled the parochial Queenslanders and many switched their beer-drinking allegiance to CUB and a new local beer put out by Power Brewing which quickly captured 14 per cent of the Queensland market by playing on its local origins and ownership. Queensland rugby league football star, 'King' Wally Lewis, would sign off his TV ads for Power's Bitter by saying, 'Sorry Bondy!'

Bond would be even sorrier as a result his decision to sell the freeholds of the many CaTs hotels in Queensland and NSW into a property joint venture called the Austotel Trust. This raised $276 million for BondCorp and the money was used to defray the $1.2-billion cost of buying CaTs. But the deal failed to acknowledge the accumulated goodwill of the CaTs publicans in their businesses in Queensland and NSW and they turned around and bit the Bond Brewing hand that wasn't feeding them. In the key NSW market — frontline of the beer war — Bond's Tooheys brand slipped from 52–53 per cent of the market to 42–53 per cent.

In the even-tougher US market, Bond's share of beer sales, through Heileman, would drop from 8.5 to 7.5 per cent in 1987–88. The only money BondCorp appears to have made out of Heileman was the US$200 million it got out of selling off the baking and snack-food sidelines when it took control in October 1987. As a trading corporation, G Heileman Brewing Co. Inc. lost US$75.6 million in 1987–88 and another US$126.7 million in 1988–89. It had severe liquidity problems because of the high cost of debt servicing, and its viability as a going concern was questioned by the auditors.

In the BondCorp accounts the brewing segment was said to have produced profits of $191 million in 1986, $202 million in 1987, $287 million in 1988 and $123.8 million in 1989. But all of these figures are suspect as they could include the results of one-off property deals and other special effects. On 15 January 1990 Bond Brewing Holdings filed a form of accounts with its US junk bond holders which painted a dismal picture of its state of affairs. According to these figures, the group lost $70.7 million, before extraordinaries, in the year to June 1989 compared with a profit of $78.8 million in the 1988 year. The 1989 loss came despite a $12.9-million tax benefit that year and a fall in interest expense from $227.4 million to $210.8 million. 'The consolidated accounts also reveal that Bond Brewing's net result in recent years has been boosted by "other income", rather than relying on its operating results after interest and tax. Bond Brewing's 1988 profit would have been wiped out had other income of $211.5 million been excluded. Half of 1988's other income was made up of a $104.1-million foreign exchange gain. Similarly, in 1987, other income of $116.6 million helped Bond Brewing post a consolidated net profit of $19.3 million. Included in other income in 1987 was a $26-million profit from the sale of shares and interest income of $69.5 million,' said a newspaper report.[275]

With $2.7 billion worth of debt riding on the back of the earnings from the breweries it was crucial that the lenders see that the businesses were making enough money to cover the negative pledge. With Bond Brewing's net interest bill believed to be running at $180 million at 30 June 1989, there was clearly insufficient cash flow on the BondCorp segment figures to keep the show on the road. The debt tortoise had caught the exhausted profit hare. The Bond group still has interests in Hungarian and Chinese breweries but they are unlikely to set the world on fire.

When the sharequake hit world markets on 20 October 1987, Bond was in the Eternal City working on the Porta di Roma project. But back home in the Infernal City that is capital of Western Australia's State of Excitement, there was much fiddling as a financial conflagration saw paper values of $55 billion go up in smoke. The two people most affected besides Bond were Bond's friend Laurie Connell and Bond's enemy Robert Holmes à Court. Bond would return to 'save' Connell and to 'bury' Hacca but both crusades would fail in their objectives and serve to position BondCorp closer to its own catastrophe.

The run started on Connell's merchant bank Rothwells

Ltd on Black Tuesday when the markets fell 25 per cent in a day. Astute depositors rightly figured that the $300 million they collectively had on deposit with Rothwells was at risk and would not be balanced by the new value of the merchant bank's high-risk lending portfolio and so they began withdrawing their money. By Thursday, $150 million had been withdrawn and the National Australia Bank refused to honour a $30-million cheque which Rothwells had drawn on the bank.

On Black Tuesday, Connell had been in the air en route to Sydney to help Warwick Fairfax's Tryart Pty Ltd cement its tragically timed and conceived takeover of the media group John Fairfax Ltd. Connell intended to retire after this 'one last business transaction' on which he was scheduled to 'earn' a $100-million 'success' fee. 'Earn' was Laurie Connell's nickname and 'success' was the name of his game. His personal pre-crash wealth was estimated to be worth $300 million, he owned four hundred thoroughbred racehorses and he had plans to build Australia's largest house, with provision for a cool room for the furs, on the site of four previous Swan riverside mansions which he had acquired for $20 million and had bulldozed.

When the extent of the liquidity crisis at Rothwells became apparent to Connell in Sydney on 22 October — he thought he was short $150 million at the time — he sent out distress signals to his three main mates who all owed 'Earn' for past services rendered. They were BondCorp, the Wardleys/ HKB connection and Brian Burke's corporatist WA Inc. All three acknowledged their indebtedness to the roly-poly dealdoer and responded to his call. If Connell, a vice patron of the John Curtin Foundation, was in trouble, so were Bond and Burke — for they were considered the joint managing directors of WA Inc. Alan Bond jumped on his corporate jet in Rome and was back in Perth by the Saturday morning to take personal charge of the rescue mission. As was his wont, Bond parked his Rolls Royce with one wheel up on the footpath opposite the Rothwells office at 77 St Georges Terrace.

Three rescue missions were mounted to save Rothwells and none of them worked. Rothwells swallowed $700 million of new money all-up and went into provisional liquidation on 3 November 1988 with thousands of innocent bystanders suffering as a result of the fallout. But none suffered more than

BondCorp and WA Inc. Their reckless interference with market forces to 'save' mate Laurie was to entangle them in a host of disastrous joint ventures — all of them over-priced and under-funded and most of them headed for the courts. Like the cloak of Nessus in Greek mythology, the Rothwells poisoned robe clung more and more tightly to WA Inc. and eventually cost Brian Burke and Peter Dowding their jobs as premiers of Western Australia. It would also cost the taxpayers of WA, who were left with the bill for the folly, at least $100 million before the WA government stopped counting.

There would be bitter recriminations among the former friends. Bond and Connell would fall out on the front pages after fifteen years of fruitful business collaboration and close personal friendship. An NCSC inquiry into the Rothwells collapse would reveal that debts of $324 million were removed from the Rothwells books just three months before Bond organised the first $370-million 'rescue' of Rothwells on the weekend after the crash. Bond claimed that his association with the Rothwells rescue had been a 'total disaster' from the beginning: 'We were a lender to them ... It was a great disappointment to us that we should be given such fraudulent figures in the first place ... There is no question he [Connell] let himself down and in the process let everyone else down.'[276] The allegations were denied by Connell.

The lasting legacy of Rothwells to BondCorp is an auditors' qualification of the 1988–89 accounts relating to the $249.4-million carrying value of a half interest in Petrochemical Industries Ltd (PCIL), a Connell company that once had fabulous plans for a $500-million plant at Kwinana. PICL was placed into liquidation on 20 September 1989 by BondCorp's PICL partner, West Australian Government Holdings Ltd (WAGH). Ironically, WAGH is the old corporate shell of what was once Bond's Northern Mining Corporation. This matter was still before the courts in February 1990. Auditors Arthur Anderson & Co. say the recovery of the investment and associated loans in PICL is dependent on the success of BondCorp's legal proceedings against WAGH, the State of Western Australia and Mr Peter Dowding.

Bond's attempt to 'bury' his fiscal foe Holmes à Court also backfired. Bond wanted to see off his one-time rival for the title of King of the West and get his hands on Hacca's famed Bell

Resources Ltd (BRL) war chest — the accumulated booty of
countless corporate raids on the world stage in the eventful
eighties. Robert Holmes à Court saw Alan Bond coming from a
mile off. He transferred all his problems (and his Bell Group
companies) to Bond's already sagging shoulders and rebuilt
his empire under the private Heytesbury Holdings Ltd banner.
Bond crowed that the deal put $2 billion in cash at his disposal
and made him the biggest financial institution in the West.
Holmes à Court taunted the victor who had appeared to pay
double the real value of the Bell assets and had assumed a
whole new swag of Bell subordinated debt to boot. That both
men were still smiling was evidence of the depth of their dislike
for each other.

Personal likes and dislikes seem to have had a debilitating
effect on Bond's ability to respond to new situations properly.
In October 1988 Bond began buying shares in Lonrho (com-
bining the words London and Rhodesia) Plc, the fiefdom of
Britain's corporate rogue elephant, Roland 'Tiny' Rowland.
According to a report in the London *Sunday Times*, the two
men met on a boat in the south of France that northern
summer to discuss possible joint ventures and both gave the
appearance that all was well between them. Tiny Rowland was
once described by then British Prime Minister Edward Heath as
'an unpleasant and unacceptable face of capitalism.'[277]

On 27 October Bond's holding in Lonrho went to 19.8 per
cent and passed that of Rowland, which was a fatal error. On
18 November, Lonrho released a report claiming that the
BondCorp group were 'technically insolvent'. It would follow
up with four other disparaging reports to which Bond never
adequately responded. Bond was obviously wounded by Rowland's about face but he had been naïve in his assessment of
his vigorous opponent in the first place. He hit back finally on
13 May 1989 at the launch of his new maxi yacht *Drumbeat*: 'It
is a great shame that we Australians listen to ... Tiny Rowland,
and give him credibility against one of your own Australian
business people.' Bond suspected Holmes à Court's hand was
involved in Rowland's foul play but he referred to the former
at the christening that day merely as 'one tall individual
here in Perth'.

There were two legs to Bond's perceived post-crash strategy. The first involved stripping the cash out of the Bell assets
and leveraging it for a tilt at a European major like Lonrho or

Allied-Lyons or both. They in turn would be stripped and
BondCorp would be left straddling the world with major operations on every continent except Africa — and Lonrho could
have provided that. It was all part of the fifty-year plan. The one
thing that Bond had learnt from dealing with Asian banks was
to think long. Thinking big came naturally.

But what he was proposing was a dream world that
depended on a never-ending stream of acquisition of debt and
debt-servicing assets. Each step on the road to building the
global conglomerate would be larger and more spectacular
than the one preceding it and each would require the confidence of the bankers in Bond's ability to pull it off. Confidence
was the cement that held Alan Bond's house of cards together.
It was the reason he paid the world's highest price ever for a
painting — $69.45 million for Van Gogh's 'Irises' in November
1987 — straight after the crash. The public didn't learn the
name of the purchaser until a lot later but the world's bankers
knew straight away. (The painting would later be repossessed.)

For one set of bankers, confidence in Alan Bond ran out
one day in late October 1989 in a boardroom high above 500
Bourke Street, Melbourne. Present were Alan Bond and his de
facto finance director Tony Oates. They had been carpeted by
Nobby Clark, the normally genial managing director of the
National Australia Bank, over alleged continuing breaches of
the BBH loan and credit agreement with the banking syndicate
for which NAB was agent. Details of the fateful encounter were
relayed to the Victorian Supreme Court by mild-mannered
bank account executive Graeme Willis during cross-examination
on 5 January 1990.

Evidently, clear-cut Clark told debt-dabbling Bond that he
and his companies had 'lost all credibility with the bank and
the bank was not prepared to tolerate continued breaches of
the loan agreement.' Bond's response was not recorded. Bond
also disputed that the agreement was breached and appealed
Justice Beach's judgment on 9 February (upholding his
appointment of court receivers and managers to BBH on 29
December 1989) to the Full Bench of the Victorian Supreme
Court. This matter was still before the court at the end of
February 1990.

On 20 October 1989 — two years to the day after the great
sharequake had rattled Bond's less-than-solid foundations —
BondCorp announced an Australian record corporate loss of

$980,180,000 for the year to 30 June 1989 and a deficit of $115.9 million in shareholders' funds. The real extent of the losses could be much larger. The auditors would express 'some doubt about BondCorp's ability to continue as a going concern' and stress that the group would be 'dependent upon the continued support from its lenders and its ultimate controlling entity, Mr A Bond.'

No doubt this information was before Nobby Clark and Alan Bond when they gathered for their traumatic *tête à tête* in late October 1989. If Willis has reported the incident accurately (it was not challenged by counsel for Bond), it had just been made patently obvious to Bond that NAB was one major lender on whose continued support he could no longer depend. If NAB had been BondCorp's only banker, the show would have been over then and there. But Bond still had the support of the HKB, and while he had some bank backing and lead in his pencil he would fight for corporate survival and to preserve his massive personal wealth. He wouldn't, he couldn't give up but he would find it extremely difficult to rebuild the credibility and confidence that he lost high above Bourke Street that day.

In his financial overview of the 1988–89 results on 20 October 1989, Bond would come as close as he ever has to admitting the fundamental flaw in his growth strategy. His partial climb-down is worth repeating for posterity: 'Over the period spanning the 1985-to-1988 financial years, total group assets grew more than seven-fold and operating revenue grew more than eight-fold. In that period Bond Group became one of Australia's best known companies for both its local and international achievements. This phase of rapid growth was substantially financed by debt. These debt levels were at the time sustainable but were dependent on the values, performance and recognised potential of the Group's assets.' Bond had never spoken truer words nor been as perceptive since he first gazed out on Lesmurdie Heights and dollar signs flashed before his eyes.

The NAB eventually made a successful *ex parte* application for the urgent appointment of receivers and managers to the assets of BBH before Justice Beach on 29 December 1989. On that day BBH announced that it was selling the brewing assets to BRL. But on Boxing Day, 26 December, Bond was at the wheel of his new $3.25-million, 26-metre, high-tech, Dallhold-owned, maxi yacht *Drumbeat* awaiting the big naval gun from the HMAS *Fremantle* to blast the start of the 630-nautical-mile Sydney-to-Hobart bluewater classic. According to the crew, Bond didn't release his vice-like grip on that wheel of fortune until *Drumbeat* was half-way down the New South Wales coast and well ahead of the fleet.

At roughly the same time as the starter's gun was to pop over soporific Sydney Harbour that day, BondCorp's Perth legal representatives, Parker & Parker, were loading their facsimile machine with an urgent missive for Mr G Willis, the agent for the participants in the BBH facility, at the NAB headquarters in Bourke Street, Melbourne. It would warn Willis that unless NAB desisted from its current course of action against BondCorp it would 'cause the liquidation of BCH (BondCorp) and the majority, if not all, its subsidiaries, possibly including Bell Resources Ltd, Bell Group Ltd, and Bond Media Ltd and enormous loss to our clients, Dalhold Investments Pty Ltd and Mr Alan Bond.'

Bond won line honours in that boat race for the first time since his first start twenty years previously. This had been the unheralded showing in *Apollo* that led to our first tilt at the America's Cup. But what a Pyrrhic victory this first Sydney-to-Hobart win finally turned out to be. Bond's lawyers and executives had failed to prevent the NAB from moving against the Bond Brewing assets in the Victorian Supreme Court; and, as his boat moved up the Derwent towards Constitution Dock on the 29th, Justice Beach was handing down the BBH orders that would cause cross-defaults in other borrowing agreements in BondCorp's $9.25-billion debt profile.

The Alan Bond story doesn't have a last chapter. As a businessman he is not finished as this book goes to press, and the legends and myths, the dazzling daring on which his career was built from nothing in the hot and dusty backstreets of Fremantle will no doubt live as long as high-flying, death-defying corporate storytelling remains a legitimate genre. But, on the balance of probabilities, it is evident that his finest moments are now behind him. What has passed is not the end of an example but the end of an era. But if BondCorp finally fails the corporate credibility test, Alan Bond will be neither the last entrepeneur to go to the wall for risking his hand against a fickle market nor the last high-risk player to be wilfully indulged without 'due diligence' by lenders and investors.

Postscript

1990: Towards the Sulan Report

On 28 February 1990 BondCorp pulled off another Houdini-like escape when the Full Bench of the Victorian Supreme Court ordered the immediate removal of receivers and managers from Bond Brewing Holdings. 'In our opinion these companies should never have been placed in receivership on December 29 nor should the receivership have been continued on February 9,' said the Full Court. Had the receivers not been removed that day, cross-defaults would have been triggered under agreements covering a number of BondCorp's Eurobond issues, some US junk bonds and other bank debt. This would have led to a demand for the acceleration (immediate repayment) of about $1.96 billion. Failure to meet this call on that day would have led to wind-up petitions against the holding company and the doubtless death of the

BondCorp group. This was Bond brinkmanship at its best.

Salvation, however, was short-lived. The 'luckiest man in the West' had apparently ended his longest winning streak (1984–1990). On 2 March the Ministerial Council for Companies and Securities (a summit of State and Federal company law ministers meeting in Adelaide) ordered a special investigation into the affairs of the BondCorp group since 1 July 1986. Adelaide lawyer John Sulan was appointed to head the special investigation and to determine by 30 June 1990 whether any civil action should be brought to protect and preserve shareholders' funds. The terms of reference are not confined to the actions and statements of BondCorp executives and officers in that time but include specific references to the group's auditors and creditors. This is a significant development in corporate-law enforcement, but it is only the announcement of an investigation, not the presumption of guilt on the part of those being investigated.

It is a tribute to the uniqueness and importance of the BondCorp phenomenon that this powerful, wide-ranging post-mortem was instigated before a corporate death certificate had been issued on any of the companies in the group. Inspectors are usually appointed after a company has collapsed — to find the reason, to lay appropriate blame (if any) and to advance legislative solutions designed to prevent repeat performances. The setting up of this special inspection will almost certainly bring about the orderly demise of BondCorp *ipso facto*, and so seeks to protect Australia's suffering international financial reputation where BondCorp's terminal struggle with its debt has become a *cause célèbre*.

At the time of writing, a Federal election campaign was in progress, in which the future of national corporate regulation in Australia, the WA Inc. losses and the level of foreign ownership allowed in the electronic media were all issues for the electorate and issues that affected BondCorp's apparently limited future. Moreover, a national debt summit was considering the international consequences of the 'cowboy antics' of our 1980s entrepreneurs and Prime Minister Hawke had said it would not be good for Australia's image if a large entrepreneur such as Alan Bond 'were to go bust'.

Inspector Sulan of the BondCorp squad appears well qualified for this unique task of national corporate policing and his report is awaited with interest. He was Commissioner for Corporate Affairs in Adelaide from 1980 to 1982, which would have given him insights into the earlier BondCorp's $180-million Santos windfall (but which does not fall within the time frame of his investigation). He has also had experience in Hong Kong as a corporate investigator, which may help his understanding of the relationship between BondCorp and BCIL.

The inquiry is expected to take twelve months and to cost the Federal and State governments jointly about $1.5 million. It has been structured deliberately to deal with the interregnum expected as the National Companies and Securities Commission is scheduled to hand over its powers and investigations to the newly established Australian Securities Commission on 30 June, but this is still subject to constitutional challenge and a satisfactory resolve of outstanding issues between the Commonwealth and the State governments. For this reason the special investigation will be conducted by Sulan and coordinated by the NCSC, in close consultation with the ASC, and a special interim report has been requested before 30 June but is unlikely to be made public.

The Sulan report will cover many of the transactions raised in the last two chapters of this book, and others which were not — for reasons which should by now be apparent. The Sulan inquest will have powers, resources and legal protection which have not been available to me as a mere small shareholder in BondCorp (disclosure: 1000 worthless ordinary shares purchased for about a dollar each in early 1989).

I undertook the writing of this book without malice and having sought my chairman's collaboration in the project. I have relied on my journalistic training in a genuine attempt to understand the Bond phenomenon and what it has meant to Australia in the sixties, the seventies and the eighties. Like many other Australians I had been deeply moved by Alan Bond's sporting feat on Rhode Island Sound in September 1983. My exhilaration was heightened by being an eyewitness to the event and a working financial journalist with some knowledge of the man's companies' activities and a burning interest to acquire more. At all times I have sought to be fair and objective and to understand the Bond position in relation to the tide of events, using where I could the very words of Mr Bond and his representatives at the time. I have had no contact with Lonrho

Plc or any of its representatives in relation to this study. I am neither sycophant nor Bond-basher, just a fascinated bystander who happens to be trained in financial news.

I am also bound by the Code of Ethics of the Australian Journalists' Association, which I have observed, and intend to observe, in relation to protecting my sources of information. While the vast majority of the material presented here is on the public record, the comments attached to them are mine. The comments are made in good faith and I verily believe them to be true and fair and definitely advanced in the public interest and with cognisance of the market's need to be fully informed. As a member of the BondCorp company I am freely exercising my right to speak out in relation to the company's affairs and management. This right is enshrined in the company's Memorandum and Articles of Association.

Bond still has the opportunity to give his personal view of the main events in his life at a later stage. However, I suspect Inspector Sulan will now get to play god confessor on any alleged shortcomings in relation to Mr Bond's management of his companies in 1986–87, 1987–88 and 1988–89 and I am content to use my humble analytical and literary skills to put the lead-up years to the Sulan Report in an economic, political and social perspective for more general consumption and as a contribution to the national debate about the growth of private and public debt in the carefree 1980s.

I would have liked to have continued my original biographical approach to Bond's life and his relationships with his wife, his children and his friends; but, during the writing, events overtook the task and it was enough to keep up with the constant stream of information coming to light about his corporate affairs. This was perhaps fortuitous. What Bond does in his private life is his business and I have no desire to repeat hearsay and innuendo or to pass moral judgment about him and his lifestyle. But what Bond does with his business and with his country's international reputation is my business and I strongly suggest it should be the business of every Australian. I have been confident enough to interpret the Bond phenomenon by reference to the figures stated in his companies' annual reports. Some of those reports are now under official investigation.

Throughout 1989 the activities of Alan Bond and his

BondCorp group were subject to the closest scrutiny ever suffered by a public figure and a private enterprise. This scrutiny had been awakened in October 1988 when Bond called off the 'grand merger' proposed in July 1988, whereby the Bond and Bell companies would be merged via a bid by BondCorp for the Bell Group, a bid by Bell Group for Bond Media and finally a reverse takeover of BondCorp by Bell Resources. Readers of this book are spared the excruciating details of this complicated series of arrangements because the deal didn't come off and because its indefinite postponement apparently led to events and transactions which have subsequently been referred to the special investigator for possible action. The ministerial council said the Bond investigation's priority should be to examine the evidence arising out of the NCSC's private hearings, adjourned on 22 December 1989, which covered *inter alia* a $1.2-billion payment by Bell Resources to BondCorp as a 'deposit' on the company's brewing assets.

The investigation will examine the audits of the Bond group accounts since 30 June 1987, and repayments to Bond group creditors since 1 January 1988. The NCSC has been ordered to investigate whether money was unlawfully or improperly paid to any Bond group creditor from funds within other Bond group companies, particularly Bell Resources Ltd.

Mr Sulan was quoted in the *Australian Financial Review* of 5 March 1990 as saying he considered his appointment a challenge. I wish him Godspeed, for I am thankful that my journey of discovery is over. I have enjoyed the ride but I am unsure about the ultimate destination.

Terence Maher, Melbourne, 5 March 1990

Notes and Sources

Chapter One

1 Bruce Stannard, the *Bulletin*, 26 November 1985
2 Jane MacLatchy, the Perth *Daily News*, 8 October 1983
3 Russell Deiley, Australian *Playboy*, September 1980
4 Stannard, *Bulletin*
5 Stannard, *Bulletin*
6 MacLatchy, *Daily News*
7 Tony Stephens & Paul McGeough, 'Captain Bond', the Melbourne *Age Good Weekend*, 5 December 1986
8 Deiley, *Playboy*
9 Deiley, *Playboy*
10 MacLatchy, *Daily News*
11 Prue Dashfield, 'Red remembers when', the *West Australian Magazine*, 8 April 1989
12 Joe Keeling, *Daily News*, 14 July 1977
13 Dashfield, *West Australian*
14 Doug Riggs, *Keelhauled*, Angus & Robertson, 1986
15 Frank Robson, 'King Bond', the *Australian Magazine*, 22–23 April 1989
16 Hugh Schmitt, the *West Australian*, 19 May 1984

53 Stannard, *Bulletin*
54 TVW7 interview
55 McIlwraith, *Weekend Magazine*
56 McIlwraith, *Weekend Magazine*
57 McIlwraith, *Weekend Magazine*
58 Riggs, *Keelhauled*

Chapter Seven

59 McIlwraith, *Weekend Magazine*
60 Trevor Sykes, *Two Centuries of Panic*, Allen & Unwin, 1988
61 Robert Gottliebsen, 'Back from the brink', the *National Times*, 11 November 1978
62 Newspaper report, 'Cheap land for houses planned', 28 July 1969
63 Sykes, *Money Miners*
64 The *West Australian*, 12 September 1970
65 Joe Keeling, *Daily News*, 7 April 1973
66 Deiley, *Playboy*
67 'Interest in WA', the *West Australian*, 4 February 1969
68 Stannard, *Bulletin*
69 Stannard, *Bulletin*
70 Don Lipscombe, 'The great survival show starring Alan Bond', the *Bulletin*, 24 February 1976 (pulped after legal action)
71 Deiley, *Playboy*
72 Lipscombe, *Bulletin*
73 Hugh D Whall ('You Do Well'), *The Southern Cross*, a publicity biography, Admiralty Publishing House, 1974
74 Austin Robertson, 'Land baron turns his eyes seaward', the *West Australian*, 16 January 1970
75 Robson, *Australian Magazine*
76 The *West Australian*, 23 May 1970
77 Lipscombe, *Bulletin*
78 TVW7 interview
79 Stephens & McGeough, *Good Weekend*
80 The *West Australian*, 10 January 1970
81 Lipscombe, *Bulletin*
82 Bruce Stannard, *Ben Lexcen, the Man, the Keel and the Cup*, Faber & Faber, 1984
83 Riggs, *Keelhauled*
84 Riggs, *Keelhauled*
85 *Daily News*, 7 October 1970

Chapter Eight

86 Australian Associated Press report, 'Cup bid may cost $4 million', 1972
87 Trevor Sykes, 'Alan Bond's sunshine empire', Parts 1–4, the *Australian Financial Review*, 19, 20, 21 & 22 February 1974
88 Trevor Sykes, 'Alan Bond's sunshine empire', Part 2, the *Australian Financial Review*, 20 February 1974
89 Sykes, *Two Centuries of Panic*
90 John McIlwraith, 'Bond bounces back', the *Australian Financial Review*, 4 October 1979
91 Gottliebsen, *National Times*

92 Interview with author
93 'On the Move', *Enterprise*, initial issue of the BondCorp quarterly house journal, Autumn 1974
94 Dr Roger Smith & Barry Urquhart, *The Jindalee Factor*, Marketing Focus, 1988
95 Smith & Urquhart, *The Jindalee Factor*
96 Smith & Urquhart, *The Jindalee Factor*
97 Stephens & McGeough, *Good Weekend*
98 Joe Keeling, 'Bond becomes national in $30 million week', *Daily News*, 7 April 1989
99 Gottliebsen, *National Times*
100 Smith & Urquhart, *The Jindalee Factor*
101 Sir Charles Court speaking on 'The Life and Times of Alan Bond', 'Background Briefing', ABC Radio National, 27 November 1988
102 Smith & Urquhart, *The Jindalee Factor*
103 The *West Australian*, 12 September 1970
104 Sykes, *Money Miners*
105 Sykes, *Two Centuries of Panic* and *Money Miners*
106 Sykes, *Two Centuries of Panic*
107 Sykes, *Money Miners*
108 Gottliebsen, *National Times*
109 Sykes, *Money Miners*
110 The *West Australian*, 6 April 1973
111 T A Mairs, 'Bond hints at the secrets of success', the *West Australian*, 18 June 1973
112 Sykes, *Two Centures of Panic*
113 'Bond can't lose in Robe share deal', the *West Australian*, 26 May 1973
114 Gottliebsen, *National Times*
115 T A Mairs (Finance Editor), 'Bond puts terms of Minsec deal', the *West Australian*, 23 May 1973
116 'Bond offer clear under Companies Act — Jamison', the *West Australian*, 13 June 1973
117 'Robe shareholders will soon know takeover finance plans', *Daily News*, 27 June 1973
118 'Victory for Bond in Minsec case', the *West Australian*, 28 November 1973
119 'Judge places clamp on Bond documents', *Daily News*, 24 October 1973
120 Sykes, 'Alan Bond's sunshine empire', Part 4, the *Australian Financial Review*, 22 February 1974
121 Gottliebsen, *National Times*
122 'Mr Bond hints at surprise', the Perth *Sunday Times*, 5 August 1973
123 Gottliebsen, *National Times*
124 Malcolm Wilson, 'Alan Bond's highly geared ship carries a breath-taking $81.6 million debt', the *National Times*, 20 May 1974
125 'WA Land to pay maiden dividend', the *West Australian*, 28 November 1973
126 'Bond points out benefits of merger', the *West Australian*, 21 December 1973
127 Reports, the *Australian Financial Review*, 9 April and 31 May 1974. Both quoted in Sykes's *Two Centuries of Panic*
128 Christopher Skase, the *Australian Financial Review*, 2 May 1974
129 Anne Lampe & Terry Ogg, the *Australian Financial Review*, 2 February 1977
130 Sykes, *Two Centuries of Panic*
131 Sykes, *Two Centuries of Panic*
132 Sykes, *Two Centuries of Panic*
133 The *Australian Financial Review*, 19 October 1974
134 Promotional brochure, Bond Corporation Group of Companies, BondCorp, 1974
135 Malcolm Maiden, 'Bond's triumphs and troubles', the *Australian Financial Review*, 4 December 1989

136 Gottliebsen, *National Times*
137 Gottliebsen, *National Times*
138 Ron Saw, the *Bulletin*, 28 September 1974
139 *Daily News*, 4 September 1974
140 John Hamilton & Antony Cheesewright, 'Bond — an empire's priceless asset', the Melbourne *Herald*, 19 October 1974
141 Quoted in Riggs, *Keelhauled*
142 Riggs, *Keelhauled*
143 Mike Ramsden, 'Southern Cross no phoenix', the *Bulletin*, 28 September 1974

Chapter Nine

144 Gottliebsen, 'Saved at the eleventh hour' ('Back from the brink', Part Two), *National Times*, 18 November 1978
145 *Sunday Times*, 13 January 1975
146 Lipscombe, *Bulletin*
147 Stephens & McGeough, *Good Weekend*
148 Ron Saw, 'Behind the great yacht flop', the *Bulletin*, 28 September 1974
149 'Bond gives Libs $21,000', Perth *Sunday Independent*, 12 March 1974
150 Gottliebsen, 'Back from the brink'
151 Stan Correy, 'Background Briefing', ABC Radio National, 27 November 1988
152 Piers Akerman, *The Cup Comes Down Under*, Angus & Robertson, 1983
153 Theodore A Jones, *Racing for the America's Cup 1974 — the View from the Candy Store*, Quadrangle, 1975
154 Stephens & McGeough, *Good Weekend*
155 Gottliebsen, 'Back from the brink'
156 Stephens & McGeough, *Good Weekend*
157 Stannard, *Bulletin*
158 Jill Sykes, 'Ill winds', *Sydney Morning Herald*, 21 September 1974
159 'Bond considered rude: Jamieson', *Daily News*, 22 November 1974
160 Michael Rafferty, 'A Political Economy of Entrepreneurship in WA — case studies of the Bond Corporation and the Bell Group', thesis submitted in the School of Social Sciences at Curtin University as partial fulfilment of the requirements for the degree of Bachelor of Arts (Honours), October 1989; and interview with author
161 Correy, ABC Radio National
162 Correy, ABC Radio National
163 Lipscombe, *Bulletin*
164 Robert Gottliebsen, 'Saved at the eleventh hour'
165 'Referendum on land: Bond', the *West Australian*, 2 July 1973
166 'Bond has talks with Canberra', the *West Australian*, 16 October 1974
167 Gottliebsen, 'Saved at the eleventh hour'
168 Gottliebsen, 'Saved at the eleventh hour'
169 Interview with author, August 1989
170 'Talks were private says Bond', the Melbourne *Herald*, 16 October 1974
171 Gottliebsen, 'Saved at the eleventh hour', and interview with author
172 Deiley, *Playboy*
173 McIlwraith, 'Bond Bounces Back'
174 Interview with author
175 Lipscombe, *Bulletin*
176 Lipscombe, *Bulletin*
177 Hugh Schmitt, 'Alan Bond the risk taker', the *West Australian*, 19 May 1984
178 Gottliebsen, 'Saved at the eleventh hour'

179 Sykes, *Two Centuries of Panic*
180 Michael Gill, 'Alan Bond has grown up', the *National Times*, 13 September 1985
181 Trevor Sykes, 'Alan Bond gets Taylors Lake project off the ground', the *Australian Financial Review*, 11 September 1975
182 Sykes, *Two Centuries of Panic*
183 Riggs, *Keelhauled*
184 Riggs, *Keelhauled*
185 'Bond drops challenge', the *West Australian*, 23 June 1976
186 Riggs, *Keelhauled*

Chapter Ten

187 Whall, *The Southern Cross*
188 Steve Harvey, 'Alan Bond succeeds by staying one step ahead', the *Australian*, 27 April 1982
189 Bill Lang, 'Bond back — and ready to go', the *West Australian*, 7 October 1977
190 'Alan Bond named top Australian', *Daily News*, 25 January 1978
191 Schmitt, 'Alan Bond the risk taker'
192 Gottliebsen, 'Saved at the eleventh hour'
193 Sykes, 'Alan Bond's sunshine empire'
194 Lipscombe, *Bulletin*
195 McIlwraith, 'Bond Bounces Back'
196 Lipscombe, *Bulletin*
197 Gill, *National Times*
198 Schmitt, *West Australian*
199 Alan Trengove, *Discovery*, Stockwell Press, 1979
200 Robson, *Australian Magazine*
201 Terence Maher, 'How Alan Bond defies the odds', *Business Review Weekly*, 19 November 1983
202 Stephens & McGeough, *Good Weekend*
203 'Vast future for gas — Bond', *Daily News*, 3 September 1978
204 Stephens & McGeough, *Good Weekend*
205 Schmitt, *West Australian*
206 Stannard, *Bulletin*
207 Geraldine Doogue, 'It's time for a major push into China — Bond', the *Australian*, 6 January 1979
208 Maiden, *Australian Financial Review*
209 Gill, *National Times*
210 'Santos stake a bonanza for Bond group', *Daily News*, 2 November 1979
211 Stannard, *Bulletin*
212 Alan Jury, 'Alan Bond taps the Asian money men', *Australian Business*, 21 January 1982
213 Brian Wills-Johnson, 'Battle looms as Bond moves in on TVW', the *West Australian*, 15 December 1979
214 R G Hamilton, report of the inspector appointed to investigate certain dealings in securities of the company Amalgamated Industries Ltd which took place on 28 April 1980, presented to the Attorney-General for the State of Western Australia on 6 April 1981
215 Riggs, *Keelhauled*
216 Hugh Schmitt, 'Boosting Australia the Bond way', the *West Australian*, 21 May 1984
217 Deiley, *Playboy*
218 John Bertrand, *Born to Win*, Bantam Books, 1986

219 Eileen Westley, *America's Cup '83 — The Complete Story*, John Fairfax Marketing, 1983
220 Riggs, *Keelhauled*
221 Bob Macdonald, 'Bond not among America's Cup challengers', the *West Australian*, 10 May 1978
222 Rob Vaisey, 'Bond in another America's Cup bid?', the *West Australian*, 5 September 1978

Chapter Eleven

223 John Arthur, 'Council split on Palace Hotel issue', *Daily News*, 13 June 1973
224 Robert Kennedy, 'Bondy swans into brewing', 24 December 1980
225 Gill, *National Times*
226 Stannard, *Bulletin*
227 Gill, *National Times*
228 Jury, *Australian Business*
229 Terry McCrann, 'Three months in the corporate life of Alan Bond', the Melbourne *Age*, 27 August 1981
230 Maiden, *Australian Financial Review*
231 McCrann, *Age*
232 John McIlwraith & Brian Robins, 'Bond's rescue bid for fellow WA entrepreneurs', *Australian Financial Review*, 14 December 1981
233 Maiden, *Australian Financial Review*
234 Jim Main, '$300,000 boost for VFL side', the *Australian*, 17 March 1981
235 Harvey, *Australian*
236 'Feeding on own bulldust', *Australian Financial Review*, 1 March 1982
237 Harvey, *Australian*
238 Jury, *Australian Business*
239 John McIlwraith & Brian Robins, 'Bond Corp states security "absolute"', *Australian Financial Review*, 26 February 1982
240 'Bond unruffled by run on shares', *Australian Financial Review*, 1 March 1982
241 Jury, *Australian Business*
242 Maher, *Business Review Weekly*
243 Terence Maher, 'Big names join Bond in the limelight', *Business Review Weekly*, 1 October 1983
244 Deiley, *Playboy*

Chapter Twelve

245 Akerman, *The Cup Comes Down Under*
246 Bertrand, *Born to Win*
247 Donald Horne, *The Lucky Country*, Angus & Robertson, 1978
248 Terence Maher, 'To the victor the spoils', *Business Review Weekly*, November 1983
249 Ali Cromie, 'The clearout at Norman Ross', *Business Review Weekly*, 16 July 1983
250 Cromie, *Business Review Weekly*
251 Jackson, Graham, Moore & Partners report on BondCorp, November 1981
252 Jackson report
253 Trevor Sykes, 'Bond's Balancing Act', *Australian Business*, 13 November 1985
254 John Hamilton, *Burkie*, St George Books, 1988
255 Hamilton, *Burkie*
256 Hamilton, *Burkie*
257 Tony Grant-Taylor, 'The deal that started with London lunches and ended in Mario's', *Australian Financial Review*, 29 August 1985

258 Stannard, *Bulletin*
259 Grant-Taylor, *Australian Financial Review*
260 David Haselhurst, 'Bond's brash brewery bid', the *Bulletin*, 30 July 1985
261 Grant-Taylor, *Australian Financial Review*
262 Gill, *National Times*
263 Grant-Taylor, *Australian Financial Review*
264 Gill, *National Times*
265 Jack Lowenstein, 'Bond dispels the myths about its finances', *Euroweek*, 30 October 1987
266 Alan Kohler, 'Rich pickings', the *Independent Monthly*, October 1989

Chapter Thirteen

267 Letter from Dallhold to the receivers of Bond Brewing, 9 January 1990
268 Paul Barry, 'Four Corners', 13 March 1989
269 Malcolm Maiden, 'Bond's triumphs and troubles', *Australian Financial Review*, 4 December 1989
270 Michael Byrnes, 'Rome investment smacks of Alan Bond's personal style', *Australian Financial Review*, 26 April 1989
271 Paul Coombes, 'Emu site valuation up in the air', *Australian Business*, 15 November 1989
272 Coombes, *Australian Business*
273 Bruce Stannard, 'The Big Aussie Battler', the *Bulletin*, 9 August 1988
274 Stannard, *Bulletin*
275 Paul Syvret, 'Heilman's assets worth $38m compared with $353m in Bond accounts', the *Age*, 24 January 1990
276 Mark Thornton, 'Rothwells figures fraudulent: Bond', the *West Australian*, 22 May 1989
277 Richard Hall, *My Life with Tiny*, Faber & Faber, 1987